AA

Essential

KU-021-542

explorer

IRELAND

Lindsay Hunt

AA Publishing

Essential

Written by Lindsay Hunt
Additional writing by Dr Peter Harbison

Edited, designed and produced by AA Publishing
Maps © The Automobile Association 1994

Distributed in the United Kingdom by AA Publishing,
Fanum House, Basingstoke, Hampshire, RG21 2EA.

The contents of this publication are believed correct at the
time of printing. Nevertheless, the publishers cannot be
held responsible for any errors or omissions or for
changes in the details given in this guide or for the conse-
quences of any reliance on the information provided by
the same. Assessments of attractions, hotels, restaurants and so forth are based upon the author's own personal experience and, therefore, descriptions given in this
guide necessarily contain an element of subjective opinion which may not reflect the publishers' opinion or dic-
tate a reader's own experiences on another occasion.
We have tried to ensure accuracy in this guide, but things
do change and we would be grateful if readers would
advise us of any inaccuracies they may encounter.

A CIP catalogue record for this book is available from the
British Library.

ISBN 0 7495 0724 1

Published by AA Publishing (a trading name of Automobile Association Developments Limited, whose registered office is Fanum House, Basingstoke, Hampshire
RG21 2EA. Registered number 1878835).

Colour separation by Fotographics Ltd

Printed by LEGO SpA, Italy

Cover picture: Ballymoe, County Galway
Page 4: near Moate, County Westmeath
Page 5 (top): cemetery, Inishmore, Aran Islands
Page 5 (left): Bunratty Folk Park, County Clare
Page 5 (right): Roundstone harbour, County Galway
Page 6: Chester Beatty Library, Ballsbridge, Dublin
Page 7 (top): lobster fishing, Connemara, Galway

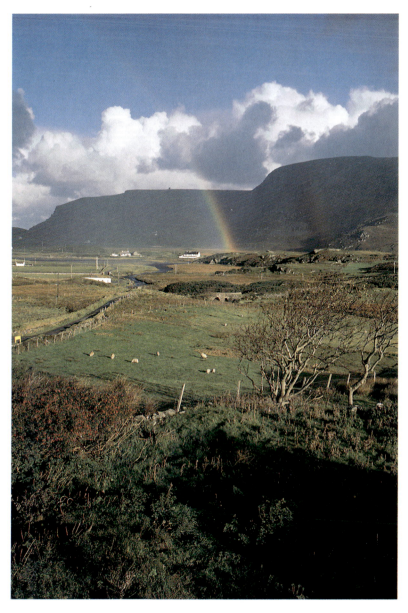

Lindsay Hunt turned to travel journalism after a career in publishing and a year spent sampling *tapas* in Spain. She has travelled extensively and researched many destinations for *Holiday Which?* magazine. She has also written, edited and contributed to numerous hotel and travel guides, including books on Spain, France, Germany, Italy and Florida.

Glencolumbcille, County Donegal

How to use this book

This book is divided into five main sections:

❏ Section 1: *Ireland Is*

discusses aspects of life and living today, from politics to peatlands

❏ Section 2: *Ireland Was*

places the country in its historical context and explores those past events whose influences are felt to this day

❏ Section 3: *A to Z Section*

is broken down into regional chapters, and covers places to visit, including walks and drives. Within this section fall the Focus-on articles, which consider a variety of subjects in greater detail

❏ Section 4: *Travel Facts*

contains the strictly practical information vital for a successful trip

❏ Section 5: *Hotels and Restaurants*

lists recommended establishments throughout Ireland, giving a brief résumé of their attractions

How to use the star rating

Most of the places described in this book have been given a separate rating:

▶▶▶ **Do not miss**

▶▶ **Highly recommended**

▶ **Worth seeing**

Not essential viewing

Map references

To make the location of a particular place easier to find every main entry in this book has a map reference to the right of its name. This comprises a number, followed by a letter, followed by another number, such as 176B3. The first number (176) refers to the page on which the map can be found, the letter (B) and the second number (3) pinpoint the square in which the main entry is located. The maps on the inside front cover and inside back cover are referred to as IFC and IBC respectively.

Contents

This quick-reference guide high-lights the features of the book you will use most often: the maps; the introductory features; the Focus-on articles; the walks and the drives.

Quick reference

The Print Room, Castletown House, County Kildare

Lord Killanin
One of the most widely known Irishmen of his generation, Lord Killanin has had a career embracing journalism, the army, movie-making, business and sports administration. Educated in Britain and in France, he holds honourary degrees from the National University of Ireland and the University of Ulster. He came to international prominence as President of the International Olympic Committee from 1972 to 1980.

My Ireland

by Lord Killanin

The Ireland that most people read about in their papers is riven with sectarian divisions which visitors are (rightly) warned to be careful how they discuss. The Ireland which greets their eyes is a very different place. The soft, glowing beauty of a magical countryside, the stylish architecture and vigorous life of the towns, the charm and wit of a warm-hearted population—these make the first impact. To them add the visual and practical importance of water.

Ireland has some 5,000km of main coastline, jagged with indentations, cluttered with coves and rocks, studded with smaller islands, green or bare. The famous Aran sweater was originally designed for the sad purpose of identifying the bodies of drowned fishermen—a different pattern for each family. The waters of springs and rivers play their part in the distillation of Irish whiskey and the making of stout, two other ingredients of Irish life by no means to be disregarded.

My family has been in Galway since the 14th century, so naturally I think first of the sea, but my career has brought me into contact with almost every important facet of Irish life, from racing and the Gaelic games (handball, Irish football, and hurling) to film-making and preserving the national heritage. I have seen changes, not all for the better (like the peculiar form of bungalow bliss spreading across the countryside), but let me end with a reassurance. The Irish, whether from the North or South, and of whatever religion or none, are agreed on one thing: that they are Irish, and nothing else. As such, whoever you are, they will give you a warm welcome.

My Ireland

by Joss Lynam

Can I separate Ireland from the Irish? Perhaps as a walker who loves solitude, I can. Alone from a Connemara summit I can enjoy a near aerial view of pale yellow beaches, surf-fringed islands and cloud shadows stippling the horizon-edged sea; from a nearby summit, I see glistening quartzite peaks, dark lakes and green and brown valleys. There are other landscapes; strangest is the Burren of County Clare, bare grey limestone, concealing in its fissures the most beautiful flowers in Ireland. Wildest perhaps are the rounded coastal hills of North Mayo and Donegal, cut off in great shattered cliffs dropping suddenly to the sea, with remnant stacks to show the angry power of the waves.

But I'm choosy; the Cliffs of Moher are diminished, made almost commonplace by the crowds. *My* Ireland demands solitude, or at most few and congenial companions, if I'm to savour to the full the awe, the fear, the joy, the excitement of the wonderful surface, shape and colours of our island.

But my Ireland is people too. Our hospitality and friendliness is a cliché, its truth only slightly dented by the vandals and thieves which, like every nation, we have to shame us. I've lived in many parts of the world, met many delightful people of many countries, but there is still something uniquely pleasurable in drifting into the welcome of an Irish pub.

Joss Lynam
Born in 1924, Joss Lynam has been climbing and walking all his life. Apart from many expeditions to the Himalaya and other great ranges, he has walked extensively in Ireland. He has written or edited many guidebooks to the Irish mountains, including *Irish Peaks*. Though born in London, his family is also from Galway, and he knows the mountains of Connemara and South Mayo perhaps better than anyone. He has been Chairman of the Cospoir Long-Distance Walking Routes Committee for some years.

IRELAND IS

■ Many of Ireland's charms are perfectly straightforward. Visitors head there for scenery, friendliness and peace – despite the Troubles. Ireland's real fascination, though, is its contrariness and ambivalence, those elements that simultaneously perplex, exasperate and bewitch – its very Irishness, if you like. Nothing is ever quite as it seems, and Irish stereotypes melt into air on closer inspection .....■

One island Is it one place or two? One part evokes all things green and Gaelic; the other is an outpost of the UK that Britain is at its wit's end to know how to manage. To enjoy Ireland, you need barely be aware of this division. On both sides of the border are glorious landscapes, plenty of friendly people, plenty of good pubs. On one side the pillar boxes are Irish green, on the other red, and for tourists (except in Belfast, perhaps) few other differences are apparent. Nor need you feel anxious about visiting the North. Statistically, it is one of Europe's safest places.

On the edge of the island perches Dunluce Castle, in County Antrim

Landscapes Ignoring the boundary, then, there are 32 counties of Ireland, each with its own distinctive character. Though at a glance Ireland may seem universally damp, mild and green, with no very high mountains and little variation of climate or landscape, it has more variety in its small confines than many larger countries. The scenery varies from rural pasturelands cut by many rivers, through wild boglands and low-lying hills, to the most spectacular mountain scenery (mostly in the west and north) sweeping down to the sea in high cliffs and craggy promontories. Offshore lie many islands, some of which are inhabited or contain ancient forts and ruined monastic

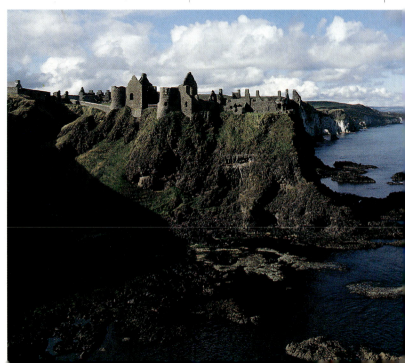

settlements; several others are bird sanctuaries.

The commonest of Irish rocks, limestone, produces great systems of porous caves, some containing stalactites and stalagmites. Volcanic activity created the highlands of the North, and the extraordinary crystalline formations of the Giant's Causeway in County Antrim. The surface of the land was glaciated during the last Ice Age, leaving classic geological features such as U-shaped valleys, corries (circular hollows), tarns (small lakes) and eskers (long, winding ridges).

Social conditions Recently great improvements have been made to many of Ireland's roads. Those in the North are financed by UK investment; in the Republic vast sums have been acquired in the form of European Community (EC) Regional Development Fund grants as part of a scheme to help the poorer countries of the EC (of which Ireland is one). Funds have also been allocated to many other projects in the North and South to develop tourism and other industries. One of Ireland's continuing struggles since the 18th century has been against economic depression and unemployment, and

The pace of life is noticeably slower to the west of the Shannon

the resulting drain of many of its most energetic and talented citizens abroad. The population has fluctuated considerably, its fecund Catholic communities producing many large families, even though they often put off marriage until late in life, especially in rural areas. Ireland now has about five million inhabitants, with a higher proportion of young people than virtually any country in Europe.

For visitors, though, Ireland still seems pleasantly old-fashioned, retaining a gentle pace of life and a generous allocation of time for almost anything – something that has been lost in so many places. Not that it is ever boring. The sociable and lively (not to say volatile) Irish are always ready to strike up a conversation, play some music or drink a jar.

If you have little time to spare, the best bet for an Irish holiday is a short break in Dublin, combined with excursions to the Wicklow Mountains, or perhaps the Boyne Valley and the antiquities of Newgrange. If you have longer, head west for Connemara, Cork, Kerry or Donegal. Longer still, see the rest of the country, including its great monastic sites and grand houses. For extensive touring, you definitely need your own transport. That could be a car, possibly a bike or even a horse-drawn caravan. You can also explore much of Ireland from a boat on its huge inland waterways.

■ 'If you think you understand Ireland,' some legendary wit once remarked, 'you've been sadly misinformed'. And indeed almost every aspect of Irish life is full of contradiction. That rule also applies to its politics, which are inextricably entwined with religion .....■

12

Paradoxes Certain elements of Irish political history may strike an outsider as surprising and somewhat contradictory:

● Some of Ireland's greatest nationalists (or at any rate critics of the English as Irish overlords) have been Protestants, some from English backgrounds. Examples include Jonathan Swift, Henry Grattan, Wolfe Tone, Robert Emmet, Charles Stewart Parnell, W B Yeats and even William Gladstone. Two of the Republic's Presidents have been Protestants.

● Both the Pope and the King of Spain supported Protestant William III's cause at the Battle of the Boyne, not the Catholic Jacobites (see page 36 for more details of this).

● Only about two per cent of the Republic's population are Protestants, yet many of its most important churches are Church of

Ministerial buildings next to Leinster House, seat of the Irish Parliament

Ireland (Protestant), including Dublin's two cathedrals.

● Northern Irish Unionists, far from being in line with the UK, are often in bitter opposition to the ruling party at Westminster. While British politicians have met, talked and reached amicable agreements with Republican leaders, the Unionists, thus far, have adamantly rejected all compromise.

Ireland's constitution The Republic of Ireland's constitution operates under a prime minister (*Taoiseach*), two chambers (senate and assembly), and a president (who is largely a ceremonial figurehead). Its main political parties sprang up during or soon after the struggle for independence in the early 20th century. Since then, parliamentary power has been dominated by Fianna Fáil (Soldiers of Destiny), the party set up by Éamon de Valera in 1926. In 1933 its more liberal and moderate (though hardly left-wing) rival, Fine

Mary Robinson, Ireland's first woman president

Gael (Tribes of Gaels), appeared. Roughly speaking, these parties mirror the positions taken by pro- and anti-treatyites during the Civil War; in other words, they either accepted (Fine Gael) or rejected (Fianna Fáil) Ireland's partition in 1921. Both parties have found it difficult to achieve majority rule recently, and the latest elections (based on proportional representation) resulted in an uneasy stalemate followed by behind-the-scenes horse-trading with minority socialist parties to form a workable coalition. The joker in the pack is Sinn Fein, the political wing of the IRA. Originally founded in 1908 (making it older than any other party), it achieved massive popular support at certain stages in its history, but now commands only a tiny fraction of Republican Irish votes. Because its leaders will not renounce the

violence of its paramilitary offshoot, the IRA, both Britain and Northern Ireland refuse to negotiate with the party – thus ironically giving it much more publicity than it deserves.

A conservative mentality The winds of change are blowing through Irish politics, a notable event being the election in 1991 of a woman president (a possibility absolutely discounted by social historians only a few years before). Mary Robinson is a liberal barrister with known sympathies for certain issues (such as the liberalisation of divorce laws) which currently perplex Ireland. The position of women in the Republic is much affected by the power of the Catholic Church and the present Pope's reaffirmation of its doctrines on contraception, abortion and divorce. Ireland ranks last among the world's developed countries in access to birth control (though the impact of AIDS has had a sharper effect than decades of religious dogma), and is alone in Europe in having no civil divorce. In 1992, the case of a 14-year-old girl made pregnant by rape and refused an abortion, or even permission to travel abroad to obtain one, hit world headlines and caused yet another complex referendum. Again, Ireland voted against liberalisation of these laws. Catholics complained justifiably of their lack of civil rights in Northern Ireland, yet the Republic's Protestants would also have an interesting case in any international court of human rights. Both sides of the border are far from a compromise – a concept rejected by both staunch Loyalists and extremist Republicans, both of whose paramilitary wings have now descended to the lowest depths of inhumanity.

13

■ Ireland's musical traditions date back continuously over many centuries, but the current scene is exceptionally lively, with a new interest in popular folk music encouraged by tourism. Irish musicians figure prominently in rock and country-and-western groups, and some Irish virtuoso performers, such as James Galway, have become world famous .....■

14

A Celtic tradition The poems and stories related by Gaelic bards at court were often accompanied by music, most typically played on the harp, Ireland's national emblem. The 12th-century historian, Gerald of Wales, praised the deftness of Irish fingerwork, and the expertise of Irish harpists was recognised as far afield as Renaissance Italy. After the Battle of Kinsale (1601), the great Gaelic clan houses declined, along with their patronage of the arts. Music was perceived by the ruling English as potentially dangerous, arousing nationalist sentiments, and it was suppressed along with other aspects of Irish culture. Musicians became itinerant, travelling from house to house to seek their fortunes at the hands of the new aristocrats; the

The tradition of live folk music lives on in countless Irish pubs

blind harpist, Turlough O'Carolan (1670–1738), was the most celebrated exponent of this tradition. The 18th century witnessed a new flourishing of musical talent in Dublin's Anglo-Irish circles, mostly influenced by European developments; Handel's *Messiah* was performed for the first time in the capital in 1742, conducted by the composer.

Meanwhile, traditional music continued to be played in Gaelic households. The ancient styles were either plaintive melodies with no distinct rhythms (possibly inherited from Spanish or North African cultures), or brisk, lively dance tunes. In 1792 a great harp festival held in Belfast aroused interest in more traditional Irish forms, and folk tunes increased in popularity. The lyric ballad, with words by such poets as Thomas Moore set to music, was sung in elegant drawing rooms throughout

Ireland. Many budding musicians left their native land, as did writers, to seek fame in England. John McCormack, the famous lyric tenor, spent most of his life in the USA (see page 240).

Irish instruments Most distinctive of the instruments used in Irish music, besides the harp, are the *uilleann* (elbow) pipes, a relative of the Scottish bagpipes but with a more plangent tone particularly suited to reflective Irish tunes. The violin (simply called the fiddle in Ireland) is held casually on the shoulder and played with only a small section of the bow. Expert Irish fiddlers are technically highly skilled, however; Fritz Kreisler is said to have declared that if he practised for a thousand years he would never be able to play as well as the Sligo fiddler, Michael Coleman. The *bodhrán* is one of the most ancient Irish instruments, a goatskin drum played with a small stick. Wind instruments include the famous tin whistle (no mere toy to a skilled player) and the flute, whose capacities have astounded worldwide audiences in the hands of the modern exponent, James Galway.

The modern scene In the 20th century Irish music has played an important rôle in the revival of nationalist sentiment and has achieved enormous popularity. The most usual venues to hear it are *ceilidhs*, where whole communities gather to dance and make music, or pubs, where *seisuns* (sessions) are held all over Ireland. The popularity of Irish music is unquestionably affected by tourism, sometimes losing both its dignity and its authenticity in the process. In the summer, when an audience is guaranteed, every pub seems to offer musical happenings. Out of season, however, they may be quite difficult to find. Doolin in County Clare is a particularly well known Mecca for groups of musicians. Other forms of music are encouraged at major festivals –

15

In Ireland, as in the Celtic areas of Britain, dance lives on as an important facet of life

Wexford's Opera Festival, Waterford's Light Opera Festival and Cork's Jazz Festival.

One of the most influential figures in Irish music in modern times was Seán O'Riada, former director of music at the Abbey Theatre, Dublin. Though classically trained, his main interest was folk music, which he greatly popularised. His group, Celtóiri Chualann, was a forerunner of the world-renowned Chieftains. The tradition continued through groups such as the Clancy Brothers and the Dubliners. Other groups took a different line of hard rock, notably Bob Geldoff's Boomtown Rats, U2, Hothouse Flowers and the Pogues. Individual performers have also hit the charts – Van Morrison, Enya, Chris de Burgh and Sinead O'Connor.

■ The Irish are famously articulate. From the loquacious Celts, alleged by Strabo (writing around the time of the birth of Christ) to be fond of 'wordy disputes' and 'bombastic self-dramatisation', through that master of empty promises the Earl of Blarney, to today's garrulous stage Irishman, words have been a constant source of delight – sometimes at the expense of action. The peerlessly eloquent Oscar Wilde said, 'We are the greatest talkers since the Greeks – but we have done nothing.' .....■

A prolific streak The Irish have written much; Ireland's contribution to English literature in all its forms – poetry, drama, novels, essays – is colossal, considering the size of its population. It seems as strong today as ever, with new talents bursting on to the stage and filling bookshop shelves with new novels and poems, while, in more ephemeral media, Irish eloquence commandeers hours of airwave time and reams of newsprint. Three writers have won Nobel prizes (W B Yeats, George Bernard Shaw and Samuel Beckett). Both speech and writings take innumerable forms, but are characterised by

Jonathan Swift, satirist and cleric

a natural flamboyance, passion, and wit, coupled with idiosyncrasy. Much of the inspiration comes, inevitably, from the tensions generated by persecution and oppression.

The Gaelic heritage Besides Ireland's outpourings in English, it has a rich Gaelic tradition (sadly inaccessible to the outside world). At various periods during the imposition of English rule, the Gaelic language was suppressed. After independence, strenuous attempts were made to revive it; indeed it was declared an official language. Éamon de Valera wanted to use it for political reasons, to assert Ireland's separate identity from Britain. Ireland's first president, Douglas Hyde, was a distinguished Gaelic scholar who loved the native

❏ Ogham script was used in Ireland from about the 4th century, but was eventually superseded by the Roman alphabet introduced by Christian missionaries. It continued to be used until after the 8th century. It was written as a series of scratched lines, and most usually appears on commemorative standing stones or monuments. Its uses for practical purposes were very limited. The key to interpreting the characters is the *Book of Ballymote*, written in 1391 in Sligo. Examples of ogham stones can be found in several places; there is a good one in the church at Killaloe (Clare) and another two in the abbey ruins of Ardmore (Waterford). ❏

16

Samuel Beckett

language for its own sake. Despite compulsory schooling in Gaelic and regular radio and television broadcasts, the natural use of Gaelic as a first language has dwindled to a few areas largely in the West, and contemporary writing is at a low ebb.

Anglo-Irish writers The first flowering of Anglo-Irish literature occurred during the late 17th and 18th centuries. Jonathan Swift (see page 62) was the giant of the age, publishing savage satires to expose the hypocrisy and injustice of life under English rule. In a lighter vein, Oliver Goldsmith, R B Sheridan, William Congreve and George Farquhar entertained English upper classes with their fizzy comedies of manners. Edmund Burke wrote philosophical and political essays in elegant prose complex enough to win present-day admirers from the whole political spectrum.

Irish writing in the 19th century came thick and fast, from George Moore and Maria Edgeworth's sharply observed novels about the Irish 'Big House', such as *Castle Rackrent,* to Shaw, Oscar Wilde and Yeats toward the end of the century, and even Bram Stoker, who introduced the world to Dracula. Anthony Trollope, though born in England, wrote many of his novels while working in Ireland; some, such as *Phineas Finn,* have Irish characters.

The tradition lives on In the 20th century, Irish writing has reflected the turmoil of independence, and a long twilight of censorship. Modern Ireland out-pruded the English Victorians, sending many great writers into self-imposed exile (James Joyce and Beckett are the two outstanding examples); J M Synge's and Seán O'Casey's plays caused riots in Dublin. Novelists and poets have proliferated within and without Ireland, however. Patrick Kavanagh, Louis Macneice and Seamus Heaney are three of its best-known poets; Molly Keane (also known as M J Farrell), Edna O'Brien, Brian O'Nolan (Flann O'Brien) and William Trevor are popular novelists. Frank O'Connor, Seán O'Faoláin, Mary Lavin and Liam O'Flaherty perfected the art of the short story, and talented modern dramatists include Brian Friel and Frank McGuinness. The disabled writer Christopher Nolan won great acclaim for his poems, *Damburst of Dreams,* and his novel, *Under the Eye of the Clock.*

The formidable George Bernard Shaw

Food and drink

■ **In today's Ireland, it seems hard to imagine the grim days of the 19th century when so many of the population starved, or that, in those days, many poor people had no clue how to prepare any food other than boil a potato. Nowadays, it is quite possible to eat both well and heartily all over the island.....■**

Changing tastes Tourism has made a vast difference to the standards of cuisine in Ireland. Until recently, there was hardly any tradition of eating out in many districts, except perhaps on very rare occasions at a local hotel. Patterns of diet were conservative, based firmly on 'meat and two veg' (somewhat overcooked), potatoes (of course) and large quantities of dairy fat. Now things are very different. Tourist demands for predictable, inexpensive fast food are met, as everywhere, with hamburgers and pizzas – a better bet being fish and chips. But more sophisticated tastes have introduced wholefoods and vegetarian restaurants (almost unheard of before), and a vast number of new eateries, often French in style, have opened in the

A traditional – and substantial – Irish breakfast

main tourist centres. Food 'events' such as Kinsale's Gourmet Festival or Galway's Oyster Festival arouse great interest. With VAT at its present rates (as much as 21 per cent for luxury goods), eating out in Ireland is expensive, particularly if you like a drink with a meal. Casual (but respectable) dress is the norm just about anywhere.

One of the best-value meals in Ireland (as in Britain) is breakfast. A 'traditional Irish breakfast' (or the 'Ulster fry' north of the border) is a brimming plateful of bacon and eggs with soda and potato breads. Accommodation rates are nearly always quoted with a full breakfast included, so you might as well stoke up for the day and get your money's worth!

Irish cuisine Whatever Irish cuisine lacks in finesse, it nearly always makes up for in copiousness, and ingredients are of a high quality. Home-grown produce includes rich dairy foods, beef, lamb and pork, a fascinating range of new Irish cheeses, and a great variety of seafood, shelled or finned. One of its great specialities is bread. Traditional Irish soda bread made with buttermilk, eaten fresh and warm, is a banquet in itself, and is automatically proffered at every meal. At mid-day, a basket of Irish bread, a bowl of seafood chowder and a glass of Guinness makes a cheap and completely satisfying lunch.

Recently there has been a welcome return to simple, hearty Irish food such as Irish stew and potato dishes. Try colcannon (potatoes with onions and white cabbage), champ (potatoes mashed with butter and chopped chives) or coddle (potatoes with bacon and onions). Black puddings use up those bits of pig not usually found on the dinner table. At teatime, look out for barm brack, a delicious sweet tea bread with dried fruit and spices.

Fish can easily be found in most of Ireland, and you don't have to be rich or posh to enjoy oysters here. If you're adventurous, try dulse or carrageen (types of seaweed), used to make various desserts – a change from the usual apple pie and ice-cream.

Whiskey and stout All alcohol (especially in the South) is highly taxed and expensive, though measures of spirits are more generous

If you wish to order half a pint, ask for a 'glass'

than in the UK. Take in your duty-free allowance if you like a drink. Pubs, though, are more than mere boozing sheds; they are the social heart of many communities and often full of life and atmosphere especially if there is some music on. Pub food is rarely very imaginative, but you can usually get snacks at lunchtime, and coffee all day. At some stage every visitor should try Ireland's 'nectar', Guinness (see panel on page 56). Some consider it tactless to request Scotch in an Irish pub – try the local Bushmills or one of the other Irish brands, neat or with a splash of plain Irish water. It is also delicious in Irish coffee, or in one of those creamy liqueur concoctions. The local lager is Harp (brewed by Guinness). If you prefer something akin to English bitter, ask for Smithwicks Ale.

19

■ The passion for competitive sports and athletics of many kinds reaches unprecedented heights all over the Republic. Its specialist games such as hurling and Gaelic football draw capacity crowds and cause vast excitement. The one thing you're unlikely to see is cricket – except perhaps in the province of Leinster and in Northern Ireland, where the games of the English are kept alive and well .....■

The big match When there's a big match on, even the least enthusiastic sportsman or woman is condemned to know about it. Flags and banners of the colours of the competing county teams sprout all over the land, on telegraph poles and gateposts, from car windows and rooftops. Switch on the radio for the news, and you will find nothing of importance has happened in the world – except the match. Needless to say, huge crowds cause boisterous disruption to everyday life (especially on the roads), and plenty of noise in the pub afterwards, but they are rarely occasions for the hooliganism often seen at British football matches. Highlights of the year are the All-Ireland hurling and football finals, held at Croke Park, Dublin, in

September, where tickets are gold-dust. In the past, however, Gaelic games were regarded as a focal point for nationalist sentiment, and were alternately discouraged or banned by English authorities and fostered by Republicans. In 1884 the Gaelic Athletics Association (GAA) was formed in Tipperary to halt the spread of anglicised games and promote Irish ones. The organisation, like the Gaelic League, was a fertile recruiting ground for political activists.

Rugby union enjoys limited popularity, but is remarkable in that the national team represents *all* of Ireland, with southern nationalist playing alongside northern Unionist.

Hurling This fast and furious game has an ancient pedigree, dating back before the Christian era. The Ulster

The distinctly Irish sport of hurling

champion Cuchulainn was renowned for his prowess at hurling, and teams of warriors are supposed to have played it for days on end. It is something like no-holds-barred hockey, played with an ash stick or 'hurley' and a small leather ball – 'sliotar'. Players (15-a-side) may strike the ball any distance and at any height, or carry it on the hurley. It's most popular in Cork and the west of Ireland, but also played in Antrim, almost exclusively by Catholics.

Gaelic football Even more than hurling, the two types of football in Ireland (Gaelic and

you need a national licence for rod-fishing for salmon, trout or sea-trout.

That other Irish passion shared by the British is racing (horses and greyhounds), and many towns have dog-tracks or racecourses. Sailing centres are mostly in the Southwest, between Youghal and Dingle, with lake and river or canal cruising focused on Lough Derg, the River Shannon, the two Loughs Erne and the Grand Canal. Walking is increasingly popular in Ireland, though in the Republic it has been discouraged by a court ruling that

soccer) are played on sectarian lines, with minimal support for the Gaelic game among Protestants. The ball is smaller than a soccer ball, and scoring is on a points system, with rules something of a cross between soccer and rugby. The game requires great physical strength and stamina.

Tourist activities As a tourist, you are unlikely to do more than watch these exciting pastimes, but there are splendid opportunities for exercise in many forms, especially golf, equestrian sports, cycling and fishing. There are over 200 golf courses, some of international class or in wildly beautiful settings. Green fees vary considerably and are more expensive in the Southwest. As a fishing destination, many claim Ireland is unparalleled, both for the quality of the sport and its low costs. Sea-fishing for shark is popular in some areas (such as Achill Island). Permits are necessary on privately owned waters (and on public waters in the North), and

Gaelic football it may be, but handling of the ball is allowed

landlords are liable for any injuries caused on their property. However, many long-distance footpaths are now in place and more accessible open spaces are planned. In the meantime, take sensible precautions before setting out. Prepare for bad weather, take the best map you can find, and let someone know where you are heading.

Both Bord Fáilte and the Northern Ireland Tourist Board produce plenty of literature on specialist sports.

■ **The bogs of Ireland once covered immense tracts of the central lowlands. To former generations, it must have seemed wholly inconceivable that they could ever disappear, or perhaps that it would matter much if they did. However, today's conservationists have recognised them as unique and precious ecosystems, and are racing to ensure that what little is left is preserved before they all vanish .....**■

24

The formation of the bogs After the Ice Age, the saucer-like bowl that forms the centre of Ireland lay awash with lakes. These gradually filled up with compost from lakeside vegetation and, eventually, peat accumulated because the micro-organisms which cause decay cannot survive in these wet conditions. There are two main types of bog in Ireland. Blanket bog, composed of dead sedge and grass, develops to a depth of around 6m in the wettest areas and is found mostly in mountainous parts of the West, or in the Slieve Bloom Mountains. Raised bog, consisting mostly of sphagnum moss, covers wider areas of the central plain, where rainfall is lower. This gradually builds up into a dome above the ground water and can reach depths of up to 12m.

Roundstone Bog, Galway, one of the last untouched bogs in Ireland

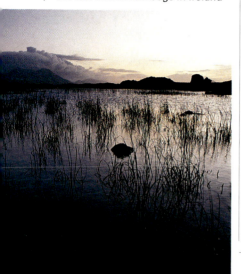

A vanishing landscape As a result of massive exploitation, the boglands have shrunk to a fraction of their original size, and are still dwindling. Ireland has almost no coal or oil reserves, so peat has always been used as fuel. In the past, turf was painstakingly cut by hand, using a spade or *sleán* – many people still have 'turbary rights' (the right to cut turf) on local bogs. The top layers of living plants are removed and replaced on the cut surface to encourage regeneration; as a result, even when Ireland's population increased, the effects of cutting peat by hand were fairly minimal.

In 1946, however, Bord na Móna (the Peat Development Authority) began mechanical digging, and now great tracts can be seen laid waste in black, sodden wildernesses, later replanted with coniferous timber. Moss peat from the surface layers is bagged up and distributed to garden centres, while peat from the lower levels is used for fuel, either in domestic fires or power stations – about a quarter of Ireland's electricity comes from peat. It has recently become obvious that if the present rate of extraction continues there will soon be none left, so a number of the best bogs are now protected as nature reserves. Currently about 14 per cent of Ireland's land surface consists of peat bog, proportionally more than any other country save Canada and Finland.

A unique ecosystem Bogland flora are fascinating and very varied. The only plants that can survive are highly specialised – some have roots reaching deep down through water-retentive mosses into a compost of half-rotted vegetation; other, fly-trapping plants supplement their diet with animal protein. Few mammals can survive true boglands (though some are havens for otters), but rare insects, flowers and birds can be seen.

The bogs are also of great interest to archaeologists. Their virtually sterile environment preserves animal and vegetable matter – tree-stumps, bog butter (see panel on page 239), even corpses, have been pulled from the bog, virtually intact, after centuries.

Safety on bogs Walking on peat bogs can be dangerous. Some deep pools may be disguised by soft mats of vegetation on the surface. It is easy to get lost as there are few paths or visible landmarks. A midge repellant is useful at some times of year, and wellingtons are essential.

Re-creation of a bog village at Glenbeigh, County Kerry

Best places to visit There are several centres where boglands are explained, for example the Peatland World centre at Lullymore, on the Bog of Allen, County Kildare (see page 88), or, north of the border, the Peatlands Park in County Armagh (see page 223). Good examples of raised bogs are Mongan Bog near Clonmacnois on the banks of the Shannon, and Clara Bog, also in Offaly. Nearby, Blackwater Bog offers an 8km circular train tour. Blanket bogs are at Roundstone in County Galway and in the Slieve Bloom Mountains on the Laois/Offaly border. Owenduff, Mayo, has the largest stretch of undisturbed blanket bog in the country. For more information, contact the Irish Peatland Conservation Council, 3 Lower Mount Street, Dublin 2 (tel: 01 722397 or 722384), the Wildlife Service, Leeson Lane, Dublin 2 (tel: 01 615666) or, in Northern Ireland, Peatlands Park, Dungannon, County Tyrone (tel: 0762 851102).

■ **The Irish tradition of storytelling can be traced back to the Celts, well before Christ, whose sagas of epic battles and great champions, gods and supernatural events were passed down orally at firelit feasts, then transcribed by early monks in manuscripts such as *The Book of the Dun Cow* or *The Book of Leinster* .....** ■

Interwoven traditions Irish mythology is incredibly complex; different accounts of similar stories are often interwoven with other traditions, and echoes of other Indo-European legends can often be found – epic tales of Greeks and Romans, for instance, or biblical stories. At first the stories were not written down, but related orally as evening entertainment, which meant embroiderings in every telling. A trained *file* (Celtic bard) was expected to be able to relate about 350 full-length tales in poetry by

The Children of Lir, see page 236

heart, and would spend years learning his art. The early Christian fathers were the first to record these legends, sometimes interspersing it with their own material and turning Celtic gods into Christian saints (St Brigid is an example).

The Celtic revival Though bardic traditions declined under English rule, interest in Celtic legends revived sharply towards the end of the 19th century under the influence of writers such as W B Yeats and the rise of Irish nationalism. The leaders of the Easter Rising were imbued with ancient myths, seeing themselves as heroes battling against dark forces of evil. Even today, paramilitary groups sometimes use mythological rhetoric to justify their appalling actions.

Celtic mythology remained alive in rural Ireland until the age of television, with a storyteller in every parish; superstitions and tales of fairy folk and monsters still abound. Ireland's leprechaun is the best known figure of popular lore – the little man in green mending shoes and guarding his crock of gold – while the banshee is a more sinister creature, a female spirit whose wailings are believed to portend a death. Places associated with ancient magic are often treated with great respect by country people, for fear of disturbing whatever spirits or fairies inhabit them.

Groups of sagas Irish sagas are classified in four main groups. The Mythological Cycle deals with pre-Celtic gods and heroes and their long-running and complicated struggles for supremacy; the Children of Lir is one of the best known stories.

A romanticised depiction of Cuchulainn by E Wallcousins

The Ulster Cycle contains the epic adventures of the Red Branch Knights of Navan Fort and their champion Cuchulainn, one of the most famous being the Cattle Raid of Cooley. The later Ossianic (or Fenian) Cycle revolves around another hero, Finn MacCool (Fionn mac Cumhaill), builder of the Giant's Causeway and Gráinne's betrothed. The Historical Cycle (or Cycle of Kings) recounts tales from various early Irish kings, and is similar to Malory's tales of

Arthur. The Celtic 'otherworld', *Tír na n'Og* (the Land of Eternal Youth, believed to lie somewhere on an island in the far West) figures in these sagas – the paradise every culture dreams of for its afterlife, where pain and suffering are no more.

The Cattle Raid of Cooley This was one of the first stories to be written down. Queen Maeve of Connaught became jealous of her husband's possessions, in particular his magnificent white bull. She tried to obtain the mighty brown bull of Cooley to match it, at first peacefully, then by force,

Flemish cartographer Ortelius chose an east–west orientation for his 16th-century map of Ireland

invading with a great army. The hero of Ulster, Cuchulainn, defended the province alone, and after a long struggle, defeated Maeve's army. But he was mortally wounded, and died strapped to a stone pillar, facing his enemies.

Gráinne and Diarmuid The beautiful Gráinne was betrothed to the ageing hero, Finn MacCool, but fell in love instead with the handsome Diarmuid. They eloped together, taking refuge under dolmens. Eventually, Diarmuid was killed by a boar on the slopes of Benbulben Mountain in Sligo. The story has clear echoes of Tristan and Isolde.

Cuchulainn, Hound of Ulster At the age of five, Setanta, nephew of King Conor, set out to join his uncle's court, taking his hurling stick and ball with him to play on the way. At a banquet held in the house of Culainn, he was attacked by a great mastiff guard-dog. Setanta hurled the ball down the beast's throat and killed it. Culainn was glad he was safe, but distressed at the death of his dog, saying 'Who will guard my house now?' Setanta promised that he would take over the role of protector, and so found his new name – Cuchulainn, the Hound of Culainn, and champion of Ulster.

See panels on pages 215 and 238.

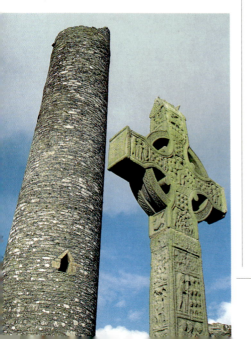

Biblical stories are carved on to 10th-century Muireadach's Cross at Monasterboice in County Louth

28

IRELAND WAS

■ **Remnants of Ireland's prehistoric and early Christian past lie scattered throughout the island, though many are shrouded in mystery and still a puzzle to archaeologists. The megalithic tombs of the Boyne valley or the ornamental jewellery of early populations show clear evidence of highly sophisticated peoples .....■**

30

Prehistoric Ireland The earliest inhabitants to have left traces of their existence probably arrived from Scotland in about 6000 or 7000BC. These were hunter-gathering peoples who slowly adopted more settled lifestyles and advanced methods of farming as the Stone Age progressed. They wove cloth, made pottery, fished from coracles (simple boats), raised stock and cleared trees to plant a few cereals. One of the earliest settlements is Glenaan, in the Glens of Antrim, where flint axe heads have been found.

The clearest legacy of the neolithic age is burial places. Between 4000 and 2000BC, many megalithic tombs (using large blocks of stone) were built. Most impressive are the passage tombs at Newgrange, but important sites can be found in Sligo and eastern Ireland (the court tombs of Creevykeel; dolmens, like those at Proleek; and wedge tombs, as at Labbacallee in County Cork). From the Bronze Age (1750BC onwards) came stone circles or mysterious single standing stones, such as those at Drombeg in Cork or Lough Gur in

Limerick. Little is known of these people, but ancient lore terms them the *Fir Bolg* (Bag Men, because they carried fertile soil to rocky fields in large leather bags), a short, dark race who lived to no more than 30 or so.

The Celts In about 700BC a new wave of invaders began to arrive on Irish shores; the Celts, a disparate group of tribes whose cousins can be found all over Europe. Driven west by the Romans, who called them *Galli,* they were known as *keltoi* by the Greeks, and became Gaels in Ireland. Their loose clan structures revolved around a leader or chieftain (*Taoiseach* – the word still used for Ireland's prime minister) who was elected rather than dynastic. As time progressed, leadership became more centralised under a single high king, though the idea of 'nationhood' never developed fully in Celtic times; clans continued to live in isolated settlements of round huts, protected by sturdy defences or by lake moats.

Celtic legacies Some aspects of Celtic culture seem to have filtered into the Irish character. The Celts were hospitable folk, who enjoyed feasting, music and story-telling. Their love of adornment is evident in the gorgeous jewellery they made – bands of decorated gold and other metals, of great artistry. Most of all they loved fighting – no mere internecine squabbles, but epic battles between warrior champions epitomised by the legendary heroes, Cuchulainn and Finn MacCool. Elevated into semi-divinities, the myths (perhaps the Celts' greatest legacy) tell of their great deeds, ringing with the clash of sword on shield,

Drombeg Stone Circle, County Cork

dripping with gore. They worshipped many gods, often adopting the sacred sites of past inhabitants for their rituals and royal residences (Tara is one of the most celebrated). Efforts to propitiate these gods were unsparing – vast quantities of treasure were heaped on the altars of the dead, and grisly sacrifices took place. One of the most chilling rituals was the 'wicker man', a huge effigy of straw and wood filled with living creatures – men, women, children, animals – and set alight.

Beyond Roman rule Ireland is unusual in western Europe in having no Roman history. The Romans gazed across at the Emerald Isle, and

Tacitus wrote, somewhat airily, 'I have often heard Agricola declare that a single legion, with a moderate band of auxiliaries, would be enough to finish the conquest of Ireland,' but they never colonised it. (Cynics say that, if they had, the roads might have been better!) As it was, the Celts held sway in their piecemeal fashion through several Christian centuries. Some recolonised west Britain in the early *anno domini* centuries, joining with the native Picts to plague the Romans along Hadrian's Wall. These Irish Celts were known as Scots, some of whose descendants are the Protestant occupants of Ulster, now regarded by some extreme Nationalists as aliens.

PREHISTORIC AND CELTIC SITES

- ● Prehistoric site
- ● Celtic site

Grianan of Aileach

Glencolumbcille

Creevykeel

Boa Island
Devenish Island

Carrowmore

Carrowkeel

Proleek Dolmen

Monasterboice

Kells

Brugh na Boinne

Hill of Tara

Book of Kells (Dublin)

Turoe Stone

Clonmacnois

Aran Islands

Gleninsheen
Poulnabrone Dolmen

Moone High Cross

Glendalough

Castledermot High Cross

Browne's Hill Dolmen

Lough Gur

Cashel

Gallarus Oratory

Staigue Fort

Skellig Islands

Drombeg Stone Circle

| 0 | 40 | 80 km |
| 0 | 20 | 40 miles |

■ After the arrival of Christianity in the 4th century (some time before St Patrick), Ireland enjoyed a golden age while the rest of Europe languished in the dark aftermath of the fall of the Roman Empire. Monasteries flourished as great cultural centres and Irish missionaries travelled back to mainland Europe to spread the good word .....■

Viking invaders The good times were not to last. From AD795 pirate raiding parties began to attack Ireland's shores, envious of the riches of the Celtic monasteries. By AD837 a wholesale Norse invasion was taking place, and this time the interlopers stayed. The native Gaels and monks built Round Towers as look-outs and refuges, and reinforced their simple wood or wattle dwellings and churches with hard stone. The Vikings caused immeasurable destruction and bloodshed as they arrived, but later settled into more peaceable habits, often intermarrying and becoming assimilated with the local population. Though illiterate, they had many skills, and founded sophisticated walled cities to defend the estuaries by which they had entered Ireland (Waterford, Wexford, Cork, Dublin, Limerick). They passed on their great knowledge of seafaring

Fearsome Strongbow now lies peacefully in Dublin's Christ Church Cathedral

and boat-building, established important foreign trade links and introduced coinage. Some converted to Christianity. The Vikings were eventually routed at the Battle of Clontarf (near Dublin) in 1014 by the famous High King, Brian Ború. Unfortunately, a retreating Viking treacherously dispatched Ború after the battle, and Ireland's chances of becoming united under a strong leader receded again.

MacMurrough and Strongbow In one of the subsequent feuds, Dermot MacMurrough abducted the wife of a rival chieftain, Tiernan O'Rourke, and the other clans set about him in revenge. In retreat, with many of his lands and his Leinster throne lost, MacMurrough sought help from abroad. Henry II of England, already considering the conquest of Ireland, and with the support of the Pope, gave MacMurrough permission to recruit from amongst his barons. Richard FitzGilbert de Clare, Earl of Pembroke, better known as Strongbow, was rewarded

The Anglo-Norman keep of Carrick-fergus Castle has walls 2.5m thick

for his timely aid with the hand of MacMurrough's daughter and great parcels of land. The Normans had arrived, and they stayed. In England, Henry II looked anxiously over his shoulder at these powerful adventurers and decided to assert his authority. He came to Ireland with his army and demanded allegiance from Irish leaders who, also fearful of MacMurrough and Strongbow, gave it. From then on, England was Ireland's overlord. Henry granted the province of Meath to his follower, Hugh de Lacy, and empowered him to act as deputy governor. English control radiated from the Dublin area, which later contracted to a small region about 50km north, south and west of the capital, defended by an earth rampart, known as the Pale.

Norman rule Irish sub-kingdoms were established further afield ('beyond the Pale'), enabling Gaelic rulers to hold sway as long as appropriate tributes were paid to England, and loyal support given in times of war. Needless to say, not all Ireland's inhabitants were content with such meek subjection, and many rebelled. Land was confiscated as punishment, leaving an enduring legacy of

resentment among the Gaelic chieftains, and great English estates began to develop, based on the feudal manorial system. All the colonisers remained free; the Irish peasantry were serfs, tied to the land. None the less, their lot in a productive demesne under strong leadership may well have been happier than before. In 1177 John de Courcy invaded Ulster and conquered it swiftly. On Strongbow's death without heirs, Henry's son, Prince (later King) John, took over as Lord of Ireland. Anglo-Norman administrative structures of government and law were set up within Ireland, great castles were built and city walls strengthened. Outside the towns, clan chiefs and Norman lords protected themselves with tower houses, sometimes enclosed by a 'bawn', a high wall with turreted corners.

Henry and his heirs consolidated their claim on Ireland by invoking heavenly allies and strengthening the position of the Church. The monasteries flourished anew, and many great churches and abbeys were built, emerging gradually from modest Romanesque to lofty Gothic as architecture progressed. The Irish Church was reorganised along Roman lines and continental monastic orders appeared – Augustinians, Cistercians, and Franciscans.

■ The Normans, like the Vikings, invaded with ferocity, but integrated with the local population surprisingly quickly. English rulers perceived a dilution of their influence as the distinctions between Anglo-Norman and native Gael blurred .....■

Catholic repression In 1366, one of the most repressive of attempts to subdue Ireland took place. The Statutes of Kilkenny aimed to quell the Anglo-Norman tendency to 'go native'. Irish citizens were prohibited from intermarrying with Normans, forbidden to enter walled cities, and their dress, language, names and customs were outlawed. Like all such measures, they were doomed to fail, and Gaelic influence continued to grow until the Pale had dwindled to a small area immediately around Dublin, despite the construction of many more castles across Ireland.

While England was enmeshed in the Wars of the Roses (1455–85), a powerful Anglo-Norman family, the Fitzgeralds, extended their influence over much of east and southeast Ireland. At first their aggrandisement was not resisted by the Tudor kings,

who saw them (warily) as allies. But when Henry VIII renounced the Catholic Church, parcelling out its land to his Protestant supporters, Lord Offaly of the Fitzgerald house of Kildare (Silken Thomas) staged an insurrection. Kildare was defeated and executed, but the precedent was set for many future stands against the English Crown. Henry tried to assert his overlordship, demanding that the mutinous lords yield their property and assume vassal status. When they refused, he grabbed their lands and gave them to the first Protestant 'planters' from England and Scotland.

The Flight of the Earls In the latter half of the 16th century, the process of plantation continued under Bloody

Fourteenth-century English settlers are brought provisions

34

THE Right Honorable and vndaunted Warrior OLIVER CROMWELL Lo: Governour of IRELAND

Cromwell in Ireland

Mary and then Elizabeth I, who fought four wars in Ireland in defence of the Reformation. Her aims were to assert the Protestant religion and to prevent any intrigues against England hatched by Ireland and Spain. The first plantation attempts were failures – more rebellions took place, led by the Desmonds of Munster, and more seriously, by Hugh O'Neill, Earl of Tyrone, a formerly compliant court protégé who had hoped to become Lord of Ulster. When he realised how little autonomy he would have under Elizabeth he joined forces with Red Hugh O'Donnell, Earl of Tyrconnell, and resisted. The final showdown came at the Battle of Kinsale (1601). Spanish reinforcements caved in under siege, O'Donnell fled to Spain where he met his death, and O'Neill was forced to sign the Treaty of Mellifont, unaware that Elizabeth had died six days earlier. All the lands of the defeated chieftains were handed to planters from Scotland, encouraged to emigrate by James I. The proud O'Neill and Red Hugh's brother and successor, unable to accept their humbled status, left Donegal for ever in 1607, in the sad exile known as the Flight of the Earls.

Plantation This cleared the way for more plantation, this time more successful. Ulster's new settlers were hard-working Calvinists, chalk to the Catholic cheese, and they have never integrated. They quickly made great improvements to the land they acquired, introducing advanced methods of agriculture. Many of the settlers were skilled craftsmen, bringing new talents to its workforce.

In 1641 the dispossessed Irish made another attempt to regain their stolen lands, rebelling violently at Portadown and killing many Protestants. Gaelic leaders allied with the 'Old English' Catholics to defend their faith, property and political rights in the Confederation of Kilkenny. Meanwhile, in England, the Civil War began. Rumours of atrocities towards Ulster planters circulated, and in revenge, Cromwell brought over 20,000 dreaded Ironsides, storming Drogheda and Wexford, slaughtering thousands and sending many into slavery. Most Catholic landowners were finally dispossessed and banished west of the Shannon ('to Hell or to Connaught', in Cromwell's phrase). When he had finished, much of Ireland was devastated and its Catholic population had dwindled to half a million, bitter beyond belief at English injustice.

35

IRELAND WAS *Anglo-Irish*

■ The agony of Cromwellian times was briefly dispelled by the restoration of the Catholic Charles II in 1660, though he was never in a strong enough position to help Irish Catholics significantly. The danger-ously Popish leanings of his successor, James II, precipitated the Glorious Revolution and William of Orange's acces-sion. James II fled to Ireland for a final stand .....■

The Battle of the Boyne James II was initially successful at drumming up support in Ireland, but his ambi-tions were thwarted when he reached Derry. Here the young trade apprentices slammed the gates of the city, and (London)Derry endured the longest siege in British history. The Protestant cause prevailed, but only after immense suffering which further polarised Anglo-Irish attitudes. In 1690 William III won his decisive victory over Jacobite (Catholic) forces at the Battle of the Boyne, and further conflicts took place at Athlone, Aughrim, and finally Limerick, where the Jacobite army eventually surrendered with honour. The Treaty of Limerick granted civil rights to Catholics, but the English reneged on it, to Ireland's everlasting disgust. Measures were taken to consolidate Protestant ownership of land and Catholic subservience.

William III scents victory at the Battle of the Boyne...

Penal laws A series of repressive laws were passed, collectively known as the Penal Code. This for-bade Catholics to practise their reli-gion publicly, or educate their children in the Catholic faith. They could not enlist for military service, buy land, nor inherit it other than by equal division among all sons. Viable estates became useless pocket handkerchiefs of land. If one child converted to Protestantism, he (or she – daughters were allowed to inherit in this case) would scoop the lot! Land ownership by Catholics tumbled to about 14 per cent by the turn of the century, and Irish lan-guage, music, literature and culture were suppressed. Once again, oppo-sition fanned the flames. 'Hedge schools' were run for Catholic chil-dren and Mass was said in secret, with members of the congregation acting as lookouts for English spies.

Georgian Ireland The 18th century in Ireland was peaceful and full of achievements – literary, artistic and economic. Many of the great country houses of Ireland date from this time (naturally, these were for the Protestant settlers, not the native Irish). Greatest of all the architects of this period was Richard Cassels (anglicised as Castle, or Cassel), from a Protestant family who had settled in Germany (see panel on page 250).
  Not just single buildings, but whole villages and towns were planned, with wide streets, tree-lined malls and grand civic buildings. Domestic architecture excelled in Dublin, with dignified terraces and squares satis-fying the new aspirations of the city-

36

dwelling middle classes. Comparatively few churches have survived from Georgian times (in particular Catholic ones), but they generally followed neo-classical patterns inspired by Greek temples. Michael Stapleton and the Swiss-Italian Francini brothers were masters of stucco work, a brilliant medium in Ireland in the mid-18th century. Literature and music flourished (see pages 58–9 and 62–3), as did many applied arts, such as silverware and furniture-making.

An attempt at reform The surface prosperity and success of the Anglo-Irish Protestant Ascendancy hid tensions seething among the underprivileged peasantry, many of whom lived in appalling conditions. The Catholics were not the only ones to suffer; Presbyterians were also disadvantaged, and during the 18th century many Ulster settlers emigrated

…while the vanquished James II flees from Irish shores

to seek their fortunes across the Atlantic. Protestants were irked by Westminster rule, and gradually a spirit arose in favour of more autonomy. The American War of Independence appealed to both Catholic and Protestant sentiment, and prosperous merchants ceased to equate their interests with those of England.

Henry Grattan, a Protestant barrister, was at the forefront of this movement. He entered parliament in the same year as the American revolt, declaring 'the Irish Protestant could never be free until the Irish Catholic had ceased to be a slave'. Westminster sat up and listened. In 1782, Grattan's Parliament was formed, an assertion of Irish constitutional independence. Measures to alleviate the lot of Catholics were passed, though nothing particularly radical. Before any major achievements could be seen, the spectre of the French Revolution intervened in 1789, and once again, England battened down the hatches of reform.

■ **Ireland caught the prevailing revolutionary mood from France and, for a while, Dublin's inhabitants went about calling each other 'citizen'. In the countryside, violence grew as secret societies dedicated to overthrowing their oppressive landlords maimed horses, burned barns and drove cattle over cliffs .....■**

Religious tensions During the days of the Penal Code Irish Catholics had learned that dissimulation and evasion were necessities for survival. To follow their faith, they had to attend secret meetings and, as they had no redress in law, they took the law into their own hands. As Cecil Woodham-Smith says in *The Great Hunger*, 'These were dangerous lessons for any government to compel its subjects to learn, and a dangerous habit of mind for any nation to acquire.' After relaxation of the laws which had prevented them from owning land, many Catholics moved to Ulster, forcing up prices. The Ulster planters began to feel threatened, and formed their own ruthless organisations. A vigilante group called the Peep o' Day Boys attacked Catholics, burning them out in dawn raids and, in 1795, the Orange Order was formed to defend Protestant interests.

Emmet prepares for the insurrection which was to cost him his life...

Wolfe Tone and Robert Emmet In 1796, the radical Protestant barrister Wolfe Tone (see page 42) set up the Society of United Irishmen in Belfast. Initially it existed as a middle-class debating society, but after its suppression by Prime Minister William Pitt, it became seditious. Tone rallied support from France and attempted a naval attack on Bantry Bay (see page 151). After its failure, Pitt imposed martial law. United Irishmen were rounded up and publicly tortured to inform on their comrades, but fury at this led to open revolt, and in 1798 thousands took up pikes and rusty swords against the English yeomanry. Over 30,000 died, and Tone was captured, later committing suicide in his cell before he could be executed.

All concessions to Catholics were withdrawn, and, on 1 January 1801, the Act of Union was passed, centralising government in London. Initially the mood was buoyant; triumphant proclamations of equality were made

...and the life of the unfortunate Lord Kilwarden, caught up in the chaos caused by Emmet's uprising

for England, Ireland, Scotland and Wales within the new legislative structure, but the high hopes were unfounded. English imports swamped the Irish economy and its industries collapsed. Ireland was now hopelessly divided between the impoverished Protestant ruling class and the dispossessed and powerless Catholics. Robert Emmet, a middle-class Protestant, staged yet another abortive uprising of United Irishmen, and was hanged. His speech from the dock inspired future generations of freedom fighters.

Daniel O'Connell Twenty years later, a new inspirational force arose in the form of Daniel O'Connell (see page 42), known as the Liberator, who championed the cause of Catholic emancipation and the repeal of the Act of Union. Voting rights were granted to Catholics in 1829, but O'Connell's attempts to change Ireland's fate peacefully failed.

In the mid-century Ireland was struck down by the complete failure of the potato crop in 1845, 1846 and 1848. Terrible famine ensued, but the British did little to help; while Ireland starved for lack of potatoes, vast quantities of beef and grain were being exported to Britain. A million died, and a million emigrated.

Charles Stewart Parnell The next great figure on the political stage was Parnell (see pages 42–3), who campaigned openly for Home Rule and reform of the oppressive land tenancy laws. Gladstone's repeated attempts to introduce a Home Rule Bill were rejected by the House of Lords, despite a groundswell of support for it. More violence took place and in 1882 the British Chief Secretary and Under-Secretary for Ireland were stabbed to death in Phoenix Park. British opinion turned against Home Rule, and, by the turn of the century, the scene was set for the break-up of Ireland. The Sinn Fein party (meaning roughly 'We Ourselves') was formed by Arthur Griffith in 1908, advocating secession from Britain. On the brink of war, Britain finally acceded to demands for Home Rule in 1914, but postponed it until hostilities had ceased. The Irish Republican Brotherhood (precursors of the IRA), unable to wait, staged the Easter Rising in Dublin (see pages 54–5); meanwhile in Ulster, the Orangemen prepared for battle.

■ Ireland's history since partition has been as tragic as it was before, at least in the North. What is particularly depressing is that the more you know about the situation, the less workable any solution seems. The two extremes seem as far apart as ever, and the atrocities continue. Hopes of some loose-knit federal structure within the EC are raised, but the details seem vague. Until intransigence mellows on both sides violence continues to seem the likeliest outcome .....■

40

The Civil War In 1918 Sinn Fein, led by the Easter Rising veteran Éamon de Valera, won a massive 73 seats at the general election, and independence was declared at a meeting of the first Dáil Eirann (Irish Parliament). The Irish Republicans (now the IRA) attempted to undermine British control, using guerrilla tactics, and British soldiers (the Black and Tans) were brought over to maintain order, which they did ruthlessly. Under the 1920 Government of Ireland Act sep-

British Prime Minister, Lloyd George, left, meets de Valera in 1921

arate parliaments were created for Northern Ireland (the Six Counties, which remained within the UK), and Southern Ireland, which was granted dominion status under Crown authority. The Anglo-Irish Treaty was signed in December 1921 by Michael Collins and Arthur Griffith. De Valera refused to accept its terms and Ireland was plunged into a disastrous and bloody civil war, a conflict between those willing to accept Ireland's partition and the rest. Many politicians, British and Irish, hoped that partition would be temporary, and that eventually the two sectors would unite peacefully when emotions ran less high. They failed to take account of Loyalist feelings in the North. Under Sir Edward Carson (see page 43), Protestant Unionists resolved to fight to the death to prevent being absorbed into the new Irish Free State.

Eire is born The new Ireland suffered badly in interwar depression, made worse by de Valera's poor relations with Britain. A tariff war with Britain made Ireland's stagnant economy virtually moribund. In 1937, political links with Britain were reduced, and the name of Eire was introduced. During World War II Ireland remained officially neutral, though its position was ambivalent. Over 50,000 citizens of the Republic enlisted voluntarily in the British armed services, but anti-British feelings were sufficiently strong to encourage some collaboration with Germany, too. Eire's refusal to order a blackout enabled the strategic target of Belfast to be pinpointed more easily, which caused many civilian losses. (Dublin was also bombed in May 1941.) De Valera, to his everlasting shame, was the only world leader to offer condolences to the Reichstag on the death of Hitler.

After the war, many people emigrated from Ireland, mostly young and talented, and ironically many chose Britain for their new home. The election of the forward-looking Sean Lemass in 1959 signalled a welcome break from the politics of Kilmainham Gaol which de Valera had symbolised. Gradually, economic prosperity increased and Ireland's stifling doldrum of artistic censorship and priest-ridden Victorian morality began to lift. Ireland dropped the name Eire in 1949, and joined the European Community in 1972. Immediate benefits were felt in agriculture, tourism and the construction industry.

The Troubles continue The upswing did not improve relations with Britain or the North. In 1968 the civil rights movement began, demanding equality for Catholics. Demonstrations and marches provoked rioting on both sides; Derry was a particular flashpoint. In 1969 British troops were sent to protect

The Irish delegation to the Anglo-Irish Treaty of 1921

the Catholics, now barricaded in ghettos, but soon their protective rôle was perceived as an aggressive one. Just eight days after Ireland joined the EC, 13 civil rights demonstrators were shot by British paratroopers during a riot (the event known as Bloody Sunday). An angry crowd burned down the British embassy in Dublin, Stormont (the Northern Irish parliament) was prorogued and the province came under direct rule from Westminster. The IRA made a disastrously triumphant resurgence in a deadly new 'Provisional' guise. The 'Provos' differed from the 'Official' IRA in having as their only goal the overthrow of British rule in Northern Ireland, by whatever means.

Since 1972, persistent attempts have been made to bring the two sides together. All have been doomed so far because the Unionists refuse to compromise with the Republic in any way. 'Power-sharing executives' come and go, at Sunningdale in 1973, and at Hillsborough (the Anglo-Irish Agreement) in 1985. Meanwhile, terrorist outrages on the British mainland have hardened opinions against the IRA and increased security measures. The hunger strike 'martyrs' of 1981 (Republican prisoners demanding political status) alienated Irish opinion still further. Talks, of course, continue – but so do the bombings and shootings.

41

Figures in Irish history

CHARLES STEWART PARNELL

NO-MAN-HAS-A-RIGHT-TO-FIX-THE
BOUNDARY-TO-THE-MARCH-OF-A-NATIO
NO-MAN-HAS-A-RIGHT
SAY-TO-HIS-COUNTRY
THUS-FAR-SHALT-THOU-
AND-NO-FURTHER

■ **It is impossible to ignore Irish history as you tour the country. Its central figures (heroes or villains, depending on your point of view) keep cropping up. What follows puts just a few of them in context, and pinpoints one or two places closely associated with them .....■**

Patrick Sarsfield, 1st Earl of Lucan (d. 1693). Hero of the 1691 Siege of Limerick, with 500 troops, he made a daring raid on William III's supply train at Ballyneety, destroying all his munitions. After the Treaty of Limerick was signed, he sailed to France (Flight of the Wild Geese), and died, fighting again, in Belgium. He was married in Portumna Castle (Galway).

Wolfe Tone (1763–98) The father of Irish republicanism, this middle-class Protestant barrister founded the United

Sir Edward Carson, as depicted in 1912

Irishmen in Belfast in 1791. After a period in America, he instigated two unsuccessful attacks using French naval support, at Bantry Bay in 1796 (see the Armada Exhibition at Bantry House, page 151), and in Donegal during the Great Rebellion of 1798. After capture at Letterkenny he was sentenced in Dublin to be hanged, drawn and quartered, but cut his throat before it could be carried out, lingering in agony for seven days.

Robert Emmet (1778–1803) A disciple of Tone, Emmet staged an abortive revolt in 1803, planning to seize Dublin Castle. Emmet was sentenced to the same grisly death as Tone, whereupon he said, 'When my country takes her place among the nations of the earth, then and not till then let my epitaph be written.' Patrick Pearse, leader of the Easter Rising of 1916, paid tribute to his sacrifice.

Daniel O'Connell (1775–1847) Known as the Liberator, O'Connell was a witty, eloquent and brilliant barrister who gave up his career at the Bar to fight for Catholic Emancipation and the repeal of the Act of Union. Elected MP for Clare (1828), he won popular support, greatly alarming British authorities, though he always renounced violence. His house at Derrynane (Kerry), is a museum to his memory.

Charles Stewart Parnell (1846–91) A political giant of the 19th century, Parnell (a Protestant) was born at Avondale House in Wicklow (see page 92). Elected MP for Meath in 1875, he campaigned tirelessly for Home Rule and agrarian reform. In 1877 he founded the Irish Land

42

Figures in Irish history

Charles Stewart Parnell

League with Michael Davitt. He used peaceful tactics, favouring 'filibustering' (disruption of parliamentary debates by long speeches), and 'boycotting' (ostracising oppressive landlords). His career ended in a scandal involving the wife of a fellow MP.

Sir Edward Carson (1854–1935) Champion of the Ulster Unionists and the architect of partition in 1921, Carson was a Dubliner, knowing little of Ulster or its people. A brilliant lawyer (he was prosecuting counsel in Oscar Wilde's trial), he organised resistance to Home Rule and Irish independence, founding the Ulster Volunteers, an armed band of Loyalists. He is buried at St Anne's Cathedral, Belfast.

Dublin celebrates the release of Daniel O'Connell, September 1844

Michael Collins (1890–1922) Born near Clonakilty in County Cork, this tall, good-looking fellow soon became a Republican hero, taking part in the Easter Rising. His tactics were ruthless and he was responsible for some brutal killings. He signed the Anglo-Irish Treaty, intended to partition Ireland peacefully. A British signatory, F E Smith, said, 'I may have signed my political death warrant.' Collins replied, 'I have signed my death warrant.' Anti-treatyites ambushed and killed him near Macroom (Cork) a few months later.

Roger Casement (1864–1916) Born at Ballymena, County Antrim, this career diplomat was knighted by the British in 1911. Involved in the Easter Rising, he landed at Banna Strand near Tralee in 1916 from a German submarine containing arms for the rebels. Executed for treason, his case was not helped in those days by the knowledge that he was a practising homosexual. His grave is in Glasnevin Cemetery, Dublin.

Éamon de Valera (1882–1975) 'Dev', the 'Long Fellow', was born in New York, but grew up at Bruree (Limerick, small museum). A veteran of the Easter Rising (pardoned because of his dual nationality) he, more than any politician, determined Ireland's course after the formation of the Free State, and was the founder of Fianna Fáil (Soldiers of Destiny). Three times premier, he was president from 1959 to 1973, but did little to heal the divisions between North and South.

43

DUBLIN

C

Ward

Dublin Airport ✈

Cloghran

Kinsaley

Malahide

Portmarnock

N1

M1

N2

Tolka

N3

Mulhuddart

Blanchardstown

Finglas

Santry

Killester

Kilbarrack

Baldoyle

Ireland's Eye

Sutton

Howth

Nose of Howth

Royal Canal

Glasnevin

National Botanic Gardens

Drumcondra

Casino

N1

Marino

Clontarf

Howth Castle

North Bull Island

Howth Peninsula

Drumleck Point

Beech Park

Castleknock

Liffey

N4

Palmerston

Phoenix Park

Irish Museum of Modern Art

DUBLIN

B

Kilmainham Gaol

Kilmainham

M50

Guinness Brewery

Waterways Visitor Centre

Ballsbridge

Royal Dublin Society Showground

Chester Beatty Library

Merrion

Dublin

Bay

Grand Canal

N7

Drimnagh

Rathmines

Donnybrook

Booterstown

Blackrock

Clondalkin

N7

Terenure

Rathgar

Rathfarnham

Dundrum

Sandycove

Dun Laoghaire

Templeogue

M50

Tallaght

Ballyboden

Stillorgan

Dalkey

N11

Kill of the Grange

Dalkey Island

Sorrento Point

A

N81

Sandyford

Leopardstown

Cabinteely

Killiney Bay

Stepaside

Killiney

N11

Shankill Cross

M11

Glencullen

0 ___ 5 ___ 10 km

0 ___ 5 miles

1 **2** **3**

44

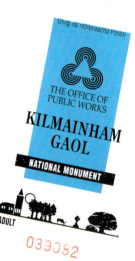

Oifig na nOibreacha Poiblí

THE OFFICE OF PUBLIC WORKS

KILMAINHAM GAOL

NATIONAL MONUMENT

ADULT

039082

Looking north up O'Connell Street, named after Daniel O'Connell, 'the Liberator' (see page 42). It was previously known as Sackville Street

Dublin For the first-time visitor, Dublin can be a perplexing experience. Its very size and city-like qualities in what is still a largely rural country make it atypical, yet it encapsulates so much that is endearing and exasperating about Ireland that it represents the Emerald Isle better than any other town. Not that the rest of Ireland necessarily thinks so; Dublin is regarded with the same mix of wistful envy and resentment by its provinces as most capital cities, and its inhabitants as a race apart. To miss Dublin, though, is to miss a colossally entertaining place, full of paradox and whimsy. It's a city of pubs, churches, grand buildings and fine museums, boozers and talkers, down-to-earth commerce and airy pipe-dreams – above all, an intimate place whose pulse must be taken at close range and over some time, possibly through a glass of Guinness, apocryphally tasting of the peaty waters of the Liffey.

The fair city? It is indeed a beautiful place, set on a broad river-basin fringed by the majestic sweep of Dublin Bay and the tantalisingly close Wicklow Mountains. Yet the 'fair city' of song was better described by James Joyce, one of its most famous citizens, as 'dear, dirty Dublin'.

The best of its Georgian architecture rivals anything that can be seen in Bath or Edinburgh, but much has been destroyed by crass development or sheer neglect. Some of the demolition is forgivable; those pretty Georgian façades often disguise impossibly friable brickwork and tottering foundations that only total reconstruction would cure. What has replaced those seemly proportions sometimes defies belief, however, especially around gap-

DUBLIN

From St Patrick's Cathedral, Dublin

Dubh linn

The *dubh linn* (dark pool) which gave its name to the city was the confluence of the Poddle and the peat-coloured waters of the Liffey. From the 9th century it was the harbour, where the original Norse settlers moored their long-ships on the low-lying banks below their fortress. A grilled opening in the south wall of the quay by Grattan (or Capel Street) Bridge shows the last remains of the River Poddle, which now runs underground for the final 5km of its course. This site was the port of Dublin until the 18th century, when a new port was built to the east by the Custom House. The original Celtic name for Dublin (still its official name in Gaelic) was Baile Átha Cliath (town of the hurdles). This name is visible on the front of some buses, on road signs and on postmarks.

The Fenian Society
This secret, militant group was formed in a Dublin timber-yard on St Patrick's Day 1858, financed by $400 donated by expatriate Irish who had emigrated to the US during the Famine years. Its members were bound by oath to loyalty to the Irish Republic. From it the Irish Republican Brotherhood, and later the IRA, developed, and it was suspected of many terrorist activities in its efforts to get the British out of Ireland. Parnell's Land League had links with the Fenians, which damaged an otherwise sympathetic hearing in Britain. Its anticlerical, Republican stance put it at odds with the Catholic Church, and known members faced excommunication. Today, Republican paramilitary groups are allegedly still partially financed by expatriate funds from America, notably Noraid, a US-based fund-raising organisation.

47

DUBLIN

The motto means 'happy the city whose citizens are obedient'

toothed St Stephen's Green or mutilated Fitzwilliam Street. The main thoroughfare on the north bank, O'Connell Street, is disappointing, its monumental dimensions and few remaining dignified buildings interspersed with seedy fast-food outlets and dull office blocks. Fortunately, though, Dublin has avoided the high-rise buildings that have ruined the skylines of other cities, and north of the river, the unsightliness is more due to dereliction than deliberate destruction. The glorious fanlit doorways that symbolise Dublin in postcards and guidebooks sometimes stand amid acres of urban desolation.

The social divide To some extent, as in London, the great divide is the river. The Liffey neatly bisects Dublin from east to west, meeting the Poddle near the Grattan Bridge and forming the *dubh linn*, or dark pool, that gives the city its name (see panel on page 46). The respectable classes enjoy elegant architecture, smart restaurants and fashionable shops now based mostly in the south around St Stephen's Green and Trinity College. In a few other areas the city's poor inhabit twilight zones of bricked-up windows and dubious backstreets where tourists are recommended not to stray. Street crime, some drug-related, some intensified by chronic unemployment, is more of a problem here than in bomb-torn Belfast, though less than in many capital cities. But in its salubrious quarters Dublin is a distinctly enjoyable and friendly place. A conversation struck up with strangers is not regarded as a sign of impertinence or lunacy, but a simple acknowledgement of fellow humanity. There is a natural friendliness about both its citizens and the whole atmosphere of the city.

The capital Though the central areas feel compact, and can easily be explored on foot, the capital is by far the largest city in Ireland. Currently the Greater Dublin area is contains about a million people, almost a third of the Republic's population, many of whom have drifted in from country areas in search of work. A large proportion of Dublin's inhabitants are under 25. It is a cosmopolitan city

Laid out by Sir Arthur Guinness in 1880, St Stephen's Green is one of the city's favourite meeting places

48

The magnificent cof-
fered dome of the City
Hall; this building, on
Lord Edward Street
near Dublin Castle,
was designed in
1769–79 by Thomas
Cooley

Billy-in-the-bowl
This extraordinary character terrorised the neigh-
bourhood of Stoneybatter,
near Arbour Hill in northwest Dublin in the mid-18th
century. Billy was born
without legs, but learned to
get about by propelling
himself in an iron bowl with
his arms. Naturally his
upper limbs developed
great strength, which he
turned to criminal use. He
lured passers-by to his
side by appealing to their
sympathy, then seized
them and strangled them
for their purses. When he
was eventually convicted
for his multiple felonies, he
was sentenced to 'as much
hard labour as his condi-
tion would allow' for the
rest of his days.

with many different nationalities and social groupings, but
there is by no means the same racial mix as, say, London.

Dublin no longer has the cachet of its 18th-century heyday, when great architecture sprouted all over the city,
when the first performance of Handel's *Messiah* was
held here, and when it was considered one of the foremost cities of Europe. Nevertheless, Ireland's recent
entry into the European Community and a vast influx of
EC funds for redevelopment have made great changes to
the city. In 1988 it celebrated its millennium (a somewhat
doubtful choice of date since its original foundation by
Viking invaders was probably in 841). In 1991 Dublin was
chosen as Europe's City of Culture, and civic ambitions
leapt, only to be dashed by economic uncertainty as world
recession deepened. Today, Dublin seems to be holding
its breath, poised uncertainly between expansion and
decline. Catch it while you can.

Traditional music in
Dublin's Brazen Head
pub

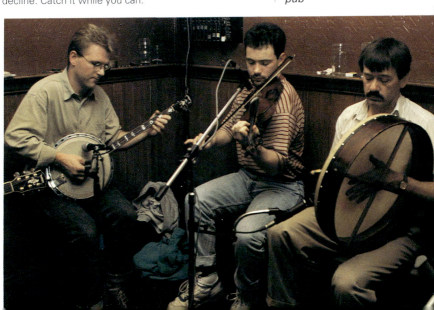

DUBLIN

St Valentine

St Valentine was a priest martyred in Rome for helping persecuted Christians. Legend relates that he restored his gaoler's blind daughter, but this availed him nothing and he was clubbed to death in about AD269. The adoption of the saint as the patron of lovers seems to have resulted from the fact that his feast-day, 14 February, was traditionally associated with various spring-time traditions, including the Roman feast of Lupercalia, when birds were believed to mate. Chaucer and Shakespeare both refer to this tradition; 'For this was on seynt Valentyne's day / Whan every foul cometh there to chese his make', wrote Chaucer in *The Parliament of Fowls*. Girls would choose their sweethearts then, and gradually a custom of sending presents and cards to loved ones developed. The crocus is St Valentine's flower.

50

From the oriental collection at the Chester Beatty Library, Ballsbridge

▶   **Carmelite Church**   46B2

57 Aungier St

Though the church stands on the foundations of a pre-Reformation Carmelite priory, nothing remains of these older buildings. What you see now dates entirely from the 19th century and is the handiwork of George Papworth, the same architect who designed Dublin's St Mary's Pro-Cathedral. Inside, it is a highly distinctive church, its spacious, light interior oddly like some municipal assembly hall, full of side-chapels and little shrines. Worshippers potter in and out between shopping to light candles to various saints, including St Valentine (see panel), patron saint of lovers, whose remains were allegedly donated to the church by Pope Gregory XVI from a cemetery in Rome and whose shrine is to the right of the nave. Hopeful couples may well add a spot more candle-wax. Others in need pass to St Albert's Well, where a relic of the Sicilian saint grants physical and spiritual healing. A 15th-century oaken Madonna and Child is also worth a look.

▶▶   **Chester Beatty Library**   47B4

20 Shrewsbury Road

Sir Alfred Chester Beatty (1875–1968) was an American mining engineer of Irish ancestry. By the age of 40 he had acquired a vast fortune, but had also developed incipient silicosis, so turned his prodigious energies to the more sedentary occupation of collecting exotic fine art. He made many trips to the Middle and Far East to add to his hoard and improve his health. He settled in Dublin in 1950, and gave his astonishing collection to the nation in 1956, living to the grand age of 93. Modern low-rise buildings in the salubrious suburbs of Ballsbridge now display his magpie genius – only a tiny fraction at a time because there is so much of it. The vivid show-cases contain outstanding examples of mostly oriental and Middle Eastern art – gorgeously decorated Chinese silk robes, Japanese *netsuki* and lacquer boxes, illuminated manuscripts and scrolled Korans, books of jade or ancient papyrus, snuff bottles and rhinoceros-horn cups, woodblock prints and miniature paintings. Apart from its academic importance, the collection is simply beautiful to look at, and should not be missed.

Christ Church Cathedral, known officially as the Cathedral of the Holy Trinity

St Audoen's Church
Under long-term restoration but visitable by appointment (tel: 01 679 1855), this ancient building can be found just west of Christ Church Cathedral on High Street. It is Dublin's earliest surviving medieval parish church, though its interior appears mostly classical and it was much altered in the 19th century. The 12th-century tower, west door and 15th-century nave and chancel are the earliest sections, and one aisle contains a font dating from 1194. In recent years the church has provided an auditorium for two audio-visual displays about Dublin, *The Flame on the Hill* (dealing with the pre-Christian era) and a recreation of Viking Dublin.

▶▶ **Christ Church Cathedral**   46B2
Christ Church Place
Oddly for a staunchly Catholic city, both of Dublin's cathedrals are Protestant. Christ Church is the seat of the Anglican Bishop of Dublin and Glendalough. It has been a Protestant church since 1551 and is inevitably closely linked with English rule of the city, though it has some rebellious streaks in its history; in 1487 the Yorkist Pretender, Lambert Simnel, was crowned here by his supporters in a counter-claim to Henry VII's throne. The cathedral stands within the original city walls, and until 1871 it was the official state church. It has a long history stretching back before the Anglo-Norman invasion to 1038 when Sitric Silkenbeard, the first Viking Christian King of Dublin, founded a wooden church on this site. This was replaced by a stone edifice in Norman times. Part of this, the south wall, collapsed in 1562, and the north wall is still half a metre out of line. Today, the buttressed grey early Gothic buildings show evidence of a ruthless 19th-century restoration which time has not yet softened. Inside, though, there is much of interest, including the so-called 'tomb of Strongbow' (Richard de Clare, Earl of Pembroke, who commanded the Anglo-Norman invasion in 1169), and the heart of St Laurence O'Toole, Archbishop and patron saint of Dublin, in the chapel of St Laud. Some of the original 13th-century tiles are incorporated into the floor, and the eagle lectern is also medieval. The crypt contains an odd jumble of quaint broken statues and the city stocks. Other curiosities include the bodies of a cat and a mouse, which apparently died in full flight when they both got stuck in an organ pipe, and the 1689 tabernacle and candlesticks of James II.

The *Bachall Íosa*
The most famous relic which Christ Church in Dublin possessed was the *Bachall Íosa*, literally the Staff of Jesus, which St Patrick is said to have used in his campaign to banish snakes from Ireland. Tradition avers that it was given to the saint when Christ appeared to him in a vision, and it became one of the symbols of office of the chief archbishop of Ireland during the Middle Ages. How exactly the *Bachall* came into the possession of Christ Church is uncertain, but we do know that it became a victim of reformational zealotry when it was burned ignominiously in 1538.

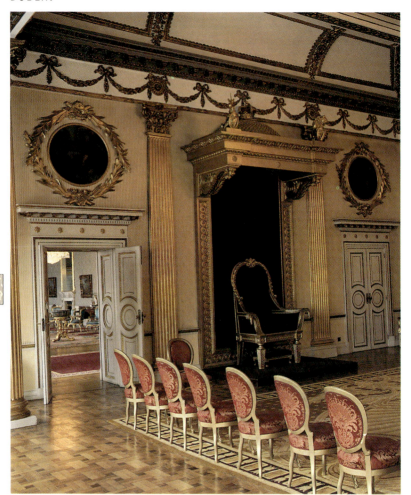

The Throne Room of Dublin Castle also contains a brass chandelier weighing more than a tonne

▶▶ **Dublin Castle**   46B2

Dame Street

This is no longer so much a castle as an assembly of courts, offices and ceremonial accommodation dating from many different periods. Though it stands on high ground that was originally a strategic site at the junction of the Liffey and the Poddle, it is now hemmed in by the surrounding buildings and doesn't offer much in the way of a city landmark. Nor does it command significant views; in fact, Queen Victoria on a visit to the city is said to have been so disappointed by the rear outlook on to slum tenement buildings that she insisted a wall be built so that she shouldn't be reminded of such indigent neighbours next time she appeared. At various stages of its history the castle has been used as fortress, prison, viceregent's residence and function rooms for important state occasions. It also serves as a useful hotel for high-risk VIPs (such as British politicians) whenever they visit to discuss Ireland's tangled affairs.

The most castle-like bit of the building still standing is

the round, machicolated Record Tower, dating from the 13th century when King John first ordered its construction. It stood on the site of an earlier Viking fortress, sections of which have been excavated and can be seen in the undercroft, along with the old moat and bits of city wall. After 1684 much of the structure had to be replaced because of fire, and much of what you see now dates from the 18th century. The church next to the Powder Tower is the Church of the Most Holy Trinity, modelled in somewhat prissy neo-Gothic and consecrated in 1814 on the site of the earlier Chapel Royal. The arms of all the viceroys from 1172 to 1922 can be seen inside. Modern buildings around the courtyard house the tax office and conference facilities. One of the most charming bits of the older buildings is the clock-towered inner courtyard.

Visits are by guided tour only, which, though informative, are somewhat impersonal. If you have time to wait it is a good idea to see the photographic exhibition in the reception building (which also does good refreshments) to get a clear idea of the layout of the complex. Inside, you see the main state apartments (provided no other functions are going on there), which are sumptuously furnished to provide a suitably opulent setting for the many dignitaries who have made use of the castle. Vast Waterford chandeliers, tapestries, hand-tufted Donegal carpets mirroring the ceiling plasterwork, and Adam fireplaces abound, revealing the palatial lifestyle led by the viceroys acting on behalf of the Crown. St Patrick's Hall is one of the most impressive rooms, all cluttered with banners and coats of arms, beneath an ornately painted ceiling. It is now used for the inauguration of Ireland's presidents. The throne room contains a massive throne believed to have been brought to Dublin by William of Orange after his victory at the Boyne. During the Easter Rising the castle was briefly threatened by an assault from the roof of the nearby City Hall. After the suppression of the rebellion, the captured rebel, James Connolly, was held (wounded) in one of the state rooms before being taken to Kilmainham to face execution.

Limited resources
As the centre of English power in Ireland, Dublin Castle was for centuries probably the most heavily guarded fortress in the country. Yet, during the Easter Rising in 1916, insurgents abandoned a scheme to take the Castle – without knowing that, at the time, it was manned only by a corporal's guard.

53

Dublin Civic Museum has a section devoted to fire-fighting. In this are a collection of fire-insurance plaques, such as the one below. They were once placed on houses to guide the insurance companies' own firemen to houses insured by them

▶ ▨ **Dublin Civic Museum**   *47B3*

58 South William Street
Housed in what was once the City Assembly House, the civic museum traces the history of Dublin from Viking times in old maps and photographs, prints, items from excavation sites, etc. The city's mercantile past is portrayed in sections devoted to various aspects of Dublin's trade and industry, and there is an interesting section on transport, including a model of the Howth tram. Temporary exhibitions on city life are held every few months. One curiosity is a sculpted head of Lord Nelson, placed here after his column was blown up in O'Connell Street in 1966 on the 50th anniversary of the Easter Rising.

The Easter Rising

■ **The Easter Rising was a curious event, tiny in comparison with the rebellion of 1798, for instance, with only about 2,000 people actively taking part in it. It was disastrously badly organised and commanded very little public support, but its martyred heroes glow in the imaginations of republican Ireland as icons in the struggle against British rule .....■**

Pearse Museum

This little museum is situated in the house once run by Padraic Pearse and his brother William as a boys' school. Their curriculum placed a strong emphasis on Gaelic studies and Irish culture. The United Irishman Robert Emmet courted his bride in the grounds. The house is now devoted to memorabilia connected with Pearse's life and the events that led to his death. It is situated in St Enda's Park in Rathfarnham, a southern Dublin suburb.

The General Post Office soon after the Easter Rising

Irish heroes The leaders were Padraic Pearse and James Connolly. Pearse, a shy schoolmaster, was an unlikely commander, but he was inspired by a kind of mystical belief that bloodshed was necessary to cleanse Ireland. He was an Irish Volunteer, a group pledged to establish Home Rule at all costs. James Connolly was a more practical man, a socialist, born into a poor Irish family in Scotland, and in the British army at 14. He founded the Irish Citizens Army, closely allied to the Irish Volunteers.

The Rising On Easter Monday, 24 April 1916, Pearse, at the head of 150 men armed with ancient rifles and farm tools, took over the General Post Office, where he solemnly read out a stirring document proclaiming the new Irish Republic. Meanwhile, volunteers took over other buildings – a brewery, lunatic asylum, factory and bakery. Many Dubliners were as bemused as the British forces by the collapse of the city into chaos, and, instead of joining the rebels, made tea for the British. The fighting lasted for six days, and on the Saturday Pearse surrendered, by when over 400 people had died. Twice as many police were killed as rebels, and four times as many civilians. Much of central Dublin lay in ruins, and the leaders of the Rising were even less popular than they had been at the start.

The Easter Rising

The tragic aftermath Then the tide turned. Instead of listening to the moderate Home Rule supporter John Redmond's advice not to execute any of the rebels, 14 of them were shot in Kilmainham Gaol, including Pearse and Connolly. From then on, they were heroes in the classic republican tradition. The release of hundreds of Irish internees later that year (among them Arthur Griffith, founder of Sinn Fein, Éamon de Valera and Michael Collins) did nothing to assuage the bitterness that surrounded the aftermath of the Easter Rising. The fact that thousands of Irishmen died just a few months later on the battlefields of the Somme, fighting in the British Army, was all but eclipsed. A bronze statue in the rebuilt General Post Office, depicting the mythical hero, Cuchulainn, at the moment of death, symbolises the glorified leaders.

Kilmainham Gaol This prison (*Inchicore Road, Kilmainham*), last used as such in 1924, is an excellent museum documenting the Irish struggle for independence. Here, many prisoners were held – United Irishmen, Fenians, Land Leaguers. A reorganisation of its exhibits has made it a gripping and memorable place, and a fascinating, if slightly partisan, insight into political and prison history. Serpent-like monsters writhe over the entrance gate. The main body of the prison, a classic barn-like shell of metal stairways and chicken-wired galleries, contains numerous display cases of items and documents. The interesting guided tour begins at the scaffold where just one prisoner was hanged, and continues to the west wing where political internees were held in tiny separate dark cells. Passing the much more comfortable room where Parnell was imprisoned for seven months, it leads, finally, to the stonebreakers' yard where 14 leaders of the Easter Rising were executed by firing squad. James Connolly had a gangrenous leg, and was shot in a chair. Another, Joseph Plunkett, was married to Grace Gifford by candlelight in the prison chapel, just two hours before he was shot. They were allowed ten minutes together.

Despite the clear dangers, life continued almost as normal for many Dubliners

The monument in the General Post Office

The children's corner at Dublin Zoo...

Guinness

Arthur Guinness established his brewery in Dublin in 1759 and soon began experimenting with a London-brewed beverage made with roasted barley, called 'porter' (after its popularity with the porters of Covent Garden). By 1799 he concentrated all his production efforts on this distinctive drink, a rich black liquid topped with that 'foamous' creamy head (as James Joyce called it). After the Napoleonic Wars of the early 19th century, an even stronger ('extra stout') beer was produced, and it rapidly reached most parts of the globe, even the South Pole (freezing is not generally recommended!). Though technology is now greatly advanced, the basic recipe of Guinness remains the same – Irish-grown barley, soft water, hops and the strain of yeast Arthur Guinness used in 1759. A highly successful marketing policy has employed many talented artists in poster campaigns. The profits from Guinness have funded many worthy enterprises, such as the Wexford Opera Festival and the Georgian Society.

► **Dublin Zoo**　　　　44B1

Phoenix Park

Established in 1830, Dublin's zoo is the third oldest in the world. If you are short of time it is not essential viewing, but as zoos go, it is attractive, set in 12ha of gardens with fauna roaming in pleasant surroundings. Its most celebrated inhabitants are the lions, one of whom achieved undying fame as the kingly beast roaring above the MGM film studios' logo before every cinematic presentation.

► **Guinness Brewery**　　　　44B1

James's Gate

Way upstream of most central sights is a Lowryesque skyline of smoking factory chimneys and giant metallic storage vats. This is the largest brewery in Europe, producing what can only be described as Ireland's *vin du pays*, though in fact it was first invented in London. Arthur Guinness's famous 'porter' is shrouded in a sort of misty-eyed Celtic mythology which declares it can never be the same drunk outside Dublin, or from a can, or that the art of pulling a pint takes years to learn. This may be nonsense, but the production process is certainly a complex one and conditions of storage are important. You can't visit the brewery itself, but in a nearby back-street (*Crane Street*), a visitor centre in a handsome 19th-century warehouse called the Hop Store tells you all you could possibly want to know about grist and malt in a well-displayed walk-round exhibition with lots of original brewing equipment, casks and posters. Thrown in with your tour is a free half-pint or so, straight from the horse's mouth, as it were. The areas immediately surrounding the brewery and the Hop Store are insalubrious and strolling through the back-streets as a conspicuous tourist is inadvisable.

►► **Hugh Lane Municipal Gallery**　　　　46D2

Parnell Square

The pictures are displayed in an elegant house designed by Sir William Chambers for the Earl of Charlemont in 1762. Today this north Dublin area is no longer very fashionable, but it was then highly desirable, and the house is a fine example of that early Georgian heyday. Its contents, however, are even more splendid – in some ways more enjoyable and intimate than the National Gallery. Luscious Corots, Courbets and Monets glow on the plain walls, along with some good Jack Yeats – and a portrait of Maud Gonne, who so captivated his literary brother. A good coffee shop adds to the gallery's attractions.

►► **Irish Museum of Modern Art**　　　　46B1

Royal Hospital, Military Road, Kilmainham

This recently opened museum certainly deserves a visit, rather more for its glorious setting than the contents themselves. The Royal Hospital is one of the finest 17th-century buildings in Ireland, constructed in 1684 as a home for retired and invalid soldiers. It is based on the style of Les Invalides in Paris, though on a much more appealing scale. It was restored by the Government in 1986 at vast cost and now, somewhat bizarrely, houses ultra-modern works of variable quality on iceberg walls. Temporary exhibitions ring the changes, along with educational and community programmes of music, theatre and visual arts. Its hearty self-service restaurant is a good reason to visit, particularly after a look at Kilmainham Gaol, just beyond the hospital's gates. Seek out the curious chapel with its remarkable riot of papier mâché decoration on the ceiling. The museum is closed on Mondays.

▶ ⬛ Irish Whiskey Corner   46C1
Bow Street
One of the bonded warehouses used to mature whiskey has been converted by Irish Distillers into a museum showing the production process of the 'water of life'. An audio-visual show and a model of an old distillery illumine the visitor, who is then regaled with a tasting to establish the difference between Scotch, Irish and bourbon. If you are touring, there are larger and better whiskey distilling attractions in Northern Ireland (Bushmills) or County Cork (Midleton). Dublin's version is in a sleazy area of the city.

▶▶▶ Kilmainham Gaol   46B1
(See Focus on the Easter Rising, page 55.)

...and the children's corner at the Municipal Gallery

Hugh Lane
When Hugh Lane went down with the *Lusitania* in 1915, he bequeathed a problem as well as a magnificent art collection. He had left his estate 'to the nation'. The difficulty was (in the light of contemporary political events) to decide which nation he meant. Britain naturally claimed he intended the collection to be British, whereas Dublin said it should stay in his native land. Eventually the dispute was settled with a classic British compromise. The collection was simply split in two parts. Half the pictures stayed in Dublin; half in the National Gallery in London, and every five years they changed over. Would that all Irish problems could be solved so amicably! (Under a new agreement, most of Hugh Lane's bequest is now actually on view in Dublin.)

A re-creation of a cooper's workshop at the Guinness Brewery

57

■ **The period from about 1714 to 1830 was Dublin's apogee, a great flowering of architecture, literature, philosophy and art. The quality of Irish craftsmanship in silverwork, glasswear and furniture, and in Dublin's superb Georgian buildings, epitomises the 'age of elegance' .....■**

58

The figure of Hope rests upon her anchor atop the magnificent Custom House

Dublin's heyday After the depredations of Cromwell's visits and the turmoil of Williamite battles, the 18th century was a time of comparative peace and prosperity in the English Pale. For the upper classes, life was highly civilised. Aesthetes and businessmen, wealthy gentry and talented artists merged resources to make Dublin one of the foremost cities of Europe. Terraces, parks, squares, imposing monuments and dignified townhouses burgeoned throughout the central parts of the city, bounded by the Grand and Royal Canals. In 1757 the Wide Streets Commission, Europe's first planning authority, established new guidelines for building development, and in 1773 the Paving Board set up sensible regulations on lighting, cleaning and drainage, making densely populated residential areas much more salubrious. This

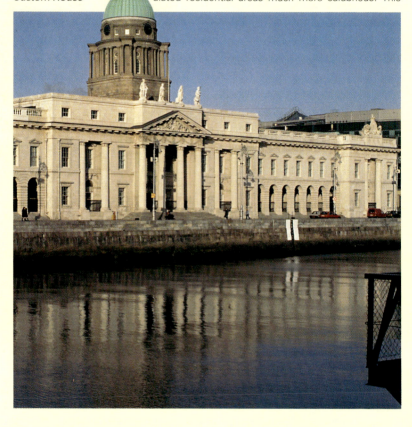

confident assertion of the good life for the Anglo-Irish Ascendancy disguised the wretched lot of the poor; in 1770 even the English viceroy was forced to admit that the Irish peasantry were 'amongst the most wretched people on earth'.

North of the Liffey In the earlier years of the 18th century, Dublin's fashionable centre of gravity lay north of the river, and the first typically Georgian housing appeared around Mountjoy and Parnell (formerly Rutland) Squares and Henrietta Street. These have not fared well since conversion to tenement buildings after the Act of Union caused a dramatic fall in property values, and the buildings now present a sad picture of neglect and decay. A few attempts at restoration have been made in some areas, such as North Great George Street, and some gems glimmer in this tarnished setting. Modest examples can be found in **Parnell Square**▶▶ (the Hugh Lane Municipal Gallery, see page 56, is in a splendid town house of the period; **Belvedere House**▶ on Great Denmark Street, now a Jesuit college, is another). Two grand set pieces north of the river, monumental buildings designed by James Gandon, can be seen to advantage from the opposite bank of the Liffey. The weighty **Custom House**▶▶ of 1791 (see panel) floats on a fragile platform of pine planks on swampy riverside land. Further west, the **Four Courts**▶ of 1785 was the seat of the High Court of Justice for Ireland. The Courts of King's Bench, Exchequer, Common Pleas and Chancery radiate from a circular central hall, liveliest at lunchtimes when bewigged lawyers hobnob with their clients. Another Gandon building stands away from the river, in Henrietta Street; the **King's Inns**▶ (1795–1827) were Dublin's Inns of Court, where budding barristers lived, studied and ate dinners. The **Rotunda Maternity Hospital**▶▶, the first purpose-built maternity hospital in Europe, has some superb stucco-work in its chapel.

South of the Liffey The best preserved and most enjoyable examples of Dublin's Georgian heritage can be seen south of the river. The shift in popularity occurred around the year 1750, after the construction of the opulent **Leinster House**▶▶ (now Ireland's parliament building) for the Duke of Leinster in 1745. At the time, he was ridiculed for his choice of a green-field site away from the hub of fashionable Dublin, but as he rightly predicted (with that self-effacing modesty typical of the era!), 'Wherever I go, they will follow.'

Dublin's Georgian heritage was largely spared aerial bombing during the World Wars, but it has fared ill at the hands of 20th-century developers and politicians. After the creation of the Free State in 1922, renovation of buildings reminiscent of English rule was not exactly a high priority. Much thoughtless and irreparable destruction took place. But there is still much to enjoy among the fanlit doorways of its 18th-century squares. A new generation of conservation-minded citizens who do not blame bricks and mortar for Ireland's disastrous history thankfully seem bent on preserving what is left.

See the following two pages for a walk around Dublin's finest Georgian buildings.

Tailor's Hall Not far from Christ Church (on Back Lane) stands Dublin's only surviving guild hall, quite different architecturally from anything else you will see in the city. It is now the headquarters of *An Taisce*, (broadly speaking the Irish equivalent of the British National Trust, see pages 230–1) which is dedicated to the conservation of historic buildings and scenic landscapes. Tailor's Hall dates from 1706 and has a fine 18th-century interior with tall Queen Anne windows and a minstrel's balcony. Admission is free.

North George Street: the lantern above the door was lit when the mistress of the house was 'at home to visitors'

Inspecting Georgian Dublin The Custom House, Four Courts, Bank of Ireland and Leinster House (while parliament is in session) are not officially open to the public. Nevertheless, it is occasionally possible to visit these buildings. If you are genuinely interested in the interiors and do not succeed in persuading a friendly official to let you in, enquire at the offices of Bord Fáilte as to whom to contact for entrance.

Walk A walk around Georgian Dublin

See map on pages 46–7.

Within the bounds of 18th-century taste, Irish craftsmen found great scope for personal expression, and the details of buildings are hugely varied and imaginative. Little touches – door-knockers, coal-hole covers, boot-scrapers – are the rewards of a sharp-eyed wander round Georgian Dublin.

College Green is a good starting point for any exploration of Dublin. This was the centre of power during the 18th century until the Act of Union centralised government in Westminster. What is now the **Bank of Ireland**►► was built by Edward Lovett Pearce between 1729 and 1739 to house the Irish Parliament. During banking hours, visitors may see the former House of Lords,

St Stephen's Green

sumptuously furnished with a Waterford chandelier, 18th-century tapestries and coffered ceiling. **Trinity College**►►►, on the other side of the Green (see page 72), dates mainly from the 18th century. Its theatrical 90m façade, attributed to Theodore Jacobsen, was built between 1752 and 1759, and the **Provost's House**►► on the corner of Grafton Street is one of Dublin's grandest Georgian mansions.

Turning down Kildare Street, Georgian **Leinster House**►►► is the most imposing of several monumental public buildings (see pages 58–9), while nearby Molesworth Street contains three interesting early Georgian houses built for Huguenot families in 1736–55. Known as **Dutch Billies**►, they are a revival of a style popular after William of Orange's conquest, featuring curvy gables and huge chimneys. In Dawson Street, 18th-century buildings include: **St Ann's**►► of 1720 (see page 70); the **Royal Irish Academy**► of 1785 housing a splendid library of Irish manuscripts; and the balustraded façade of the Lord Mayor's residence, **The Mansion House**► (1705, actually a Queen Anne building), is sometimes open for exhibitions. **St Stephen's Green** is one of the landmarks of the Georgian city, though its buildings date from many periods and its park was not laid out until Victorian times (see page 68). The best of the Georgian buildings are: the **Royal College of Surgeons**►► (1806) scarred by the Easter Rising; **Newman House**► (Nos 85 and 86 on the south side), original home of the Catholic university (one of these houses, ironically, was built for a vehement anti-Catholic, Thomas 'Burnchapel' Whaley, by the great 18th-century architect Richard Castle); and **Iveagh House**►► (1736), now the Department of Foreign Affairs (not open). Off St Stephen's Green, **Harcourt Street, Ely Place** and **Leeson Street** contain many attractive and well-preserved domestic townhouses.

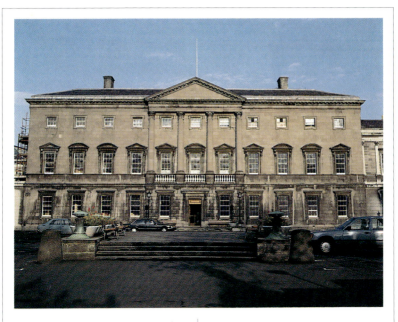

Leinster House, designed by Castle

61

Fitzwilliam Street▶ contained the longest stretch of Georgian buildings in Europe until an astonishing piece of civic vandalism in the 1960s permitted a hideous office block to tear a hole in it. The Electricity Supply Board (whose administrative headquarters it is) have now sheepishly rebuilt one of the houses they tore down. **Number 29▶** is open (free) as a little museum, and its elegant rooms re-create something of the atmosphere of late Georgian times. **Fitzwilliam Square▶▶**, though not the largest or most famous Georgian example, is actually one of the best preserved. Many fanlit doorways retain original features such as glass recesses for lamps, and anti-burglar spikes set in the walls. A glance down Mount Street reveals the attractive late-Georgian church of **St Stephen's▶▶**, known as the Pepperpot from its unusual dome. In the mid-18th century the **Grand Canal** beside the church would have been a bustling highway of commerce and passenger traffic.

Merrion Square▶▶▶ is the final great 'set piece' on this walking tour. The blue plaques all around many of the houses commemorate famous former occupants, suggesting how fashionable it once was. Planned in 1762 for Lord Fitzwilliam, it is unquestionably one of the finest of all Dublin's squares. Oscar Wilde's parents lived here, along with Daniel O'Connell, the statesman, W B Yeats, and many other worthies.

Georgian elegance in every detail

■ **Dublin is an emphatically literary city. Most great (and many not-so-great) Irish writers gravitated here at some stage so, to some extent, the literary history of Dublin is the literary history of Ireland. The ghosts of Yeats, Shaw, Synge, Beckett, O'Casey, Wilde, Swift and others haunt its streets and bookshops. The National Library, near Leinster House, contains a splendid collection of first editions and works of 17th-century Irish authors, as well as later writers, including Swift, Goldsmith, Yeats, Shaw and Joyce .....■**

Top: a fanciful depiction of Oscar Wilde

James Joyce Tower
The 22-year-old Joyce spent only a week or so here in the August of 1904, though he later immortalised it in the first chapter of his masterpiece *Ulysses*. The Martello Tower belonged to Oliver St John Gogarty, an ebullient surgeon and poet, who invited Joyce to stay with him there. For more details of his eventful stay in the tower, see page 96–7.

Stella and Vanessa
Jonathan Swift's women friends are immortalised in his letters and other writings under pseudonyms. 'Vanessa' was Esther Vanhomrigh who lived in Celbridge, County Kildare (at Barberstown Castle, see Hotels and Restaurants, page 271). Swift met her in London in 1708 and may even have fathered her child. She followed Swift to Ireland but broke off her friendship with him when he became involved with 'Stella'. The second great attachment of his life was another Esther (Johnson), with whom he had a deep but apparently platonic relationship. Memorials to Swift and Stella can be seen in St Patrick's Cathedral (see page 71).

Georgian flowering Along with its architecture, Dublin's literary scene blossomed during the 18th century, a time of great intellectual ferment and scientific discovery. One of the giants of the era was the Dean of St Patrick's Cathedral, Jonathan Swift. Probably the greatest satirist in the English language, he is most famous for *Gulliver's Travels*. He was a Protestant and obviously part of the Anglo-Irish Ascendancy, but some of his bitterest invective was directed against the cruel and unequal conditions of the Irish poor. In *A Modest Proposal* he attempted to stir up the complacent attitudes of the time by suggesting, deliberately outrageously, that Irish children should be fattened up for English tables.

Swift's contemporaries included William Congreve and George Farquhar, both of whom were educated at Trinity College, Dublin. Like many other Irish writers, however, they soon left for London, as did the later authors, Oliver Goldsmith and Richard Brinsley Sheridan. During the 19th century, dramatists who achieved greatest fame were Oscar Wilde and George Bernard Shaw (who lived on until 1950), both of whom, following the usual pattern, left their native land to dazzle London society.

The Gaelic Revival Meanwhile, however, another strand of writers began to receive attention in Dublin. At the end of the 19th century a renewed interest in all things Irish (the Gaelic Revival) was inspiring artists such as W B Yeats and his friend George Russell; Celtic myths interweave their work. The turn of the century saw a great flourishing of theatrical talent, this time a home-grown version using Irish, specifically Gaelic themes. John Millington Synge's works for the Abbey Theatre were among these, followed by the pacifist works of Sean O'Casey. Both these writers were controversial, and aroused much furore when they broke away from the norms of light social comedy.

James Joyce The literary giant most closely associated with Dublin, James Joyce (1882–1941), is surprisingly not among its three Nobel-prize-winners (Beckett, Shaw and Yeats), all of whom have strong links with the capital too. Joyce however, lived and breathed the place, though he

Literary Dublin

always had a love–hate relationship with it and spent most of his adult life abroad. He referred to his native city as the 'centre of paralysis': 'How sick, sick, sick I am of Dublin. It is a city of failure, of rancour and unhappiness. I long to be out of it,' he wrote. The works in which Dublin appears, almost as the central character, are *A Portrait of the Artist as a Young Man*, *Ulysses*, *The Dubliners* and *Finnegan's Wake*. Ironically, Joyce, spurned and hounded into exile while he lived, is now fêted by the tourist authorities as one of the city's greatest ambassadors – every step of his Dublin-set masterpiece *Ulysses* carefully documented in self-guided walks and wall plaques. Keen followers of his work can buy a map and follow the route taken by Leopold Bloom on that famous June day. The trail leads well out of the city centre to the southeast suburbs of Dalkey and Sandycove, where you can find the James Joyce Tower which features in the opening chapter of *Ulysses*. Inside is a museum set up in 1962 by Sylvia Beech, original publisher of his great novel, containing Joycean memorabilia and some letters. Next to the tower is the Forty Foot Pool, where Buck Mulligan (based on Gogarty, see panel) swims at the start of *Ulysses*. Nearby Dalkey was the subject of Flann O'Brien's novel *The Dalkey Archive*.

The prolific George Bernard Shaw

Brendan Behan

Of all the characters who trod Dublin's literary stage during the course of this century, few were more rumbustious than Brendan Behan – variously remembered as a loveable rogue or an arrogant sot – whose over-draught of Guinness contributed to his untimely death in 1964 at the ripe young age of 41. During his creative years, the pubs in Dublin were officially closed on St Patrick's Day, and one of the few places where one could openly get a drink was at the annual dog show in the Royal Dublin Society's premises in Ballsbridge. On repairing there one St Patrick's Day, Behan is said to have bitched 'Who the hell brought a ****ing dog into a place like this, anyway?' – or words to that effect.

William Butler Yeats (1865–1939)

▶▶ **National Gallery** *47B4*

Merrion Square West

The National Gallery is a fine collection, though not in the first rank of European art galleries. About 2,000 works are on show at any one time, representing Irish, US and all major European schools of art up to the 19th century. More recent works are on display at the newly opened Irish Museum

The intricate beauty of the Tara Brooch, housed in the Treasury of the National Museum. Despite its name, it has no known connection with Tara in County Meath

of Modern Art in the suburb of Kilmainham (near the gaol) and at the Hugh Lane Municipal Gallery (see pages 56–7).

The National Gallery first opened 1864, with only a tiny fraction of the paintings it now possesses. Much of it was due to the energies of William Dargan, a railway magnate largely responsible for building Ireland's rail network. He was the moving spirit behind the Dublin Exhibition of 1853, using the profits to found the gallery, and his statue stands on the lawns near the entrance gate. The building was designed by Francis Fowke, who also designed the Victoria and Albert Museum in London.

The collection contains a number of painterly works by Jack B Yeats, brother of the poet, W B Yeats, which make a gritty contrast to the sentimental productions of other members of the Irish School. Other highlights include Degas' *Ballet Girls* and Sir Joshua Reynolds' *Earl of Bellamont*. The Impressionists are well represented, as are Italian and Dutch schools and earlier French artists from the 17th century onwards. A fascinating collection of Irish portraits lines the grand staircase, culminating in the fiery Countess Markiewicz who was furious at being pardoned for her part in the Easter Rising (see pages 54–5). The gallery has an attractive coffee shop and restaurant. Admission is free, and it is open every day (until 9p.m. on Thursday).

Viking foundations
One of the first additions to the National Museum's collections was a Viking sword which appropriately came to light when the builders were digging the foundations for the museum just over a century ago.

▶▶▶ **National Museum** *47B3*

Kildare Street

This museum houses many of the finest masterpieces of Irish Celtic art from the Bronze Age to the Middle Ages. Its greatest treasures (appropriately housed in the Treasury) include the Tara Brooch, the Ardagh Chalice, the Cross of Cong, the Shrine of St Patrick's Bell, and many other exquisite pieces of gold jewellery and croziers. The Tara Brooch is perhaps the most important and most copied of all Celtic jewels. It dates from the 8th century and is made of white bronze, silver-gilt, amber and glass, and though it measures only about 5cm across, it is intricately decorated with scrolls and spirals and strange beasts on both sides. The Ardagh Chalice, from about the same period, is inspired by Byzantine art – a shapely wide goblet of gilded bronze, chased with gold filigree and studded with coloured glass.

A department called *Ar Thoir na Saoirse* (The Road to Independence) contains mementoes of the Easter Rising and the Civil War. Other sections contain superb porcelain of Irish, English, European and Asian origins, many items from Japan, rare textiles and old musical instruments such as Irish harps and uilleann pipes. A particularly interesting recent addition to the museum's collection is the evidence of Viking settlement by Wood Quay, near Dublin Castle. Excavations were carried out here before the hideous – and much opposed – council offices (known popularly as the Bunkers) were built on this important historic site. The finds are on display in an annexe towards the rear of the museum. A testament to more amateur archaeologists, the Derrynaflan Hoard was discovered by a group of metal-detecting enthusiasts in County Tipperary. Like the National Gallery, admission is free (closed Monday).

► **Natural History Museum**   *47B3*
Merrion Street
This is part of the National Museum (and has the same opening hours), but is housed in a separate building. In a large hall, a crowded display of taxidermy can be seen, including a comprehensive collection of Irish mammals, birds, fish and insects, together with various mineral exhibits. Upstairs are animals from other parts of the world, while whales once stranded on the Irish coast now hang from the roof.

Shavian generosity
Today we associate the name of George Bernard Shaw so much with drama that it may come as a surprise to find his statue (by Trubetzkoy) on the lawn of the National Gallery of art. There is, however, a very simple explanation. The statue was erected by a grateful nation in recognition of Shaw's generous gesture of bequeathing one third of his estate to the gallery because, as he said himself, he was 'educated' there. Through the royalties accruing particularly from *My Fair Lady* after his death, his posthumous philanthropy helped the gallery to fill gaps with some remarkable acquisitions in the 1960s and 1970s.

67

The gallery of Dublin's Natural History Museum

Parks and Gardens

■ **Weather permitting, it is never difficult to find a place to get away from the traffic noise in Dublin. The Georgian layout of the city naturally produced a system of spacious squares and landscaped gardens around its principal monuments, and Dublin is full of green open spaces, neat and municipal, or wilder and more natural .....■**

Short-term tenancy
The apocryphal story is told of a prominent and somewhat self-opinionated 20th-century Irish politician who went to Glasnevin Cemetery in search of a suitable plot for himself. On being offered one in the poshest part of the grounds, he declined, saying that it was far too good for him. The official then came up with a more medium-priced alternative, which was also spurned – to the growing surprise and frustration of the cemetery office. But all turned to smiles when a much cheaper one was suggested and promptly accepted. 'After all,' said the politician, 'I only need it for three days.'

The Three Fates quietly watch life pass by from their vantage point in St Stephen's Green

Town squares The most famous of the Georgian squares is **St Stephen's Green**, which was formerly common land. In 1880 Lord Ardilaun (heir to the Guinness fortunes) paid for the present gardens to be laid out, and they now encompass 9ha of lawns, flower-beds, paved walks, shrubberies and an ornamental lake with wildfowl. Bandstands, statues and pergolas dot it at intervals; its various monuments include Henry Moore's memorial to Yeats and a statue of Wolfe Tone amid stone slabs ('Tonehenge'). The gardens are open during daylight hours when they become one of Dublin's most popular spots for strolling and having a lunchtime sandwich.

Merrion Square is another attractive open space dating from Georgian times, and has the restored Rutland Fountain inset in its railings. During the Famine years (1845–8) a soup kitchen was set up in this well-heeled residential square to feed starving refugees who poured in from the devastated country areas. Today you are more likely to find artists selling their wares at weekends.

Phoenix Park At the west end of the city lies the huge open space called **Phoenix Park**. It stretches along the Liffey for about 5km, and covers 712ha, about five times the size of London's Hyde Park. The park's name comes from the Gaelic *fionn uisce*, meaning 'clear water', referring to the spring in the Furry Glen. In it are lakes, woods, fields, a racecourse and sports grounds. It also contains Dublin Zoo (see page 55), and the headquarters of the *Garda Siochána*, or Irish police force. Its most striking monuments are the 60m obelisk to Wellington and the Phoenix Column, erected in 1747 by Lord Chesterfield, a former lord lieutenant. The parklands once belonged to Kilmainham priory, until seized during the Reformation, and later became a deer park owned by the Duke of Ormonde (deer still roam the park, descended from the original herd). During the 18th and 19th centuries it was a fashionable place with desirable residences, one of which now houses the Irish President. The so-called '15 acres' (now playing fields) were well known as a duelling place in the 18th century. Phoenix Park's popularity suffered when in 1882 Lord Cavendish, the Chief Secretary, and Burke, the Under-Secretary, were stabbed here by obscure malcontents called the Invincibles. The assassination caused a great furore at Westminster, where the question of Home Rule for Ireland was at last being seriously debated. The park's main entrance lies at the southeast corner, off Parkgate Street.

69

Other green spaces A little way east lies **Arbour Hill Cemetery**, a quiet memorial garden where the leaders of the Easter Rising are buried, their names carved in stone beside a copy of the stirring proclamation of independence. Dublin's other interesting cemetery is in **Glasnevin**, in the north of the city, where lie the graves of Éamon de Valera, Gerard Manley Hopkins and Roger Casement (see page 43). Close by are Dublin's **National Botanic Gardens►►**, set up in 1795, and containing about 20,000 species of plants and trees, including specialist rose and vegetable gardens. The ornate glasshouses known as the Curvilinear Range were constructed by Richard Turner, a famous 19th-century iron founder also responsible for producing the Palm House in Belfast. Riverside walks lead through bog and peat gardens and the arboretum.

One of Dublin's wilder spaces is **North Bull Island**, a strip of dunes and beaches off the coast, reached from the road to Howth. It is now a nature conservancy area, but visitors can walk out along the causeway to the lighthouse. Many species of birds can be seen here and further information can be gleaned either from the guided tours or at the interpretive centre.

The Curvilinear Range of greenhouses at the Botanical Gardens

Poet James Mangan, St Stephen's Green

*St Ann's is built
from pale granite
interspersed with
single courses of red
brick*

▶ **St Ann's Church**   *47B3*

Dawson Street
This church's Italianate façade of
1868 in neo-Romanesque granite
disguises an 18th-century interior
of polished wood balconies and
ornate plasterwork. Wooden
shelves beside the altar were constructed to hold loaves of bread for
the poor, a bequest left by Lord
Theophilus Newtown.

▶ **St Francis Xavier's
Church**   *47E3*

Upper Gardiner Street
This classical Jesuit church was
constructed as soon as Catholic
emancipation was achieved in
1829. It is built in the shape of a
Latin cross, and has an Ionic portico. Inside its most striking features are its fine coffered ceiling
and the green *faux* marble altar-
piece brought from Italy.

▶ **St Mary's Abbey**   *46C2*

off Capel Street
The remains of the Pale's most prominent Cistercian
monastery, founded by the Benedictines in 1139, lie here.
Much of the stone was removed to build Essex Bridge
near by and only the chapter-house still stands.

▶ **St Mary's Pro-Cathedral**   *47D3*

Marlborough Street, east of O'Connell Street
Dublin's most significant Catholic church has never been
granted full cathedral status. Originally destined for the
site occupied by the General Post Office, it actually

Silken Thomas
In 1534 the 10th Earl of
Kildare, known as Silken
Thomas for his love of fine
clothing, mutinied against
Henry VIII and declared
vengeance on him at St
Mary's Abbey for his apos-
tacy against the Catholic
Church and the supposed
beheading of his father (a
false rumour). Thomas was
captured and executed in
1537.

*Some believe that
one of the mummi-
fied bodies in St
Michan's Church is
that of a medieval
Crusader*

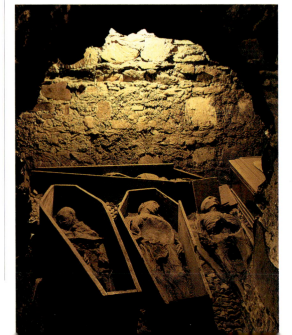

stands in a fairly undistinguished site off O'Connell Street, its dome and Doric façade barely visible among discount shops and street markets. Inside, its 1820s Renaissance interior has some dignity, though few points of major interest. John Newman first avowed his conversion to the Catholic faith here in 1851, and the famous tenor, John McCormack, was a member of the Palestrina choir here.

▶ **St Michan's Church** 46C1
Church Street
This little church (begun in 1095) in a run-down area at the back of the Four Courts attracts a certain ghoulish excitement for the mummified corpses in its vaults, which are on display to anyone who cares to peer through a hatch. Their remarkable preservation is due to the hygroscopic action of the surrounding magnesian limestone, plus a few whiffs of methane gas from some subterranean rubbish-tip. Handel is supposed to have played the organ here, and at the 'penitent's pew' malefactors knelt to make their offences public.

▶▶ **St Patrick's Cathedral** 46B2
Patrick's Close
The precise status of this cathedral is a puzzle. Just a few hundred yards down the road stands another Church of Ireland cathedral, Christ Church. The two have always been great rivals. St Patrick's is the national cathedral, the home of the first university in Ireland (1320–1520), and is Ireland's largest church. It is legendarily associated with St Patrick because of a neighbouring well, where the saint was believed to have baptised many converts. From 1191 onwards the original church was replaced by the present building, much restored in the 1860s on the proceeds of Guinness. The cathedral stands in a desolate wasteland of forlorn housing estates and looming cranes, without the city walls. By far its most celebrated incumbent was Jonathan Swift, author of *Gulliver's Travels*, who was Dean here for over 30 years (1713–45) and is buried in the cathedral beside his beloved 'Stella', Esther Johnson. A plaque is inscribed with Swift's self-penned epitaph which, translated from the Latin, reads: 'Where fierce indignation can no longer rend the heart,/ Go traveller, and imitate, if you can, this earnest and dedicated champion of liberty.' Near by is a memorial verse from Alexander Pope dedicated to Swift, and Swift's death-mask, chair and writing-table can be seen in the north pulpit. At the west end of the church is a 17th-century monument to the Boyle family, typical of the period, the demure parents presiding over a multitude of neatly replicated offspring. The young Robert (the scientist who was later to formulate Boyle's Law) is somewhere on the lowest tier.

Next to St Patrick's is **Archbishop Marsh's Library▶▶**, similar to (but smaller than) the Old Library of Trinity College. The barrel-vaulted upper room houses a wonderful collection of ancient leather-bound tomes in dark floor-to-ceiling cases. Several fascinating manuscripts, such as old herbals with beautiful plant illustrations, are separately displayed. Swift's annotated copy of Clarendon's *History of the Great Rebellion* is here among 25,000 other volumes. Cages where readers could be locked to consult valuable books can also be seen.

St Patrick's has no crypt because the River Poddle flows directly beneath the cathedral

►►► Trinity College 47B3

College Green

This single-college university was founded by Elizabeth I in 1592 on confiscated monastery land, ostensibly 'to civilise Ireland with both learning and the Protestant religion'. Small wonder, then, that it became a source of division in the city. Catholics were always allowed entry to the college, and free education – provided of course they converted; up until 1966, Catholics had to obtain a special dispensation to attend on pain of excommunication. Now, however, the proportion of Catholic students at TCD, as it is known, is about 70 per cent. The roll of honour is impressive; Edmund Burke, Jonathan Swift, Oliver Goldsmith, Bram Stoker, Wolfe Tone, William Congreve, J M Synge, Samuel Beckett have all passed through these hallowed portals.

Today TCD occupies a prime location at the heart of Dublin, in an oasis of gardens and parks. Little remains of the original buildings; the imposing, classical façade and Corinthian columns give it an unmistakeably 18th-century feel. Inside, like ancient English universities, its buildings are arranged around quadrangles of lawns and cobbles. The theatre, examination hall, chapel, dining hall, and the old brick accommodation blocks known as the Rubrics can be seen as you pass from the Front Court to the Library Court. The campanile, by Charles Lanyon, marks the site of the original priory. To the right is the Old Library, where the *Book of Kells* is housed.

Since 1801 Trinity College has had the right under copyright law to claim a free copy of all British and Irish publications, and now houses nearly 3 million volumes in eight buildings. Even on a selective basis, about a kilometre of new shelving is needed every year to keep up with all the new publications, these days housed off-site.

Coach parties roll up to visit Trinity's concession to the tourist industry, a 40-minute video called *The Dublin Experience*, which gives a potted history of the city in a new building behind the library, from late May to October.

*Above: the Old Library of Trinity College
Below: TCD's frontage extends for over 90m*

The Book of Kells

■ After over a thousand years, the intricate decoration and bright colours of this Latin text of the Gospels gives a clear proof of the inventive skill and dedication shown by those early Irish scholars. The glowing patterns illumined not merely the pages of the text, but the whole of the Christian world .....■

The Old Library of Trinity College houses about 2 million volumes, stacked in a double-decker layer of floor-to-ceiling shelving in twenty bays of a splendid cathedral-like hall called the Long Room, measuring 64m by 12m. The building was designed by Thomas Burgh in 1712; its barrel-vaulted ceiling was added in the 19th century to provide more shelf space. At the far end of the library are two harps, one traditionally associated with the great Irish king Brian Ború, though actually from the 15th century. By far the most famous and precious of all these treasures is the 8th-century illuminated manuscript of the four gospels known as the *Book of Kells*. Inscribed in Latin on vellum parchment, its pages are magnificently ornamented with patterns and fantastic animals. The designs closely resemble the interlacing patterns found on Celtic metalwork and are obviously influenced by those traditions. Although the manuscript was certainly kept at the monastery of Kells in County Meath, there is some doubt whether it was actually produced there, some authorities believing it may have been copied in Iona or Lindisfarne. Its 680 pages were rebound during the 1950s into four separate volumes. Two of these are generally on display in the Old Library, the pages turned every so often to give a different view. Conservation of this priceless document is a constant battle, and you may have to be content with a facsimile version. Downstairs, however, is a fascinating exhibition showing how the *Book of Kells* and manuscripts like it were produced – what ingredients went into the ink dyes, what implements and brushes were used, and how the monks worked to produce these truly remarkable effects. Besides the *Book of Kells*, several similar manuscripts are kept at Trinity – the *Book of Durrow*, the *Book of Dimma* and the less colourful *Book of Armagh*.

The startlingly beautiful and complex Book of Kells

73

An ancient theft
The *Book of Kells* was stolen one night from the western sacristy of the great stone church of Kells (Meath) in 1007. The *Annals of Ulster* tell that it was recovered after two months and twenty nights, 'its gold having been taken off it and with a sod over it'.

■ Genealogy is now big business in Ireland. Hundreds of visitors from the New World annually attempt to find their roots. It's a significant market – around 60 million people, mostly in North America and the Antipodes, are estimated to be of Irish descent. Of these by far the largest number live in the US (40 million or so), 5 million live in Canada, and another 5 million in Australia and New Zealand. The rest, hard to assess precisely, are somewhere in the UK or scattered throughout the globe .....■

Before it became the Heraldic Museum, No 2, Kildare Street was the home of a gentlemen's club. On one of its columns (and visible from the road) are two monkeys playing the gentlemanly sport of billiards

74

An exhibit at Dublin's Heraldic Museum, showing the Irish harp

Finding your roots Ancestor-tracing is particularly popular in Dublin, where most of the records are held, and in the west of Ireland which saw vast emigration during the Famine years. Ulster also has strong links with the New World; many 'Scotch-Irish' Protestant settlers have made their homes in Canada or the USA. In September 1992, Ireland staged a large cross-border Homecoming Festival throughout the country. Along with the *ceilidhs* (evenings of folk music and dancing) and the 'crack' (fun) went many more earnest events such as clan rallies and history seminars, and lots of hints on the tracing of forebears.

The great interest in origins is fostered by recent research overseas. Canada, for example, has carried out a detailed survey on Irish settlement of its Atlantic seaboard. For many people, a visit to Ireland is a chance to see the Old Country, to track down the family town or homestead, and perhaps look up a few living relatives.

Irish archives A burgeoning number of organisations and centres throughout Ireland will now help you draw your family tree. Increasingly, family records and databases are being computerised and interlinked, making it much quicker and easier to track down records that would have taken hours of patient poring over documents in the past. Inevitably, there's a cost involved, but unless your roots are particularly elusive, the charges are generally quite modest. You could just pay a few pounds for a five-year search through the births, marriages and deaths certificates, or up to IR£150 for a detailed survey of several generations, neatly documented. Research concentrates mainly on civil and parish records, census forms, wills, papers dealing with land or property transactions, etc.

Emigration records Irish data is somewhat patchy. In 1922 at the start of the Civil War the Public Record Office, then housed at the Four Courts in Dublin, was shelled and many documents were lost (fortunately some copies were kept elsewhere). During the Famine years, scant records were kept of those who emigrated or died on the way – such was the despair and chaos of those times. The best bet is to start at the other end, where detailed immigration papers were completed in most American and Australian ports of entry. Seven volumes of immigrant records list every arrival into New York from 1846 to 1851 (*The Famine Immigrants*, published by the Baltimore Genealogical Publishing Company). Australia's records are also good, particularly of those who left Ireland on 'assisted passage' schemes, or who were deported for a criminal offence (often this was a trivial misdemeanour or political involvement – the chances of unearthing some serial killer in the family archives are small). Contact the National Library in Canberra, or the Mitchell Library in Sydney.

If you want to track down your Irish roots, try to do as much research as you can before you arrive. Living relatives, family papers and records in your own country are the first sources to tackle. Build up as complete a picture as you can of the ancestors who emigrated – full name, trade, religion, and which town or county they came from. (Many emigrants named their new homes after their former parish or town, which can be a clue). When you arrive, visit one of the organisations or genealogy centres in the county of origin. It is wise to make an appointment in advance, especially during the summer. The Republic's tourist office, Bord Fáilte, produces an information sheet (No 021) on tracing your ancestors, which contains useful advice, lists of publications and addresses.

Banners in the Heraldic Museum

Northern Ireland addresses
Public Record Office of Northern Ireland, 66 Balmoral Avenue, Belfast BT9 6NY (tel: 084 661621).
Ulster Historical Foundation, 68 Balmoral Avenue, Belfast BT9 6NY (tel: 084 681365).
Irish Heritage Association, 162a Kingsway, Dunmurry, Belfast BT17 9AD (tel: 084 629595).
(Please enclose international reply coupons if you write for advice.)

Provincial addresses
Clare Heritage Centre, Corofin, County Clare (tel: 065 27955).
Mayo North Family History Research Centre, Enniscoe, Castlehill, Ballina (tel: 096 31809).
Roscommon Heritage and Genealogy Centre, Strokestown, (open only from May to September) (tel: 078 33380).
Irish Family History Foundation, 1 Clarinda Park North, Dun Laoghaire, County Dublin (tel: 01 2808571).
Irish Family History Society, PO Box 36, Naas, County Kildare.

Dublin addresses
Genealogical Office, 2 Kildare Street, Dublin 2 (tel: 01 6618811).
The Heraldic Museum – full of arms, banners, crests, etc. – is at the same address.
National Library, 2 Kildare Street, Dublin 2 (tel: 01 6618811).
National Archives, Bishop Street, Dublin 8 (01 4783711).
Births, Deaths and Marriages, Joyce House, 8–11 Lombard Street East, Dublin 2 (tel: 01 6711000).
Registry of Deeds, Henrietta Street, Dublin 1 (tel: 01 8732233).
Hibernian Research Company Ltd, PO Box 3096, Dublin 6 (tel: 01 966522; fax: 01 973011).

Accommodation

The Shelbourne Dublin's grandest hotel is no less than an institution. The 19th-century Shelbourne, on the most fashionable 'Beaux Walk' stretch of St Stephen's Green, is part of the nation's heritage; in Brian Moore's novel, *The Lonely Passion of Judith Hearne*, it is the ultimate proof of wealth and status. The Irish Free State's constitution was drafted here in an upper room. Today it forms part of Mr Forte's hotel empire, and is pleasantly unstuffy. Everybody is welcome, at least for a coffee or a drink in the Horseshoe Bar. For the restaurant, you are advised to dress up a little, and remember your wallet.

Cheaper alternatives If you find the Shelbourne's tariffs are a bit steep, there are plenty of other options. The best bet if you want somewhere within reach of most of the sights and shops is to stay south of the river, somewhere around the St Stephen's Green area, or further out in the pleasant residential suburbs of Ballsbridge. Many attractive Georgian townhouses have been stylishly converted into guest-houses and small hotels, where you can glimpse something of Dublin's former glory in an appropriate setting. The Georgian House is probably one of the best, and best-located, of these, with a lively seafood restaurant. Others include Longfield's, Stephen's Hall and The Grey Door. An excellent and refreshingly different style is provided at No 31, Leeson Close, in an architect's former home.

Further south, the tariffs will be lower and the buildings more recent, probably Victorian or Edwardian. Be prepared for a bus- or taxi-ride to the centre. Some of the best are Simmonstown House, Raglan Lodge, Ariel House and Merrion Hall. Elsewhere in the city, pick your location with care: some areas are not particularly pleasant for walking after dark. The seedier dives around Connolly Station and off upper O'Connell Street are best avoided, and not even particularly cheap. The Gresham Hotel, one of Dublin's best and longest-established, once in a prime location on O'Connell Street, now suffers from run-down surroundings.

ISAAC'S

This popular hostel, also known as the Dublin Tourist Hostel, is located a block or two behind the Custom House on the north bank of the Liffey. It is an agreeable conversion of a wine warehouse dating back to the early 1700s, and as far as possible its architectural features have been kept intact. For simple accommodation at a low price it is hard to beat. The self-service restaurant (open to non-residents) stays open all day from 7.30a.m. and serves cheap, filling fare with an emphasis on wholefoods and vegetarian dishes. There is music laid on in summer. A similar hostel (with the same name) exists in Cork.

The Shelbourne faces St Stephen's Green

Number 31

One of Dublin's most surprising guest-houses lies hidden behind a secluding stone wall in a quiet cul-de-sac off Leeson Street. The former home of a leading architect, Sam Stephenson, it is now a coveted, small B&B. The centre of these double townhouses has been gutted to create a large, sunken sitting-room with a small bar. Vast breakfasts are served in an upper dining-room overloking a roof garden billowing with exotic vegetation, while intriguing objects bestrew the house. The rooms are simple, but all have good bathrooms. The atmosphere is civilised, but relaxed.

77

If you want a hotel with all the trimmings, modern business hotels such as the Conrad or the Westbury are well located. Buswell's, a favourite haunt of politicians and journalists, has more character, and a certain 18th-century cachet. Jury's, the Dublin flagship of a well-known Irish hotel chain, or the Burlington can provide all possible facilities, including lively nightlife, in modern box-like premises south of the river.

Further out If you have a car, consider staying even further out in the more peaceful suburbs, or on the coast, say in Dalkey or Blackrock. Parking in the centre is always difficult and a car is a constant security risk. Avondale House in Scribblestown is a good out-of-town choice, a former hunting lodge dating from the 1720s with a country-house atmosphere. There are many cheaper B&Bs in the coastal areas. You will find it difficult to enjoy Dublin's night scene (or its pubs) staying this far out, however.

Hostels and self-catering If you are on a tight budget, and want to stay centrally, consider a hostel. You may have to share a room, but an increasing number of decent, privately-run hostel-style rooms are now available. ISAAC'S is a good bet for young travellers. For slightly more comfort, Avalon House in Aungier Street (near the Carmelite Church) offers simple but stylish accommodation and a pleasant coffee shop.

Apartments and houses can be rented on a self-catering basis at all price levels, some with maid service. If you prefer more independence or perhaps have children, this may be the ideal solution. A number are listed in Bord Fáilte's self-catering guide. There are no central campsites 'in Dublin – the nearest you'll get is somewhere south of Dun Laoghaire or in Donabate to the north of the city. Unofficial camping is not recommended and could also be risky.

Book ahead Accommodation in Dublin is plentiful, but the best is not cheap and can fill up rapidly during special events or conferences. Book ahead if you can. The tourist office provides a booking service and will telephone round (for a fee) if you turn up on spec. (See also Hotels and Restaurants, pages 269–283).

Food and drink

No visit to Dublin should pass without a sampling of the famous Guinness

A wider choice The eating scene in Dublin is immeasurably better now than it used to be, with a far wider choice of cuisine, and more emphasis on healthy, high-quality ingredients rather than filling, high-fat stodge (though Ireland cannot claim to be the gastronomic capital of the universe). Needless to say, there is plenty of fast food available, especially in areas north of the river. Most outlets are predictably indifferent, with the exception of a couple of good fish and chip shops (Leo Burdock's or Beshoff Ocean Foods) and pizza joints (Bad Ass Café or Fat Freddy's). For gourmets, the city has plenty of choice in the smart town-house restaurants around St Stephen's Green, most of which produce classic French or nouvelle cuisine dishes, but you can expect to pay handsomely for the privilege there. The best of these (Patrick Guilbaud, The Commons, Le Coq Hardi, Les Frères Jacques) have earned their high reputation; others verge on pretension.

For a number of years now Dublin has been home to a number of very good ethnic restaurants – the Rajdoot and Shalimar produce interesting Indian food, the Imperial and the Sichuan are the best of the Chinese restaurants, while, for Italian food, Kapriol and Caesar's are recommended. Besides foreign cuisine, though, traditional Irish cooking is making a healthy comeback, you may try a Dublin coddle (sausages, bacon, onions and potatoes in a thickened sauce) or oysters and Guinness. One of the most unusual restaurants serving Irish food is Gallagher's Boxty House, in the lively Temple Bar quarter. (A 'boxty' is a sort of Irish potato pancake with all kinds of savoury fillings.) The ambience and décor are agreeable and the prices not at all expensive, hence its popularity.

Dublin coddle
4 back rashers of bacon
4 large sausages
black pepper
2 onions, sliced
cornflour
Place the bacon, sausages and onion in a pot and cover with cold water. Bring to the boil and simmer gently for 1–2 hours until the meat is cooked. Thicken with cornflour, season with black pepper and serve immediately with fresh soda bread.

Pubs Dublin pubs concentrate on the drinking side rather than food, but the demands of tourism have meant that more and more serve snacks at lunchtime, though it is rarely particularly imaginative. A civilised touch, however, is that most will serve coffee at any time of day, including, of course, an Irish coffee. The mystique surrounding the serving of Guinness is less overt here than you might expect, but if you look as though you would appreciate it, a shamrock will be etched deftly into the creamy head.

The Powerscourt Centre, off Grafton Street, good for cafés

Two Irish specialities, oysters and Guinness

Brown soda bread
625g wholemeal flour
150g white flour
1 teaspoon salt
1 teaspoon bread soda
60g oatmeal
550–600ml buttermilk
Sieve all the dry ingredients together. Make a well in the centre, pour in the buttermilk and stir until the mixture forms a soft dough. Turn on a floured surface and knead lightly to form a round disc roughly 35cm in diameter. Cut a deep cross into the dough with a sharp knife. Place on a buttered baking dish and bake in the middle of the oven, 220°C, for 15 minutes, then reduce the temperature to 180°C for a further 25 minutes until rich and crusty. Cool on a wire rack.

Cafés For lunchtime snacks some of the most attractive restaurants are in museums or shopping centres – National Gallery, Hugh Lane Municipal Gallery, Dublin Castle, Kilmainham Hospital, Kilkenny Design Centre, and the Powerscourt Centre. One place that cannot be ignored is that great institution known as Bewley's Café. There are four of them in Dublin altogether, set up by a Quaker family of tea and coffee importers over a century ago to enable customers to sample their products. The most famous, Bewley's Oriental Café, is on Grafton Street, a wonderful dark and mysterious emporium of stained glass and mahogany serving good food and staying open late. Upstairs is a quieter café area with a small museum.

Other options If you don't want to spend too much in the evenings, head for Temple Bar, which is young and upbeat, but rather more enticing than the sectors north of the river. Many of the restaurants here come and go with the wind, but some of the more long-lasting ones include the Boxty House (see above), Fat Freddy's Pizza Warehouse and the Bad Ass Café.

If you fancy an excursion, there are several excellent restaurants in some of the coastal resorts; Na Mara in Dun Laoghaire, Il Ristorante in Dalkey or King Sitric in Howth are perhaps some of the best. Seafood is usually excellent. Check what days they close if you plan your excursion visit around them.

On Sundays, Dublin can be a desert as far as eating goes. Many of the good places are closed, and those that stay open are likely to be fully booked. If you are in the city at a weekend, think about eating well ahead of time and make sure you have a table.

Cuisine more Italian than Irish is advertised on this wall in Cecilia Street

Shopping

Markets At the north end of Grafton Street is an eye-catching statue in bronze, affectionately known to Dubliners as 'the tart with the cart'. The subject, of course, is the famous Molly Malone (see panel), wheeling her wheelbarrow. To find today's Molly Malones, you will need to head for the old-fashioned street markets held in Moore Street (mostly selling fruit and vegetables, off Henry Street near the General Post Office), or alternatively the Liberties in Meath Street beyond Christ Church Cathedral, where dozens of stalls of cheap clothing and household goods are on colourful sale.

Shops for visitors Most tourist shopping, however, is done in rather different surroundings, either in the safe, if highly priced, confines of a modern hotel or in one of the city's specialist shops. The main shopping area in the centre of town lies between Grafton Street and O'Connell Street. The big department stores are here – Clery's and Eason's north of the river (along with Marks and Spencer and bargain basement stores like Dunne's in the Ilac Centre, or Arnotts), and more exclusive Switzers or Brown Thomas in Grafton Street. Many international chain shops like Benetton, Next, Principles, etc, can also be found around pedestrianised Grafton Street. Smaller side-streets contain most specialist craft and fashion shops. Nassau Street is a particularly good area to head for if you are looking for typical Irish craft products such as ceramics, knitwear, tweed, linen, crystal, or Celtic jewellery. The outlets range considerably in classiness, one of the more upmarket being the excellent Kilkenny Design Centre, a branch of the enterprise based at Kilkenny Castle. Others worth checking out (also in Nassau Street) are the exclusive tweed and clothing store, Kevin and Howlin, the Sweater Shop for Aran knitwear, Blarney Woollen Mills and the Best of Irish. For traditional Irish music, Claddagh Records (at 2 Cecilia Street) is one of the best shops.

Dublin boasts a number of new shopping precincts. One of the best is in the imaginatively reconstructed shell of

Molly Malone
In Dublin's fair city where the girls are so pretty I first set my eyes on sweet Molly Malone.
She wheeled a wheelbarrow through streets broad and narrow
Crying 'Cockles and mussels, alive, alive Oh'.

Nassau Street has a fine range of shops, from second-hand bookstores to retail outlets more geared to tourists

an 18th-century town house, called the Powerscourt Centre, with splendid plasterwork ceilings and exterior façade (just off Grafton Street). This complex houses many individual shops, restaurants and cafés. Another central shopping mall is on St Stephen's Green, an unmissable, modern, greenhouse-like structure with yet more shops and cafés. Tierney's has one of the better craft displays here.

Bookshops are legion in this literary city, most of them around St Stephen's or College Greens or the quaysides. Several of these sell collectable second-hand volumes. Fred Hanna's (27/29 Nassau Street), Green's (Clare Street), Hodges Figgis (54 Dawson Street), the Winding Stair (40 Lower Ormonde Quay) are some of the best-known, besides the larger and more general retailers, Waterstone's and Eason's. For antiques, head for Francis Street in the Liberties (beyond Christ Church Cathedral).

Beyond the centre Out of the city centre, the suburbs of Blackrock or Dalkey have their own shopping complexes and markets, not necessarily worth a special trip. Closer into town on Pearse Street (take a bus two or three stops from Pearse Station) is the Tower Design Centre, a 19th-century sugar-refining tower now run by the Irish Development Authority and housing about 35 separate craft enterprises producing souvenirs in fashions, stained glass, painted silk, knitwear, jewellery, etc. Visitors are welcome to wander round the complex and watch the artists at work. There is no pressure to buy.

Practicalities Shopping hours in Dublin are generally Monday to Saturday, 9–6, with some of the smaller shops geared to tourists opening on Sundays as well. For non-EC residents, the VAT waiver scheme called Cashback makes high-taxed Irish goods more attractive, although there is a fair bit of red tape involved in claiming this back at Dublin or Shannon Airport. Collect a form as you buy the goods and have it stamped as you leave the country.

Shopping is an enduring pastime for these two Dubliners

81

A crowd-pulling display in Brown Thomas, Grafton Street, one of Dublin's most famous shops

Nightlife

Decisions, decisions Dublin is famous for its pubs – over 800 of them if you care to count, or are capable of it – and for its theatre. These therefore form the core of the city's evening entertainments. Like most capital cities , however, it can offer much more – many kinds of music, from rock to classical, around two dozen cinema screens, and a host of night-clubs and wine-bars. Some larger hotels offer well advertised cabaret shows, Jury's being the most widely publicised. There is always plenty going on if you know where to look, but most parts of the city can seem pretty quiet after midnight, and a few are unsafe.

The main concentration of night-clubs is in Leeson Street. Most of them are basement bars so the seemly Georgian façades are not at all rowdy. Generally they don't charge entrance, but drinks are pretty expensive. They are at their liveliest at weekends (Thursday to Sunday) and get going after 10pm.

Pubs Pubs and bars are scattered all over the city and take innumerable forms, some modern and plastic, others ancient and Victorian, most of them somewhere in between – suitably 'modernised' for tourists. The pub of the moment is difficult to pin down with fashions changing, though regulars may stick to one or two favourites all the time. Most of the well known places are very busy at night despite the high cost of alcohol in Ireland. They seem generally good-tempered, though they can be very noisy and boisterous. Some have notable gay scenes; others may be popular with drug users, of which Dublin has many. Though predominantly masculine, Dublin's bars are not unfriendly towards women, who will usually get a civilised welcome.

Some of the best-known and most 'characterful' bars on the south side are Doheny and Nesbitt (5 Lower Baggot Street), O'Donoghue's (Merrion Row), Toner's (139 Lower Baggot Street), Neary's (1 Chatham Street); further west, the Stag's Head (1 Dame Court, off Dame Street), and Mother Redcap's (Back Lane, off High

Joycean pubs
In The Bailey (Duke Street) Joyce fans can find the door of No 7 Eccles Street, the fictional home of Leopold Bloom in *Ulysses*, rescued by the pub's proprietor, John Ryan, from a builder's skip. At Davy Byrne's, you can be served a faithful version of the lunch Bloom enjoyed there on 16 June 1904 (Bloomsday) – a glass of burgundy and a Gorgonzola sandwich.

The capital has a thriving youth culture as Dubliners U2 and Bob Geldof might suggest

In 1897 the Star of Erin music hall changed its name to the Empire Palace. A few years later it became the Olympia Theatre, as it remains today

The Abbey Theatre
The Abbey is one of Dublin's most classic traditions, yet it has staged some controversial productions. The first performance of J M Synge's *The Playboy of the Western World* in 1907 caused riots because an Irishman used the word 'shift' (meaning petticoat) on stage. Police had to be called to protect Synge from the outraged audience for over a week. In 1926 O'Casey's play *The Plough and the Stars* caused a similar uproar when the national flag was shown in the presence of a prostitute. After a later production of this play in 1951, the theatre burned down (accidentally).

Street). Near the Liffey, upriver from O'Connell Street, the Brazen Head (20 Lower Bridge Street) and Ryan's (Parkgate Street) are now in fairly sleazy areas, but have retained their old-fashioned interiors. Ryan's is a confection of mahogany and brass unchanged since 1896. The Brazen Head claims to be Ireland's oldest, where Wolfe Tone and Robert Emmet plotted England's downfall. Davy Byrne's and the Bailey (both in Duke Street) have Joycean associations which keep them eternally popular.

Music and theatre Many of the pubs offer evening music sessions, Irish traditional, jazz, etc. One specialising in music is Bad Bob's Backstage Bar, a trendy night-spot in Temple Bar. Dublin, of course, has launched many a rock or pop star on the way to fame and fortune; U2, the Chieftains, the Dubliners, Sinead O'Connor and Chris de Burgh have all performed in Dublin's night-spots on many occasions. For more traditional music, head for the National Concert Hall in St Stephen's Green; the Royal Hospital at Kilmainham also stages a number of concerts and evening events. One of the theatres offers music at weekends – Midnight at the Olympia on Fridays and Saturdays involves disco dancing between aisles of plush red seating. Earlier in the evening (and during the week) it usually offers an assorted range of light entertainment. The Gaiety is similarly popular. For more heavyweight theatre, head for the Gate or the Abbey, where Dublin's great theatrical tradition started. The annexe to the Abbey, called the Peacock, and the Project Arts Club in Temple Bar, specialise in avant-garde or experimental work.

Film There isn't much of an art film scene in Dublin, though some films may be released earlier in the Republic than in London. Most of the two dozen screens on or near O'Connell Street are fairly run-of-the-mill or downright seedy. For an alternative to commercial cinema, head for the Lighthouse Screen, or the Irish Film Centre in Temple Bar. There are very few cinemas in the suburbs.

To find out what's going on in Dublin, get the *Irish Times* which has daily listings, or the magazine *In Dublin*, on sale in any newsagent

Practical points

The Rubrics at TCD,
see page 72

see page 72

Sightseeing tours
Dublin Bus runs sightsee-
ing coach tours of Dublin
using open-top vehicles
(covered in wet weather).
The heritage tour visits ten
locations near city sights,
and with an all-day ticket
you can hop on or off at
any point. Buses run hourly
between 10 and 4 in high
season.

84

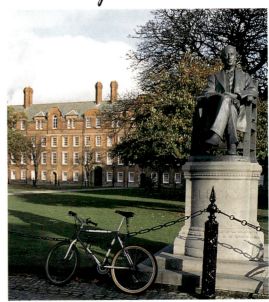

*Dublin's coat of arms
embellishes this
street sign*

What's on offer Dublin is an exceptionally friendly city and most people will be only too happy to help you out. The main tourist office is at 14 O'Connell Street, open weekdays 9–5, tel: 8747733. It is usually crowded, but there are many leaflets to pick up, not all of which are free. Walking tours around the city are also advertised here, and can be fun and informative. Another useful start to city orientation is the Dublin Experience show at Trinity College, on view during the summer months.

If you are short of time, plan carefully and cut out extraneous attractions. Some of the big sights close for part of the weekend or on Monday, and Dublin Castle is occasionally shut altogether. Ask before you set off. Things not to miss are the Castle, Trinity College and the National Museum and Gallery. Try to catch some of the Georgian architecture around Merrion Square and St Stephen's Green, and the two cathedrals to the west of the city. If you can, visit Kilmainham Gaol and Hospital, and walk in Phoenix Park. Art-lovers will want to find Hugh Lane's Gallery, and, if the lighter side of culture appeals, head for the Guinness Brewery Hop Store Museum. Choose a promising-looking day for excursions to Howth or Dalkey; the best beaches lie around Killiney Bay or Sandymount (some dangerous currents). There is also a magnificent stretch of sand on Bull Island, a peaceful nature reserve.

If you happen to be in Dublin during a big match, you'll certainly be aware of it. Gaelic games are played at Croke Park, north of the city centre. The All-Ireland Hurling and Football Finals take place in September. St Patrick's Day (17 March) is a fine time to be here, with parades and other happenings, but celebrations are smaller than those in New York and Boston, for example. To find out what's going on, get a listings magazines (the best is *In Dublin*).

City transport A bus map is worth getting. Although the central areas are reasonably compact, Dublin can make you footsore, and hopping on a bus occasionally may be welcome. The routes, if not always the schedules, are more or less adhered to. Most of them start from Busáras, the main station, just north of the river near the Custom House, or from the streets near College Green. If you plan to do much exploring, it is worth getting a Day Rambler ticket. The words *An Lár* on the front of a bus indicate it is going to the city centre. For longer trips, contact Bus Eireann's offices just across O'Connell Street from the tourist office. A branch of Thomas Cook (118 Grafton Street, tel: 677 1721) can answer general travel inquiries. For youth travel, student discounts, etc., contact the USIT office on Aston Quay.

For travel to the nearest coast, the DART (Dublin Area Rapid Transit) route, a single rail line between Bray and Howth, is an entertaining excursion with fine coastal views. You can catch the DART trains at Connolly, Tara Street or Pearse stations. For train services further afield (between Dundalk and Arklow) you should head for the main station, Connolly. Heuston Station serves the western and southern regions.

Taxis are not generally hailed on the move, but stand in ranks in some of the main streets, and are fairly expensive. Parking is always difficult and costly in the city centre. Always park in official places, not in quiet backstreets, where the incidence of vandalism and theft is very high. Never leave anything remotely valuable inside.

Crime The problems of urban life have caused a sharp rise in street crime generally, exacerbated by economic depression and drug and alcohol abuse. Conspicuous tourists are easy prey. Don't carry too much money and don't stray into unknown areas off the main tourist trail. The streets west of St Patrick's Cathedral, or many north of the river, are not advisable for unscheduled sauntering.

Rock 'n' Stroll
Self-guided walks round Dublin inevitably focus on its Georgian architecture or literary associations, or perhaps pub crawls for the thirsty. An alternative themed walk is the Rock 'n' Stroll Guide, which leads its followers to the principal places in Dublin associated with the contemporary music scene. Revisit The Chieftains' first gig at the Gresham Hotel, Mary Black's stamping ground at the Olympia, or U2's launch-pad in Mount Temple Comprehensive School! Pick up the tour guide in any tourist office.

85

O'Connell Bridge, at the heart of the city

EASTERN COUNTIES

Newtown Butler · Clones · Newbliss · MONAGHAN · Derrymore House · Bessbrook · Hilltown · Newcastle · 852m Slieve Donard

Belturbet · Butler's Bridge · Drum · Cootehill · Ballybay · Castleblayney · ARMAGH · Newtownhamilton · Newry · D O W N · Mourne Mts

Ballyhaise · Lough Oughter · Crossmaglen · Warrenpoint · Rostrevor · Annalong

Cavan · Stradone · Shercock · Kilcurry · Omeath · Carlingford · Kilkeel · Greencastle

C A V A N · Kilnaleck · Baileborough · Carrickmacross · Mullabony · Dundalk · Dooley Pen

Kingscourt · Dun A Rí Forest Park · L O U T H · Castlebellingham · Dunany Point · Dundalk Bay

Lough Sheelin · Ballyjamesduff · Virginia · Ardee · Drumconrath · Dunleer

Finnea · Lough Ramor · Oldcastle · Castletown · Monasterboice · Collon · Mellifont Abbey · Drogheda

Coole · Castlepollard · Crossakeel · Kells · M E A T H · Hill of Slane · Slane · Battle of the Boyne · Dowth · Balbriggan

Tullynally Castle · Fore Abbey · Clonmellon · Navan · Knowth · Newgrange · Duleek · Skerries

Lough Derravaragh · Delvin · Athboy · Bective Abbey · Ardcath · Rush

W E S T M E A T H · Ballivor · Trim · Hill of Tara · Boyne · Naul · Donabate · Lambay Island

Mullingar · Killucan · Dunshaughlin · Ashbourne · Swords · Newbridge · Malahide

Lough Ennell · Kinnegad · Clonard · Summerhill · Royal Canal · Dunboyne · Dublin Airport · Portmarnock

Tyrrellspass · Enfield · Kilcock · Maynooth · Lucan · M1 · Howth

Edenderry · Celbridge · Castletown · M50 · DUBLIN

Daingean · Bog of Allen · Robertstown · Straffan · Clane · Clondalkin · Tallaght · Dun Laoghaire

Geashill · Clonbulloge · Lullymore · Sallins · DUBLIN · James Joyce Tower · Killiney

Bracknagh · Grand Canal · M7 · Naas · Brittas · Powerscourt · M11 · Bray

Portarlington · Irish National Stud Japanese Gardens · Droichead Nua (Newbridge) · Enniskerry · Kilruddery House & Gardens

Monasterevin · Kildare · Russborough House · Blessington · Greystones

Mountmellick · Kilcullen · Poulaphouca Reservoir · 848m Mullaghcleevaun

Portlaoise · Fontstown · Dunlavin · W I C K L O W · Wicklow

Stradbally · L A O I S · Athy · Baltinglass · Glendalough · Laragh · Ashford · Mount Usher Gardens · Rathnew

Abbeyleix · Ballylynan · 926m Lugnaquilla Mts · Rathdrum · Wicklow · Wicklow Head

Ballinakill · Newtown · Castledermot · Rathvilly · Avondale · Avoca

Castlecomer · Carlow · Hacketstown · Aughrim · Woodenbridge · Mizen Head

Ballyragget · Tullow · Tinahely · Arklow

K I L K E N N Y · Dunmore Cave · Old Leighlin · C A R L O W · Leighlinbridge · Ballon · Shillelagh · Carnew · Kilmichael Point

Kilkenny · Muine Bheag · Bunclody · Gorey · Courtown Harbour

Gowran · Borris · Ferns · Ballycanew

Kells Priory · Dungarvan · Kiltealy · 734m Blackstairs Mts · Slaney · Cahore Point

Stonyford · Thomastown · Graiguenamanagh · W E X F O R D

Knocktopher · Jerpoint Abbey · Inistioge · St Mullins · Enniscorthy

The gentler aspect of the Wicklow Mountains

EASTERN COUNTIES

Eastern Counties The counties immediately around Dublin constitute the Pale, the area most strongly influenced by English rule from Norman times onwards. What lay beyond the Pale was less easily subjugated and often perceived (accurately) as a threat to English interests. The pull of the capital ensures these eastern counties still receive a steady flow of visitors, though scenically (with the exception of Wicklow) they are not Ireland's most exciting regions. There are, though, a good many reasons to spend time here. They are enormously rich in history, layer upon layer of it from prehistoric to recent times. The famous passage graves at Newgrange are Ireland's best-known neolithic site. Then there are Celtic High Crosses, the evocative monastic settlement of Glendalough, many later abbeys and churches, castles and several of Ireland's grandest houses and gardens. Horse-lovers will want to visit the Curragh at Kildare and the nearby National Stud. For walkers, the heather moors and wooded glens of the Wicklow Mountains bristle with opportunities. If you are thinking of a beach holiday in Ireland, the drier sunnier climate of the Southeast makes a seaside stay a reasonable gamble instead of a long shot. The best beaches in this region are in County Wicklow.

County Louth is the smallest of the 32 counties of Ireland. Inland, it echoes the drumlin country of those other border counties, Cavan and Monaghan – a gentle, placid landscape of little hills and lakes. Its easterly section is more dramatic, a precursor of the Mountains of Mourne that loom enticingly across Carlingford Lough. The Cooley Peninsula, setting for one of Ireland's greatest epics (*Táin Bo Cuailgne* – the Cattle Raid of Cooley) makes a fine excursion, where the lakeshore village of Carlingford is one of the most delightful low-key holiday bases, managing to avoid (for the most part) the strains of other border towns such as Dundalk or Monaghan. Drogheda, Louth's other main town, seems to have weathered its Cromwellian torments more resiliently than most and amply repays a stop, or even a stay. All around

EASTERN COUNTIES

The little gentleman in black velvet
This favourite Jacobite toast during the reign of Queen Anne is still drunk in certain nationalist and Catholic circles. The little gentleman is the mole that is alleged to have killed William III when his horse Sorrel stumbled on a mole-hill and threw him on 21 February 1702, badly fracturing his collarbone. The king died in London a fortnight later. If this sounds a heartless tradition, the anti-Catholic toasts of the Orange Order are much more savage. The 19th-century British Prime Minister, Sir Robert Peel, apparently drank to these in his early life, and became nicknamed 'Orange Peel' by the Irish.

it, stretching into County Meath, is a rich cluster of pre-historic and Celtic sites, great abbeys and castles, the Hills of Slane and Tara suffused with legends and national symbolism. The River Boyne is a place of pilgrimage for many tracing the progress of that famous battle of 1690 along alternate banks, though this was only one of numerous skirmishes between Jacobite and Williamite troops in those troubled years.

Dublin's hinterlands Closer to Dublin, the coast is studded with small fishing ports, most fairly dull. Howth and Malahide are the ones to visit – the first for its breezy headland views and castle gardens, the second for an interestingly furnished castle and art collection. The capital's immediate hinterland is County Kildare, where the rolling springy grassland provides pasture and an exercise track for dozens of fine-boned thoroughbreds. This is the heart of Ireland's bloodstock industry, one of the more solid mainstays of Ireland's shaky economy. Keen followers of form may want to time their arrival carefully to co-incide with one of the big annual races. Naas holds its big race meeting in April, at Punchestown Racecourse. The Curragh, famed for horse-racing since time immemorial, hosts all of Ireland's classic events – the Oaks, the Derby and the St Leger.

Naas, Kildare's county town is near enough to all this to benefit from horse-borne prosperity and far enough from Dublin's suburban tentacles to have a spirit of its own. It makes one of the best places to pause and plan a route. If horses aren't your scene, you can search for Round Towers and Celtic High Crosses, follow the great canal routes that criss-cross the county or investigate the mournful Bog of Allen (an interesting new interpretative centre explaining the significance of bogland ecology has recently opened up at Lullymore, near Rathangan, tel: 045 60133 for details). Kildare's most important stately home is Castletown, one of Ireland's largest Palladian houses.

South of Dublin lies County Wicklow, one of the capital's favourite 'lungs'. A glance at its topography soon indicates why – the Wicklow Mountains reach a significant altitude by Irish standards (Lugnaquilla is Ireland's

The lonely Vale of Glenmacnass in the Wicklow Mountains just south of Dublin. Glenmacnass means 'the valley of the sons of Neasa'

third-highest peak at nearly 1,000m) and contain some very beautiful and unpopulated scenery. The coastline, too, has attractions – breezy headlands and great sweeps of sand stretching from Bray southwards, the best being Brittas Bay south of Wicklow Head. A journey over the central heights is most rewarding; choose one of the routes around the Sally Gap and take in the awe-inspiring views around Glencree and Glenmacnass, or seek out the hidden lakes of Tay and Dan. Powerscourt Gardens and Russborough House shouldn't be missed; ensure you time your visit to find them open. The other 'unmissable' is Glendalough, a collection of ancient monastic buildings in a gorgeous setting. Wicklow's impressive range of sights also includes the great gardens of Kilruddery and Mount Usher, and Charles Stewart Parnell's house at Avondale, now a forest park and museum to his memory. There is no shortage of excellent accommodation or restaurants in County Wicklow; its nearness to Dublin ensures a steady year-round trade and it has a quietly prosperous air. The most famous bits of the Boyne valley and the holiday resorts of the east coast are also pretty well equipped, and County Kildare has a number of good places to stay or eat. The less popular regions of Louth and Meath, however, offer rather patchy choices and it needs some planning to stay anywhere pleasant. Dundalk is a particular desert – if you have the time, it's worth reaching Carlingford.

The tower of Trim Abbey, as seen from the town's castle

89

Leinster taboos
In ancient Ireland, the lives of kings and other notabilities were hedged in by taboos, doubtless going back into the mists of pre-history. Death was the inexorable outcome of these being violated one by one, a subject beloved of the dramatic story-tellers of medieval Ireland. Five taboos recorded for the king of the Leinstermen included those forbidding him from:
❏ travelling widdershins (anticlockwise) around the Wicklow Hills on a Wednesday;
❏ sleeping between Dublin and the Dodder River with his head facing to one side;
❏ setting up camp for nine days on the plains of Cualu (Bray);
❏ travelling alone on the road to Dublin on a Monday;
❏ riding on a dirty, black-hooved horse over the plain of Mullaghmast (County Kildare).

The meaning of the interwoven spirals, found on several stones at Newgrange, remains unclear

THE BOYNE VALLEY

Drive   **From prehistory to 1690 along the Boyne valley**

A drive through the past from prehistoric times to Ireland's most significant battle-site whose divisive echoes reverberate more than 300 years later in the streets of Belfast and London. (It is recommended that you follow the precise route of this drive on a detailed, large-scale map.)

Head north from Drogheda on the N1. Clearly signed to the west are the High Crosses and Round Tower of **Monasterboice** (see page 105). Looping back south again by the Mattock valley, watch for signs to the remains of **Mellifont Abbey**, in a maze of quiet lanes (see page 105). About 7km west of **Drogheda** (well signed off the N51 from the town) is the historic **King William's Glen**, site of the famous Battle of the Boyne in 1690. An orange and green sign by the river marks the main site of conflict. A waymarked trail from the Townley Hall Estate (the extensive grounds of a Georgian mansion) leads to a viewing place above the battle-

ground showing where the opposing armies camped, and where William's army crossed the river from the north at two separate points, taking the forces of James II on the southern banks by surprise. An explanatory diagram and display board outlines the battle manoeuvres. It is worth getting a leaflet or map (from local tourist offices) showing the battle-sites if you want to explore in detail, since dodging back and forth across the river can be disorientating. The battle route passes the Boyne Navigation Canal, part of a grand scheme to connect Ireland's major waterways.

The battle was a historical landmark for many reasons, a minor point of interest being that it was the last conflict in Europe in which opposing monarchs played an active military rôle; William III himself narrowly escaped death from a sniper's bullet on the morning of the battle. William's soldiers used sprigs of leaves to distinguish themselves from the Jacobite forces, since they wore

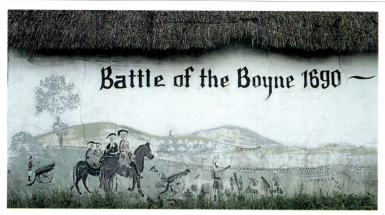

A mural on a cottage near Drogheda celebrates the famous battle

no clearly recognisable uniforms. As they crossed the river they played the Orange marching tune *Lillebulero*. Gradually, James's forces were pushed back south towards **Duleek**, where one of Ireland's oldest stone churches once stood. St Ciarán's was built in the 5th century soon after Christianity first reached Ireland. The remains now visible date from later centuries. The final skirmish of the Battle of the Boyne took place at Duleek, and William is thought to have spent the night after the battle near here. Buried in the churchyard is Lord John Bellew, a Catholic who died at the subsequent Battle of Aughrim. He was shot in the stomach, and so must have died bravely, facing his enemies.

Further west lie some of Ireland's most important neolithic remains, including the passage graves of Dowth, Knowth and Newgrange, collectively known as **Brugh na Boinne** (see pages 108–9). Besides the main tombs, at least 40 other burial places are believed to lie in and around this fertile farmland within a strategic bend of the River Boyne. Some of these sites have not yet been excavated, though from the Newgrange tomb several strange humps and mounds are clearly visible in the surrounding landscape.

Kells (formerly known as **Ceanannus Mór**), up the Blackwater valley, is best known for the *Book of Kells*, a splendid illuminated manuscript now housed in Trinity College Dublin (see page 73). Many other antiquities and sacred sites are clustered along the Boyne valley around **Slane**, **Navan**, **Tara**, seat of the High Kings of Ireland, and **Trim** (see their respective entries throughout this chapter; the Hill of Tara is on page 107). Castles dating from more recent times are scattered throughout the region. Trim itself has an enormous fortress – the largest dating from Norman times. The evocative ruins of **Bective Abbey** are also worth looking out for on the peaceful meadows by the river between Trim and Navan.

This simple church at Kells dates from the first millennium

Avoca Handweavers give daily demonstrations of their craft

Parnell and Kitty O'Shea
Parnell fell in love with Kitty, wife of Captain Willy O'Shea, by whom she had three children. It was not a successful marriage, however, and the two spent long periods apart, constantly impecunious. She first met Parnell outside the House of Commons in London, and the attraction was instant. Within a short time the two were secretly living together, and Parnell fathered her remaining children. O'Shea put up with the situation at first, hoping for the inheritance from Kitty's wealthy aunt. When his chances were dashed, he sued for divorce. (See also pages 42–3.)

► **Avoca** 86B3

Avoca, a pretty hamlet of neat white cottages in a wooded setting by the meeting of the Avonbeg and Avonmore Rivers, is the home of Avoca Handweavers, who produce some of Ireland's most energetically marketed craft products from a group of whitewashed buildings containing the oldest surviving handweaving mill in Ireland, dating from 1723. The business was built up over 40 years by the Wynne sisters, who claim to have invented the car rug! Bright tweeds of natural fibres are manufactured (mostly on modern machinery) and made into hats, suits and voluminous cloaks. High-quality Avoca products can be found all over the country. Coach parties converge to watch weaving demonstrations, enjoy good lunches or teas in the café, and (perhaps) take something home with them.

►► **Avondale** 86B3

Deep in one of County Wicklow's most beautifully wooded areas is the Georgian birthplace and home of the 19th-century politician Charles Stewart Parnell, now a museum dedicated to his memory. Parnell was one of Ireland's greatest campaigners for democracy and land reform. Though at first regarded as a dangerous revolutionary because of his association with the Irish Land League, he eventually won Gladstone's abiding respect and persuaded many people that Home Rule was a viable option for Ireland. His career foundered abruptly after his long-standing liaison with the wife of a fellow Member of Parliament became public knowledge (see panel). Soon after divorce proceedings were instituted, Parnell was ousted from his political position and died of strain and ill-health. A film relates the background to Parnell's life-story and the history of the house, which is most interestingly furnished and contains many touching mementoes and political cartoons. Some of his eloquent love letters to Kitty O'Shea are framed on the walls, as is the extensive Parnell family tree, many of whose members died tragically of madness, vaccination, fevers or grief.

The grounds were taken over by the state in 1904 as a forestry school. Much research on arboriculture is conducted here and the forest park is full of fine and flourishing trees of many different species. Walks lead through the 214ha park by the riverside.

Bray *86C3*

Bray is a convenient place for Dublin's citizens to gain a breath of sea air, though it cannot be described as the most exciting bit of Ireland's coastline. It is the southerly terminus of the DART suburban railway line from Dublin, so is easily reached without a car. The best views are from Bray Head, the final excrescence of the Wicklow range, from where the Great and Little Sugar Loaf Mountains can be seen. North of Bray is the long sandy beach of Killiney Bay.

Bray has literary associations with James Joyce, who lived briefly at 1 Martello Terrace, which featured in *A Portrait of the Artist as a Young Man*. It is now privately owned and not generally open to the public. A more accessible place of interest is **Kilruddery House and Gardens▶** to the south of the resort, a rare example of 17th-century landscaping. Ponds, avenues, parterres and hedges are laid out with mathematical precision. The house dates from the 1650s (extensively remodelled in the 1820s) and contains many interesting features – Grinling Gibbons carving, Chippendale furniture and a water-powered stable clock (open May, June and September, afternoons only).

▶▶ Carlingford *86E3*

The most enjoyable place on the Cooley peninsula (see page 96) is Carlingford, between the green slopes of Slieve Foye and the blue waters of the lough, with the Mourne Mountains beyond. This delightful village is by far the best base in the area, with several excellent, inexpensive pubs and guest-houses. For its modest size, it has some imposing monuments, indicating that it was a place of some significance during the Middle Ages. King John's Castle stands on the north side of the harbour, a massive D-shaped fortress dating from the 13th century. Its opposite number is Greencastle, on the Northern Irish side of the lough. In the village itself are Taafe's Castle and the Mint, both fortified houses, and the old town hall, or Tholsel, an arched gateway.

93

Avondale House is famous as the birth-place of Charles Stewart Parnell. In the surrounding Forest Park you may be fortunate enough to catch sight of an otter

Drogheda ale

'Of one part of its manufactures, every traveller must speak with gratitude – of the ale namely, which is as good as the best brewed in the sister kingdom… And while satisfying himself of this fact, the philosophic observer cannot but ask, why ale should not be as good elsewhere as at Drogheda: is the water of the Boyne the only water in Ireland whereof ale can be made?'

William Makepeace Thackeray (1842)

The banner of a local fishermen's guild now in the Museum of Local History, Drogheda

▶▶ **Castletown House**   86C2

This huge stately home is rated as one of the finest examples of Palladian (classical) architecture in the Republic. It has many intriguing features, but its restoration seems sadly underfunded, despite the noble efforts of the Irish Georgian Society. It was built in 1722 for William Connolly, Speaker of the Irish House of Commons, who made a colossal fortune from forfeited estates after the Battle of the Boyne – it is hardly surprising that local attitudes to the house have been somewhat ambivalent. Designed by Alessandro Galilei in the style of an Italian villa, it contains wonderful plasterwork by the Francini brothers, and a sumptuous Pompeiian Long Gallery with splendidly hideous Murano chandeliers. The extensive grounds feature clipped yew trees and a folly obelisk. Though it is no longer lived in, its contents clearly reveal the character and tastes of its former owners. Lady Louisa Connolly, who married in 1758 at the age of 15, was one of its most influential collectors and decorators. An extravagant woman in some ways, she appears more compassionate and socially aware than many of her class, declaring when faced with the gargantuan banquet menus of the time, 'It can never be right or useful that one set of people should be gorged with food and the other part in want.'

▶▶ **Drogheda**   86D2

This was originally a Viking town, later expanded into one of Hugh de Lacy's principal Norman strongholds, though little remains of the old town walls. In 1412 the two parts of the town on either side of the Boyne were united by charter to become the largest English town in Ireland; something of this ancient medieval pattern can still be seen in the hilly streets. The Millmount to the south side is topped by an 18th-century military barracks and fort, with a fine view of the northern part of the town and the railway viaduct spanning the river.

Drogheda stands at the lowest bridging point of the River Boyne, just a few kilometres from the site of the famous battle of 1690. Wartime violence was nothing new; in 1649 Drogheda saw one of Cromwell's bloodiest assaults. Women and children who took refuge in one of its churches were burned alive and the defending garrison, driven south of the river to the hilltop Millmount Fort, were ruthlessly massacred after their surrender. The garrison commander, an English royalist, was battered to death with his own wooden leg. 'I think that we put to the sword altogether about 2,000 men,' Cromwell wrote smugly, 'It is right that God alone should have all the glory.' Today the Millmount Fort houses a strangely peaceful collection of items in the excellent, privately run **Drogheda Museum of Local History**▶▶ – medieval guild banners, old trade machinery and tools, and a coracle made of willow and leather. Other sections of this garrison have been converted into craft studios and a restaurant.

Over the river again, several buildings in the densely packed main town catch the eye: the 1224 Magdalene Tower, last remnants of a Dominican friary; the fine 13th-century Lawrence Gate, surmounted by two drum towers; the little chapel of the Siena Convent; and the Tholsel, an 18th-century town hall now used as a bank. The two churches of St Peter's are also worth a look, the Protestant one for its grim 'cadaver' gravestone, the Catholic one for the famous shrine of St Oliver Plunkett (see panel on page 114), Primate of all Ireland, whose blackened head was rescued from the flames after his execution at Tyburn (London) for high treason (his crime was simply unrepentant Catholicism).

Despite these somewhat grisly memories, Drogheda is an attractive place, with some good music pubs (notably Carbery's on North Strand and McHugh's on Lawrence Street) and a lively, purposeful air. It makes a convenient and pleasant base for exploring the rich heritage of the Boyne valley, which contains some of Ireland's most impressive antiquities.

Drogheda and Cromwell
The atrocities committed by Cromwell's troops are well documented in many sources, though the precise number of casualties is hard to establish. Yet the municipal records of Drogheda on both the day before *and the day after* the alleged massacre in 1649 deal with the vexatious topic of street lighting, and make no mention of Cromwell's frightful conduct – even in cowed acquiescence. It is indeed an odd omission. There is no doubt that some of Cromwell's actions have been exaggerated for propoganda purposes, though he amply earned his hated reputation in Ireland.

95

Castletown House, considered by some to be the finest 18th-century mansion in the Republic

EASTERN COUNTIES

The Long Woman's Grave
Near the Windy Gap on the Cooley peninsula a plaque relates the strange tale of the Long Woman's Grave. A man courted a tall Spanish beauty, telling her he owned all the lands that could be seen from a high place. She married him and came to Ireland, then asked him to show her his inheritance. He brought her to the Windy Gap, where the views are closely obstructed by cliffs. She died of shock and is buried in the Long Woman's Grave.

Dundalk 86E2

Dundalk is an unenticing place, congested with traffic and vaguely threatening. It is a border town, too close to the most sensitive section of the Northern Ireland frontier for comfort, and is not recommended as a base. Nevertheless, it has a few features of interest, the most noteworthy building being its **Cathedral of St Patrick▶**, a pastiche of King's College Chapel, Cambridge, with rich mosaics inside. The monument outside the neo-classical court-house declares itself in faded letters to be dedicated to the 'martyrs in the cause of liberty who fought and died in the struggle against English tyranny'.

Just outside the town is the huge bird reserve at **Dundalk Bay▶**, where thousands of wading birds search for food and shelter among the mudflats. North of the town, a few minutes' drive takes you into the lovely scenery of the hilly, granite **Cooley peninsula▶▶**, attractive in its own right, but overlooking tempting views of the Mountains of Mourne across the lough which divides the Republic from Northern Ireland. Cooley is associated with one of Ireland's best-known myths, the Cattle Raid of Cooley, in which Queen Maeve, jealous of her husband's prize white bull, attempts to take the brown bull of Cooley by force. Cuchulainn, the Hound of Ulster, is the hero of the hour, but is mortally wounded during the battle (see pages 27–8). Curiosities on the Cooley peninsula include the giant Proleek Dolmen, accessible via a footpath from the Ballymascanlon House Hotel, and the Windy Gap, a mountain pass closely hemmed in by cliffs and crags, and scene of an incident in the Cattle Raid epic.

Colimore Harbour in Dalkey, not far south of Dun Laoghaire

Dun Laoghaire's coat of arms clearly shows the town's seafaring connections

JOHN POWER & SON
SMITHFIELD, DUBLIN 7
ESTD. 1791
IRISH WHISKEY
DISTILLED AND BOTTLED IN BOND BY
John Power Son
DUBLIN
PRODUCT OF IRELAND
40% vol
750 ml

97

▶ **Dun Laoghaire**   86C3

Weary ferry travellers from Britain usually have difficulty either spelling or pronouncing the name ('Dun Leary') of this major entry port into the Republic. Its former name (Kingstown) commemorated the English George IV, who visited in 1821. Its Irish name refers to an earlier monarch, the 5th century High King of Tara, Laoghaire, who allowed St Patrick to set up his mission in Ireland. When the harbour was constructed by the Scot, John Rennie, in the early 19th century, its vast granite piers were the largest in the world. Besides its commercial traffic, Dun Laoghaire is a prestigious yachting centre. Apart from catching ferries, visitors stray to this Victorian town of brightly painted houses to look at the **National Maritime Museum▶**, in the former Mariners Church on Haigh Terrace, which houses a French longboat captured at Bantry, County Cork, in 1796, and the old optic from the Baily Lighthouse on Howth Head, used until 20 years ago.

The **James Joyce Martello Tower▶** at Sandycove is another place of interest. Joyce spent a brief and disturbing time here with the poet-surgeon, Oliver St John Gogarty, who later appeared as Buck Mulligan in *Ulysses*. Apparently, one of the guests had a nightmare and fired several shots into the fireplace of the room where they were sleeping. Gogarty then shot at a row of saucepans above Joyce's head, shouting 'Leave him to me!' Joyce, tempering valour with discretion, left next morning. The Martello tower houses a small museum set up by Sylvia Beech, with Joycean memorabilia, including a tie given by Joyce to Samuel Beckett. The gunpowder magazine now houses the Joyce Library and Joyce's death mask made on 13 January 1941 (open April–October).

A detail from the Christ in Majesty sculpture, in Dun Laoghaire

Close by is the Forty Foot Pool mentioned in *Ulysses*, a natural seawater swimming hole where nude bathing was once permitted, for men only. Women are now allowed, but togs are required – by order! Nearby Dalkey▶ (pronounced Dawkey) is an attractive resort with ancient fortified mansions and summer boat trips to Dalkey Island, a bird sanctuary and home to a herd of wild goats.

Kildare, popular with canal enthusiasts

High Crosses
South Kildare contains several well preserved High Crosses. The best are at Moone and Castledermot. The Moone example stands over 5m and depicts biblical scenes (lane signposted near post office). There are two crosses at Castledermot, again carved with scriptural themes. Both sites stand in the ruins of ancient monasteries.

Canal trips
County Kildare is traversed by two great canal systems, the Royal and Grand Canals, which connect Dublin with the interior lakelands and the Rivers Shannon and Barrow. They were major arteries of trade during the Industrial Revolution until the 1801 Act of Union stifled Ireland's economic development. The place to find out more about the canals is Robertstown. Here, trips run from the restored Old Canal Hotel (exhibition), which was built in 1803 to serve canal-borne passengers; candlelit dinners with music are sometimes held in summer.

A range of shoes is on offer to Kildare's four-footed residents

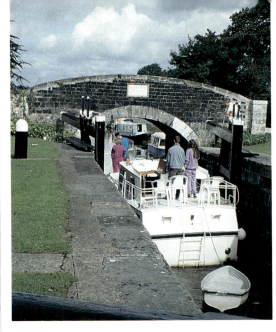

▶▶ Kildare
86C1

The town has a village-like air; gaily painted shop-fronts, old pubs and of course a betting shop cluster round its market square by the sturdy tower of **St Brigid's Cathedral▶**, dating from the 13th century, but much altered since. Stained-glass windows depict Ireland's great saints – Brigid, Patrick and Columba. During the 5th century Kildare was one of the few religious houses in Ireland exclusively for women. The cathedral is flanked by a tall **Round Tower▶**, which you can climb in summer for extensive views of this rolling horse country. Immediately outside town is the wide, springy, gorse-speckled plain called the Curragh, which will immediately stir the heart of any racing *aficionado*. The Curragh is Ireland's largest military camp, where the armoured vehicle that carried Michael Collins to his fatal ambush in 1922 is on display.

If you are at all interested in horses, one place you will certainly want to see is the **Irish National Stud▶▶**, based at Tully just outside the town. Visitors can tour the neat buildings and see the horses being exercised and groomed, or at ease in carefully fenced paddocks. These valuable animals enjoy a standard of living many humans would envy, and their occupation may appeal, too. The stallions stay hard at work from January to July; the rest of the year is their 'holiday'. They have to perform as stalwartly in the covering sheds as they ever did on the racecourse.

The stud was set up in 1902 by the British, and transferred to the Irish state in 1943. Its eccentric founder was Colonel William Hall Walker, who believed that the stars influenced the horses' form. The stallion boxes are built with lantern roofs to allow heavenly bodies their full effect on the horses. Every time a mare foaled, Colonel Walker would cast its horoscope, and race or sell the progeny accordingly. The system, it is said, was uncannily successful.

Spring and early summer are the most interesting times to visit, when you will see new foals with the mares. The foaling area contains a special unit in which orphan foals can be safely fostered. Later in the year the Sun Chariot Yard holds promising yearlings whose paces are just about to be tested. Veterinary research is carried out at the stud, along with all aspects of the complex and rarified science of horse-breeding. The animals are not pets and should not be approached; apart from their extreme value, they can be fierce and may bite or kick, while mares with foals can be particularly savage.

The ornamental lake near the stable units provides mineral-rich drinking water for the horses, said to encourage good bone structure. Also in the grounds are the ruins of the Black Abbey, dating from the 12th century, along with the **Irish Horse Museum**▶, dedicated to all aspects of the equine species. The skeleton of the legendary steeplechaser Arkle is on display, as well as Pat Taafe's whip and the Duchess of Westminster's racing colours.

Next to the Stud is a completely different attraction, though it can be visited on a joint ticket. The **Japanese Gardens**▶▶ symbolically depict man's progress from birth to eternity, via a series of landmarks representing disappointments and failures on the road to enlightenment and final happiness. On the way, visitors pass such features as the Marriage Bridge, the Hill of Ambition and the Tunnel of Ignorance. The intricate landscaping makes the gardens seem much bigger than they really are. They were created by the Japanese gardener Eida and his son between 1906 and 1910. A garden centre offers bonsai trees for sale, and tea rooms provide sustenance. Open daily in season.

Two bodies
A saint's relics were of huge importance to the economy of a monastery because of the pilgrims who came to venerate them, and strife between monasteries for the possession of such relics was by no means uncommon. One recorded instance concerned the relics of St Abban, a south Leinster saint. His medieval *Life* tells of a struggle between the monks of Killabban (his County Kildare birthplace) and those of his monastery at Maganey, for the possession of his body. The former claimed it because they were his first followers, while the latter based their claim to it on the fact that the saint had lived and died amongst them. Divine Providence, however, stepped in and settled the matter satisfactorily by bestowing an identical body of the saint on each of the communities!

101

The elegant Japanese Gardens are a surprising find next to the National Stud

■ **The English and the Irish probably come closer to understanding each other through their mutual love of horses than in any other way. Ireland is currently estimated to have about 55,000 horses, including 15,000 race-horses .....■**

Laytown Races
The much loved and highly unusual Laytown Races are held just once a year in either July or August. The course is a gently shelving beach of soft sand in a little coastal resort in County Meath, near Drogheda. As soon as the tide goes out the six-furlong track is quickly marked and the horses thunder across the strand, amid a lively seaside atmosphere of candy-floss stalls and paddling children. The competitors race not only each other, but the advancing tide!

102

A focal point of Ireland's racing country is Punchestown racecourse, County Kildare

A land of horses Ireland is the heart of the bloodstock industry, where many of the world's best thoroughbreds are reared and trained. It also has facilities for every type of equestrian sport: flat-racing, steeple-chasing, show-jumping, eventing, hunting or trekking. Equestrian centres abound, and hunting (not politically correct in much of the UK), is alive and well, with packs from Connemara's Galway Blazers to the Fingal Harriers of Dublin. For other aspects of the horse world, turn up at the jolly Connemara Pony Show (Clifden, August), the fashionable Dublin Horse Show (August), or the horse fairs in Buttevant (County Cork, 12 July) and Ballinasloe (County Galway, October), where all classes of horseflesh change hands amid an arcane code of palm-slapping and luck money.

Irish breeding Horses thrive in Ireland's mild climate and lush, unpolluted pastureland. The grass overlies a base of limestone, which produces the calcium needed for healthy bones. The native Irish horses are Connemaras, those cheerful animals that survive on saltmarsh grasses and seaweed in the far West. Romantic legends tell how Spanish Arab horses escaped from Armada vessels shipwrecked off the Galway coast in the 16th century and intermingled with the native stock, producing a taller, faster and more elegant breed. The two other distinctively Irish equines are the powerful draught horses, used to plough fields and draw carts, and the charismatic creature of the turf, the long-limbed thoroughbred. Cross-breeding between draught and thoroughbred produces the sturdier but athletic animals used for hunting or show-jumping.

Horses

The lure of the turf Horse-racing is more than a mere sport in Ireland; it is a passion, consuming and generating vast sums of money. The Irish bet about IR£90 million a year on the turf, and thousands are avid studiers of form. The bloodstock industry turns over staggering amounts, aided by favourable government tax-breaks. Many British breeders, trainers and owners now base their operations across the water. Racing, however, was known in Ireland many centuries ago. The legendary Red Branch knights of Ulster raced, as did later Gaelic warriors, though it was then mainly a sport of kings. The Normans and Elizabethans loved it; Cromwell, with his characteristic lack of *joie de vivre*, tried to ban it as the work of the devil – possibly one of his less popular moves in Ireland. During the 18th century racing was all the rage, and two neighbours in County Cork coined a new phrase with their epic cross-country dash between the spires of Buttevant and Doneraile churches – 'steeplechasing'.

Today, racing 'over the sticks' still has a great following, though not nearly as much money is involved as in flat-racing. Jumpers are usually gelded, so when their sporting days are over they cannot retire gracefully to sire lucrative strings of winning progeny, as flat-racers do. None the less, the courage and stamina needed of both horse and rider in steeplechasing make it an exciting and highly respected sport.

Ireland has nearly 30 racecourses, and meetings are held somewhere on about 230 days of the year, including Sundays. They vary enormously from state-of-the-art Leopardstown, just outside Dublin, to the quaint Laytown Races (see panel). Ireland's most celebrated flat-racing venue is the Curragh in County Kildare, 2,400ha of gorsy plain where any visitor will see strings of racehorses testing their paces on the springy turf. The great national hunt (steeplechasing) courses are at Fairyhouse (where the Irish Grand National is held), Punchestown, Navan and Galway. You can find full details of the racing calendar in any Irish paper, or from the tourist board. The most valuable race is the Irish Derby; the winner, whose progeny will be closely watched for hereditary swiftness, commands a guaranteed place in the annals of racing history.

The tack room at one of Ireland's many riding schools; this is at Donacomper, near Celbridge in – almost inevitably – County Kildare

National Stud
Tully, near Kildare, is home to the Irish National Stud (see pages 100–101). Set up by the British in 1902, it passed to the Irish in 1943, and now welcomes visitors to look round the palatial quarters inhabited by Dancing Dissident or Broken Hearted and their precious offspring. The National Horse Museum is also here, exhibiting the skeleton of the peerless Arkle, three times winner of the Cheltenham Gold Cup.

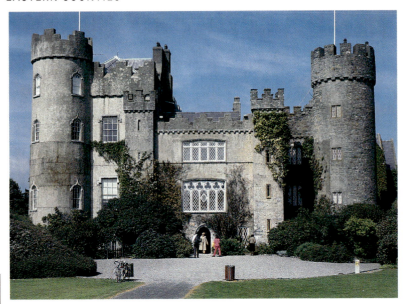

Inside Malahide Castle highlights include the Oak Room, full of intricate panelling from the 16th and 17th centuries

Newbridge
Beyond Malahide, in Donabate, lies the former home of the Cobbe family. Designed by George Semple, Newbridge is an 18th-century house set in wooded parkland. Guided tours are available; the drawing room is an authentic example of Georgian décor, and the areas 'below stairs' contain original utensils and equipment. More unusually, the much-travelled Cobbes built up a charming little museum of curiosities from many foreign places. Craft workshops and period transport displays are on show in the courtyard. (Open April–October, closed Mondays).

▶▶ **Malahide Castle**   86D3

With the exception of a brief spell under Cromwell, this romantic-looking building was the seat of the Talbot family for nearly 800 years before it was bought by Dublin County Council in 1976. The Talbots were Jacobite supporters and fared badly in the Battle of the Boyne. It is said that the 14 cousins who sat down to breakfast at Malahide on the morning of the battle were all dead by nightfall. The tour of the building enables you to see its transition from a simple fortification to a charmingly domestic country house in elaborate Gothic style; the present turrets and battlements are entirely ornamental. It contains many original furnishings, mostly 18th-century, and a fine collection of portraits which now form Ireland's National Portrait Gallery. The structure of the house dates from several periods, the oldest section being its 14th-century tower. The Great Hall is especially noteworthy, the only one in Ireland to be preserved in its original form.

The beautiful gardens around the castle contain a remarkable botanical collection; beyond lie many hectares of well-kept parkland. In the castle yard is the **Fry Railway Museum▶**, with engines and rolling stock hand-made by a Dublin railway engineer, Cyril Fry. The 'O'-gauge railway is an amazing scale model with stations, bridges, trams, buses, barges, the River Liffey and the Hill of Howth. There are also perfect models of Cork and Heuston Stations, O'Connell Bridge, the Halfpenny Bridge and the Guinness loading wharf.

▶ **Marino Casino**   86C3

If you are on your way to Malahide or Howth, this little Georgian gem is worth tracking down in Dublin's northern suburbs, though it is perhaps a long trek from the centre to see this one building. The Casino has nothing to do with gambling, but was built for Lord Charlemont (who lived in what is now the Hugh Lane Municipal Gallery, see page 56). It was simply an exuberant bit of neoclassical frivolity, a skittish aside to a villa in which he planned to house some of the works of art he brought home from a grand tour. The villa no longer exists, but the restored Casino survives, flamboyantly decorated with urns concealing chimneystacks. Nearby Marino Crescent (also known as Ffolliot's Revenge) was built by a painter out of spite to block Lord Charlemont's view of the sea. The backs of the houses were made particularly hideous with ill-proportioned windows and scruffy sheds.

Maynooth   86C2

If you are touring west of Dublin you will probably drive through Maynooth at some point, a pleasant Georgian town with a ruined castle and, near by, the famous seminary and lay university of St Patrick's College, where many of Ireland's priests are trained. During the Reformation it was suppressed, but reopened in 1795 after the repeal of the harsh Penal Laws against Catholics. It can be visited by appointment (tel: 01 628 5222), and contains an ecclesiastical museum. The town's main square is in Victorian Gothic style and was designed by Pugin. Close to the town, but secluded behind forbidding walls, is the large estate of Carton House, a fine Georgian mansion currently undergoing redevelopment.

▶▶ Mellifont Abbey   86D2

Remains of the first Cistercian church in Ireland, founded in 1142, stand in a maze of quiet lanes by the River Mattock. Built by St Malachy, Archbishop of Armagh, its design was heavily influenced by the French Cistercian monastery at Clairvaux, where St Malachy had stayed and befriended the abbot, St Bernard. There's a fairly good overview of the ruins from the car-park area, but a modest entrance fee is charged if you wish to take a closer look. The most striking section of the ruins is the Romanesque octagonal lavabo, or washing place, about half of which is still standing.

A Tasmanian connection
The late Lord Talbot de Malahide was also the owner of another Malahide – in Tasmania, where his sister still lives. Inspired by his family's interests there, and by his own fascination for botany, he wrote the definitive multi-volume work on the plants of Tasmania. He also introduced to the Irish Malahide garden plants from his antipodean property, as well as others from Africa, North and South America, China, Australia and Mexico – which makes it a plantsman's paradise.

105

Portraits from the National Gallery in Dublin now hang in the imposing setting of Malahide Castle

Mount Usher Gardens make the most of their position on the River Vartry

The Hill of Tara, once a site of pagan importance, is one of many such places to have been 'Christianised'

▶▶ **Monasterboice** 86E2

North of Drogheda, off the N1, is one of the best examples in Ireland of a carved High Cross. This is the 10th-century Cross of Muiredach, nearly 6m high, which bears numerous biblical scenes in deep relief, such as Cain slaying Abel, David and Goliath and the Last Judgement. The west face is devoted to the life of Christ, including the arrest in the Garden of Gethsemane, and the risen Christ returning to meet St Peter and St Paul. At the bottom of the Cross is an inscription in Gaelic saying 'A prayer for Muiredach by whom this cross was made'. Two other more eroded High Crosses can be seen on the site, along with a fine Round Tower and a pre-Gothic sundial. Two ruined 13th-century churches stand within the enclosure.

▶▶ **Mount Usher Gardens** 86B3

These lovely gardens stand in 8ha of well-watered land on the banks of the River Vartry. Water forms an essential part of the scenery, with cascades and bridges visible in just about every section. It is quite possible to get utterly lost if you forget which way the water is flowing. They were laid out by Edward Walpole, a Dublin businessman, and his sons, from 1868, as a wild garden, and contain about 5,000 species, including many rhododendrons and eucalyptuses. The gardens offer fine displays of colour throughout the summer opening period. The maples in late September and October are especially striking. Several craft and clothing shops stand by the entrance, where there is a tea-room.

▶ **Navan** 86D2

Navan occupies a strategic site on the Boyne. Not compelling in itself, it makes a good base for seeing several places in the area. Within the town, the most interesting sight is **Athlumney Castle▶**, over the bridge. This 15th-century tower-house was apparently burned down by its last owner, Sir Lancelot Dowdall, a devout Catholic who refused to let it fall into William's hands after the Battle of the Boyne. He is said to have watched his home blaze all night from the opposite banks, then set off into exile.

Thirteen kilometres south of the town is one of Ireland's most famous antiquities, the **Hill of Tara**▶▶. This shows evidence of occupation from many different periods, and was the symbolic seat of the High Kings until the 11th century. Its history is steeped in legends, but archaeological evidence suggests that some grim events must have taken place here. Various ring forts can be seen, though some were damaged in recent years by British Israelites searching for the Ark of the Covenant (see panel). The site has probably always been associated with religious cults of some kind, though its influence waned after the arrival of Christianity. It was from this hill that King Laoghaire and the Druids first noticed St Patrick's defiant fire on the nearby Hill of Slane.

The Hill of Tara is now just a grassy flat-topped hill grazed by sheep, reached by a field path from the parking place. It rises only 100m or so from the surrounding land, but the views over the plains are very extensive. Various inconclusive mounds and earthworks indicate the locations of the old palaces, banquet hall, and Bronze Age burial sites, and many artefacts have been unearthed and removed from the site for display in museums. Tara's most significant event in recent times was a mass meeting called by the nationalist leader Daniel O'Connell (see page 42) which is said to have attracted over a million people. This alarmed the British Government, who suppressed O'Connell's activities and thus put one more nail in the coffin of a peaceful Anglo-Irish settlement.

South of Tara is **Dunsany Castle**▶, a private residence originally built in the 12th century by Hugh de Lacy to defend Anglo-Norman territory. It contains a fine collection of art and some unusual Jacobite relics (the Lords of Dunsany are the Plunkett family to which the famous Saint Oliver belonged). The castle is open in high season, mornings only (tel: 046 31845 for more details).

Today, visitors to the Hill of Tara are thankfully more inclined to appreciate the views than dig vainly for the Ark of the Covenant

The Ark of the Covenant
In 1899, the purchase of a book on Charing Cross Road in London led a group known as the British Israelites to the belief that the Ark of the Covenant lay buried on the Hill of Tara. One of their number, a Mr Groome, came to Ireland to excavate in furtherance of his biblical quest. When he found nothing, some locals took pity on his disappointment and placed some Roman coins where he would dig on the morrow and where, inevitably and to his own delight, he duly discovered them the next day. But after a singular lack of success in locating what he had set out to find, he packed his bags and returned to England. The Ark still remains undiscovered on the Hill of Tara – or anywhere else.

▶▶▶ Newgrange 86D2

Newgrange is unquestionably one of Ireland's most important archaeological sites, and is perhaps the most spectacular passage-grave (the tomb takes the form of a long passage covered by a vast mound) in Western Europe. Dating from *c.*3000BC, it is possibly 1,000 years older than Stonehenge. The tumulus stands in a sloping field above the road, overlooking the glittering snake of the Boyne and a vast sweep of quiet farmland. It is easily spotted because the front retaining walls of the grass-covered mound are faced with brilliant white stones of quartzite. The nearest source for these stones is the Wicklow Mountains south of Dublin, so thousands of tons of material must have been dragged huge distances. Egg-shaped grey stones are studded at intervals among the white ones, though the original pattern of these (if there was one) is a matter of speculation. The mound itself measures about 100m across, and is over 10m high at its central point. Over the years it had completely collapsed and was reconstructed during the 1960s, using careful measurements to determine its precise dimensions. In the front of the mound is a low entrance formed by slabs of rock, and above it another rectangular opening, the roof-box. This sophisticated device is constructed with a narrow slit in the stone so that, once a year, for about 15 minutes on the morning of the winter solstice, the rays of the sun illumine the interior of the tomb. All around the edge of the tomb is a low wall of large boulders, some carved with spiral shapes. The significance of these is unknown; they may have been purely decorative.

You can walk all round the mound (the white wall does not go all the way) to see what remains of a circle of standing stones. A guided tour takes you into the inner

108

The entrance to the passage-grave, with the roof-box above the lintel

The sparkling white of the quartzite lends added drama to Newgrange

stone chamber of the tomb from which three recesses lead. The magnificent dovetailed structure of the vaulted roof still keeps the water out. Other mysterious patterns are carved on the inner stones, some invisible from outside and presumably for some cult purpose. Stone basins contained the bones of the cremated dead with offerings of beads and pins. At the end of the tour an artificial light is switched on to recreate an approximation of the solstice phenomenon.

Newgrange is open all year and is besieged by school parties and visitors in high season. During the winter solstice (21 December and several days around that date), access is virtually impossible; places are booked many years in advance to see the phenomenon within the tomb. Tourism at this sensitive site is carefully managed, but even so, erosion is occurring. The Office of Public Works has controversial plans afoot to place a new interpretative centre near the site with a replica of the tomb to reduce the pressure of visitor numbers.

Newgrange is by no means the only local antiquity. The nearby mounds of Dowth and Knowth also contain passage tombs. As you look from Newgrange, over the lush pastureland enclosed by this sheltered bend of the Boyne, the shapes of numerous strange humps and tumuli are visible – these are other burial sites, about 40 in all, some of which have not yet been explored. The Irish name for this giant graveyard is *Brugh na Boinne*, the palace of the Boyne. Its builders were a farming community who were apparently fairly settled and peaceful, clearing forests and raising stock. The looping River Boyne furnished them with a useful artery of communication and a natural defence barrier.

Many aspects of the tombs are puzzling and myths and theories abound. The fatally wounded Diarmuid, lover of Gráinne, is alleged to have been brought here 'to put aerial life into him'. Other legends declare these tombs (inaccurately) to be the burial places of the Kings of Tara, while the sun-cult rituals echo those discovered in ancient Egyptian tombs, though these graves probably predate the pyramids by several hundred years.

There are several inscribed stones at Newgrange; this one is at the back of the mound

Tomorrow never comes
In early Irish mythology, Newgrange was associated with the Dagda, the good god of the Celts, his wife Bóann (the divinised River Boyne) and his son Oengus – all supernatural beings belonging to the Tuatha Dé Danann (peoples of the goddess Danu), who had defeated the Fir Bolg people (see page 30) and had occupied Ireland before the Celts. The 12th-century *Book of Leinster* tells the tale of how Oengus used a verbal trick to get possession of the great mound at Newgrange from his father. The Dagda, it seems, was persuaded to let his son have it for a day and a night, and when he asked his son to return it the next day, Oengus replied that a day and a night meant forever – so he kept it. He had probably argued, with impeccable Irish logic, that tomorrow never comes as every day is today.

EASTERN COUNTIES

Daniel Robertson
The terraces of Powerscourt Gardens were indelibly stamped by the unsteady hand of this gouty and eccentric architect who, in 1840, was commissioned by the 6th Viscount Powerscourt to draw up new plans for the garden. Apparently Robertson's *modus operandi* was to be trundled around the gardens in a wheelbarrow, directing staff while swigging intermittently at a bottle of sherry. Once the bottle was empty he ran out of ideas and all useful work for the day ground to a halt. Robertson's habits were expensive, and he was constantly in debt. Whenever the sheriff called, he used to hide in the copper dome of the house.

110

▶▶ **Powerscourt**   *86C3*

The pretty village of Enniskerry and the theatrical backdrop of the Wicklow Mountains add greatly to the appeal of this great estate, which covers about 5,500ha. Even the entrance drive is impressive – over a kilometre long. James I granted the land to the 1st Viscount Powerscourt, Sir Richard Wingfield, in 1609. A magnificent house was designed by Richard Castle, whose Palladian handiwork can be seen all over Ireland. Unfortunately the great edifice burned to a shell in a disastrous accident in 1974 just after a long programme of restoration. Plans are afoot to recreate the house, but the phenomenal cost of the exercise has so far daunted enthusiasts. All that can be seen now are the splendid gardens, laid out on the south-facing slopes in front of the house which overlook the Great Sugar Loaf Mountain. They were first created in the mid-18th century soon after the completion of the house, but redesigned in the 19th century by the redoubtable Daniel Robertson (see panel) with classical parterres and Italianate statuary. They contain glorious lakes with spouting fountains and winged horses, and magnificent specimen trees which grow to a prodigious height in this mild climate. Unusual touches include a Japanese garden (1908) on reclaimed bogland sporting little scarlet bridges, a pet cemetery dedicated to many faithful friends (Jack, Sting and Taffy), mosaic terraces made of beach pebbles from Bray, and neat, homely kitchen gardens. A garden centre, pleasant tea-room and a gift shop maximise tourist revenue.

An additional attraction about 6km away (separate entrance charge) is the **Powerscourt Waterfall**▶▶, which plunges about 120m in a mare's-tail plume down a jagged rock face. There are excellent local walks around the valley below and, to make the most of the entrance fee, take a picnic and make an outing of it. Kiosk refreshments and picnic tables are provided.

The Great Sugar Loaf Mountain forms a memorable backdrop to the gardens at Powerscourt

▶▶ Russborough House *86C2*

Like nearby Powerscourt, this grand Palladian mansion shows the Anglo-Irish ascendancy in the Pale at its most confident and powerful. It was designed by the ubiquitous Richard Castle (and, after his death, Francis Bindon) for the 1st Earl of Milltown, a wealthy Dublin brewer. The structure is palatial; two huge semi-circular wings stretch from the main body of the building to two side pavilions. Inside, the grandeur continues in magnificent plasterwork by the Francini brothers. Some of it, like elegant cake icing, swirls round exquisite oval sea scenes by Claude Vernet, commissioned specially for the house.

Today the house is owned by the nephew of Alfred Beit, the German co-founder (with Cecil Rhodes) of the De Beer Diamond Mining Company. Besides a multitude of antiques, tapestries, and valuable porcelain, his fabulous collection of art (strong on Spanish, Dutch and Flemish schools) is now held at Russborough. At least, some of it is, for Russborough has suffered two major burglaries. The first was in 1974 when, in a *cause célèbre* that hit all the headlines, Dr Bridget Rose Dugdale stole 16 paintings for her IRA lover (the haul was recovered, undamaged, later). In May 1986 another break-in occurred and this time the owners were not so lucky. Now the house is under a fair degree of surveillance and, if you turn up outside normal opening times, you are likely to get a less than courteous reception. There is, however, still plenty that makes the house well worth a special visit. The grounds consist of woodland and a large artificial lake (actually a reservoir), with views of the Wicklow Mountains beyond.

Nearby **Blessington▶** is one of the most charming villages in the Wicklow Mountains, and makes a popular base for exploring the area. Its wide street is flanked by tall trees and dignified Georgian buildings. Blessington was once a staging post on the coach route from Dublin to Carlow. Dame Ninette de Valois, founder of the Sadler's Wells Ballet Company, was born near by.

Apart from a wonderful collection of paintings, Russborough House is also the home of some unusual dolls

A dramatic display
When King George IV announced his intention of visiting Powerscourt in 1821, a path was hurriedly laid out from the great house to the waterfall in the grounds, and an artificial lake with sluice gates created at the top of the fall to make a more dramatic cascade for the King to admire. But the delights of the luncheon table in the mansion gave His Majesty insufficient time to visit the waterfall, and when the sluice gates were subsequently opened, the great onrush of water destroyed the wooden platform on which the King should have been standing. So the English monarchy has reason to be thankful to Powerscourt – and a good lunch!

Skerries is so-called because of the islands lying just off the coast; the name means 'sea rocks' in Gaelic

The road to Slane
The reason, it is said, why the road from Dublin to Slane was made so straight (unlike most in Ireland) was to minimise the time it would take King George IV to reach his mistress in Slane Castle when he visited Ireland in 1821.

A shield set into the walls of Slane Abbey

Skerries   86D3

This is one of the biggest resorts on the northeast coast, mostly visited by Dubliners. The strange indentations at Red Island are claimed to be the footprints of St Patrick. Boat trips to St Patrick's Island enable visitors to explore a ruined church where a national synod was held in 1148. Just south is the pretty fishing village of Loughshinny.

► Slane   86D2

The town was built on the instructions of Viscount Conyngham in the 18th century, around a crossroads. For its modest size it has considerable historic interest, and is a pleasant grey-stone place of agreeable Georgian proportions. The demesne of Slane Castle, former home of the Conynghams, lies behind firmly locked gates, though it can be glimpsed occasionally from nearby roads. Open-air rock concerts were recently held in the castle grounds, but it is not generally open to the public and has been damaged by fire. The Marchioness Conyngham was rumoured to have been George IV's last mistress, and he apparently spent a good deal of time here. Near the riverside is a mill and small transport museum containing a collection of vintage and veteran cars. The four identical Georgian houses set at equal angles to the crossroads in the village centre have given rise to one of those appealing Irish tales that are almost certainly untrue.

The houses were supposedly built for four quarrelsome spinster sisters whose exasperated brother became so fed up with their wranglings under one roof that he insisted they live separately. Whether or not the story is true, the houses are fine examples and deserve a close look.

A humble labourer's cottage a short distance from the centre of Slane was the birthplace of the lyric poet Francis Ledwidge. A plaque outside displays one of his most haunting verses, written after his friend Thomas MacDonagh was executed for his part in the Easter Rising of 1916:

'He shall not hear the bittern cry
In the wild sky, where he is lain,
Nor voices of the sweeter birds
Above the wailing of the rain.'

Ledwidge himself was killed soon after this – at Flanders, fighting on the British side. He was only 30 and is now lamented as a great loss to literature, though his work was not widely read at a time of such political upheaval.

Outside the village is the **Hill of Slane▶** on which the ruins of a monastery stand. The site is famous as the place where St Patrick lit paschal fires to challenge the pagan king, Laoghaire, who had forbidden flames to be kindled within sight of his palace at Tara (see page 107).

▶ Straffan *86C2*

This village on the banks of the Liffey has two tourist attractions, though both are open only in high season. The **Butterfly Farm▶** is the only one of its type in Ireland, with tropical species fluttering about in a hothouse full of exotic plants. The **Steam Museum▶** documents the history of the steam age in Ireland, showing how it revolutionised industrial as well as agricultural practices such as butter-churning and corn-threshing. Working steam engines are on display, including Richard Trevithick's prototype steam-powered road vehicle. The engines stand in the courtyard of an 18th-century house. Phone in advance if you want to attend a 'live steam day' (tel: 01 627 3155).

Swords *86D3*

This is now a bustling modern town where new housing takes some of the commuting overspill from central Dublin. But it has an ancient pedigree, and was formerly the site of a monastery founded by St Columba in the 6th century. Swords Castle stands at the north end of town, a fortified manor built in about 1200 by the Archibishop of Dublin. Two towers can be seen in the grounds of the Protestant church – a Round Tower from the 11th century, and the last vestiges of a 15th-century church.

Garrick Castle
Sited near the Boyne a few miles upriver from Slane is the ruined castle of Garrick. Close by was a weir and, so the story goes, fish caught in a net there touched a wire connected to the castle kitchen, so that the cook would know when to serve up the freshest of salmon on the menu.

113

Slane Abbey was founded in 1512 for four priests, four clerks and four choristers

Land of saints

■ **Christianity reached Irish shores during the late 4th century, not with Roman fire and sword, but through the persuasive urgings of an extraordinary band of missionary monks who brought the glad tidings to the pagan Gaels. Many of these early Christian teachers and founders of monasteries are now Irish saints .....■**

St Oliver Plunkett (1629–81) One of the most interesting of all Ireland's saints was canonised very recently, in 1976. St Oliver Plunkett, Archbishop of Armagh and Primate of All Ireland, had the misfortune to live during the troubled years of the 17th century, when Catholicism was rigorously suppressed by English authorities. He was on friendly terms with the Protestant clergy of Ulster, who had a high regard for his sincerity and achievements, but false allegations by Titus Oates in 1678 over a 'popish plot' to bring French soldiers into Ireland resulted in his arrest, though the charges were blatantly absurd. On 1 July 1681 he was executed in London for 'treason', his offence being simply that he was an unrepentant Catholic. At his trial the Lord Chief Justice declared, 'The bottom of your treason was your setting up your false religion, than which there is not anything more displeasing to God.' Plunkett's severed head was rescued from the flames and brought back to Ireland, where it resides in a shrine in the Catholic Church of St Peter, Drogheda.

Saintly lives Innumerable saints are encountered on any visit to Ireland. Most of them are obscure (who now remembers St Gobnet or St Lurach?) and the patterns of their lives are often very similar – they renounced the world, founded monasteries and did good works. The achievements of these early monks, however, are hard to over-estimate. The trials they endured, the distances they travelled in uncharted terrain and their dazzling artistic talents are truly staggering. Christianity was indeed a faith that moved mountains. The Christian message was mainly interpreted by men, just as it is now, and attitudes to women were extremely misogynistic. Just a few intrepid women saints braved this exclusive and hostile masculine preserve, among them St Brigid, who founded one of the earliest of Ireland's nunneries at Kildare.

In today's Ireland, the saints still play an active rôle in the lives of many devout Catholics. You will find candles burning at every shrine, votive offerings in sacred places and eager pilgrims praying for their intercession in everyday affairs or for the perpetual forgiveness of sins. Factual evidence about most of the early saints is sparse. Their lives are but shadowy, and wreathed in legends or miraculous tales. Some of them are composite figures or even Christian incarnations of pagan Celtic gods. The most famous Irish saint, of course, is St Patrick, the most effective of all the early missionaries (see page 226 for more details of his life, and of places associated with him).

St Columba (*c.*521–97) Also known as Columcille (meaning 'dove of the church') St Columba was born at Lough Gartan in Donegal. He was a high-ranking member of the O'Neill clan, a scholar, poet and natural leader. After training as a monk at Moville and Clonard, he founded the monasteries of Derry and Durrow, possibly also Kells. In 563 he left Ireland with 12 companions to found a monastery in Iona, an island off the Scottish coast, but retained his links with Ireland. He was a charismatic figure, tall and striking, well educated, persuasive and ardently committed to his cause. Some of his actions seemed less than saintly. This endearingly human paragon was, by all accounts, a thief and a cheat – stealing a ceremonial cross from a neighbouring church and secretly copying a psalter he borrowed from a friend. This resulted in the deaths of thousands at the Battle of the Books (see page 210).

St Ciarán (*c.*512–45) The founder of the great monastery of Clonmacnois, St Ciarán had an auspicious pedigree as

Land of saints

a Christian leader – he was the son of a carpenter. His first monkish years were spent on the Aran Islands with Enda, the islands' most famous saint. Later he went to Scattery Island, in the mouth of the Shannon, and finally to Clonmacnois further upstream, where he died soon afterwards. Apparently he aroused such jealousy among his fellow clerics that they prayed he would die young – and he did! But his good works lived on, and the influence of Clonmacnois spread far and wide, surviving until 1522, despite many Viking raids.

St Brendan the Navigator (*c.*486–575) This famous Irish saint was the founder of a monastery at Clonfert in County Galway, and also Ardfert in Kerry. His sister was (another) St Brigid. His missions took place mostly in western Ireland, but he is best remembered as a great traveller. His epic voyage is chronicled in the 10th-century romance, *The Navigation of St Brendan*, in which he set sail with 12 disciples in search of an earthly paradise in the Atlantic Ocean. The journey lasted over seven years, and it has been suggested that his account of 'crystal columns' (icebergs?) and 'curdled seas' (the Sargasso?) may pinpoint him as the first to cross the Atlantic. St Brendan's supposed voyage was imaginatively recreated in similar conditions by the modern explorer Tim Severin, and the wood-and-leather boat he sailed across the Atlantic in 1976 can be seen in the history theme park of Craggaunowen, County Clare (see page 183).

Clonmacnois, founded by St Ciarán, was for centuries the intellectual capital of Ireland

115

This little church at Glendalough is familiarly known as St Kevin's Kitchen as the small bell-tower resembles a chimney

St Kevin (died *c.*618)
Founder of the great monastery at Glendalough, County Wicklow, St Kevin came from a noble Leinster family and was educated by monks from childhood. After his ordination he adopted a hermit's existence at Glendalough. His quest for solitude was in vain, however, for crowds of disciples soon gathered around him and he became the leader of a great and influential community. He is alleged to have murdered a woman who attempted to seduce him, shoving her from his rock-ledge cave into the lake below. The tale conveniently bolsters the early fathers' belief that women were the source of all corruption.

The stark silhouette of the Yellow Steeple; near by stands a section of Trim's town walls

Michael Dwyer's escape
The year 1798 witnessed great upheavals against English rule, especially in the Southeast. During the harsh winter of 1798–9 the Wicklow-born rebel Michael Dwyer took refuge in a cottage in Derrynamuck, in the Glen of Imaal. Over 100 English soldiers surrounded it, but he declined to surrender, though he requested the owners of the house be freed. The army allowed this, then battle commenced. A fellow-rebel, Sam McAllister, sustained a broken arm and could fight no longer, so offered to sacrifice himself to give Dwyer a chance to escape. He showed himself at the door and drew the English fire. He was immediately killed, but while the soldiers were reloading their muskets, Dwyer was able to slip away. The cottage is now a folk museum.

Captain Robert Halpin
Robert Halpin (1836–94) was one of Wicklow Town's most prominent citizens. His main achievement was as commander of the *Great Eastern*, Brunel's iron steamship that laid the first transatlantic telegraph cable. A granite obelisk commemorates him in the town, and a plaque at the church of St Lavinius, but for further insights, head for his former home, Tinakilly House, 3km north of town, now a luxury hotel and restaurant.

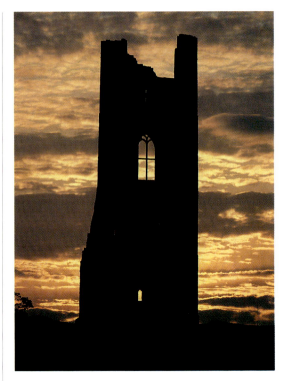

► ▬▬▬ **Trim** *86D2*

Trim Castle is one of the most imposing Anglo-Norman fortresses in Ireland, and as it stands in the centre of the town by the River Boyne it is easy to get a good idea of its size and layout. The ruins cover about a hectare and include a vast keep flanked by rectangular towers. Sections of curtain-wall are interspersed with sally-gates. The original castle was built by Hugh de Lacy in 1172, though the present structure dates from a later period. Some sections are fenced off and undergoing restoration; otherwise you can wander round freely. Near by are the ruins of the Royal Mint and a gaunt skeleton called the Yellow Steeple, dating from the 14th century, the last remnants of an Augustinian abbey, destroyed in 1649.

Bective Abbey►►, between Navan and Trim, is one of the earliest examples of a Cistercian foundation in Ireland. Hugh de Lacy was buried here in 1195, and it was obviously a place of some significance (its abbot sat in the English House of Lords). Most of the extant ruins date from the 15th century and stand in a gloriously peaceful setting in a field by the Knightsbrook River.

► ▬▬▬ **Wicklow** *86B3*

The county town of this much-visited area is small and unassuming, but it makes a pleasantly unstressful base, as its name, meaning 'Viking meadow' suggests. Its history, however, has been far from untroubled. In AD432 St Patrick had an unfriendly reception when he landed at Travilahawk Strand. One of his entourage had his teeth knocked out and became known as Mantan (the toothless one). Irish clans (O'Byrnes and O'Tooles) slugged it out with the Anglo-Norman Fitzgeralds for centuries and after the rebellion of 1798 many of the participants were tried in the town's court-house; those who evaded capture took to the hills. Wicklow's main features of interest are the scanty remains of the Black Castle by the road above the harbour, a fine headland for coastal walks, a ruined 13th-century friary and a heritage centre in the town jail (local history and genealogical research). The Protestant **Church of St Lavinius►**, topped by a Byzantine dome, has several unusual details, including a romanesque doorway and a fine roof. In Norman times the slopes to the River Vartry were planted with vines, a testimony to Wicklow's comparatively sunny climate. The harbour area is oddly severed from the main town; beyond it stretches a long, shingly beach trapping a brackish lagoon (Broad Lough), which makes a sheltered habitat for wildfowl.

►►► The Wicklow Mountains   86B2

These wild hills on Dublin's doorstep are a great boon to city dwellers. From the southern suburbs you can gaze at them on clear days; by public transport or a car they take just half an hour to reach. If you have time enough you can even walk there on the 132km Wicklow Way, starting just outside Dublin in Marlay Park. The route is not very clear in places, and the mountains can be dangerous in misty conditions. The rounded hills of ice-eroded schist and granite enfold a strange mixture of bleak, awesome glens and boggy plateaux, interspersed with welcoming Shangri-La valleys like Glendalough or the Vale of Avoca. The improbable cones of the Great and Little Sugar Loaf Mountains protrude suddenly from the surrounding contours, their granite caps more resilient than the rest. The wildness and emptiness of the mountains made them good hiding places after the 1798 rebellion and during those troubled times they were full of insurgents. One of the main arteries through the region, the military road linking Rathfarnham and the garrison at Aghavannagh, was constructed by English forces in yet another attempt to impose control on recalcitrant Ireland.

The Duke of Wellington
A monument in Emmet Street, Trim, commemorates Arthur Wellesley who lived as a boy here before being, as the Duke of Wellington, the victor at Waterloo. He had been born in Dublin in the same year as his great adversary, Napoleon. But he seems to have had no very high regard for the capital city of his birth, if we can judge by the answer he gave when asked what he thought of Dublin, 'If a man is born in a stable, that does not make him a horse.'

117

Wicklow was one of the bases used by the Vikings on the east coast of Ireland

Killimor • · Banagher · Kilcormac · Bracknagh •
O F F A L Y · Clonaslee · **Portarlington** · Irish National St
Woodford · **Birr** · Kinnitty · **Mountmellick** · Monasterevin · Japanese Garder
Portumna · Carrigahorig · 528m ▲ · **Kildare**
Borrisokane · Cloughjordan · Mountrath · Portlaoise · Stradbally · **K I L I**
Mountshannon · **Roscrea** · Castletown · **L A O I S** · Fontstown
Lough Derg · Borris-in-Ossory · Abbeyleix · **Athy**
Portroe · **Nenagh** · Donaghmore · Rathdowney · Ballinakill · Ballylynan · Castledermot
▲ 532m ▲ 462m · Toomyvara · Durrow · Newtown · **Carlow**
Killaloe · Templemore · Castlecomer · **CARL O**
694m ▲ · Borrisoleigh · Urlingford · Freshford · Ballyragget · **Dunmore Cave** · Old Leighlin · Leighlinbridge
Newport · **Thurles** · Muine Bheag
Boher · Holycross · **Kilkenny** · Borris
Cappamore · **T I P P E R A R Y** · Clonoulty · Gowran · Dungarvan
Pallas Grean · Ballingarry · **Kells Priory** · Graiguenamanagh · Blackstai
Herbertstown · Golden · **Cashel** · Killenaule · Callan · Stonyford · Thomastown
Tipperary · Newinn · **Ahenny High Crosses** · Fethard · Knocktopher · **Jerpoint Abbey** · Inistioge · St Mullins
Bansha · 720m ▲ · Kilmaganny · **New Ro**
Ballylanders · 920m ▲ · **Slieve Naman** · **Clonmel** · **Carrick-on-Suir** · Mullinavat · Glenmore
Mitchelstown · Ballylooby · **Mitchelstown Caves** · Comeragh Mts · Mooncoin · **John F Kennedy Park** · Dunganstown
Kildorrery · Barryporeen · Clogheen · 791m ▲ · **WATERFORD** · **Dunbrody Abbey**
Knockmealdown Mts · Fauscoum · Kilmeaden · Ballyhack · Arthurstov
▲795m · **Mount Melleray Monastery** · Kilmacthomas · Passage East · Fethard
Fermoy · Ballyduff · Cappoquin · **W A T E R F O R D** · Waterford Airport · Dunmore East
Rathcormack · Lismore · Bunmahon · **Tramore** · Hook Head
CORK · Tallow · Clashmore · Annestown · Ring (An Rinn)
Watergrasshill · **Dungarvan** · Mine Head
Killeagh · **Youghal** · Ardmore
Midleton · Castlemartyr · Youghal Bay
Passage West · **Fota Island** · **Cobh** · Cloyne
Carrigaline · Whitegate · Ballycotton · 2 · 3

An attractive thatched cottage at Kilmore Quay; travelling around modern Ireland, you are more likely to see whitewash than thatch

M7 Naas
Droichead Nua
(Newbridge)
Powerscourt
M11 Bray
Kilruddery
House & Gardens
Russborough House
Kilcullen
Blessington
Enniskerry
Greystones
Poulaphouca
Reservoir
848m
Mullaghcleevaun
WICKLOW
Dunlavin
Wicklow
Laragh Ashford
Mount Usher Gardens
926m
Glendalough
Rathnew
Lugnaquilla
Wicklow
Wicklow Head
Baltinglass
M t s
Rathdrum
athvilty
Avondale
Hacketstown
Aughrim
Avoca
Mizen Head
Tullow
Tinahely
Woodenbridge
Shillelagh
Arklow
Carnew
Kilmichael Point
Gorey
Bunclody
Courtown
Harbour
Ferns
Ballycanew
iltealy
WEXFORD
Cahore Point
Enniscorthy
Clonroche
Oilgate
Blackwater
Ferrycarrig
Irish National Heritage Park
Curracloe
Wexford Wildfowl Reserve
Taghmon
Wexford
addington
Wexford Bay
Johnstown Castle
Rosslare
Duncormick
Rosslare Harbour
Lady's Island Lake
allyteige Bay
Kilmore Quay
Carnsore Point
Saltee Islands
St George's Channel

0   10   20   30 km
0   10   20 miles

4   5

SOUTHEASTERN COUNTIES

119

Southeastern counties In contrast to the wildness of western Ireland, the Southeast is mostly low-lying and docile. Rich pastureland watered by brimming rivers extends gently to a quiet coastline of long sandy beaches, estuarial mudflats of wading birds and low cliffs fringing deep bays. Ireland's most fertile farmland lies in the Golden Vale, making Tipperary one of the most prosperous inland counties. There is a great deal to see and do, though to reach all its scattered attractions you will certainly need a car. The sunny, drier climate of the Southeast attracts both Irish and foreign visitors for summer holidays, and there is an excellent choice of beaches.

120

Tacumshane, near Kilmore Quay, has the rarity of a thatched windmill in working order

Travelling people
There are about 3,000 itinerant families in the whole of Ireland, amounting to a population of around 20,000. Many live in illegal roadside camps in conditions of great squalour. Notices discouraging 'travellers' can be seen as you approach many towns and villages. The origins of the true 'traveller' may date back to the 18th century, when many families were dispossessed by the harsh Penal Code, and took to the roads as tinsmiths (hence the old term 'tinker') and dealers. They ranged far and wide, gathering together at events such as the Ballinasloe Horse Fair, where their 'king' was elected. Recently, economic decline has resulted in a sharp increase in homeless families, and today's travellers represent a considerable social problem, for large groups of disruptive itinerants prove unpopular even amongst a race as tolerant as the Irish.

Town and cultural attractions Development here remains low-key; Tramore is the only significantly built-up resort, offering amusement parks and a costly multi-media attraction themed on the Celts. If this atypical brashness doesn't appeal, it is easily avoided. The Southeast's other resorts are all small and village-like, even the county town of Wexford. Waterford is the only 'towny' place, a thriving port and commercial centre where derricks unload cargoes on the wharves and industrial complexes hum. Most famous is the crystal factory a couple of kilometres out of town. This is the largest of its kind in the world, and its annual turnover is boggling – though recession and competition from other production plants have dented Waterford's trade badly. Nevertheless, there is no shortage of visitors on the free guided tours, even if few leave clutching a chandelier (see page 143).

The other sizeable towns of the area are medieval Kilkenny, an up-market tourist town with enough attractions to act as an excellent base, and Tipperary's prosperous county town, Clonmel, where Georgian influences are more noticeable. Carlow, however, is disappointing: neither the town nor the county have much to detain you.

County Tipperary's great tourist honeypot is the Rock of Cashel. Coach tours flock to this atmospheric outcrop of limestone in the middle of lush plains to admire the majestic ruins clustered on its summit. If abbeys and monasteries interest you, this is certainly an area to explore – the great settlements at Holy Cross (County Tipperary), Duiske, Jerpoint (both County Kilkenny), Dunbrody and Tintern (both County Wexford) are some of the finest. Castles, too, stud the bridging points in these great river valleys – no significant town is without some bristling fortress or other. Cahir, Kilkenny, Lismore, Nenagh and Enniscorthy are among the most impressive.

Activity holidays As well as for conventional touring or seaside breaks, the Southeast is a splendid area for activity holidays. The flatter coastal terrain makes walking and cycling holidays less strenuous than in some parts of the country, though inland the hill ranges of the Comeragh, Blackstairs or the splendidly named Knockmealdown Mountains have plenty of visual drama. The South Leinster Way through Carlow and Kilkenny takes in some of the most beautiful scenery around the Nore and Barrow rivers. The Munster Way meanders along the borderland of Tipperary and Waterford over the spectacular high point known as the Vee Gap, and the lovely valley of the Nire. You can link the two routes (they meet at Carrick-on-Suir), or pick up the Kildare Way along the River Barrow towpath from Graiguenamanagh. Bird-watchers should head for the reclaimed Wexford Slobs, Hook Head peninsula or the Saltee Islands.

For fishing holidays, the region is excellent; the rivers teem with brown trout, salmon and coarse fish of all kinds, particularly the Blackwater River. Dungarvan and Dunmore East are the best centres for deep-sea fishing. Lough Derg in the far northwest of County Tipperary is another good location for water sports, including cruising, though the main centres are in Clare or Galway (Killaloe, Mountshannon and Portumna). Equestrian sports are naturally popular in this horsy country; hacking and hunting can be arranged. Tipperary breeds some of Ireland's finest bloodstock, and the interest in racing is evident from no fewer than four racecourses, while greyhound racing centres on Clonmel. Competitive sport is a passionate preoccupation throughout Ireland, but the traditional games of Gaelic football and hurling are played in Tipperary with special enthusiasm. It is no surprise to discover the Gaelic Athletic Association (GAA) was founded here by the sportsmanlike Archbishop of Cashel.

A turbulent history The Vikings held sway over this region for many years, finding those broad estuaries and inviting harbours easy landings from which to torment the native Celts with pillage and nose taxes ('Pay up or we'll cut your nose off'!). Following their example, Strongbow invaded Ireland for the Anglo-Normans via Waterford in 1169, ostensibly to aid Dermot MacMurrough regain his Leinster throne. In return, Strongbow received the hand of Dermot's daughter, the first dynastic alliance between Irish and Norman. But the Normans stayed on and their power grew. The Gaelic MacMurrough Kavanaghs resented the curtailment of their influence, and remained a thorn in the English side, rebelling every so often with unexpected ferocity. Cromwell finally broke their resistance, and is remembered with even less affection in this part of Ireland for his slaughter of hundreds of unarmed citizens at Wexford. The Southeast was relatively peaceful through the 18th century, but the surface calm disguised many ill-feelings. When a confrontation with the yeomanry fanned smouldering passions in 1798, the people of Carlow and Wexford erupted in fury, wielding pikes in a brave but hopeless stand against English cannon-fire at the decisive battle of Vinegar Hill, Enniscorthy.

121

The Vee Gap, near Mitchelstown in County Tipperary, looks especially dramatic in 'Irish weather'

Ardmore's Round Tower; at 30m, it is one of the finest (and latest) in Ireland

Ardmore's Round Tower

'The tower… is said to have been built by St Declan in one night; that when it had arrived at its present height, a woman coming to gather herbs, looking up, asked the Saint what he was doing, upon which he threw down his trowel and killed her, and coming down he threw her upon the top of the tower, where a part of her remained till a few years ago. It is certain, however, that the tower was never raised higher than it is, which it is said it would have been, had not the woman interrupted the Saint in his pious work.'
P D Hardy: The Holy Wells of Ireland (1836)

► **Ardmore**　　　　*118A2*

Ardmore is an attractive little resort at the foot of high cliffs, where simple hotels and a guest-house or two command awesome views over the bay. A blue-flag award for its clean beach and a 'tidy town' commendation indicate a sense of local pride. One of its best-known residents is the popular novelist Molly Keane. An ancient place, Ardmore saw the foundation of Ireland's earliest Christian settlement when St Declan arrived here from Wales, some 30 years before St Patrick. His bell and vestments were miraculously borne across the water by a glacial boulder, now tiptilted on a little spur of rock on the beach. It promises wondrous healing powers for all agile enough to creep beneath it.

Excellent views can be seen from the monastery. Most of the remains date from after Declan's time; a well-preserved Round Tower and cathedral are largely 12th century. The cathedral displays clear and vigorous carvings of biblical scenes, such as the Judgement of Solomon and the Weighing of Souls. Inside are several ogham stones (see page 16). St Declan's Oratory is an older structure which may contain the saint's remains, the surrounding earth much pillaged for its restorative properties. St Declan's Well and another ruined church where the saint spent his final years can be found along the cliff walk signed from the village.

►► **Cahir**　　　　*118B1*

The fortress in the centre of this small town on the Suir River is in fine condition after recent restoration work. Cahir Castle►► dates mainly from the 15th century with many later alterations, and was formerly a stronghold of the powerful local Anglo-Norman Butler family, Dukes and Earls of Ormonde. Queen Elizabeth I's favourite, the Earl of Essex, rammed a few cannon-balls into its masonry in 1599, but it survived Cromwellian times little scathed. The huge walls enclose three separate 'wards', outer, middle and inner, the inner one guarded by a gate with a portcullis. Rooms in the keep are whitewashed and contain armour displays and period furnishings from the 16th and 17th centuries. The hammer-beamed great hall dates only from the 19th century. An audio-visual presentation fills in some local background.

Cahir's fortunes waxed and waned through the centuries, but in peace time it developed an important milling industry introduced by local Quakers. The town is something of a time warp, and some of its shops and houses appear little changed for decades. One of them, Keating's Draper's Shop, traded in pre-decimal currency until it closed down a couple of years ago. Another agreeable feature of the town is its evident lack of religious or political bigotry. Protestants and Catholics used to worship simultaneously in its ruined church, separated only by a curtain wall. Somewhat unusually, in the main square is a war memorial dedicated to the many local men who joined Irish regiments and fell in the Great War. Throughout most of the Republic, the World Wars seem unmarked, and the people who gave their lives in these conflicts are forgotten.

The other curiosity in Cahir is the **Swiss Cottage**▶, lying just outside the town on the Clonmel road. This quaint thatched building with its eyebrow windows and corkscrew timbering looks like something out of Hansel and Gretel rather than the Swiss Alps. It was designed in about 1810 by the Royal Architect, John Nash, for a scion of the Butler family, in a then-fashionable genre known as a 'cottage *orné*', a sort of rustic summer-house or hunting lodge in which the wealthy gentry relaxed and amused themselves in what they imagined to be rural simplicity. The cottage was rescued from dereliction by various enthusiastic conservationists and extensively restored recently; the original hand-painted French wallpapers and fabrics have been faithfully copied, and it is now elegantly furnished with many fascinating period details. It stands in pretty woodland gardens by the riverside.

123

Cahir Castle was once thought to be impregnable, but Cromwell took the castle in 1650

At around 100 tonnes, the capstone of Browne's Hill Dolmen weighs heavy upon its supporting stones

Carlow
118C3

Though a county town, Carlow is disappointingly lacklustre apart from a few nice old shop-fronts (Cigar Divan on Dublin Street is a fine example of authentic Victoriana). It lies on the east bank of the Barrow in the once tempestuous borderland at the edge of the Pale, old warehouses lining its former quays. Its castle, standing in the grounds of a mineral-water bottling plant, is perilously ruinous after the misguided attempts of a Dr Middleton in 1814 to reduce the thickness of the walls in order to convert the castle into a lunatic asylum. Unfortunately he understood little of the explosives he was using for the purpose, and the walls were well and truly modified, becoming so unsafe that some parts later had to be demolished. Also worth a brief look in the town is the county museum with various reconstructed farm interiors. The 19th-century Gothic cathedral is easily spotted by its unusual lantern spire, looking like a crown of thorns. It contains an elaborate pulpit and a finely sculpted marble **monument to Bishop Doyle**▶, or JKL (James of Kildare and Leighlin). The story goes that the artist, John Hogan, forgot to include the bishop's ring, and was so mortified by this omission that he committed suicide.

Three kilometres east is the impressive **Browne's Hill Dolmen**▶, clearly visible across a field, though it stands some way from the road. The tilted granite capstone is enormous, weighing around 100 tonnes, and is thought to be the largest of its type in Europe. It poises on its supporting stones as delicately as a ballerina. A fenced path leads from the parking place round the edge of the field.

▶ Carrick-on-Suir
118B2

A border town straddling the counties of Tipperary and Waterford, Carrick is noteworthy for its beautiful Tudor mansion. This is all the more remarkable because such buildings are a rarity in Ireland, in comparison with literally hundreds of fortresses and abbeys. Despite its name,

An intriguing shop-front in Carrick-on-Suir

Ormonde Castle, quite one of the finest examples of an Irish manor house

Ormonde Castle►, the house is completely unfortified, perhaps in misplaced expectations of less turbulent times. The building was commissioned by 'Black Tom', a swarthy-faced 10th Earl of Ormonde, in anticipation of a visit by his cousin Queen Elizabeth I (who never turned up). Tom was a great favourite of the Queen's, a potent reason for an attempted poisoning by his rival the Earl of Leicester, which he survived. Tom remained an ardent royalist and contributed greatly to the maintenance of English rule in Ireland during this troubled period, though his Anglo-Norman Fitzgerald relations were at logger-heads with the English by this stage.

Behind the grey-stone, gabled exterior pierced with many mullioned windows lies lovely stucco work, particularly fine in the 30m Long Gallery where royal coats of arms surmount the fireplace. The timber roof contains no bolts, only carpentry joints. Marks can be seen in the attic-room beams, where garrisoned soldiers would stick their knives before retiring for the night.

There is probably no truth in the legend that Anne Boleyn (Queen Elizabeth's mother) was born at Carrick. Today the town is much prouder of a more recent hero, Sean Kelly, the racing cyclist, who was ranked world champion for five consecutive years. He won many major events, including the 1988 *Tour de France*. A square in the town is named after him.

Just outside Carrick (on the N24) a well-signed thatched roadside showroom indicates the factory of **Tipperary Crystal►**. Visitors are welcome to look around the production plant and of course buy the hand-decorated glass-ware. The founders of this enterprise learned their trade at the much more prestigious Waterford factory, but were laid off during hard times and used their redundancy money to set up a rival company, using similar techniques. Prices are slightly lower, and Tipperary Crystal has been successfully competing with Waterford – a gratifying piece of vengeance for those redundant workers.

A literary ransom
The Butler family of Carrick Castle had many notable warriors, but it also included men of letters, notably one Émonn mac Risderd Butler. He employed scribes to write for him, and one of their manuscripts, dating from the middle of the 15th century, is now preserved in the British Library in London. So highly prized were his manuscripts that two were given to the Earl of Desmond in ransom for Émonn's life after he had been defeated in the Battle of Pottlerath in 1462.

SOUTHEASTERN COUNTIES

▶▶▶ **Cashel** 118C2

Gaelic Athletic Association
This largely rural movement was first founded in 1884 in Thurles, 18km north of Cashel, under the sponsorship of the Archbishop of Cashel, Thomas William Croke (1824–1902). The GAA's purpose was ostensibly to popularise traditional Irish pastimes such as hurling, handball and Gaelic football, and today it remains Ireland's most important sporting association. Though not party political, it has proved a fertile recruiting ground for Republican activists, and in the past has been suspected of IRA sympathies. Most of the hunger-strikers of 1981 were GAA members.

The Rock of Cashel rears up from the fertile plains of County Tipperary

Stories tell how the devil bit a huge chunk out of the Slieve Bloom Mountains, then spat it out in disgust here in the Golden Vale when he saw St Patrick preparing to build a great church. This erratic outcrop of limestone among the patchwork plains of rich cattle pasture looks almost freakish enough to justify such a tale. The Rock of Cashel is a mere 61m high, but approached from below, the craggy outline of towers and gables crowning the hilltop looks most ethereal, especially in certain conditions of light or weather. Close up, the romantic image fades a little under the pressure of tourism. It is one of Ireland's most popular sights and is always besieged by visitors in high season. The little town of Cashel has managed to avoid the worst excesses of commercialised religiosity, however, and remains a pleasant country town of tastefully restored shop-fronts and pubs and several additional minor sights to complement the Rock itself.

Cashel has long been a place of great significance, and rivalled Tara as a royal seat for the kings of Munster from the 4th century AD. St Patrick arrived in about AD432 and converted King Aengus, who became Ireland's first Christian ruler. Among many legends associated with this event, St Patrick is alleged to have used a shamrock leaf to illustrate the nature of the Holy Trinity. During Aengus's baptism, St Patrick accidentally drove his sharp crozier through the king's foot, but he did not complain and his wound was discovered only after the ceremony. A

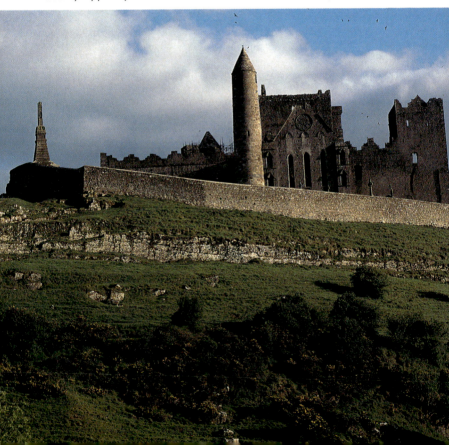

shocked St Patrick asked why he had said nothing, and the king replied that he had assumed the suffering was some sort of initiation rite, emulating the pain of Christ.

The buildings now visible on Cashel date mainly from the 12th and 13th centuries. Earliest of these structures is probably the **Round Tower▶**, remarkably preserved, with an entrance doorway 3.5m above ground level. **Cormac's Chapel▶▶,** ornately carved with beasts and human figures, begun in 1127, is in excellent condition and displays the Irish Romanesque style clearly. A sarcophagus in the Chapel is said to be the tomb of Cormac, the bishop-king of Munster, who presided during Cashel's great time of influence in the 12th century. The roofless 13th-century **cathedral▶▶,** the largest building on the Rock, with tall lancet and quatrefoil windows and a later central tower on Gothic arches, witnessed a particularly unpleasant act of Cromwellian barbarism when Lord Inchiquin besieged the town in 1647. The citizens fled to sanctuary in the cathedral, whereupon turf was piled up around the walls and set on fire, roasting hundreds of unfortunate townspeople to death. Various attempts were made to repair the building, but it gradually declined and in 1749 Cashel's main place of worship was moved down to the town. The first building visitors encounter, where the ticket office is situated, is the **Hall of the Vicars▶**, a 15th-century residence for privileged members of the choir. It now contains a museum with St Patrick's Cross and Coronation Stone. From the Rock the Cistercian ruins of Hore Abbey are visible.

In the town, a small **folk village▶** attracts many tourists. It features reconstructions of 18th-century buildings and displays artefacts of the period. The **GPA-Bolton Library▶▶** in the grounds of the Protestant Cathedral is an unusually gripping collection of old tomes; it contains over 12,000 volumes, including part of Chaucer's *Book of Fame*, printed by Caxton, and a collection of church silver. Not to be missed is a glance at **Cashel Palace▶**, a splendid brick edifice, former home of the Archbishop of Cashel, and now a luxury hotel (see Hotels and Restaurants, page 274). Non-residents can take advantage of the basement Buttery Restaurant, one of the cosiest places in town for a hearty meal or quick snack. A path leads from the hotel gardens up to the Rock.

An inflammatory priest
The building of the cathedral on the Rock of Cashel began in the 13th century, but funds must have run out, as the nave was curtailed very considerably and its western end was constructed as a palace for the archbishop. The cathedral was set on fire during the 15th century by Gerald Fitzgerald and, when asked by King Henry VII why he had done such a thing, he replied that he thought the archbishop was inside!

St Patrick's Cross

Miler Magrath
Buried in the cathedral at Cashel is Archbishop Magrath, a noted pluralist who enjoyed the best of both worlds. Born around 1523, he began his religious life a Franciscan friar, soon becoming Catholic Bishop of Down and Connor, an office he later combined with being Protestant Archbishop of Cashel. At his death (1622) he had amassed 70 livings, four bishoprics, two wives and numerous offspring.

Inside the museum at the Rock of Cashel

SOUTHEASTERN COUNTIES

Charles Bianconi
This adopted citizen of Clonmel was born at Tregolo in northern Italy on 24 September 1786. He was dispatched to Ireland by his father to avoid a scandal at the age of 16 after he had fallen in love with a neighbour's daughter who was destined for a marriage with the nobility. On 6 July 1815 he began a one-horse cart service between Clonmel and Cahir, which rapidly grew into a thriving mail-coach business and reputedly the world's first public transport system. His vehicles were known as 'bians' (after Bianconi) and ran thousands of miles each day all over Ireland, despite competition from the railways. His headquarters were in Hearn's Hotel in Parnell Street (recently restored) and he became Mayor of Clonmel twice.

The attractive harbour at Dunmore East continues…

▶▶ **Clonmel**   *118B2*

Clonmel is Tipperary's county town, a prosperous and pretty place with plenty of life and, if home-grown novelist Laurence Sterne's writings are anything to go by, some whimsically rum goings-on. Sterne lived during the 18th century and is best known for his novel, *Tristram Shandy*. Other novelists have connections with the town; Anthony Trollope worked for a while in the local post office, and George Borrow, the 19th-century traveller and writer, was at school here. There are no outstanding sights in the town, but it has lots of pleasant shops and eating places, and stands on the edge of some extremely picturesque touring country. The **circular drive**▶▶ to the south, along the Nire and Suir valleys, is very well worth taking on a fine day. So are trips into the unspoilt Comeragh Mountains.

The town was once an important stronghold of the powerful Butler family. Its Main Guard replaced the courthouse destroyed in the Cromwellian siege. The West Gate dates from 1831 and stands on the site of an earlier medieval gateway. Near St Mary's Protestant church are sections of the old 14th-century walls which defended the town against Cromwell for longer than any other Irish town. A few churches have minor points of interest; several have eye-catching 19th-century, 'streaky bacon' coloured brickwork.

Clonmel is famed for its field sports, notably fox-hunting and hare-coursing. It is a great centre of the greyhound world, and the slim animals can often be seen being exercised along the road, much as racehorses are in Kildare.

▶ **Dungarvan**   *118A2*

A bustling fishing port and resort on the Colligan estuary, Dungarvan is surrounded by low cliffs and gentle hills. The setting is rather more appealing than the town itself, but it lends itself to simple family holidays with an excellent beach at Clonea Strand. The centre of the town is Grattan Square, flanked by stately buildings. Down by the harbour a maze of tiny alleyways laces between warehouses towards the quayside, where several attractive old inns serve good seafood. Old Market House contains a museum of local history, where the sad tale of the *Moresby*, shipwrecked in Dungarvan Bay, is recounted. Close to the town the remains of Dungarvan's Castle, built by King John, can be seen, and on the east bank of the Colligan is an Augustinian abbey overlooking attractive **Helvick Head**▶▶. The drive round the bay to this headland leads through the tiny Gaelic-speaking village of **Ring**▶, with fine coastal views on the way.

▶▶ **Dunmore East**   *118A3*

This substantial village at the seaward end of Waterford Harbour is now a popular resort and sailing centre, but tourism is a secondary interest. Dunmore has its own *raison d'être* dating from 1813, when it was chosen as Waterford's mail packet station.

Bright fishing boats crowd the pretty harbour of what is obviously still a well-used port. Visitors are warned that they approach the waterside at their own risk; ropes and steel hawsers bestrew the workmanlike quays. The setting is lovely – red sandstone cliffs, topped with vivid emerald turf and golden gorse, catch the sun, while beneath lie sheltered coves of soft sand. A lighthouse guards the headland. The picturesqueness has encouraged an influx of well-heeled visitors and the village has been used more than once as a film-set. Waterford residents retire or escape here in spacious architect-designed bungalows, and more transient holidaymakers stay in thatched holiday homes. The core of the old community is still visible closer to the harbour, in a pleasing assembly of well-kept Georgian and Victorian cottages. The village boasts an exceptionally good range of reasonably priced accommodation and unpretentious eating places, and is an excellent place to stay to explore Waterford City or any of this attractive coast.

Master McGrath
At a fork in the road 5km northwest of Dungarvan stands a splendid commemorative monument – to a greyhound. It was erected by local sportsmen to Master McGrath, winner of the Waterloo Cup three times (1868, 1869 and 1871) and victor in all but one of the 37 courses he ran. Doubtless they were keen to honour both his triumphs and the bets he won for his backers.

...to be the mainstay of the local economy

129

From the Wexford County Museum in Enniscorthy

An impostor
The Round Tower which dominates the Irish National Heritage Park at Ferrycarrig gives the impression that the hill on which it stands was the site of an early Irish monastery, to which Round Towers normally belonged. However, a plaque in the wall gives the game away; the tower is a 19th-century copy commemorating the men of Wexford who died in the Crimean War (1853–6).

► **Enniscorthy** 119B4

The market town of Enniscorthy on the banks of the River Slaney is remembered for a terrible battle in the troubled year of 1798. On 21 June about 20,000 rebels, including many women and children, armed with agricultural implements and metal bayonets or swords, gathered on Vinegar Hill just outside the town. They had held it for nearly a month, but English troops under General Lake, finally losing patience, strafed the insurgents with continuous cannon-fire. Exactly how many were killed is not known (many slipped quietly down the far side of the hill), but the massacre remains vivid in the minds of Irish nationalists. The Battle of Vinegar Hill effectively marked the end of the 1798 uprising, but Enniscorthy played an active anti-British rôle in the Easter Rising of 1916. A fascinating collection of items connected with the battle can be seen in the **Wexford County Museum►**, housed in the sturdy square-towered castle. This impressive Anglo-

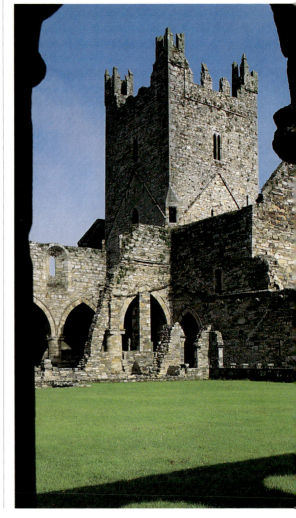

In its heyday, Jerpoint Abbey was surrounded by a small town, but few, if any, traces of this now survive

Norman building was briefly leased to the Elizabethan poet and politician, Edmund Spenser, during his inglorious period of office in Ireland. From the castle you can see the slopes of Vinegar Hill, golden with gorse most of the year, and crowned with the stump of an old windmill which served as the rebels' HQ. The town is the centre of the Southeast's soft-fruit industry, and every July a Strawberry Fair is held. Enniscorthy's other noteworthy building is its Gothic cathedral of St Aidan's, designed by Pugin, architect of the Houses of Parliament in London.

A few kilometres up the road lies **Ferns►**, now just a village but formerly the capital of Leinster. Its eye-catching ruins are the remains of a fine 13th-century castle and an Augustinian abbey.

►► Ferrycarrig   119B4

Just where the River Slaney broadens into tidal mudflats west of Wexford, a popular new attraction draws the crowds. The **Irish National Heritage Park►►** recreates many aspects of daily life in Ireland through about 9,000 years of history up to the Anglo-Norman period. Full-scale models of lake settlements, ring-forts, burial places and a Norman motte-and-bailey castle lie hidden among hazel groves and reed-beds in a large park. This is 'theme-park Ireland', but of its kind it is well done, informative and naturalistic, helping to put into context many of the scattered antiquities you will find as you travel around Ireland. An audio-visual presentation is available at the visitor centre, along with a wide selection of guidebooks, good snacks and teas. It rewards a visit, particularly if you have children to amuse.

► Holy Cross Abbey   118C2

Holy Cross Abbey, about 7km south of Thurles, is set in peaceful water meadows by the River Suir. It was founded in 1169 and restored in the 15th century. After that it fell into decay until 1971, when much rebuilding and interior whitewashing made it usable again as a parish church. The abbey's great treasure which attracts thousands of pilgrims to its wall shrine is an alleged splinter of the True Cross, thought to have been given to Murtagh O'Brien, King of Munster, by a 12th-century pope – yet another fragment of that ubiquitous piece of carpentry! The Ulster clan chiefs O'Donnell and O'Neill stopped off to pray here on their way to Kinsale, but the True Cross was apparently not on their side (see page 162). The interior contains a rare wall-painting of a Norman hunting scene and some fine stonework.

►► Jerpoint Abbey   118B3

These evocative Cistercian ruins seem to have a much more authentically medieval ring about them than somewhat commercialised Holy Cross, the tweedy stone tower and battlements erupting suddenly on a quiet bend south of Thomastown. Quite a lot can be seen by peering through the gaps in the walls, but if the visitor centre is open it is worth the modest entrance charge to wander round the cloisters and chancel for a close-up of the vivacious carvings of medieval figures and strange beasts on capitals and tombs. The **glassworks►** at Jerpoint produce a plainer style than most Irish crystal factories.

Near Enniscorthy
'Before dinner had a most delicious walk by myself along the banks of the River Slaney, which, for two or three miles out of the town, are full of beauty, and this sunny evening was quite worthy of them. It was likewise delightful to me to be alone in such a scene, for it is only alone that I can enjoy Nature thoroughly; men and women disturb such scenes dreadfully.'
Thomas Moore: *Diary*, 25 August 1835.

Two characterful figures adorn one of the tombs at Jerpoint Abbey

THE VEE GAP

Drive **The Vee Gap**

A roller-coaster drive between southern Tipperary's two ranges of hills, with panoramic views of fertile plains.

From the mundane agricultural town of **Tipperary**, an important dairy-farming centre, a scenic route is marked via the **Glen of Aherlow**▶▶. A road through dappled woodland meanders up to a sharp hairpin bend giving a breathtaking vista down the Aherlow valley. This beautiful glen is about 18km long, following the course of the Aherlow River. Shortly afterwards it joins the Glen of Aherlow road with grand glimpses of the Slievenamuck Hills to the north, and the shallow-

pitched ridge of the Galtee Mountains on the southerly side. The highest summit is Galtymore Mountain, at 920m. The Cahir Way and numerous forest trails lead through the hills, past ancient cairns and glacial tarns. The region is noted for its food products, so look out for traditional farmhouse cheeses, Galtee bacon and sausages, hams and even venison. **Mitchelstown** is a good place to buy.

From **Bansha** a good main road (N24) leads south-east to the town of **Cahir** (described on pages 122–3). At Cahir the minor R668 runs down towards the old market town of **Clogheen**▶, where you can join the spectacular **Vee Gap Drive►►** through the Knockmealdown Mountains. The Vee road winds steeply up through larch and rhododendron, and at its most spectacular loop several safe parking bays offer irresistibly photogenic views. Far below, the Suir valley and the Golden Vale of emerald fields lie as flat and placid as an embroidered quilt beneath vast skies. Black-and-white cattle graze amid a sprinkling of farmsteads. Just south of these viewpoints the road climbs over heather-, bracken- and gorse-covered slopes to the V-shaped pass which forms the boundary between Tipperary and Waterford Counties. A tarn is visible below the road, and a couple of stone shepherds' shelters. Beyond the pass, the road descends past **Mount Melleray Monastery** (see page 136) to **Cappoquin**.

►   **Kilmore Quay**   *119A4*

Just offshore lie the Saltee Islands, Ireland's largest bird sanctuary. Boats run from the harbour from May until mid-July, the nesting season for thousands of sea-birds. The pretty village of thatched and whitewashed cottages vies with Kinsale by hosting a seafood festival in July – the Wooden House pub is one of the better bars offering traditional music. An old lightship moored in the harbour contains a small maritime museum. The westerly sandspit of Ballyteigue is another important nature reserve, with rare plants.

►►   **Lismore**   *118A1*

The **castle►►**, looming above the dense woodland of the Blackwater valley, is one of Ireland's most evocative fortresses. Built by Prince John in 1185, it was extensively remodelled in the 19th century, when Joseph Paxton (designer of the Crystal Palace in south London) was commissioned to recreate a Tudor-style residence for the 6th Duke of Devonshire from the medieval ruins. It was planned on an opulent scale; the gorgeous **gardens** are open to the public during the summer (though you can't see inside the castle). Sir Walter Ralegh lived here for a time, selling it to Richard Boyle, father of the famous chemist who was born in the castle. It also functioned as an archbishop's palace, eventually passing in 1753 to the Cavendish family, the Dukes of Devonshire, whose Irish seat it remains to this day. For many years Lismore Castle was the home of Fred Astaire's sister, Adele, who married a Cavendish.

The other main buildings of interest in Lismore are the two cathedrals. **St Carthage's►**, the Anglican one, is mostly 17th century, its notable features including the splendidly carved Mac Grath tomb dating from 1548, and two bright lancet windows by the pre-Raphaelite artist, Sir Edward Burne-Jones. The Catholic Cathedral, built in 1881, contains many ornate decorations in Italian Romanesque style.

An award-winning **heritage centre►►** has appeared in Lismore's stone court-house. An excellent audio-visual production on the history of the town and the local area dwells particularly on its importance as a monastic settlement and university in the 7th century. Today Lismore is proud of another local celebrity, the travel writer Dervla Murphy, who acquired her wanderlust by cycling around this beautiful wooded valley where she was born.

Surprising Lismore
Lismore Castle is a place of surprises. James II, on looking out of the window over the River Blackwater in 1689, was so amazed at the drop that he started with a fright; the spot is pointed out to this day. In 1814, when workmen were repairing the castle, they found a crozier of *c.*1100 in a wall, along with a later medieval manuscript containing the lives of early Irish saints. Both were probably hidden when the castle was besieged and burned in 1645. They are now in the National Museum, Dublin.

135

A figurehead at the Maritime Museum, Kilmore Quay

Mitchelstown Caves lie in a limestone trough between the Knockmealdown and Galtee Mountains, and are the unexpected home of a very rare spider, Porrhoma Myops

▶▶ Mitchelstown Caves   *118B1*

This cave system is believed to be the largest system of river-formed limestone caverns in Ireland. Though privately owned, they remain pleasantly uncommercialised. You buy your ticket at a simple roadside farmhouse, and the 3km tour round a small section of the caves is conducted on an amateur family basis, with many references to fancifully named formations ('Is it an old man, a pig, an elephant?'). Minerals in the rocks have caused spectacular colourations. The caves served as a hiding place for the Earl of Desmond during the 16th century. Today, occasional special events take advantage of the acoustics.

▶ Mount Melleray Monastery   *118B2*

This austere, grey monastery was founded in 1832 by the Cistercian order who have industriously turned a barren hillside into fertile and productive land. The community (which consisted mostly of Irish monks) was expelled from its original home in France and granted 240ha here. Visitors are welcome to the main church and can stay in the guest lodge by prior arrangement. Just south of the monastery is a grotto shrine where miraculous visions of the Virgin have been seen, plaster statues weep and rock, and the faithful gather to light candles and pray.

▶ New Ross   *118B3*

There are few reasons to visit New Ross specifically, but it has such a strategic location that you will almost certainly find yourself driving through it at some point if you are in the Southeast. It commands the lowest bridging point on the River Barrow so you must either take the car ferry between Passage East and Ballyhack or pass through New Ross to travel between Counties Wexford and Waterford. Views of the town from either of the stepped hills rising sharply from the waterfront overlook its busy wharves. It is a very old settlement, founded in the 13th century by Strongbow's son-in-law, William le Marshall, on an ancient monastic site. A few bits of the ancient city gates remain. The waterfront can be pleasantly explored from a boat-deck; river cruises up the Barrow are organised in summer on the Galley Cruising Restaurant. Failing that, almost any direction from New Ross is a rewarding excursion, particularly north, towards Inistioge and St Mullins. Flower-dappled lanes potter through ancient villages studded with crumbling castles and abbeys. Sparkling rivers snake through the meadows, and the gentle contours of the Blackstairs Mountains, brown, green or heather-coloured, rise in the background.

The drive northwest through the beautiful Nore valley leads past Inistioge▶ to Thomastown▶▶ and Jerpoint Abbey (see page 131). Inistioge is a picturesque little town, with lime trees planted in its main square beside the bridge, a pretty river frontage and a jumble of 18th- and 19th-century houses on the lane twisting up from the town centre. There are ruins of a Norman castle and an Augustinian monastery. Thomastown, once a medieval walled town of importance, is now a lovely place with mellowed grey-stone buildings and a few ruins. The Ladywell Water Garden▶ at Thomastown is best in early July. Return to New Ross via Graiguenamanagh and St Mullins (see page 141). Graiguenamanagh, in a spectacular position beside the river, is a little market town, famous for Duiske Abbey▶, a much restored 13th-century Cistercian foundation, once the largest in Ireland. The effigy of a knight stands beside the abbey's entrance, and a magnificent Romanesque processional door may be found down the steps from the south transept.

South of New Ross lies the J F Kennedy Park▶▶, a vast arboretum occupying over 240ha of forest and landscaped gardens with about 5,000 types of carefully grouped and documented specimen trees and shrubs. Nature trails lead through the grounds and visitors can drive to a viewpoint on the summit of Slieve Coillte. Much botanical and arboricultural research is carried out here.

The J F Kennedy Arboretum, near New Ross

Irish-American presidents
Two recent and memorable US presidents have roots in southeast Ireland. President Kennedy's great-grandfather was born in a cottage in Dunganstown, just south of New Ross in County Waterford, and descendants of the family still live there. A memorial arboretum to John Kennedy has been planted close by. Ronald Reagan's folk probably hailed from the tiny, one-horse town of Ballyporeen, near Mitchelstown in County Tipperary. President Reagan visited Ballyporeen in 1984 and brought great fame to it. A visitor centre documents this historic moment, though as time wears on it is of less pressing interest.

The Irish in exile

■ 'As long as Ireland produces men with sense enough to leave her, she does not exist in vain.' George Bernard Shaw's remark is unkind, but apt. Irish-born people or, more accurately, people of Irish descent, have had a most disproportionate influence in many fields, particularly in the arts, media, sport and politics. But they have often shown this after they have left the island .....■

Top: Ireland's best-known literary exile, James Joyce

The Flight of the Wild Geese
After the final victory of William III's forces at the Battle of Limerick in 1691, many Jacobite officers accepted the terms of surrender at the Treaty of Limerick and sailed away down the Shannon to join the armies of Catholic Europe (perhaps with the hope one day of returning to defeat the old enemy). Among these aristocratic mercenaries was the hero of the Battle of Limerick, Patrick Sarsfield, Earl of Lucan. Like the earlier Flight of the Earls in 1607, this exile of leaders dealt a great blow to Gaelic power in Ireland. Their estates and castles were quickly snatched by Protestant settlers.

A constraining influence Somehow, Ireland seems to breed a listlessness and apathy at home which often crystallises into formidable energy, talent and purposefulness abroad. Of course, people with the most get-up-and-go are the ones likely to leave any country to better their lot, and the Irish who stay at home are by no means devoid of talent. Nevertheless, many periods in Ireland's history have militated against pioneering spirits; the long doldrum since the Irish Free State was formed in 1922 is one of the most noticeable of these in recent times. After English shackles were shaken off, Ireland had everything to play for – high ideals, a young and vigorous population and a new nation to form. Under de Valera's rule and the constricting influence of a peculiarly oppressive form of Catholicism, Ireland remained fossilised in a twilight zone of romantic mythology, social divisiveness and economic gloom. Many people have left Ireland since, ironically for the land whose rule they have so roundly rejected.

Artists and Ireland Artists and writers have deserted Ireland for centuries in search of havens where their work would receive a better reception than in the reactionary climate of their birthplace. After World War II, the Irish government tried to stem the tide by offering writers tax-free status in the Republic. The hugely successful novelist Frederick Forsyth was one of the most notable acceptors of this bribe, though other writers found it odd that a government should encourage literary enterprise with fiscal measures and then censor it on religious or moral grounds. A vast number of Irish writers have made their homes abroad. One, Cecil Day-Lewis, even became an English poet laureate. The novelist Edna O'Brien, herself an exile in London from Tuamgraney, County Clare, described the claustrophobia of Irish provincial life. 'Hour after hour I can think of Ireland, I can imagine without going too far wrong what is happening in any one of the little towns by day or by night.' For a visit, for a holiday, the pace of Ireland is refreshing, endearing, delightful. For a lifetime, many have found it stultifying.

Enforced emigration Reasons for the steady haemorrhage of Irishmen abroad range from general 'grass is greener' aspirations to the most dire and desperate emergencies. Most drastically, the Famine years of the late 1840s resulted in massive emigration, mostly from the West. Whole communities were decimated and many

The Irish in exile

have never recovered. In earlier times, religious persecution was often the spur, famously in the exile of leading Catholic families after the confiscation of their lands (The Flight of the Earls in 1607, see page 34–5), or after defeat in battle ('The Wild Geese', after the Battle of Limerick in 1691, see panel). The Ulster Presbyterians emigrated in great numbers in the late 18th and early 19th centuries to seek their fortunes in the New World. The best place to learn about this phase of Irish history is at the Ulster-American Folk Park in County Tyrone (see page 234).

The Kennedy homestead in the JF Kennedy Park near New Ross shows what early American homesteads looked like

Influential exiles To see evidence of Ireland's influence abroad, you need look no further than the list of US Presidents. Over a quarter of them are of Irish descent – mostly of Ulster Protestant stock. More recently, John F Kennedy and Ronald Reagan have partly redressed the balance with their origins in Counties Waterford and Tipperary. Canada, too, has had Brian Mulroney as Prime Minister. Today over 40 million citizens of the USA can claim Irish ancestry.

Irish representatives overseas can be found in just about any field you care to name: John Field the composer; Dame Ninette de Valois, founder of Sadler's Wells; James Hoban, architect of the White House; Field Marshall Montgomery, military hero of World War II; Sir Hans Sloane, founder of the British Museum; John McEnroe, the tennis star – and a host of others.

The excellent Ulster-American Folk Park near Omagh, County Tyrone, Northern Ireland

Old Leighlin
118C3

A few minor sights make this village worth a brief stop. One is the squat crenellated tower of the 13th-century Anglican church known grandiosely as St Lazerian's Cathedral, with, near by, a 7th-century monastery and Lazerian's well which attracts many pilgrims. The simple cathedral has a Gothic door and two fonts. Leighlinbridge to the east, as its name suggests, is a bridging point over the Barrow (the original bridge here dates from 1320). The scanty remains of the Black Castle can be seen on the east bank, one of the earliest Norman defences in Ireland.

►► Ring of Hook
118A3

The quiet peninsula on the east side of Waterford Harbour is a strange low-lying place full of deserted villages and migrant birds. The straight, empty roads lead through Ballyhack, where a small shuttle ferry cuts out the long trek inland via New Ross, then through **Duncannon**, a peaceful small seaside resort with a sandy beach and a reputation for fine sea fishing. Military remains indicate its former strategic importance; a fortress built by the Anglo-Normans stands by the waterfront, strengthened to guard against the Spanish Armada in the late 16th century, and during Napoleonic times the British built three Martello Towers to deter the French. The big house here, Loftus Hall, was built by the 4th Marquis of Ely for his bride-to-be, Victoria, the Princess Royal, who called off her engagement for mysterious reasons. It is now a hotel, capitalising on a ghostly legend that the Devil once escaped through the roof here after a game of cards, leaving cracks that are impossible to repair (a good excuse for leaving them alone, anyway!).

At the craggy, desolate tip of the peninsula stands an ancient lighthouse, the oldest in Ireland. Warning lights for shipping have been kept here for over 1,400 years, but the present, zebra-striped version dates from Norman times. Even earlier than this, a Welsh monk called Dubhand is thought to have kept a form of lighthouse by hoisting a cauldron of burning pitch to a high platform. On stormy days the sea sends dramatic columns of spray through blow holes in the rocks. During high season some enterprising families seek out

By Hook or by Crook
The origin of this phrase is much disputed, but Cromwell is alleged to have used it when he was planning his assault on Waterford, declaring he would take the city 'by Hook ...' (on the eastern side) '... or by Crook' (just below Passage East on the west side of the harbour).

140

The lighthouse on Hook Head has ancient origins; it was built by one Raymond le Gros in 1172. The sea at Hook Head is also noted for the beauty of the corals found growing on the limestone

these quiet beaches around Fethard and Booley Strand; at other times of year you can enjoy them almost unchallenged. The village of Slade is especially charming and is a well-known scuba-diving centre. The remains of some 18th-century salt-houses can be seen on the pier (where salt was extracted from sea-water by evaporation.

Rosslare   119B4

Well-known as a ferry terminal for traffic from Normandy and Wales, Rosslare Harbour is actually 8km south of the town, which is a popular seaside resort capitalising on its long, sandy beach and relatively sunny climate. However, there is little of interest in the place, except perhaps for golfers (it has an excellent links course).

Just south of Rosslare is Our Lady's Island, connected to the mainland by a causeway, where the ruins of an Augustinian priory and a Round Tower can be seen (the tower leans more precariously than that at Pisa). There is an annual pilgrimage to the Marian shrine from 15 August to 8 September. Some pilgrims crawl round its 5ha on their knees; others walk with one foot in the water.

▶   St Mullin's   118B3

A monastery was founded here in the 7th century by St Moling, a monk of high birth and apparently artistic talents. The watercourse that he dug with his own hands to power a mill is still there, but the monastery buildings have since disappeared and the remains visible now date from medieval times. In the churchyard are a penal altar, used surreptitiously when Catholic services were banned, and the graves of several Leinster kings, including the fearsome warrior Art Mac Murrough, scourge of the Anglo-Normans. St Mullin's is scarcely worth visiting for its remains alone, which are minimal and hard to track down, but the village itself is at a most beautiful spot by a stream with the Blackstairs Mountains rising behind. Many places around here, or in Graiguenamanagh▶▶ upstream where the more impressive monastery of Duiske Abbey▶ stands, are ideal for walks and picnics.

A cannon still guards the busy port of Rosslare

Captain Myles Keogh
Captain Keogh, from Leighlinbridge, was an adventurous soul. He fought for the Pope in the 1860s when Garibaldi was uniting Italy, then joined the American Civil War on the Union side. His third military adventure was with Colonel Custer's 7th Cavalry, where he fought gallantly at the Battle of Little Big Horn against the Sioux Indians in 1876. He was apparently one of the last to die, and as a mark of respect was not scalped after the battle. His horse Comanche was the only survivor on the army's side.

Waterford City has been a bustling centre since the Vikings settled here in the middle of the 9th century

Waterford mutiny
The citizens of Waterford were a fairly pugnacious lot, it seems. Mayor Briver had to be rescued by his wife in 1641 when a riot took place. Mrs Briver wrote that when she heard swords being drawn against her husband, 'I ran oute into the streete without hatt or mantle and laid my handes about his necke and brought hem in whether he wud or no.' Later this same mayor lost three fingers from his hand – bitten off by an angry mutineer.

▶▶ **Waterford** *118B3*

Waterford is by far the largest town in the Southeast and one of the few prospering industrial centres in the Republic. It too, has suffered badly from world recession, however, and signs of depression are evident even in its famous glassworks. Other industries include light engineering, electronics, paper manufacture, and brewing. Some visitors find the overtly workmanlike quaysides offputting after rural towns in Ireland, but Waterford has a grand history and plenty to explore.

Waterford is essentially a Viking city, with many reminders of this period of its history among the buildings lying immediately behind the waterfront. **Reginald's Tower▶** was built in 1003 as part of the old city walls by a certain Reginald (an unlikely sounding name for a Danish city governor), and served subsequently as royal residence, fortress, mint, prison and air-raid shelter. It is now the Civic and Maritime Museum, containing many municipal documents and regalia.

The most interesting churches are St Patrick's Catholic church of 1750, well restored in terracotta and white after being used as a corn store during penal days, and the Protestant Christ Church Cathedral, built in 1770 and containing a weighty colonnade of Corinthian columns and fine stucco ceiling decorations. A grim memorial to James Rice, a mayor who died in 1490, depicts the process of posthumous decomposition in graphic detail. The Catholic Holy Trinity Cathedral also has a remarkably sumptuous interior.

Later civic buildings worth a glance are the 1849 courthouse, with a massive classical portico, the **city hall▶** of 1788 with magnificent Waterford crystal glittering in the public assembly rooms and the **Chamber of Commerce▶**, a town house of 1795 with a spectacularly beautiful stairwell. You can glance at all this free of charge.

One of Waterford's most interesting recent developments is the **heritage centre▶▶** housed in the disused church of St Peter's in Greyfriars Street, where the best finds from Waterford's Viking and medieval past (excavated during preparations for a new shopping centre) are excellently displayed.

FOCUS ON — *Waterford Crystal*

■ **A visit to the crystal factory on the N25 Cork road, about one kilometre from the centre, is the most popular tourist activity Waterford has to offer. Free factory tours take place every weekday during the mornings. At busy times of year you should reserve a place .....■**

The tours are indeed interesting, and take about 40 minutes (a good plan for a wet day: to reserve a place contact the tourist office on 051 75788). You are taken round each stage of manufacture. Basic ingredients of glass are silica and potash; lead crystal also requires a significant quantity of lead oxide in powder form (safety regulations must be strictly adhered to with this toxic substance). The lead gives the glass its particular qualities of brilliance and capacity to refract light, and also makes it very heavy. The ingredients are heated to about 1,200°C over many hours, then hand-blown and skilfully shaped before cooling. Finally the glass is cut with deep grid-like patterns, the air filling with minute particles and the screech of carborundum and diamond wheels. You will see Waterford Crystal in grand houses throughout Ireland; today, a modern version of one of those glittering droplet chandeliers costs several thousand pounds.

The plant now covers a site of about 16ha, and worldwide sales top IR£86 million. By far the largest market for Waterford Crystal is the US, and American tastes are therefore strongly reflected in the ornate designs. Waterford now has many home-grown rivals throughout Ireland, though Waterford still claims the edge for its high quality (no inferior produce is ever sold; it is simply smashed and melted down again), its purity of colour and its deep cut. Certainly, if you want to find out about crystal, this is the place to do it. Prices start at around IR£18 for a tiny liqueur glass.

The history of Waterford Crystal
The history of Waterford glass started in the late 18th century, when George and William Penrose set up a factory here in 1783. It flourished for 68 years, before the disastrous economic conditions of 1851 caused its closure. A century later, Waterford once again became home for a glassworks, modest at first, but expanding to prodigious dimensions within only 40 years.

143

A master cutter concentrates on his task

SOUTHEASTERN COUNTIES

Wexford's Main Street is typical of many of Ireland's shopping thorough-fares

Wexford Opera Festival
This event has been held during October at the Theatre Royal for over 40 years, now attracting opera buffs from far and wide, as well as many international stars. It tends to favour rare or neglected works, and so has a pleas-antly off-beat, avant-garde tinge. If you manage to get tickets, you may of course discover why some of these works are rare and neglected! For all that, it's the social event of the year in Wexford, festive but unsnobby, where local people dress up and drink champagne. Book well ahead for seats; they are gold dust (box office tel: 053 22240 or 22144). If you can't get a ticket, many other events will be going on too – concerts, revues, recitals, jazz in pubs, etc. Many travel companies offer package tours to the festival.

►►   **Wexford**   *119B4*

For all its bloody history, Wexford has a peaceful air. First glances may suggest it is all too dull, basking in its muddy estuary like some somnolent reptile. But it is by no means moribund. Present traces of a proud past are admittedly vestigial, but a bustling small-town charm and sense of life outweigh any initial disappointment. If you catch it during October when the acclaimed opera festival is in full swing, you will be left in no doubt that Wexford rates itself pretty highly, and why not, achieving full-page write-ups as it does in all the national papers?

The Viking name *Waesfjord* (harbour of the mudflats) is apposite. The River Slaney and several tributaries empty their silt-laden waters into the sea here, and Wexford's practicality as a deep-water port has long since been over-taken by its rival in the next county, Waterford. But the mud is not all bad. North and south of the town, large areas on either side of the estuary provide a habitat for many thousands of wading birds. The **Wexford Wildfowl Reserve**►► is a must for ornithologists. The 'Slobs', as the mudflats are known locally, are *polders*, or reclaimed land lying lower than sea level. Follow the signs for the reserve from Wexford's coastal exit roads and you will reach a research station with a visitor centre, a lookout tower, identification charts and hides. Entrance is free. The neighbouring dunes around Raven Point are also an important nature reserve with rare plants and insects, as well as birds.

The town itself straggles along the waterfront, several blocks deep. The helpful tourist office can be found slap in the centre of the seafront, where Crescent Quay takes a bite from the shore. The bronze statue outside commem-orates Commodore John Barry, the brilliant naval officer who avenged his Irish ancestors by emigrating to Philadelphia and trouncing the English during the American War of Independence. Wexford is best ex-plored on foot (historic walking tours are advertised) when narrow alleys and one-way streets prove no obstacle. The old centre of town is a cheerful mix of agreeable pubs, old-fashioned shops and plenty of decent down-to-earth eating places. The main historic monuments are the **Westgate▶**, dating from 1300, and the remains of **Selskar Abbey▶**, where the Anglo-Irish treaty was signed after the Norman invasion, and where Henry II spent many Lenten hours atoning for the murder of St Thomas à Becket. A couple of modern Gothic churches can be seen, interesting only because they are virtually identical. That's really about it, though keen historians will note the Bull Ring, where Cromwellian troops slaughtered about 300 hapless citizens as they prayed for mercy. Many others were put to the sword in one of the most appalling massacres of the Ironside invasion. When Ireland rebelled again in 1798, Wexford's inhabitants were among the most vigorous pike-wielders, as the statue in the Bull Ring indicates.

Two other sights are well worth a visit if you are in the vicinity of Wexford. The Irish National Heritage Park is described above (see Ferrycarrig, page 130). Towards Rosslare is another museum, in the massive Gothic-revival building called Johnstown Castle, constructed as a private residence around the core of a 15th-century tower-house. This contains the **Irish Agricultural Museum▶▶** (the rest of the building serves as an agricultural college). It is the largest collection of its kind in Ireland, full of attractive displays of intriguing implements like furze rooters, barley hummlers and turnip knives. The veterinary section displays fearsome horse gags and drenching horns. Little workshops have been recreated showing how the tools would have been arranged and used by wheelwrights, coopers, etc. There are also displays of ancient domestic appliances and butter-making equipment. The grounds around this imposing castellated and mullioned grey stone building are beautifully landscaped and open to the public.

White-fronted geese
The Wexford Slobs attract 40 per cent of the world's population of Greenland white-fronted geese for about eight months of the year. Farmers are not too thrilled by this, since, protected from all predators, the geese munch their way through the same amount of grass as a herd of several hundred cattle. Their diet is supplemented with specially provided helpings of sugar beet in frosty weather. The film-show at the research station shows how the birds are ringed to study their lifestyles and migration patterns. Many other species join them on the Slobs at various times of year.

145

The Irish National Heritage Park

Fungi the dolphin
This half-tame creature has captured the hearts of thousands in the past few years. His behaviour suggests he may have escaped or been released from a marine park at some stage. He cavorts in Dingle Bay to the delight of all onlookers and the great pleasure of the tourist authorities, and has apparently no fear of humans or their boats. He will frolic beside wet-suited bathers, jump over boats and really gives the impression that he enjoys company. Fungi seems to have become completely fixated by his human visitors and will chase off any rival dolphin who encroaches on his territory. Boat trips from Dingle Harbour virtually guarantee a sighting during the summer.

The predictable, but pleasant, face of tourism on the Muckross Estate near Killarney

annual gourmet festival raise both standards of cuisine and the region's popularity with continental visitors. The high quality of local ingredients helps; seafood, good beef and rich dairy products now available everywhere belie the terrible sufferings of the Southwest during the Famine years.

The massive emigration from these counties to the New World results in a backwash of third- or fourth-generation visitors migrating back to the land of their forebears searching for roots. Shannon Airport welcomes transatlantic visitors, who converge on Limerick and Killarney. Many foreigners from continental Europe approach via Cork and some have settled here permanently, adding new flavours to the area's restaurants and bringing fresh artistic talents with them.

A warm welcome English attempts to subjugate this old Irish province of Munster produced a mass of fortifications all along the coast, ever-watchful for popish plots from Spain and France using Catholic Ireland as an unlocked back door from which to invade the mainland. Today, however, the tricky Anglo-Irish interface leaves little mark here.

The Southwest has two of Ireland's largest cities, Cork and Limerick. These are certainly worth seeing, but the rural areas are far more appealing. The coastline is, in places, particularly beautiful, and generally more exciting than the lush inland scenery, cut by its great easterly flowing rivers. An exception is Killarney's National Park, a highspot in any itinerary. Less well known, but also worth exploring, is the forest park of Gougane Barra, on the remote inland borders of Cork and Kerry. It is a place, of wildlife, of tumbling streams and the hermitage of St Finbarr. Founded probably in the 6th or 7th century – although the ruins beside the modern church date from

Youghal beach, Cork

the 18th century – the hermitage of Cork City's patron saint is set on an islet in the beautiful Gougane Barra Lake, the source of the Lee, which eventually reaches the sea at Cork. The county of Limerick is the Cinderella of the three, with little to lift its flattish landscapes from mediocrity. Killarney and Blarney are perhaps the only blatant examples of mass tourism in the region. Elsewhere, the tourist scene is low-profile. Kinsale, Kenmare, Dingle, Youghal and Bantry all make charming and very much classier bases for exploring the coast.

A mild and verdant land Few would argue that the islet-strewn peninsulas that trail westwards to the Atlantic are the places to visit for the best scenery, where the blue water of never-distant sea sets off the brilliant rain-washed emerald of fields and mountains. Here the pace of life is slow and gentle, and the ambience unmistakably Irish, perhaps most noticeably in the Dingle peninsula, one of the largest Gaeltacht (Irish-speaking) regions. Traditional Irish music can be heard all over the region, particularly in Dingle and some of the villages of south Cork, such as Leap and Clonakilty.

The influence of the Gulf Stream keeps frost permanently at bay and, though Atlantic storms can be severe, sheltered regions lend themselves to superb subtropical gardens and a great range of flora and fauna. Flower-spotters will be in their element, but even the least botanically minded can scarcely fail to be impressed by the lush fuchsia hedges, dripping scarlet all summer, or the arbutus trees that grow wild in the valleys of Iveragh. Water-lilies and rare bog plants colonise the reedy pools of Cork's quieter peninsulas. The Southwest is a good place for birdwatchers, too – first landfall for myriad exhausted migrants in spring and autumn on Clear Island or the wild Skellig Islands, the moors, mountains and lakes of Kerry and the sheltered, muddy estuaries around Timoleague on the south Cork coast.

Rose of Tralee Festival
This is held in the last week of August and is a great tourist attraction for the region. Six days and nights of solid merriment take place, including pipe bands and parades. The main event is a beauty contest which anyone of Irish origins can enter. Visitors from around the world compete for the honour of being crowned Rose; details from the Festival Office in Lower Castle Street, Tralee (tel: 066 21322).

The Spaniard, a pub in Kinsale, Ireland's gourmet capital

The enormous, conical, whitewashed beacon near Baltimore acts as a marker for boats

An enterprising bar in Bantry has erected this elaborate and informative advert-isement for its wares

1796

NOTICE
THIS ANCHOR WAS TAKEN IN A TRAWL
BY THE MOTOR TRAWLER 'SAOIRSE',
SKIPPERED BY PAT DEASY ON THE 11th
SEPTEMBER, 1964. EXPERTS BELIEVE
THAT IT IS ONE OF THOSE ANCHORS LEFT
BEHIND WHEN THE FRENCH FLEET UNDER
WOLFE TONE, WHICH WAS COMING TO
ASSIST THE IRISH REBELS IN 1796, WERE
FORCED TO CUT THEIR ANCHORS IN A GALE
AND RETIRE. THE ANCHOR WEIGHS 17 CWT.
NOT QUITE SO HISTORICAL BUT EQUALLY
INTERESTING IF YOU ARE DYING OF THIRST IS
THE ANCHOR BAR WHICH ERECTED THIS SIGN

► **Baltimore** 146A3

Baltimore combines salty fishing-village charm with a sturdy castle and several good restaurants. Trips are also available to Sherkin Island where there is a 15th-century friary, and to the Fastnet Lighthouse on the outermost scrap of Irish territory. In June 1631 Baltimore witnessed a curious and tragic incident, when Algerian pirates stole into the harbour and attacked the village, killing a number of residents and abducting about 200 as slaves to North Africa. Some believe the raid may have been orchestrated by the fierce O'Driscoll clan to frighten off English set-tlers. If so, it worked; many of them moved upstream where they felt less threatened. The poet, Thomas Davis, wrote a rollicking poem about the raid in 1844:
'The yell of "Allah" breaks above the prayer and shriek and roar,
Oh Blessed God! The Algerine is Lord of Baltimore.'

► **Bantry** 146B3

Most people who tour south Cork pass through this fish-ing and market centre on the main coastal road. The town stands at the head of the long haven of Bantry Bay, shel-tered by two of the hilly peninsulas that trail southwest from Cork's mainland. A statue of St Brendan gazes seawards from its square by the harbour. Bantry was twice an unsuccessful target for French invaders hoping to establish a base in a friendly Catholic enclave from which to over-throw the English. In 1689 a French fleet called in, offering support for James II, only to be rebuffed by Williamites. In 1796 the revolutionary Wolfe Tone arrived with another French fleet (see panel), but was driven back by fierce storms. An alert local landowner, Richard White, sent urgent warnings to the English forces and was rewarded for his loyalty by a peerage. His descendants still live in the splendid mansion of **Bantry House►►**, one of the most beautifully located houses in Ireland. The terraced Italianate gardens overlook a gorgeous sweep of Bantry Bay. The house amply repays a visit, its sumptuous rooms full of fascinating contents. The hospitable present owners offer a classy brand of B&B (alas no longer inexpensive) in a separate wing of the house (see Hotels and restaurants, page 273), and another recent attraction is the **Bantry 1796 French Armada Exhibition Centre►►** in a renovated side courtyard. This lively museum recounts the history of Wolfe Tone's failed rebellion and displays articles recovered from the wreck of the frigate *La Surveillante*, which sank during the storms and was excavated in 1982.

Minor diversions in the town itself are a museum of local history, and the **Kilnaruane Pillar Stone►**, carved with mysterious early Christian symbols of four men rowing, and a cross.

►► Blarney 147B4

Everyone has heard of Blarney and, when coach parties clog the village, it seems as if everyone has come to see it, too. Tourists arrive for two reasons – to kiss that stone in Blarney Castle and to visit the large gift and craft centres that have sprung up near by. Quite why the Blarney Stone exercises such fascination is hard to fathom, but the superstition that kissing it endows you with Irish eloquence or 'blarney' is certainly appealing.

The stone is an oblong block of limestone located high among the battlements of a fine 15th-century tower-house, once a stronghold of the Mac Carthys, former kings of Munster and Lords of Blarney. A Cormac Mac Carthy supposedly strung Queen Elizabeth I along with honey-tongued promises and prevarications, until she exclaimed in exasperation, 'Blarney, Blarney! What he says he does not mean,' and thus the word entered the language. To reach the stone, visitors must clamber up the tower steps (over 120 of them), join the inevitable queue (in high season, at least), and then lie down and lean backwards over a sheer drop. It looks awkward but is actually quite safe, even without the two strong-armed retainers there to grab your ankles. The stone is swabbed down regularly enough to prevent transmission of any nasty ailments. Some tout will offer to take your photograph while you are kissing the stone, but be warned, it isn't a flattering angle!

The lush water gardens by the River Lee and the 19th-century Rock Close (a rock garden with fanciful wishing

151

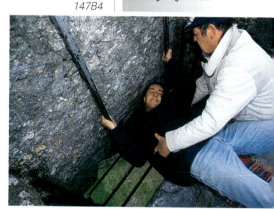

Whatever one gains from kissing the Blarney Stone, one loses one's dignity

There's more to Blarney than the stone

The sinking of the *Lusitania* Recent speculation about this has made disturbing reading. In World War I the ship, sailing from New York to Liverpool , was sunk, off Cobh, by the Germans, who claimed that she was carrying arms, as well as civilians. This was denied, but evidence now suggests that it was true. More disturbing is the theory that the Allies contrived the episode to persuade the US to enter the war. The German government had placed advertisements in New York papers warning passengers not to take the sailing, implying that the vessel was not a random wartime target. Both suspicion and casualties were increased by the unusual absence of patrolling British warships. She sank in 20 minutes, leaving passengers floundering in the water. Some survived by clutching floating debris, one sitting in a cane chair. The submarine that had sunk the ship did nothing to save passengers, though knowing many were American civilians, not a remotely legitimate target.

steps and druidical associations) make an attractive foil for the romantic ruin, and behind the castle is an elaborate Scottish baronial mansion called Blarney Castle House (visitable on a joint ticket), furnished in Victorian style.

In the village, craft and knitwear shops catch the purse strings, the most advertised being Blarney Woollen Mills, now a colossal hypermarket with a restaurant, hotel and coach-park attached. The smaller shops are rather more enjoyable than this bargain basement, but there's certainly a wide range of merchandise from all over Ireland.

► **Castletownshend** 146A3

The literary cousins, Edith Somerville and Violet Martin, lived in Drishane House and are both buried in the grey stone church of St Barrahane where Edith was organist. They are better known as Somerville and Ross, authors of the *Irish RM* stories. The village is most pretty, its main street sloping steeply up from the quayside. If you career down it too fast you are in danger of hitting a tree carefully preserved in the middle of the road. Near by is an excellent quaint old pub called Mary Ann's. The Townshend family still live in the local castle, where idiosyncratic B&B evokes the atmosphere of the *RM* books.

►► **Clear Island** 146A2

The frayed coastline at Ireland's bottom left-hand corner disintegrates into a scattering of islets around Baltimore. From here, or from Schull further along the coast, you can take a boat to Ireland's most southerly community, Clear Island, where the Irish-speaking population of less than 200 is greatly outnumbered by the birds. An observatory enables visitors to delight in the multitude of streaming migrants – all kinds of gulls, shearwaters, storm petrels and rare songbirds, even an occasional disoriented albatross. Other sights pale beside the bird-life: the well and church dedicated to St Ciarán, born here in the 6th century; a wind-driven electricity generator financed by the EC; and a small folk museum. It is possible to stay on the island, though amenities are spartan.

►► **Cobh** *147B5*

For many hundreds, probably thousands, of Famine emigrants, the scenic panorama of **Cork Harbour**►► and the colourful houses of Cobh must have been their last glimpse of the Emerald Isle. Many perished *en route* in the dreaded 'coffin ships'; others never had a chance to return from the New World where they made their homes. The name Cobh (pronounced 'cove') means 'haven' in Irish. Besides emigrant ships, Cobh berthed some of the great transatlantic liners, including the ill-fated *Titanic* and the *Lusitania*, torpedoed offshore on 7 May 1915 with the loss of 1,198 lives (see panel). Many victims are buried in the local cemetery, and the story of the sinking is told in a new heritage centre. Today Cobh is a fishing port, holiday resort and sailing centre, its well-restored buildings and slightly raffish air giving it great character. **St Colman's Cathedral**►► is the most striking landmark, set high on the hilltop, its spire honed to an impossibly slender point. It was designed by Pugin in 1868, and is an exuberant masterpiece of Victorian high Gothic, decorated with intricate marble and mosaics, and full of atmosphere. Harbour trips are available in summer.

   Situated in the estuary at the mouth of Cork Harbour and connected by bridges to the mainland, **Fota Island**► may be reached via the Cork–Cobh railway line. It includes a wildlife park and an important arboretum with many rare specimen trees. Fota House, a Regency-style hunting lodge, is being redeveloped as a leisure centre.

Built to last?
A 16th-century tower-house at Castlehaven near Castletownshend was built by the O'Driscolls, who gave it to the Spaniards before the Battle of Kinsale in 1601. When the Spanish were defeated, they yielded the castle to the English. Before *they* could occupy it, the O'Driscolls retook it and were about to blow it up when in turn they were surprised by the English, who prevented the destruction. It survived until 1926, when Edith Somerville, one of the literary combination of Somerville and Ross, was out for a walk; she heard a rumble, and found that the castle had collapsed into a heap of rubble behind her.

153

St Colman's Cathedral sits perkily on top of the Georgian seafront

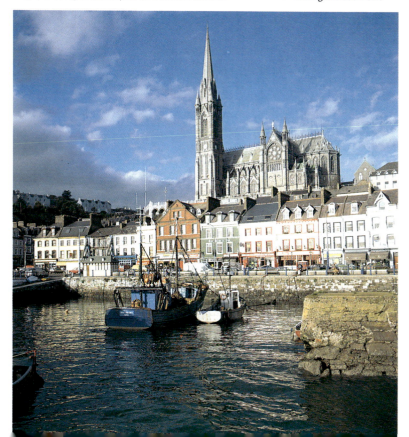

Subtropical gardens

■ The Venerable Bede was one of the first to remark on Ireland's favourable weather: 'Ireland is far more favoured than Britain by latitude, and by its mild and healthy climate ... there is no need to store hay in winter ... and no lack of vines.' The typical Irish 'soft day' of gentle drizzle and sunshine is ideal for plants – small wonder, then, that Ireland contains such a fine collection of gardens of all types in which many rare and tender species flourish. Many of these are open to the general public in summer, or can be visited by arrangement with the owners .....■

Strawberry tree
This plant is most closely identified with Killarney and the lush countryside of south Kerry, where it grows to prodigious heights. It is also known as the arbutus tree, *Arbutus unedo*, and has waxy white flowers and dark green glossy leaves. It flowers in the autumn and is then hung with slow-ripening strawberry-like fruits. A song of 1890 commemorates the tree:
    My love's an arbutus
    By the borders of Lene,
    So slender and shapely
    In her girdle of green.

Ilnacullin Gardens
Annan Bryce, a Belfast-born MP, purchased Ilnacullin from the British War Office in 1910. His dream to build a mansion and lay out gardens on this bare island off Glengarriff in County Cork was ambitious: the soil was shallow and infertile, the terrain exposed. To realise his project he enlisted the help of Harold Peto, an advocate of the Italian style of garden design and architecture in an age when less formal wild gardens were all the rage. Ilnacullin is a blend of both styles, containing a wide range of oriental and southern hemisphere plants, and many architectural features complementing the splendid natural setting.

A long tradition In early Christian times a major activity of any monastery was gardening – mostly for food or medicines, but also for decorating churches. With the arrival of the Normans horticulture became much more complex and widespread, with new and varied foodstuffs. Sir Walter Ralegh's foreign travels introduced important plants from the New World – tobacco, cherries and, of course, the potato. His friend, the Earl of Cork, laid out one of Ireland's first Renaissance pleasure gardens in the estates of Youghal. During the latter part of the 17th century gardening was on a grand scale, influenced by the gardens of Versailles, designed by Le Nôtre. Exotic plants began to arrive from abroad, and Dutch immigrants brought innovative botanical techniques. The 18th century was a great age for gardening, as for most aspects of civilised living, passing from baroque formality to the naturalistic landscapes of 'Capability' Brown. The Royal Horticultural Society of Ireland was founded in 1816.

During Victorian times botanical tastes diversified, many gardeners concentrating less on design and more on accumulating specimens; several important botanic gardens were planted at this time. Two great gardeners of the age were Daniel Robertson (see page 110) and William Robinson, who introduced a new style of 'natural' gardening based on a close observation of landscape. Many smaller, intimate gardens appeared too, some influenced by the English style of Gertrude Jekyll – two gorgeous creations are Beech Park and Butterstream, both fairly near Dublin. During the early 20th century a passion for oriental gardens developed; the Japanese Gardens at Tully, Kildare, are one such example (see page 101).

Period landscapes One of Ireland's most interesting gardens, historically, is Kilruddery, outside Bray (see page 93), which retains its 17th-century canals, parterres and statuary. Representing an earlier era, the lovely gardens around Lismore Castle were laid out in Jacobean times. Greatest of the Georgian gardens surround houses such as Florence Court, County Fermanagh (see page 230) and Castletown, County Kildare (see page 94). A fascinating late-18th-century example is Emo Court, County Laois, where lawns dotted with neat, clipped yews and statues provide a foil for James Gandon's neo-classical mansion.

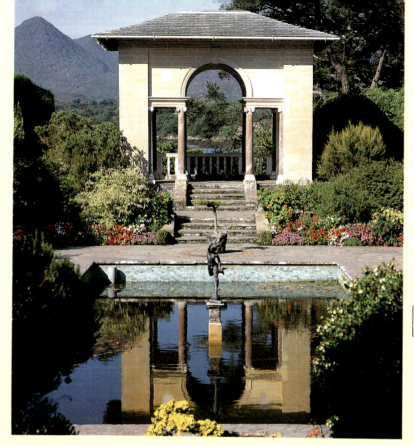

Spectacular gardens Despite its latitude, some of Ireland's most celebrated gardens are in the North, several in the care of the National Trust, among them Mount Stewart and Rowallane (see page 231). In the Southwest, Anne's Grove near Castletownroche represents some of the best work of William Robinson – shrubs, magnolias, rare mallows and water plants flourish in hedged compartments and walled gardens. The Italianate gardens of Bantry House, set by the sea, are a must for keen gardenspotters too, as are the castle gardens of Timoleague and the grounds of Muckross House in Killarney's National Park, where vast rhododendrons and exotic trees (including the strawberry tree, see panel) grow against a mountain backdrop. Derreen Gardens, on the road between Kenmare and Castletownbere, luxuriate in woodland with many subtropical species, tree-ferns mingling with bamboo and eucalyptus. Near by are the gardens of Dunloe Castle, with more rare trees (Chinese swamp cypresses and the pungent 'headache tree', *Umbellularia californica*). One of the most enjoyable of all the Southwest's gardens is Harold Peto's masterpiece, Ilnacullin, on an island reached by boat trips from Glengarriff, in County Cork (a landing charge). On a fine day in May or June this Italian garden of Grecian temples and an orderly jungle of flowering shrubs makes a marvellous excursion (see panel).

Bord Fáilte produces a useful leaflet containing information about Ireland's best gardens.

Ilnacullin gardens on Garinish Island

The glorious colours of Rowallane Gardens

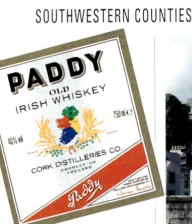

St Fin Barre's Cathedral looks down over the southern branch of Cork's River Lee

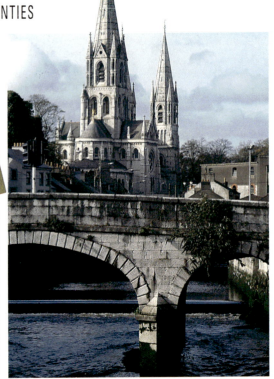

The *Cork Examiner*
Cork's daily newspaper seems to epitomise the independent spirit of the city. The *Cork Examiner* (just called 'the paper' locally) is a distinguished and dignified piece of journalism. The first edition appeared in August 1841, shortly before the Potato Famine. Many of the population were illiterate and certainly too poor to afford newspapers, so it was a brave venture. The first edition proclaimed it devoted 'to the welfare and interests of the whole community', and that it seems to be, read by all classes of society. It survived attacks by anti-Treaty demonstrators in 1922 when all the machinery was smashed, and has never lost a single day's printing through strikes, wars, or technical problems.

► ► **Cork**   *147B4*

Cork has no compelling sights, nor is it especially beautiful, and an initial reaction to the Republic's second city may be one of disappointment. None the less, visitors generally come away well pleased with the place, perhaps infected by the vehement enthusiasm of its inhabitants for their city. The way *not* to enjoy Cork is to drive through panicking about the check-in time at the airport or harbour. A map shows why the city, first bridging point on the Lee estuary, is a bottleneck. Traffic is invariably congested during working hours, and parking is by disk only: leave the car in one of the official parking-places and walk.

Cork takes pride in being the cultural and economic centre of the Southwest, constantly challenging Dublin's supremacy. It has always favoured ousting British rule, becoming known as 'rebel Cork' after supporting Perkin Warbeck (a Flemish impostor who in 1492 claimed to be Duke of York), and was a base for the Nationalist Fenian movement in the 19th century. Its prosperity was based on trade in hides, textiles, butter and wine. Industries such as ship-building and motor-manufacture are no more, replaced by skills such as the computer business. The centre's streets reveal Cork's mercantile past – tall 18th-century bow-fronted houses and fine warehouses. Many now quake beneath the demolition crane.

The centre is built on reclaimed marshes ('Cork' comes from the Irish meaning 'marshy place') and the older part of the city is on an island embraced by two arms of the River Lee. The land rises steeply towards the heights of Shandon; several imposing church spires pierce the skyline, Victorian Gothic being the prevailing style. **St Fin**

Barre's▶ was designed by William Burges in a flourish of white limestone steeples. Inside it is richly decorated – angels gazing down from a starry apse. On the Shandon side of town, **St Anne's Church▶** soars to a red and white pepper-pot tower surmounted by a golden weather-vane in the shape of a salmon. It houses the famous eight-bell carillon immortalised in the corny ballad known as 'The Bells of Shandon'. You can climb the tower and, for a fee, 'play' the bells. The nearby neo-classical **Butter Exchange▶** contains several smart craft studios, making jewellery, ceramics and traditional porcelain dolls.

On the island, Cork's commercial heart beats along the main thoroughfares of Grand Parade and St Patrick's Street. Old-fashioned department stores jostle trendy clothes boutiques, but the newer and most chic shops are around the pedestrianised area near St Paul's Street, where you can find interesting bookshops (one, Mainly Murder, is devoted exclusively to thrillers and detective fiction), and good crafts shops. Classy Donegal rainwear and equestrian clothing are also sold in these side-streets. To the west lie elegant Georgian malls and the university. The **City Museum▶▶** – Republican history features prominently – is in the grounds of Fitzgerald Park by the Mardyke Walk, an attractive riverside breathing space.

Cork has plenty of nightlife, from raucous pub discos to avant-garde theatre. Its opera house (not a pretty sight) is a 1960s addition to municipal culture; other arts venues are the **Triskel Arts Centre▶** and the **Crawford Art Gallery▶** (worth a visit just for its restaurant – see Hotels and Restaurants, page 281). At the end of October, the city is thronged for its acclaimed international jazz festival. Eating in Cork is a pleasure, with plenty of choice, from imaginative, cheap wholefoods to gourmet French cuisine. Accommodation in Cork ranges from civilised Georgian town-houses to well-run, good-value hostels.

▶▶▶ **Dingle peninsula**   *146C1*
See pages 158–9

Elizabeth Aldworth
This young lady from County Cork achieved fame as the only woman ever to be accepted into the bizarre and secretive world of Freemasonry. The local lodge met at her family home in Doneraile (her father was a Mason), but naturally she was always banished during the proceedings. One day in 1712 curiosity got the better of her and she hid in a clock-case to find out what went on, but she was discovered. Once the Masons had got over their anger, they decided the only way to keep her quiet was to enrol her, and so she became the order's one and only female member. Her grave is in St Fin Barre's Cathedral.

157

Better things to come
'Limerick was, Dublin is, and Cork shall be
The finest city of the three.'
Recorded in 1859 as 'the old prophecy'.

The Coal Quay open market in Cork City

THE DINGLE PENINSULA

(map of the Dingle Peninsula showing Tralee, Tralee Bay, Brandon Bay, Dingle, Dingle Bay, Slieve Mish Mountains, Castlemaine, Blasket Islands, Slea Head, Ventry, Dunbeg, Gallarus Oratory, and roads including N21, N70, R559, R560, R561)

Drive The grandeur of the Dingle peninsula

A tour round this remote, Irish-speaking westerly extremity offers many things: superb coastal scenery with peaceful beaches and scattered islands; grand mountains and lush, fuchsia-splashed countryside; a fascinating assortment of antiquities; and a lively scene of music and excellent seafood restaurants based on the charming fishing port of Dingle.

Starting points for this drive are Castlemaine (north of Killorglin), or Tralee. For scenic drama a clockwise

The shrine at Slea Head

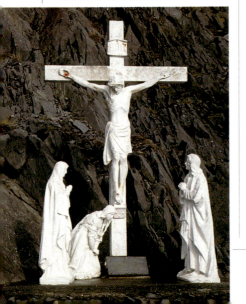

tour is recommended (although the scenery at first is quiet and undramatic) with good dune beaches at Inch and small hamlets like **Anascaul;** the strange, secretive tarn to the north, **Anascaul Lake►**, is worth a brief detour. **Dingle►►** is the peninsula's main tourist centre, constantly lively during the summer. It is by no means undiscovered, as anyone arriving during the Dingle Cultural Festival (mid-July) will note, but it never seems as overcrowded or touristy as Killarney, and it's a great deal classier. Out of season, though, many of its good restaurants, craft shops and hotels are closed, and no boat trips run. The town is extremely well-kept, with restored shop-fronts and colourful inn-signs. The harbour is particularly appealing – bright fishing vessels moored in a lovely natural haven. In former centuries smuggling was a major source of income. The Old Presbytery houses a local history exhibition.

Beyond Dingle is **Ventry**, where you may see upturned *currachs* (canvas-covered canoes) on the beach. Follow the road marked Slea Head Drive round Ireland's most westerly point. The whole area is riddled with forts, souterrains, standing stones and crosses; you need a good detailed map to explore them all. On the hillsides you will pass a number of strange little stone huts known as beehives or *clochans*. There are over 400 in the area altogether. Some farmers may charge you to visit these, and the more perfect specimens may have been reconstructed from the original stones as storage places (or for their more recent value as tourist attractions). **Dunbeg▶**, near Ventry, is one of the best sites (an Iron Age cliff-top fort with beehive huts near by).

If archaeology does not thrill you, the scenery certainly will, especially when the wild **Blasket Islands▶▶** appear as you round the **Slea Head** promontory. The Blaskets are uninhabited now, though one belongs to the former Irish Prime Minister Charles Haughey and is used as a holiday home. The last inhabitants moved to the mainland in 1953, the local women no longer willing to confine their marriage prospects within this tiny community. The Blaskets have inspired a thriving literary tradition: Maurice O'Sullivan's *Twenty Years a'Growing* and Tomás Ó Crohan's *The Islandman* are two of the best-known accounts of island life. Summer boat trips visit the islands from **Dunquin▶**, where the film *Ryan's Daughter* was made. **Ballyferriter▶** contains a heritage centre illustrating many aspects of life on Dingle, including its antiquities, Blasket literature and scenes of rural

activity such as turf-cutting.

Towards the ragged northwest of the peninsula are two interesting historic monuments. One is the **Gallarus Oratory▶▶**, a tiny but perfectly preserved church built of neatly packed unmortared stones. It dates from between AD800 and AD1200 and still keeps the rain out, though its roof-line is sagging slightly. A couple of kilometres up the road is **Kilmalkedar▶**, another early church from about the 12th century, roofless but bearing fine Romanesque carvings in purplish stone. By returning to Dingle again, you can start the final dramatic leg of this drive, over the **Connor Pass▶▶** (best tackled on a clear day), past the 953m summit of Mount Brandon. Once over the pass, **Brandon Bay▶** opens in a fantastic geological model of lakes, rivers and rock-strewn contours. The seafaring monk St Brendan set sail from these shores in the 5th century. In 1976 Tim Severin recreated his voyage in a similar craft of wood and leather to discover whether he could have reached America before Columbus (see the Craggaunowen Project, page 183). Once down near sea level, the northern coastal strip is a quiet and easy drive past long beaches and humdrum farmland.

159

Dunbeg promontory fort, Ventry, dates from between 400BC and 50BC

Ross Castle

Ross Castle is a fine ruin dating from the 15th century; a tower-house and later dwelling house still remain (restoration work, however, has kept it closed recently). Home of the local chieftains, the O'Donoghues, Ross Castle was the last place in Munster to fall to Cromwellian forces in 1652. The story goes that General Ludlow, hearing of a superstition that Ross Castle would never be taken by land, bought ships to sail up the lake, whereupon the defenders, hitherto defiant, immediately gave up their arms.

From Ross Castle, it is possible to take boat tours of the lake (these are non-stopping) or, alternatively, to hire a rowing boat for a landing on Innisfallen Island. Here, against a landscape of gentle valleys and dark woods, are the ruins of Innisfallen Abbey dating from AD600.

KILLARNEY ENVIRONS

Kate Kearney

A well-known pub on the way up to the Gap of Dunloe, Kate Kearney's Cottage is named after the colourful local beauty who dispensed illegal *poteen* and other favours to travellers passing through the gap during the mid-19th century. She was apparently in constant trouble with the law, but was finally vanquished by the potato blight which made *poteen* distilling impossible. One night, she simply vanished.

▶▶ **Killarney**   146C3

Every visitor to the Southwest has to see Killarney. The town itself, however, is disappointing. Once a seemly little place with a soul of its own, it is now given over wholly to tourism. It becomes hopelessly congested in summer, is very commercialised and, apart from the tall-spired Catholic **cathedral of St Mary's**▶, designed by Pugin in flamboyant high Gothic, has no outstanding features of interest. However, the immediate surroundings of the **Killarney National Park**▶▶▶ are not to be missed and, if you can evade the milling coach parties and wheedling 'jarvey-men' (pony-trap drivers), it takes on the grandeur of genuine wilderness. Macgillycuddy's Reeks, Ireland's highest mountains, lie just outside the National Park, but are clearly visible on fine days. Killarney is the usual starting and finishing point for the popular excursion drive known as the Ring of Kerry (see pages 170–1) though if you have your own transport you can just about avoid the town centre. The tourist office (slap in the middle!), however, is very helpful with maps and detailed local information. The Kerry Way is a 60km footpath leading through the mountains from the National Park towards Glenbeigh on the Iveragh peninsula.

Once out of the town, the choices for exploration are bewildering. To the south (the east shore of Lough Leane) lie the Muckross estate and various well-known beauty spots on the Kenmare road up to the pass called Moll's Gap. On the way, you may be diverted by the 14th-century **Ross Castle**▶ (see panel) by the lakeshore, and **Muckross Abbey**▶, a 15th-century ruin surprisingly well-preserved after a Cromwellian visit in 1652. The main pull, however, is **Muckross House**▶▶ and the surrounding gardens and parkland. No cars are allowed within the estate, but you can park by the house. To explore the extensive grounds, you can either accept a ride from one of the jarvey men (negotiate the fare carefully before you set off), or hire a bike. Muckross House is a furnished 19th-century neo-Tudor mansion designed by William Burn. Attached to it is a folk museum, where craftsmen demonstrate their trades. The lakeside gardens have wonderful rhododendrons and azaleas, best in early summer. The Meeting of the Waters is a popular spot between the Upper Lake and Lough Leane, where arbutus trees flourish in the mild climate. Lake boats 'shoot the rapids' here, and close by is the Torc Waterfall▶, plunging 20m down a mountainside. All these make excellent picnic sites if you can avoid the crowds. There is also a good tea-shop at Muckross House.

Beyond Muckross House the road winds on through woods, heather moors and mountains, becoming ever more beautiful but needing care at hairpin bends and tunnels. Ladies' View▶▶ is a place to pause for an unforgettable vista across the lakes of the National Park towards the Gap of Dunloe. (The 'ladies' were Queen Victoria and her ladies-in-waiting, who presumably caught this view on a fine day and were duly impressed.)

The Gap of Dunloe▶▶ is Killarney's other great tourist attraction, a rugged glacial pass between the mountains, providing magnificent views of tarns and cliffs. It lies on the west side of the lake and is reached by heading north from the centre of Killarney. Once again, the jarvey-men will be only too happy to stir their bored nags into action from the centre of town, but you will save time and money by driving at least as far as Kate Kearney's Cottage (see panel). From here vehicular traffic is banned, so you must walk or hire a pony or jaunting car. Most of the tourists head no further than the Gap itself, but if you want more seclusion you can continue on foot through the lonely Black Valley down past Lord Brandon's Cottage (a tea-shop) to the lakeshore and pick up a boat past the caves of Middle Lake and over to Ross Castle.

Killarney wildlife
Ireland's last wolf was killed near Lough Leane in 1700 and the wild mountain landscape of the National Park, backed by Macgillycuddy's Reeks, has always been home to many species of wildlife, some quite rare. Ireland's only herd of red deer may be found here, together with wild goats, Japanese sika deer, otters, badgers, foxes, hares and hawks. The remote Black Valley attracts many birds. Whooper swans, with their shiny black legs, yellow-and-black bills, and whooping, bugle-like call, visit every winter; hooded crows and the rare chough can also be seen.

161

Ladies' View, near Killarney, justly one of Ireland's most famous panoramas

SOUTHWESTERN COUNTIES

Kinsale Gourmet Festival
During the first week in October, Kinsale is even more packed than usual, though its visitors may look more sleek and well-heeled than at other times of year. Kinsale's Gourmet Festival extends the normal tourist season nicely and is well publicised throughout Ireland, attracting a good many discerning foreign palates, too. This is a time for eating, when the town's excellent pubs and restaurants vie with each other to produce gastronomic delights. The emphasis is on local seafood, and the places to look out for are clearly advertised, displaying the Kinsale Good Food Circle sign. See Hotels and Restaurants (pages 269–83) for some suggestions of where to go.

162

Kinsale fishermen tend their nets

▶▶▶   **Kinsale**   147A4

Kinsale has attractions out of proportion to its modest size and so is very popular, though it has managed to maintain a more exclusive image than Killarney. Its setting is seductive – tall slate-roofed houses sprinkled among the steeply wooded estuary slopes of the River Bandon. Its historic interest and fishing-village charm make it an appealing place both to stay (it has excellent accommodation) and to eat (see panel). From Kinsale you can easily explore both Cork City and the glorious coastal or inland scenery of south Cork. It is also a notable sailing and fishing centre.

During 1601–2 a Spanish force occupied Kinsale and were besieged by English troops. Irish allies of the Spaniards were routed, a significant step towards the establishment of the English order (and the decline of Gaelic power) in 17th-century Ireland. Soon afterwards the main players in this struggle, the O'Neill and O'Donnell clan chieftains, fled to Europe and abandoned their lands to English settlers. The town was spared a Cromwellian hammering, wisely backing the right side. Later that century James II landed at Kinsale with French forces in an attempt to regain his throne, and from here he finally left Ireland, defeated. Kinsale became an important English naval base, and Desmond Castle held many French prisoners in Napoleonic times. The town is evidently proud of its history, which is well recorded in the local **museum**▶, a Dutch-style 17th-century town hall in the centre of town. Some of its most interesting exhibits relate to the sinking of the *Lusitania* (see page 152). The court-room in which the inquest was held is a memorial to the 1,198 victims of the disaster.

Of Kinsale's two fortresses the most interesting is **Charles Fort**▶▶ on the east side of the estuary, built in the late 17th century to guard the harbour entrance. One of the best-preserved examples of a star fort in Europe, it remained garrisoned until 1921. You can clamber over the ramparts (keep an eye on children) and visit a military exhibition. The views of Kinsale from this headland are superb; the parking-area makes a good picnic spot.

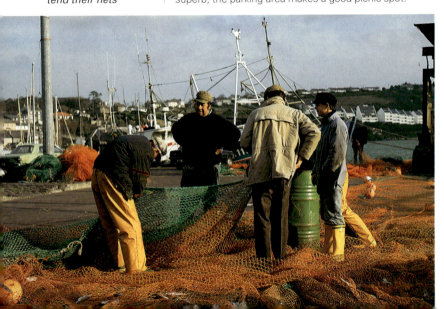

The South Cork coast

■ **From Kinsale to Mizen Head is by no means undiscovered, but seems far less obligatory and overdone than excursions such as the Ring of Kerry, when you take your place in a convoy of coaches. Meandering along tiny coastal roads through small villages, and undoubtedly getting lost amid Irish signposting, is one of the most delightful ways to enjoy the Emerald Isle .....■**

The Old Head of Kinsale is a lonely headland on which stands a ruined fortress; offshore is the wreck of the *Lusitania* (see page 152). From Timoleague to Clonakilty – the Seven Heads peninsula – is a massively convoluted shoreline. Hidden away down these lanes from all passing trade is a fine restaurant, the Dunworley Cottage (see Hotels and Restaurants, page 281). **Timoleague**▶, known for its gardens, is also remarkable for its skeletal Franciscan abbey. Here the coast is utterly peaceful, but beautiful. Wading birds paddle in the estuary, and the shores are full of unusual plants. **Clonakilty**▶ is an engaging place. There's little to see, but it has a lively feel, the main street lined with painted shop-fronts and old-fashioned bars. Traditional music, street theatre, festivals and crafts add to its attractions. Outside town is the birthplace of Michael Collins (see page 43), whose exploits are recounted in O'Donovan's Hotel. Seemingly endless, unspoiled sand graces the vast beach at **Inchydoney**▶.

The drive through the fuchsia-splashed villages of Ross Carbery, Glandore and Unionhall is glorious; creeks and lagoons mirror wooded slopes and fishing cottages with sandy coves tucked bib-like under their chins. **Leap** is famous for Irish music, based at Connolly's Bar. Beyond lie the pretty village of **Castletownshend**▶ (see page 152), tidal Lough Hyne and a scatter of islands in Roaring Water Bay. After **Skibbereen** are the colourful villages of **Ballydehob**, **Schull**▶, **Goleen** and the spectacular 220m cliffs of **Mizen Head**▶▶, guarded by an O'Mahoney stronghold. Barleycove is a fine beach. To the north, Sheep's Head peninsula is a lovely tour if time permits. The Beara peninsula, is unfairly neglected in favour of the Ring of Kerry, but is as rewarding and less crowded. Highlights include the rugged copper-mining country around **Allihies**, and the **Healy Pass**.

Drombeg Stone Circle
Between Glandore and Ross Carbery, and not too difficult to search out, is the Drombeg Stone Circle, a good example from the early Bronze Age. Charred bones were buried in the middle of this stone circle. Nearby is a *fulacht fiadh*, or cooking trough, heated with stones from a fire.

163

The lighthouse at the Old Head of Kinsale was unable to prevent the wreck of the Lusitania

■ **Many of Ireland's historic houses fell into decay or were destroyed during the 20th century, but a heartening number have survived, and those too large to make comfortable family homes have been sympathetically converted for other purposes. Some of them are now splendid hotels, giving many visitors a chance to experience a grandeur granted at one time to only a handful of privileged folk .....■**

A cricketing prince in Ireland
Set in glorious countryside beneath the Twelve Bens in Connemara, but far, far away from any cricket pitch is Ballynahinch Castle, now a comfortable hotel. At the beginning of this century, when still a private residence, it was owned by Prince Ranjitsinhji, a characterful Indian nobleman who played cricket for England on many occasions. See Hotels and Restaurants, page 275, for more details.

Top: Bantry House
Below: Ashford
Castle, County Mayo

164

A taste of the past These hotels are all highly individual, but fall into several types. There are the great baronial castles favoured by the ultra-wealthy (mostly more or less latter-day fakes, but none the less with some interesting history and contents, and palatial comfort). Then there is the legacy of the Georgian era spanning 170 of Ireland's most prosperous years. These may be mansions in rolling parkland, or pleasingly modest rectories or glebe houses. Then there are Victorian properties with famous family histories. Just a few examples can be mentioned ; for further suggestions see Interesting Places to Stay (pages 242–3) and Hotels and Restaurants (pages 269–83).

Grand castles Shannon Airport attracts many well-heeled transatlantic visitors who desire nothing more than to stay in a real Irish castle. This need is satisfied by several large, expensive, luxury hotels within easy reach. Nearest, at 13km from the airport, is **Dromoland Castle**, a vast mock-Gothic pile on a 150ha estate. The estate dates back to the 16th century, when it was the seat of the O Brien family, descendants of the great High King, Brian Ború, but the original house was replaced in the 1820s and the interior has recently been given a New York-style facelift by decorator Carlton Varney. **Ashford Castle** is another Hollywood dream also under American ownership, this time on Lough Corrib, predictably furnished in sheer luxury, and with superb grounds. Once the home of the Guinness family, it incorporates a 13th-

Historic hotels

century castle and a later French-style château in its opulent 19th-century shell. Also within reach of Shannon is **Adare Manor**, past seat of the Earls of Dunraven. Again it is Victorian and grandiose with vast mullions and fireplaces and colossal state rooms. On a somewhat smaller scale is **Markree Castle** in Sligo, home of the Cooper family since 1640, and last altered substantially in 1802. Its hotelier owner is a member of the original family, and an accomplished restaurateur. The castle has welcomed literary lights such as Lady Gregory and W B Yeats. **Waterford Castle** has a special brand of seclusion. It is set on an island in Waterford Harbour, and must be reached by its private car ferry. The core is a genuine 17th-century castle, with oak panelling, antique furniture and tapestries.

Elegant country houses One of the earliest period houses in Ireland now open as a hotel is **Assolas Country House** in Kanturk, County Cork. This peaceful place was built about 1590, but is now largely 17th century in style and has gorgeous gardens and fishing rights. If Georgian elegance is to your taste, one fine example is **Enniscoe House**, near Crossmolina (Mayo), a mid-18th-century mansion with fascinating period features. The perfectly proportioned façade conceals an earlier structure with a different layout of floor levels and room sizes. Its owner, Susan Kellett, is a descendant of the original family. **Carnelly House (**Clare) is also Georgian but was built in Queen Anne style by Francis Bindon. The tall windows, Francini ceilings and Corinthian pillars give a gracious air to this creeper-covered brick house. **Cashel Palace** is an exceptional building of the same period (1730) and for 200 years was a bishop's palace. It stands beneath the Rock of Cashel, and has an ancient mulberry tree on the lawn. **Coopershill** in County Sligo dates from 1774, but echoes earlier times in its utterly relaxing rooms. Regency-period **Marlfield House** (1820) is in Gorey, Wexford. This is the former dower house of the Courtown Estate, later the seat of the Earl of Courtown and a great focus of social life. It retains the tradition of lavish hospitality amid elegant and sumptuous furnishings.

Adare Manor, County Limerick

Tinakilly House, Wicklow
This is one of the most interesting Victorian houses in Ireland. It was built in the 1870s for Captain Robert Halpin, Commander of the *Great Eastern* steamship which laid the first telegraph cable linking Europe and America. Halpin was granted a substantial pension by a grateful government, and retired here to this grand mansion in 3ha of sheltered gardens by the sea. Unfortunately he barely lived long enough to enjoy it. After a dangerous life of shipwrecks and dubious escapades in the American Civil War he succumbed to blood-poisoning at 58, after cutting his toenails! A splendid staircase, mahogany inlaid doors, Italian fireplaces, oil paintings and seafaring memorabilia preserve something of the atmosphere of this flamboyant house, and its larger-than-life owner.

SOUTHWESTERN COUNTIES

Lough Gur

Limerick's countryside is not especially noteworthy, but there is one little jewel tucked away in the southeast. Lough Gur is a beautiful crescent-shaped lake around which evidence of many early civilisations has been found. Antiquities include a wedge-tomb and a large stone circle at Grange. Cartloads of remains were discovered after the partial draining of the lake in the 19th century. An interpretative centre has been set up overlooking the reedy lake, with a visitor centre and museum in two replica thatched *crannóg* huts of the neolithic era.

▶ **Limerick**   *147D4*

Limerick is a significant city in terms of industry and population , currently vying with Galway for third place in the Republic. It has a rich historical background and plenty of interesting sights, and, as a result of its strategic location at the lowest bridging point on the Shannon, most visitors to the Southwest find themselves enmeshed in its traffic systems at some point during their stay. But few people choose to stay long here. Somehow, modern Limerick doesn't quite work and, with rather dull scenery on its doorstep, its attractions as a base are limited. Much of the city seems run down and unemployment is rife. It has a higher crime rate than most Irish provincial cities, and there are places not to leave your car for long, or to wander at night. Appealing accommodation is scarce, good restaurants few and far between. Its sad history seems to have left a legacy of bitterness and apathy that dies hard, despite energetic attempts to revitalise the centre with new development of its wharves and warehouses, careful conservation of its Norman and Georgian heritage and an upbeat marketing profile.

For all that, it is certainly worth half a day of anyone's time, more if you are interested in Irish history. Limerick was originally a Viking settlement, due to its strategic location at the mouth of the Shannon. Brian Ború, High King of Ireland, eventually conquered the Danes, many of whom settled down quite happily in Ireland and intermarried with native Gaels. The Norman era was important for Limerick. The Normans expanded the town and built huge fortifications with curtain walls, King John's Castle being one of the most impressive. In Cromwellian times it suffered terribly under the onslaughts of General Ireton, Cromwell's son-in-law and commander of Ireland, who besieged the city walls for over six months. Later that century Limerick was one of the last Jacobite bastions after the Battle of the Boyne, the hero of the period being

King John's Castle is unusual in that it has no keep

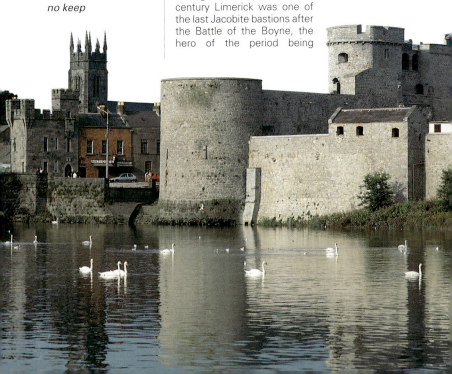

Patrick Sarsfield who made a daring raid on William's ammunition wagons and supply trains.

Eventually, however, Limerick capitulated, and the infamous Treaty of Limerick was signed in 1691. Few incidents in Ireland's history illustrate the role of 'perfidious Albion' more clearly than this. Within two months the English reneged on their promises to grant the Catholic population religious and property rights, and instituted draconian measures against them. The **Treaty Stone▶**, on which the agreement was signed, became a symbol of all that was hateful about English rule. It can still be seen at the west end of Thomond Bridge, now sand-blasted clean in an attempt to erase the memories. Today Limerick is a vehemently Catholic and Nationalist city, still locked in its unhappy past.

Within the town centre the most notable monument is **King John's Castle▶▶**, near Thomond Bridge. First built in 1200, it still looks the part of a medieval Norman fortress, though much restored after its 17th-century battering during the Siege of Limerick and subsequent alterations. The tower is the oldest section, and housed a British garrison until the birth of the Irish Free State in 1922. An excellent and imaginative newly-opened visitor centre now reconstructs the story of Limerick and its castle, and outside in the castle yard lie various curious engines used in medieval siege warfare – find out how the magnonel and trebuchet worked.

For more history, Limerick's city **museum▶** in two restored 18th-century houses documents the city's prosperity in Georgian times, when it produced fine silverware and lace. Even more worthwhile is the **Hunt Museum▶▶**, outside the centre in the university campus area at Plassey. The art historian and antiquarian, John Hunt, donated a magnificent collection of Celtic and medieval art, including the Antrim Cross and a Bronze Age shield. **St Mary's Cathedral▶**, in the centre, is the city's most appealing religious building, and its oldest, founded in 1168 but dating mainly from the 15th century. Unexpectedly in this strongly Catholic city, it is a Protestant church. Its most interesting features include black oak choir stalls with carved 15th-century misericords (see photograph and caption, above right).

An ornately carved misericord from St Mary's Cathedral. They were so-called (misericordia is Latin for pity) because they afforded clerics some form of rest when standing through lengthy services. They perched on these small seats, rather than standing unsupported

167

Inside St Mary's

The Midleton Distillery even ran to having its own fire-engine

► ▬▬ **Midleton Whiskey Distillery** *147B5*

In the pleasant little town of Midleton, an impressive 18th-century industrial complex of stone mills and warehouses has been restored to enlighten visitors about the fine art of whiskey distilling. The Jameson Heritage Centre is an entrepreneurial venture by Irish Distillers, emulating the successful Northern Irish attraction at Bushmills. For a fee (which includes a tasting) you can tour the modern distillery together with the Old Midleton Distillery, in use for 150 years from 1825 to 1975. The world's largest pot still, with a capacity of over 150,000 litres, stands by the reception building. Despite the heritage centre's name, it was the brand known as Paddy, rather than Jameson's, which was distilled in Midleton from the 19th century; John Jameson's whiskey was always produced in Dublin.

► ▬▬ **Rathkeale and environs** *147D4*

Castle Matrix►, just outside Rathkeale, is a 15th-century tower-house containing an important collection of documents and an intriguing museum. It can still be visited (on certain days in high season, tel: 069 64284), but since the owner's recent death the future of the contents is uncertain. The farmland of west Limerick and the Shannon estuary is tame compared with the grandeur of Cork or Kerry, but if you have been around the Dingle peninsula you could well find yourself driving through it. A few sights are worth a detour. **Ardfert►**, north of Tralee, has some roofless monastic remains, currently being restored. The beach near by is Banna Strand, where Roger Casement's abortive adventure took place (see page 43). Hugging the Shannon coast, **Glin Castle►**, seat of the Knights of Glin, is a fine 18th-century house with Victorian Gothic additions, and the interior contains delicate plasterwork and mahogany furniture. Official hours are very restricted (May only), but you can visit by appointment at other times (tel: 068 34173 or 36230), or even stay there if you are wealthy enough. Further along, and probably the most worthwhile stop of all, is **Foynes Flying Boat Museum►►** in the terminal of the original Shannon Airport. During the 1930s and 1940s, Foynes was the operational headquarters for seaplanes travelling to and from the US, and for any aviation freak, the museum, with its fascinating collection of film footage, instruments, photos, logs, etc., is a must. Foynes claims to be the original home of Irish coffee, and you can sample a reviving glass in the café. **Adare▶**, a notably pretty village of thatched cottages on the main Limerick road, contains the ruins of three ancient abbeys and of 12th-century Desmond Castle. Adare Manor, a lavish Gothic mansion, is now a country house hotel (see Hotels and Restaurants, page 275).

▶▶ Youghal   147B5

Youghal stands by the winding Blackwater estuary, right on the border between Counties Waterford and Cork. Pronounced 'yawl', this ancient walled seaport has a rich history and several interesting buildings. Its resilient, salty character is striking, and in 1956 it impressed the director, John Huston, sufficiently to use it as a film location for *Moby Dick*. Its most illustrious resident was Sir Walter Ralegh, once mayor of the town. The 15th-century college warden's house known as Myrtle Grove was Ralegh's house and, though there is little evidence that he spent much time here, the town has enthusiastically adopted him as its standard-bearer. A somewhat contrived Potato Festival is held here each late June and early July to mark Ralegh's supposed introduction of the Virginian tuber to Irish shores. A citizen with a more genuine claim to the town's attention was Richard Boyle, father of the famous scientist who formulated Boyle's Law, and builder of the almshouses in the town. **St Mary's Collegiate Church▶** is Youghal's most impressive building, containing many tombs and effigies, including one to the fantastically wealthy Earl of Cork and his 16 children (by three wives). Other buildings to look out for are: the Georgian **clock tower▶** bridging the main street; the dilapidated tower house, **Tynte's Castle▶**; and the **Red House▶**, a Dutch-style merchant's house. The **town walls▶▶** are some of the best examples in Ireland, with large sections still in fairly good condition. Another good reason to pause for a while in Youghal is to visit its excellent seafood restaurant, Ahernes (see Hotels and Restaurants, page 281).

Rose of Tralee

The pale moon was rising
 above the green mountain,
The sun was declining
 beneath the blue sea;
When I strayed with my love
 by the pure crystal fountain,
That stands in the beautiful
 Vale of Tralee.

She was lovely and fair as
 the rose of the summer;
Yet 'twas not her beauty
 alone that won me;
Oh no, 'twas the truth in her
 eyes ever dawning,
That made me love Mary,
 the Rose of Tralee.

William Mulchinock

169

The lighthouse at Youghal

WESTERN COUNTIES

Red Mary

Máire Rua (Red Mary) O'Brien, who lived in the 17th century, was apparently a perfectly harmless person, although one tale described her as a woman of great lust who had many suitors. Before giving her hand, she would demand that a suitor should prove his worth by riding her fierce stallion – which then promptly raced out over the Cliffs of Moher and deposited his rider in the Atlantic below. All perished except one, who succeeded in bringing the stallion back to Máire Rua whereupon she closed the gates of her castle. In trying to leap over the gateway the horse died, thus explaining the name of her castle – Leamaneagh (*Léim an Eich*, or horse's leap), though neither history nor legend record that she married the brave horseman.

A Celtic cross is silhouetted against the darkening sky on Inishmore, the largest of the Aran Islands

Ballyshannon
Inishmurray
Cliffony
Creevykeel
Bundoran
Belleek
Castle
Caldwell
Forest
Park
Grange
Garrison
Lough
Melvin
Sligo
Bay
Lissadell
House
527m
Benbulben
Rosses Point
Killala
Bay
Easky
Parke's
Castle
Manorhamilton
Ilala
Enniscrone
Dromore
West
Strandhill
Queen Maeve's
Grave
Sligo
Carrowmore
Creevelea
Dromahair
Glenfarne
Slieve Gamph
(Ox Mts)
Ballysadare
Colloooney
Lough
Gill
Dowra
LEITRIM
allina
Moy
Bunnyconnellan
SLIGO
Drumkeeran
ugh
nn
Ballymote
ugh
llin
Foxford
Tobercurry
Lough
Arrow
Lough
Allen
Drumshanbo
Curry
Carrowkeel
Keadue
Swinford
Charlestown
Boyle
Lough
Key
Leitrim
rlough
Kiltimagh
Connaught
Regional
Airport
Lough
Gara
Lough Key
Forest Park
Carrick-on-
Shannon
Drumsna
Balla
Knock
Ballaghaderreen
Frenchpark
Lough
Boderg
Ballyhaunis
Castlerea
Elphin
Claremorris
Tulsk
Strokestown
Ballintober
Ballindine
Ballymoe
Lanesborough
Kilmaine
Dunmore
Roscommon
rule
Glenamaddy
Fuerty
ROSCOMMON
Tuam
Ballygar
Lough
Ree
Headford
Mount
Bellew
Caltra
Thomas
Street
Kiltoom
GALWAY
Monivea
Ballybaun
Ahascragh
Athlone
alway
Athenry
Kilconnell
Ballinasloe
Oranmore
Clonmacnois
Craughwell
Suck
Clonony
Kilcogan
Clonfert
Cloghan
Dunguaire
Kinvarra
Thoor
Ballylee
Loughrea
Eyrecourt
Banagher
Aillwee
Caves
Coole
Park
368m
Killimor
Shannon
Kilmacduagh
Gort
Lough
Cutra
Slieve Aughty Mts
Woodford
Portumna
Birr
Carrigahorig
Corofin
Lough
Graney
Borrisokane
Cloghjordan
yssert O'Dea
Castle
Crusheen
Mountshannon
CLARE
Tulla
Taurngraney
Lough Derg
Portroe
Nenagh
nnis
Knappogue
Castle
532m
Craggaunowen
Quin
462m
Toomyvara
larecastle
Killaloe
Templemore
Newmarket-on-
Fergus
Sixmilebridge
694m
Shannon
Airport
Bunratty Castle
& Folk Park
Newport
Borrisoleigh
TIPPERARY
er Shannon
LIMERICK
Golden
Thurles
Askeaton
Boher
Cappamore
Vale
Holycross
Adare
Patrickswell
Pallas Grean
Clonoulty
Rathkeale
3
Lough Gur
Herbertstown
4

Connemara ponies

The qualities of this versatile breed make it popular with horse-lovers all over Britain and Ireland. At most times of year they can be seen roaming the harsh terrain of Connemara, surviving on a diet of brackish grass and seaweed. In August many are brought to Clifden for the Connemara Pony Show to have their withers examined by local dealers. Resilience is an obvious characteristic, but these ponies are also good-tempered and biddable. A subtle admixture of Arab blood lends style to the sturdy native stock and, when well groomed and smartened up, they are handsome, elegant creatures in any show ring.

Dún Aengus, on Inishmore, arguably the finest ruin in the Aran Islands

Irish cabins

During the early 19th century standards of living in Connaught were extremely poor due to overpopulation and the oppressive land laws of the time. A description in 1823 gives an idea of how many people lived: 'a room fifteen feet by nine, no window, no chimney, not even the sign of a fireplace, a mud floor sunk considerably below the level of the road by the side of which it stands, originally ill made and in this wet season covered by almost one foot of water, in one corner are a few lighted sods of turf which, while they afford but little warmth to the wretched group around them, fill the room with volumes of smoke.'

Western counties Oliver Cromwell's famous declaration that Irish rebels could go 'to Hell or to Connaught' suggests he didn't think much of this western region. In times when soil fertility and accessibility were important considerations, these rain-swept, isolated outposts of barren limestone or waterlogged bog must have held few attractions. Famine struck western Ireland particularly hard and emigration from Counties Galway, Clare and Mayo has been high. Until the 18th century, British influence was minimal, and the area is still firmly Gaelic in outlook, its population in tiny scattered rural communities rather than towns and villages. The Irishness shows through, in speech, music, crafts, sport and attitude. Now, it is the West's very distinctiveness that many visitors find so appealing, and, above all, its scenery. These three counties encompass a colossal variety of landscapes and sights. Scenic highlights are unquestionably the ghostly grey-white expanses of bare limestone in the Burren, and the wild coast and mountains of Connemara, where the Twelve Bens loom over flattering mirrors of water amid moorland and blanket bog. Mayo, to the north, is quieter and less popular, though its peaceful scenery has always appealed to a discerning minority. Achill Island is one of its loveliest (and most visited) spots.

Tourist attractions Tourism, low-key at first, has boomed and become much more commercialised since the opening of Shannon Airport, near Limerick. This is still a mandatory, though controversial, touchdown for all transatlantic passenger aircraft flying into Ireland.

Worryingly, the importance of tourism to the region's economy may threaten some of its most sensitive sites. Recently, the Office of Public Works planned to build a new visitor centre in one of the most remote parts of the fragile Burren. The scheme was roundly condemned by ecologists world-wide, and the impact of new road systems, pollution and erosion was not accurately assessed. There was a serious danger that here, as in other parts of Ireland, the temptation to capitalise on tourist revenue would ultimately destroy those very things that visitors came to enjoy. This plan, at least, was rejected by the Irish Supreme Court, but there will doubtless be others.

Out of season (October–April) most of the West is quiet, with all but the busiest attractions closed and less choice of accommodation available. To tour the area in any depth, it is essential to have a car. If you don't drive, the best base is Galway City, which has plenty to do all year round and opportunities for nearby excursions. One of the most interesting trips is to the Aran Islands – stay a day or two, if you can, and see them all. For an activity holiday, golf, riding and fishing are all well provided in the West.

The ideal time to visit the Burren is May or June when its fantastic variety of flowers are at their best. For birdwatching, however, spring and autumn are good times, particularly on the Cliffs of Moher and Downpatrick Head. Inland, huge expanses of water also attract thousands of wildfowl. Pontoon, between Loughs Conn and Cullin, is an especially good place to watch them. So too are the lonely bogland and mountains of the Connemara National Park and the strange turlough lakes of Galway and Clare – one month, a sheet of water, the next, just an emerald patch of freshly watered vegetation, brilliant with flowers, as the giant underground aquifers steadily fill.

Knappogue Castle in County Clare runs medieval banquets in season; see below for more details

Medieval banquets
These are a popular tourist attraction in the Shannonside region of Counties Clare and Limerick. Three castles are highly promoted for medieval entertainments of various kinds, with costumes, music, feasting and fun: Bunratty, Knappogue and Dunguaire (see Hotels and Restaurants, pages 269–83). Don't expect anything authentic or highbrow, but they are greatly enjoyed by many visitors, especially those using Shannon Airport. Ask at any tourist office for information – leaflets are widely available explaining how to book a place.

Currachs
These traditional keelless rowing boats are made of tarred canvas stretched over a light wooden frame (originally made of hazel rods and cowhide). The stern is flat, the prow high, so the boats ride high in the water and are extremely buoyant in the roughest seas, though very fragile. Most carry three oarsmen. They are carried to and from the water's edge upside-down over the crew's heads to avoid damage by rocks, which gives a most curious insect-like impression to a spectator. They are still used for inshore lobster-fishing and collecting seaweed, but the popular sport of *currach*-racing on the west coast of Ireland also helps to keep these unusual craft afloat. (See photograph on page 194.)

Typical Aran cottages, with the ubiquitous dry-stone walls marking the field boundaries

▶▶ **Achill Island**   *172D1*

Mayo's western seaboard seems on the verge of disintegration, its straggling peninsulas anchored to the mainland only by a thread. Achill is the largest of these semi-islands, a rough triangle with sides about 24km long, linked to Curraun (itself a peninsula) by a modern road bridge over Achill Sound. Its quiet beaches and spectacular mountain scenery make it an appealing holiday destination; touring, by car or bike, surfing and angling are the main activities and in summer boats make trips to coastal caves or in pursuit of the harmless basking sharks that haunt this coast. Keel is the main village, boasting shops, simple accommodation and a splendid sandy beach, with some dramatic formations known as the Cathedral Rocks at its furthest end. The most scenic parts of the island can be seen from the Atlantic Drive (signed from the main road near the bridge) which leads past awesome cliffs, heather and gorse moors, and white cottages sprinkled against dark rocks. Beyond Keel, the road stretches towards Achill Head, rearing towards the Atlantic like a sea-monster.

▶▶▶ **Aran Islands**   *172B2*

The cracked limestone terrain of the Aran Islands, lying about 45km out in Galway Bay, links them geologically with the Burren, in County Clare. The islands are flattish, but tilt towards massive sea cliffs in places. Making a living on these bleak rock platforms, virtually treeless and exposed to the full brunt of Atlantic storms, has always been a struggle. Large areas have no natural depth of soil and the islanders have painstakingly created fields from a mixture of sand and seaweed compost, protecting them with an intricate network of dry-stone walls.

Today's dwindling population of islanders (about 1,500 in all) subsist on their age-old livelihoods of fishing and farming, and, increasingly, on tourism. Many speak Gaelic and a very few still wear traditional Aran dress. The canvas fishing boats called *currachs* are used, though have outboard motors now. Aran has always inspired a strong tradition of literature and oral story-telling; J M

Traditional shop-front, Bunratty Park

Castles and abbeys
The Shannon region has many ancient buildings, often carefully restored to achieve full tourist potential. Besides well-known Bunratty, there are tower-houses at Knappogue, a Mac Namara stronghold, and Dunguaire, near Kinvarra. Less touristy are Aughnanure, on Lough Corrib, and Portumna, on Lough Derg. Some of the best monastic sites include: the Franciscan friaries of Quin and Ennis; Clonfert, which has a lovely Romanesque doorway; Ballintubber, founded by a Connaught king; Ross, near Headford; and the remains at Kilmacduagh, with its leaning Round Tower and cathedral. Cong Abbey, in Mayo, housed the great processional Cross of Cong, now in Dublin.

177

Synge set his play *Riders to the Sea* here, and the classic film, *Man of Aran*, made by the Irish-American director, Robert Flaherty, in 1934, is regularly shown on Inishmore.

Most visitors, on a day-trip to one island, will have time to appreciate only a faint whiff of Aran's cultural background; by staying in the islands' simple accommodation, you will absorb far more. Several ferry companies serve the Aran Islands from Galway City, Rossaveal, Spiddal and Doolin (County Clare). Aer Arann fly tiny aircraft to all three islands. All transport services may be affected by weather and you should check schedules carefully.

Inishmore►►► is the largest and most visited island. You can explore by bike, on foot, take a mini-bus or hire a pony-trap ride along its 12km spinal road. Inishmore has a wealth of ancient monuments, notably one of Ireland's outstanding prehistoric sites, the remarkable cliff fort of Dún Aengus, though access is currently under review. Three concentric horseshoe rings of stone perched atop mighty cliffs seem an odd place of refuge, so exposed to the elements and with a sheer drop to the roaring sea below. Its precise age and purpose are still a mystery. The smaller islands are **Inishmaan►►** and **Inisheer►►**, both of which have small fortresses, churches and folk museums to visit.

►► Bunratty Castle and Folk Park   173A3

Bunratty, on the main tourist route from the west coast to Shannon Airport, is now a highly commercialised venture, dragging in coach parties by the thousand for 'medieval' banquets and 'traditional Irish nights' of fiddle music and Irish stew. For all that, the 15th-century castle is genuine enough and well worth seeing.

Set in the castle grounds, the Folk Park re-creates rural Irish life at the turn of the century by means of a series of 'typical' village buildings of the sort you will rarely see in Ireland outside folk theme parks. Chickens cluck around the cottages and costumed staff demonstrate traditional skills. Extraneous attractions include exhibitions, gift and tea-rooms, and the famous tourist pub, **Durty Nelly's**, obligatory viewing for any coach tour. There's a good (smart) restaurant above it called Mac Closkey's.

Stone gates
Despite there being a high density of fields and walls on the Aran Islands, wooden gates are thin on the ground, since trees are scarce. The islanders' answer is to use small gaps in the wall, filled with stones. When access is needed the 'gate' is dismantled and then reassembled. Some gates are topped with a branch of thorn to dissuade the occupant of the field from pushing the gate over. See above for an example.

THE BURREN

Drive The eerie beauty of the Burren

A moon buggy may seem more appropriate for this eerie landscape than a conventional car. Geologists, botanists and antiquity-hunters will be in their element.

From a distance parts of this treeless limestone plateau in north Clare look bleak, but a closer exploration reveals that the area is astonishingly rich in plant-life, playing host to over 1,100 of the 1,400 species found in Ireland. Although the stone surfaces have been scraped clean by the elements, every crack and hollow contains some fragile vegetation, absorbing moisture and nutrients from minimal resources. Alpine species flourish next to those from Mediterranean shores: rare saxifrages, gentians, maidenhair ferns and orchids. The best time to visit the Burren for flowers is undoubtedly in May or June.

Within a couple of hours you can drive across the Burren on the major road from Ennis to Ballyvaughan – and get an idea of the landscape of ancient domed hills and grey-white crazy paving. But this moonscape reveals its real charms only to the sharp-eyed observer on foot, so take a picnic, and leave your vehicle at some stage. Walkers on the Burren should wear sensible footwear and

Bloody cranesbill, which grows commonly all over the Burren

take great care. A 30km waymarked trail, the Burren Way, runs from Ballyvaughan towards Doolin.

Ballyvaughan▶ is an attractive centre from which to explore the Burren; other bases with accommodation are **Killinaboy, Corofin** or **Ennistymon**. The southern section of the Burren is characterised by seasonal lakes called *turloughs*, which ebb and fill as the region's water table changes. Gradually, rainwater falling on this limestone plateau finds its way underground into a maze of caves and subterranean channels. Most are too dangerous for novice investigations, but one has been opened and is worth a visit; the **Aillwee Caves**▶▶, south of Ballyvaughan are a commercial operation, but the caverns themselves are left reasonably natural apart from pathways and illumination. Near the cave entrance a shop sells local cheeses and other produce.

Parts of the Burren are reasonably fertile, supporting some farming and herds of feral goats. Other areas seem inhospitably bare, a shock after the lushness of most of Ireland. For centuries before the advent of tourism the sparse population of the Burren lived in grim poverty.

The best way to find out more about the Burren's unique flora and geology is to visit the privately run **Burren Display Centre**▶▶ at Kilfenora, beside the partly ruined church known as **St Fachtnan's Cathedral**▶▶.

Other sights worth looking for as you cross the central spine of the Burren are ancient tombs, such as the 4,500-year-old **Poulnabrone Dolmen**▶, or the **Gleninsheen wedge-tomb**▶, easily spotted beside the R480 near Caherconnell. The ruins of **Leamaneh**, a 17th-century mansion owned by the O Briens, are a prominent landmark near Kilfenora. Another curiosity is a slightly faint *sheila-na-gig* on the ruined church at **Killinaboy**. These carvings of female figures in indelicate poses were perhaps an ancient fertility symbol, or a dire warning of the sins of the flesh.

Slieve Elva, where the Burren meets the sea

■ **There are no snakes in Ireland, as every Irish schoolchild knows. But its four national parks, 68 national nature reserves (plus 44 in Northern Ireland), 60 bird sanctuaries and 12 forest parks provide a remarkably rich and varied collection of habitats for a vast number of other species, including creatures that are now very rare in Britain, such as corncrakes or otters .....■**

180

The Burren
This unusual terrain soaks up the rays of the sun like a giant storage heater and releases it gently throughout the winter, keeping temperatures a vital fraction higher than the surrounding area. It supports an amazing variety of plants, including many fragile, low-growing types that would be swamped in the average meadow. Species to look out for include the deceptive fly orchid (resembling an insect), gentians and alpine saxifrages. Mountain avens and wild thyme grow everywhere on the Burren, forming colourful sheets in early summer. Needless to say, visitors are requested not to pick or uproot any plants.

Fly orchid

An unspoilt land Ireland is a predominantly rural country, but like everywhere else, is steadily becoming more built up. Land use is changing, usually to the disadvantage of native flora and fauna, but there are still huge tracts of unspoilt countryside where ancient farming patterns prevail. Migrant birds return year after year to safe haunts, rare orchids and obscure insectivorous plants flourish in specialised niches, and lichen grows thick on walls or tree-trunks in unpolluted air. Bird-watchers and plant-spotters, or anyone who appreciates country life, will much enjoy an Irish holiday. Remember your binoculars, and a reference book for identifying unusual species. If you plan to walk any of the long-distance footpaths of Ireland, or visit specialist regions like the Burren, check what to look for at an information or visitor centre before you set off. Bord Fáilte's leaflet, *Ireland Naturally,* outlines the main nature reserves and places of interest.

Abundant wildlife Practically any part of Ireland offers the keen-eyed naturalist a good selection of species, but a number of locations are especially noted for unusual wildlife. Ireland has fewer mammals than the UK (no moles, for instance), but those that are there can often be found more abundantly. Otters colonise many rivers and streams, even quite near towns. Pine martens, red deer and red squirrels can be found in the newly designated forest parks. The last remaining native woodlands can be seen in the national parks of Killarney and Glenveagh.

Exotic plants If you are interested in plants, the best region to head for is the mysterious limestone wilderness of the Burren in County Clare (see panel, and pages 178–9). Other areas special for plants are the sand-dune habitats, such as the Raven National Nature Reserve in County Wexford (wild asparagus, round-leaved wintergreen and lesser centaury), and the lush, sub-tropical oceanic lands of Kerry and Cork, where wild fuchsias bloom and the strawberry tree grows to unusual size. Mosses and ferns thrive in the moist, mild air. Ireland's boglands support a unique ecosystem of wetland plants, including sundews and butterworts (see pages 24–5).

Rare birds Bird-watchers have an immense choice of habitats. There are many exciting coastal reserves, first landfall for rare migrants which cross the ocean to breed or overwinter in Ireland. Spring nesting seasons begin early for native birds, followed by an influx of species

Wildlife

The Irish yew
Every example of this tree ultimately comes from cuttings taken from the mutant discovered in the gardens of Florence Court in County Fermanagh. The branches have an unusual upright habit instead of the normal spreading growth. The original tree was identified and first propagated in 1767, and the Irish yew is now planted widely in graveyards and formal gardens.

Marine reserves
For marine habitats, head for Strangford Lough near Belfast, or Lough Hyne in south Cork, where sheltered sea inlets have fostered unique colonies of creatures usually found in more tropical waters. Giant skate and basking shark glide through the narrow straits, carpeted with bright corals and sponges.

There are pine martens in the forest parks, but you will be lucky to see one

Corncrake

from Africa. In autumn rare American waders appear in ones and twos, and in winter great numbers of waterfowl fly in from Northern Europe and the Arctic or Canada. Manx shearwaters glide close to Belfast towards dusk, with an eerie cry that once unnerved the Vikings, and nest on Light House Island. Greenland white-fronted geese arrive in huge flocks on the 'slobs' (reclaimed *polder* mudflats) of Wexford. Puffins nest in just a few rocky places on the west and southwest coast (the Cliffs of Moher, Clear Island or Puffin Island). Terns colonise the sheltered inland sea of Strangford Lough. Several of the most famous bird reserves are islands; Ireland's Eye, just off Howth near Dublin, the Copelands near Belfast and the wild Skellig Rocks off the southwest tip of Cork. Clare Island and the Saltees are both accessible by boat at the most interesting times of year. Other good bird-watching locations are the quiet estuarial coast of Waterford and Wexford (particularly around Hook Head, Kinsale Old Head or Kilmore Quay), the muddy flats of Timoleague, and the wild rocky fastnesses of Clare, Mayo, Rathlin Island and Donegal, where seabirds gather in vast numbers on cliff ledges, at spots such as Horn Head (Donegal), the Cliffs of Moher (Clare), or Downpatrick Head (Mayo). Inland, many of the larger lakes and river systems support huge colonies of waterbirds – godwits, avocets and swans. Birds of prey can be seen wheeling in lonely circuits around the Wicklow Mountains, the Slieve Blooms, the Sperrins (in the North) or Macgillycuddy's Reeks.

WESTERN COUNTIES

A justifiably famous Irish viewpoint shows Clifden in its glorious setting by the Twelve Bens, most of which are visible below. Leaving Clifden on the Sky Road (on a clear day) and looking back after a kilometre or so reveals the full panorama

▶▶ **Clifden**   *172C1*

The 'capital of Connemara' occupies a glorious position at the head of Clifden Bay, with the Twelve Bens mountain range a dramatic backdrop (see photograph below). Clifden is little more than a large village with a population of 1,400 or so, but its location makes it a popular base. It is also an agricultural and market town, but much of the land around is too poor to farm, and the region's income derives mainly from tourism. It has a range of affordable accommodation, lively bars and fine sandy beaches. An arts festival is held in late September, though a more traditional event is the August Connemara Pony Show.

Cottages and bungalows have sprung up all around the 19th-century core of the town, founded in 1812 by the local landowner, John d'Arcy, descendant of an Anglo-Norman family who converted from Roman Catholicism to avoid dispossession under the Penal Laws. He built the ruined Gothic castle visible from the Sky Road. The town consists of two main streets of attractively restored colour-washed shop-fronts displaying the names of Connemara families, notably Joyce. Main landmarks include two grey-spired churches, one Catholic, one Protestant.

The best views of the town and the surrounding landscape are seen from the Sky Road, a narrow circuit around the Kingstown peninsula to the northwest. This scenic corniche skirts the hillsides, overlooking plunging vistas of white farms, emerald fields and sapphire sea.

▶▶▶ **Cliffs of Moher**   *172B2*

Sheer, dark walls of rock stretch dramatically for 8km along the coast of Clare, an even-topped curtain, in places as much as 200m high. These remarkable cliffs are home to a great variety of seabirds, including a colony of puffins, and on clear days there are splendid views of the Aran Islands and the mountains of Connemara. A cliff path leads to the southerly extremity of Hag's Head, fenced as the cliffs are so friable. The rocks are basically limestone of the same sort as the Burren, but shale and sandstone have formed on top, and are subject to rainfall erosion and the pressure of many feet; keep back from the edge. You can park near the depressingly commercialised visitor centre. Not far away is a folly viewpoint built by the 19th-century MP, Sir Cornelius O Brien, where a telescope gives a close-up of the huge rock-faces and sea stacks, standing in the lazily moving waves which, from this height, are almost inaudible.

► Corofin   173B3

This village amid the pretty turlough lakes of the southern Burren is a fine base for exploring the area. Accommodation consists mainly of B&Bs, with one good private hostel in the centre. Even if you don't stay, visit the **Clare Heritage Centre►►** housed in the former Protestant church. It has a moving exhibition connected with the Famine period, when this part of Ireland suffered particularly badly. In a building close by, a genealogical centre has been set up, containing half a million baptismal records of over 2,500 families. Descendants of émigré families flock here to find their roots (see pages 74–5).

►► Craggaunowen Project   173A3

This historic reconstruction vividly brings to life Ireland's pre-Christian past and remains one of the best of its kind, very well explained with a good visitor centre, coffee shop and picnic area. The art historian and archaeologist, John Hunt (see page 167), restored the 16th-century tower-house of Craggaunowen Castle during the 1960s, then turned the grounds to imaginative use. A Bronze-Age *crannóg* (island dwelling) stands in a reedy lake; other exhibits include a ring-fort and a stretch of Iron-Age timber road. Also on display is the leather-covered boat called the *Brendan*, in which Tim Severin and his crew sailed the Atlantic in 1976–7, in a putative repetition of St Brendan's 6th-century voyage to the Americas (see page 115).

183

Fun on Judgement Day
When two imaginative girls were growing up in Chile in the early 1900s, each wrote a poetic epitaph for the other, agreeing that whoever lived longer would place her poem on the other's tombstone. Subsequently both came to live near Corofin. When Audrey Douglas (née Sharman) died in 1968, she was buried in the grounds of the Church of Ireland church in the village (now the Clare Heritage Centre). Faithful to her pact, Vanda Cutler inscribed the following on the tombstone, visible for all to read:

Here, as ever, sleeping sound,
Lies our Audrey in the ground.
If she wakes, as wake she may,
There'll be fun on Judgement Day.

CONNEMARA

Drive Mountains, beaches, untouched bogland and a fjord

If you're lucky with the weather, this magnificent drive offers superb coastal and mountain scenery, a 2,000ha national park, and one of the best areas of blanket bog in Ireland.

Connemara is the westernmost section of County Galway, beyond Lough Corrib. Inland are moors and looming hills, lakes and streams fringed by vivid green vegetation, and a massively indented but placid coastline. One main road, the N59, leads through the centre of Connemara and round the northern area, but though scenic enough, it's best to deviate from this for at least part of the way to take in some of the coast. If you start at Galway you take the main road for the first section (via Oughterard).

Oughterard▶ is some way inland, but is surprisingly a great fishing centre, serving the resort area of Lough Corrib, Ireland's second largest lake (40km long) which virtually splits the county in half. If you have time a detour along the lush lake-shore towards Curraun is a pleasant option. From Oughterard it's a straightforward and beautiful journey past

Roundstone, a quiet village on the peaceful Connemara coast

mirror-like pools to **Maam Cross**, where the monthly cattle fair is about the only sign of life. Here you have a choice between exploring the mass of islets along the coastal peninsulas, or pressing on to the small, unremarkable settlement of Recess. Further on, call in at **Ballynahinch Castle▶** (now a luxury hotel, see panel on page 164), in fine parkland by a lake. A detour via the peaceful coastline of **Cashel Bay▶▶** is a recommended alternative here. Sheltered from Atlantic gales and storms, this quiet bay sprouts luxuriant subtropical vegetation at every turn.

Roundstone▶ has a particularly attractive setting at the foot of Errisbeg with wonderful views of the Twelve Bens; its tourist industry is taking over from fishing. If you cut across the peninsula instead of following the coast you will see at close quarters one of the best remaining stretches of Irish blanket bog, now at last recognised as an important ecosystem, rather than something to be dried and burned. It's a lonely road with an uneven camber, so drive carefully, especially towards nightfall. The bog is haunted by the ghost of a traveller murdered by two old women who offered him shelter; not good for the local B&B trade!

Clifden▶▶ is the 'capital' of Connemara. There's not much to the town, but it has magnificent scenery all around, best seen from the immensely scenic Sky Road▶▶, signed

Kylemore Abbey; there can be few more dramatically sited schools

to the northwest. Just past the seemly Quaker village of **Letterfrack** is the entrance to the **Connemara National Park▶▶**, containing some of the West's finest mountain scenery. There's a visitor centre here with a slightly disappointing exhibition on local natural history and bogland. Staff can suggest short hikes through the park; guided walks are organised in summer. For more challenging walking, follow one of the routes given in *The Mountains of Connemara; a Hillwalker's Guide*, on sale, a couple of kilometres further on, at the shop at **Kylemore Abbey▶▶** whose fairy-tale towers are reflected in a clear lake. Kylemore is a latterday Tudor folly, the creation of a 19th-century English shipping magnate. It now houses a girls' boarding school, but welcomes visitors to its craft shops and tea rooms. The road to **Leenane▶** is especially scenic, running past the long inlet called Killary Harbour, where controversial fish-farming is taking place. Leenane recently achieved cinematic fame as the setting for the film, *The Field*. A brief drive over the bridge to **Aasleagh** gives a view of a series of waterfalls, a salmon leap, and the gateway to County Mayo. If you want to return towards Galway from Leenane a couple of routes potter through Joyce Country around Lough Corrib.

WESTERN COUNTIES

Oysters and Guinness at the International Galway Oyster Festival, held in late September each year

The Lynch Memorial
This marble plaque over a Gothic doorway can be found near the Collegiate Church of St Nicholas in Market Street. It commemorates a poignant, though almost certainly fictional, legend that a former city mayor, James Lynch FitzStephen, tried and convicted his own son, Walter, of killing a Spanish rival for the affections of his beloved. The boy confessed to the crime and Judge Lynch felt morally obliged to condemn his son to death as he would any other citizen guilty of murder. But no-one would carry out the sentence, so he was forced to hang his son himself. After the execution the mayor retired into seclusion, a broken man.

Claddagh rings
These ornaments of silver or gold originated in The Claddagh, once a close-knit fishing community just outside Galway's old city walls, now a neat suburb. Claddagh rings depict two hands holding a heart surmounted by a crown, symbolising a promise, or a hope, of eternal love and friendship. The precious heirlooms were handed down the female line and, depending which way round the ring was worn, showed whether a girl was engaged, or still on the marriage market.

► ►   **Galway**   *173C3*

Galway has been one of the fastest growing conurbations in Europe, soon to be the Republic's third city, but in 1993 a major employer, IBM, closed its factory. Despite its size, it has an intimate, village-like atmosphere and seems a place where everyone knows everyone else, though this may be an illusion, as much of its population consists of temporary visitors (tourists or students). Besides its prestigious 19th-century university, where students can take their degrees in Gaelic, Galway has several Irish language schools. None of its sights is essential viewing, but the town seems to add up to more than the sum of its parts, and is a good centre for entertainment and shopping (especially second-hand books and classy crafts).

There is always plenty going on, both low- and high-brow – a festival just about every month, an innovative theatre, concerts, lively pubs and restaurants. In short, it is perhaps Ireland's most enjoyable and upbeat city, full of vivacity and character and increasingly frequented by younger visitors in search of 'good crack' (fun). It hosts high-calibre Irish folk groups and its sporting prowess is a source of pride, particularly in traditional games such as Gaelic football and hurling. The Galway Races (a six-day meeting in July) and its Regatta Festivals are some of the oldest regular events. Beside its own attractions, Galway is a good base for exploring local areas – Connemara, Lough Corrib, the Aran Islands and the Burren.

Galway's prosperity was founded on its strategic location at the lowest bridging point of the River Corrib, a waterway once used by many vessels, now mainly by spring salmon who leap the falls by the **Salmon Weir Bridge►**. Founded by the Anglo-Normans in the 13th century, Galway became known as the City of the Tribes, a reference to the 14 leading families who held sway quarrelsomely in its early history. In its heyday, Galway was a significant port and European trading centre; its traditional vessels, the elegant lateen-rigged Galway hookers, traded food and fuel for livestock from the Aran Islands, or smuggled contraband from France and the Channel Isles. By the western mouth of the river are the remains of a Gaelic-speaking fishing community known as **The Claddagh▶** (see panel). The cottages have now been replaced by tidier municipal housing, but old photographs and artefacts displayed in the city's **museum▶** show how it looked. The museum is in a stone structure called the **Spanish Arch▶**, erected by the harbour to protect ships off-loading Iberian cargoes of wine and brandy.

Up towards the centre of town the most striking monument is the bizarre and hideously modern **Roman Catholic Cathedral of Our Lady Assumed into Heaven and St Nicholas▶**, a vast limestone structure in neo-Renaissance style, all seeping copper and flashy marble. The unorthodox (amorous) behaviour of its former bishop (Eamonn Casey) which raised eyebrows in 1992 has apparently failed to dent local faith. More seemly buildings lie in the medieval quarter of the city, where wandering through its delightful streets of well-restored shop-fronts and stone town-houses is recommended. Sixteenth-century **Lynch's Castle▶**, now an Allied Irish Bank building, was once the seat of the Lynch family and its mullioned façade is decorated with exotic escutcheons and gargoyles. The dignified **Collegiate Church of St Nicholas▶** has seafaring associations, including a legend that Christopher Columbus prayed there. Eyre Square is a welcome space after the confinement of the tiny old lanes. Dedicated to President Kennedy, it contains several monuments, the most interesting being the crested Browne Doorway, a disembodied portal dating from 1627, removed from a grand mansion in 1905. Bits of the city walls are incorporated into the new Eyre Square shopping centre. Nora Barnacle, James Joyce's wife, hailed from Galway, and her tiny house (now a shop) can be visited in the Bowling Green.

Oysters and ale

Galway's native oysters raised in the calm tidal waters around Clarinbridge are world-famous, and it is an ideal place to acquire an expensive taste – whenever there's an 'r' in the month. In fact, most Galway oysters are perfectly affordable, being farmed ones from Portuguese stock which, unlike the native oysters, can be eaten in any month. Though carefully prepared, these are served with no pretentious ritual. Wash them down with a pint of Guinness if you like. Each year in early September the Clarinbridge Oyster Festival is held. The best places to try them are Paddy Burke's pub in Clarinbridge, or the quaint waterside restaurant called Moran's Oyster Cottage. You can walk downstream to see the beds when the tide is right. They take about four years to reach maturity.

The beach at Salthill, west of Galway, looks south towards the Burren

Knock
173D3

Knock's pedigree dates back over a century, when it was suddenly transformed from a humdrum little bog village into one of the most revered Marian shrines in Christendom. It is now the 'Lourdes of Ireland' with a vast new basilica, constantly thronged by pilgrims. Its present high profile in the Catholic world is due in large part to the energies of a local priest, Monsignor James Horan. He battled with the authorities for an airport which, despite early descriptions as 'a foggy, boggy white elephant', has greatly opened up the northwest region to tourist traffic since its eventual inauguration in 1986, seven years after Pope John Paul II made a celebrated visit to Knock. The commercialised religiosity of innumerable souvenir stalls may offend the purist, but today Knock attracts more pilgrims than ever, around a million a year.

On a dark and stormy night in 1879 two village women saw an apparition of the Virgin Mary, with St Joseph and St John, on the gable of the parish church. Scarcely able to believe their eyes, they called other villagers, who also saw the vision. It lasted a couple of hours, then faded away gradually. All 15 witnesses were interviewed and cross-examined by a commission of enquiry. Some 50 years later, three surviving witnesses were again independently interviewed, and firmly maintained every detail of what they had seen, giving an unnerving veracity to their story.

The original church still exists, the gable where the vision had appeared now preserved behind a glazed oratory. It has fine features inside, notably stained glass by the ubiquitous Harry Clarke (1889–1931). The new church, designed to hold a congregation of many thousands, was completed in 1976. Though fairly hideous to an unpartisan eye, the hexagonal building contains inter-

Knock's position on the world pilgrimage trail was confirmed by the visit of Pope John Paul II in 1979

Croagh Patrick
The brooding, conical outline of this mountain dominates the skyline all around southwest Mayo. It is associated with St Patrick, the site of his Lenten fast and legendary 'Pied Piper' act with the snakes. Each year, on the last Sunday in July, pilgrims make an arduous ascent, some barefoot. On clear days, the summit gives magnificent views over Clew Bay to the Partry Mountains and Connemara. If you are sensibly shod, you can climb Croagh Patrick in a couple of hours. (See also page 226.)

esting examples of modern art and architecture. Its 32 ambulatory pillars each contain stone from a different Irish county, and the windows represent each of the four provinces: Connaught, Leinster, Munster and Ulster.

Knock's religious significance dwarfs any other reason to come here, but there is a good little **folk museum▶** in the village illustrating life in the west of Ireland and giving some background on the shrine.

Lisdoonvarna
172B2

Ireland's only spa stands in this curious village on the edge of the Burren, emitting sulphurous and radioactive iodine-filled springs alleged to cure numerous ills. The bath-house facilities will seem primitive if you frequent posh health clubs, but the old-fashioned bath-tubs and massage rooms have a certain historic fascination. Needless to say, the water tastes ghastly.

Grandiose spa hotels and villas indicate the spa's one-time popularity, but today the village is more renowned for its Matchmaking Festival, held annually in September after harvest time. The festival has an honourable history; wealthy farming families used to pair-off their eligible sons and daughters via a 'matchmaker' for appropriate dowries of cattle or horses. Later the festival became a dating agency for the famously shy and sexually repressed bachelor farmers of rural Ireland, who often had few social outlets and little opportunity to meet potential brides. Many failed to marry until very late in life, if at all. These days, however, the festival has become a tawdry and depressing event, at which lonely singles turn up for a drunken grope and a one-night stand rather than a soul-mate. Unusually in organised dating circles, the proportion of men is far higher than women (about three to one). There's plenty of good 'crack' (fun), though, and it's certainly worth a visit as a social curiosity. If you're on the lookout, who knows, you may get lucky!

At the **Lisdoonvarna Smoke House▶**, signed from the village centre, visitors may observe fish being smoked, amid a choking salty fug of charring wood chippings. You can have a brief look round, watch cheerful women deftly filleting and trimming massive sides of salmon (wild and farmed), and buy some of the products here, or try them in the Roadside Tavern next door.

Monsignor James Horan
The guiding light behind Knock International Airport may ultimately be super-natural, but its earthly inspiration took the shape of Mgr James Horan, an indefatigable local priest. He it was who first raised the idea of upgrading the grass airstrip to jumbo-jet capacity. After the Pope's visit in 1979, Mgr Horan was convinced the shrine would draw vast numbers of pilgrims. Decried by sceptics as a foggy, boggy white elephant, the airport nevertheless opened in 1986, soon proving popular with both tourists and pilgrims. Indeed the Lourdes–Knock run is used by many French visitors wishing to fish in the lakes of the West!

189

Captain Charles Boycott
The man whose surname has entered the English language as a word meaning to ostracise was land agent for Lord Erne in County Mayo in the late 19th century. He lived at Loughmask House, on the lough's eastern shore. During the 1879–82 Land War (Parnell's campaign to reduce land rents by 25 per cent) he was isolated by the local community 'as if he were a leper' for his refusal to co-operate. No one would work for him, or even speak to him, and eventually he was forced to leave Ireland.

WESTERN COUNTIES

Thoor Ballylee, Yeats's retreat from the frantic events of 1920s Ireland

Coole Park
Yeats's patron lived here – the redoubtable Lady Augusta Gregory (1859–1932), a wealthy widow who encouraged many writers and artists at the turn of the century. The house fell into neglect after her death and was demolished during World War II, but the splendid grounds are now open to the public as a national park and are a marvellous place for walks and picnics. The 'autograph tree', a copper beech on which many famous visitors carved their initials, can be seen behind railings in the peaceful walled garden. In the park is the turlough lake that inspired Yeats's poem *The Wild Swans at Coole*.

▶▶ **Thoor Ballylee**   173B3

An ancient bridge and a more ancient tower,
A farmhouse that is sheltered by its wall,
An acre of stony ground,
Where the symbolic rose can break in flower.
                    (*Meditations in Time of Civil War*)

In 1917 W B Yeats found this evocative 'ivy-covered tower', conveniently close to his friend and patron Lady Gregory, who lived at Coole Park. Thoor Ballylee was a fortified residence built by the Anglo-Norman de Burgo family during the 14th century. Then in his 50s and newly married to his young bride George Hyde-Lees, Yeats purchased the derelict tower-house for £35 and spent intermittent periods of the next decade there with his new family, converting the interior into simple, but stylish living and sleeping quarters. The 'winding stair' image which repeatedly appears in his poetry refers to the stone steps leading up the tower. From the battlemented rooftop, views extend over the placid meadows by the nearby millstream to the Slieve Aughty Mountains. Many of Yeats's more mystical writings were produced here, notably *The Tower* and *The Winding Stair* (not generally his most admired work); by this stage his disillusion with the Irish political scene was taking effect and he sought relief in seclusion and mythology. In 1928 Yeats abandoned the damp tower for warmer climes and died in France in 1939. The Kiltartan Society took over the decaying tower in 1961 and fully restored it in Yeatsian style, putting many documents, first editions and manuscripts on display. The audio-visual show gives a good background to the poet, the house, and the turmoil of the times.

▶▶ **Westport**   172D2

One of the most charming towns in Ireland's western region, Westport shows its Georgian origins clearly in its broad streets and canalised river flowing through a lime-fringed avenue called The Mall. It is set on an inlet of Clew Bay, where the Carrowbeg River flows into the sea. Many

Setting the world to rights in Westport

of its fine buildings remain, some carefully restored. The Protestant church is late Victorian (about 1880) and has charming art nouveau influences.

Westport was originally laid out as part of a great estate and, at the turn of the 18th century, prospered greatly from its textile industry. In 1801, though, the Act of Union made local businesses collapse as cheaper products flooded in from England. By 1825 Westport's linen industry was virtually finished. Today, Westport is a market town and fishing centre, with a few good beaches near by. Many visitors pass through, stopping at its main sight on the way.

Westport House▶▶ stands in fine parkland about 3km outside the town, near Westport Quay. Designed by those great architects of the 1730s, James Wyatt and Richard Castle, it is the seat of the Brownes, Marquesses of Sligo, and is County Mayo's only stately home open to the public. Though somewhat commercialised in an attempt to meet the colossal running costs, it is still a remarkable house, beautifully furnished inside with Irish Georgian and Victorian silver and antiques, Waterford Crystal, Chinese wallpapers and a fine collection of paintings, including a *Holy Family* by Rubens. The doors are made with Jamaican mahogany (the 1st Marquess spent time as a governor there, apparently one of its more benevolent rulers, who freed many slaves). The dungeons beneath the house date from an earlier dwelling, allegedly a castle belonging to the pirate queen, Grace O'Malley. These now provide but one of the many attractions and side-shows set up in the park and grounds, which include a zoo, gift shops, boating lake, a model railway and horse-drawn caravans. The Browne family have lived in Westport House for over 400 years.

Westport Quay, just outside the main entrance gates to the house, has several good restaurants, and there is a range of accommodation in the town. A couple of summer festivals (arts in October and a street festival in July) and good music pubs are other reasons to head here. The Wyatt Theatre (in season) puts on some amateur productions of Irish drama.

'My wife George'
W B Yeats was something of a pessimistic visionary at times, foreseeing the places he lived in going to rack and ruin after he left. On a plaque set into the wall of the tower at Thoor Ballylee, he inscribed the following verse:

I, the poet William Yeats,
With old mill boards and
  sea-green slates
And smithy work from the
  Gort forge,
Restored this tower for my
  wife George;
And may these characters
  remain
When all is ruin once
  again.

191

Westport House also has an attractive modern church in its grounds

■ **Any glance at Ireland's antiquities – its great churches, the jewellery worn by the Celts, the intricacies of illuminated manuscripts like the *Book of Kells* – will show what a long tradition of sheer artistry exists there, what a delight in pattern, shape and texture. This continues today, encouraged strongly by tourism .....■**

Bog-wood carvings

An artist with a highly individual product is Michael Casey, who works at Barley Harbour in County Longford and has achieved an international reputation. He has made a speciality of carving bog wood (blackened timber preserved for thousands of years beneath boglands) into imaginative sculptures of figures or animals. It is a long process. First the wood has to dry out – taking almost two years. Then it is carved, and finished carefully with sandpaper and beeswax to a remarkable sheen. The wood used is mostly yew, pine or oak.

192

The labour-intensive and highly skilled craft of lace-making, here practised in Monaghan

Souvenir hunting Ireland's craft industries are a major source of revenue. They vary from huge enterprises employing hundreds of workers, like Waterford Crystal, to tiny artisan studios where one person practises woodcarving or jewellery-making. Some crafts are still cottage industries – much knitting or lace-making, for example, is still done at home. Most visitors will want to take at least one reminder of Ireland home, and there is now a wide and attractive choice of souvenirs to suit all purses; shop around for price and quality. Prices can be high in Ireland with VAT at its current swingeing rates. If you live outside the EC, consider reclaiming this tax on anything valuable.

Many craft centres and even factories now welcome tourists, and free tours are provided at several large enterprises, such as Waterford Crystal, Tyrone Crystal, Belleek Parian ware, Foxford Woollen Mills in County Mayo, Donegal Parian China and Magee's tweed factory in Donegal Town. These are often elaborately set up with guided tours, audio-visual shows, refreshments, and showrooms where you can inspect, and of course buy, the product. Packing and shipment arrangements can also be made if you live abroad.

Kilkenny is an attractive place to buy crafts. The Kilkenny Design Centre, set up in old stables opposite the castle, provides a high quality outlet for many of Ireland's best producers. There is also a branch in Dublin (see page 80).

Craft villages Smaller studios have developed (mainly in the west of Ireland, notably in Donegal, Connemara and Dingle), where economic conditions have justified a special focus of attention on employment opportunities. Artists can rent small workshops in these 'craft villages' to produce jewellery, knitwear, pottery, woodwork, handweaving, etc. Connemara marble, a greenish stone, is fashioned into innumerable souvenirs near Moycullen. Several potters in Cork and Kerry have been particularly successful; Stephen Pearce's modern pottery in terracotta colours with abstract stripes of white is a typical example. Produced at Shanagarry, east of Cork City, it is now available in smart stores in Dublin or the West End of London. Robin and Jane Forrester's Bandon pottery is also very popular – in blue with a fruit pattern.

Glass and crystal Few visitors will be able to take a stained glass window home, but in many of the churches of Ireland you will see the work of artists Harry Clarke or Evie Hone, who brought about a revival of this craft in the earlier part of the century. There are good examples at

Crafts

Carrickmacross in Monaghan, Ardara in Donegal, or at Kingscourt, Cavan. Ireland's brand of deep-etched, brilliant lead crystal is most famously produced at Waterford, but now has many competitors – in Tipperary, Cavan, Athlone, Donegal, Tyrone and Galway. Jerpoint Glass, made in County Kilkenny, is plainer.

Linen and wool Textiles have always been a staple of Ireland's craft industry, linen and wool being the two main fibres used. Today's flax production is quite limited, but high quality tea-towels and tablecloths are available all over the island, subtly woven in damask patterns or more crudely stamped with shamrock motifs. Lisburn has linen trails and a linen museum. Centres of the lace industry are Carrickmacross and Clones in the border counties of Cavan and Monaghan (see panel on page 246) and Limerick. Both produce so-called 'mixed lace' which is sewn on to cotton net. Genuine hand-made lace is expensive. Knitwear is ubiquitous. The classic Aran sweater is now produced all over Ireland in many different designs.

One of Ireland's most famous products is tweed. Manufacture still centres on Donegal, where those classic, hard-wearing fibres in soft peaty colours are woven in factories such as Magee's. Other natural fabrics are woven by Avoca Handweavers (see page 92).They are one of the most high-profile of Ireland's craft enterprises, producing soft worsteds and mohairs in bright, jewel-like colours of blues and pinks, mostly for women's fashions.

Limerick, too, is renowned for its lace

Stephen Pearce
Stephen Pearce's pottery is at Shanagarry, near Cork, and is open to visitors. Only three designs are made, each in a simple, yet sophisticated style, from local clay. One is a black-and-white glazed earthenware range called Shanagarry, another a terracotta range, and the third a blue-and-white design. There may be only three ranges of pottery, but in all these contain over 400 separate items.

Glass factories
Many of Ireland's lead-crystal manufacturers welcome visitors to look around and watch the glass being blown and cut by hand. Most famous is Waterford (see page 143), but other companies such as Tipperary Crystal, Tyrone, Galway and Cavan will also allow visitors (contact local tourist offices for details). If you prefer a more modern, plain form of glass, one of the most interesting studios to visit is Jerpoint Glass, at Stoneyford in Kilkenny (tel: 056 24350).

Belleek pottery dates back to 1857

Lough Derg

This lake, set in desolate bog and moorland east of Donegal, is a popular destination for pilgrims who converge in droves on a tiny island, ostensibly for inner peace and solitude, although Station Island now is virtually covered by buildings – an octagonal basilica and several hostels. St Patrick is said to have spent 40 days praying and fasting here, and now the island receives up to 15,000 visitors a year. During a three-day summer vigil of prayer and contemplation only black tea and dry toast may be consumed; no sleep is allowed on the first night. Pilgrims walk barefoot around the island's shrines. If this sounds an interesting sort of weekend break, be warned that penitents come here from all over the world. Book early to avoid disappointment!

Traditional currachs are still widely used on the west coast

Inishtrahull

Malin Head
Inishtrahull Sound
Ballyhillin
Clonmany
Malin
Culdaff
Fanad Head
Camdonagh
Horn
Head
Fanad
nfaghy
Fort
Dunree
Moville
Cresslough
Doe
Castle
Lough Swilly
Inisbowen
Rathmullan
Buncrana
Carrowkeel
Milford
Lough Foyle
Rathmelton
Eglinton
Airport
Limavady
Glenveagh
National Park
Grianan
of Aileach
Eglinton
Globe
House
Church
Hill
Letterkenny
DERRY/LONDONDERRY
Colmcille
ritage Centre
St Johnstown
LONDONDERRY
DONEGAL
Claudy
Dungiven
ts
Lifford
Mts
Ballybofey
Stranorlar
Strabane
683m
Sawel
Sperrin
Sion Mills
Plumbridge
ough
ske
Castlederg
Gortin
Newtownstewart
Ulster
History
Park
Ulster-American
Folk Park
TYRONE
Lough
Derg
Drumquin
Omagh
Carrickmore
Pettigoe
Beragh
Pomeroy
Castle
Caldwell
rest Park
Kesh
White Island
Seskinore
Lower
Lough Erne
Dromore
Fintona
Ballygawley
Castle Archdale
Country Park
Irvinestown
Simpson
Grant
Ballinamallard
Aughnacloy
Devenish Island
Clogher
Augher
FERMANAGH
Fivemiletown
Caledon
Enniskillen
Castle Coole NT
Emyvale
Belcoo
Lisbellaw
Middletown
lenfarne
Blacklion
Maguiresbridge
Marble Arch
Caves
Florence
Court NT
Lisnaskea
Upper
Lough Erne
Rosslea
Monaghan
Swanlinbar
Derrylin
Smithborough
Rossmore
Forest Park
Clones
ron
Mts
Newtown
Butler
Newbliss
MONAGHAN
IM
Belturbet
Drum
Ballybay
Ballinamore
Butler's Bridge
Ballyhaise
Cootehill
Fenagh
Killashandra
Lough
Oughter
Carrigallen
Killy Keen
Forest Park
Cavan
Stradone
Shercock
Mohill
Arvagh
CAVAN
Bailieborough
Drumod
Kilnaleck
Kingscourt
Lough
Gowna
Ballyjamesduff
Drumlish
Virginia
LONGFORD
Lough
Sheelin
Lough
Ramor
Oldcastle
Moynalty
ewtown
orbes
Ballinalee
Granard
Finnea
Longford
3
4

NORTHWESTERN COUNTIES

The Stolen Child

'Where the wave of moon-
light glosses
The dim grey sands with
light
Far off by furthest Rosses
We foot it all the night,
Weaving olden dances,
Mingling hands and
mingling glances
Till the moon has taken
flight;
To and fro we leap
And chase the frothy
bubbles,
While the world is full of
troubles
And is anxious in its sleep.
Come away, O human
child!
To the waters and the wild
With a faery, hand in hand,
For the world's more full of
weeping than you can
understand.'

W B Yeats (1865–1939).
(See page 201 for The
Rosses.)

Northwestern counties Donegal's spectacular scenery is often considered the best in Ireland, though its location keeps it remote. Outside a brief, intense summer season, when tourists flit through like butterflies, these northern regions (Counties Sligo, Donegal and Leitrim) can seem forlorn and windswept. All through the year clouds scud rapidly in from the Atlantic, bringing lashing horizontal squalls or drizzling sea-mists. Just as suddenly these are followed by shafts of sunlight and vivid rainbows which alchemise its glens, cliffs, mountains and beaches into the landscapes of Irish holiday brochures. Here, in these far-flung peninsulas, you will find that elusive rural idyll – softly domed ricks of hand-turned hay and whitewashed thatched cottages with scarlet doors. The postcard scene disguises a history of constant struggle against the elements and economic deprivation. In many of these areas emigration is rife and the population ageing. There is little industry other than the old cottage-based crafts of knitting and weaving, though these are now organised to catch the tourist's eye in village-like studio complexes or factories such as Magee's of Donegal Town. Most of the region's income comes from tourism and not all the side-effects are beneficial. On some sections of coastline, insensitive development has resulted in a garish outbreak of modern white bungalows which bear little relation to their surroundings. Numerous seaside resorts amuse those hardy enough to chance the weather. Bundoran's kiss-me-quick image evokes a bygone era of traditional family holidays. Today, some of these splendid unpolluted beaches have achieved a new cachet as Ireland's best surfing spots.

Northern extremities

Tenuously attached to the Republic by a thin isthmus of land between the coast and its severed Ulster neighbours, Donegal waves its tattered banner even further oceanwards than the Six Counties, constituting Ireland's northernmost extremity. Its cliffs at Slieve League are the highest in Europe and

The sturdy Irish Draught is especially useful where vehicles cannot venture

several wild promontories make important habitats for sea birds. It scores not only with incomparable coastal scenery, but also with inland Glenveagh National Park, where massive glacial valleys carve grandly through grouse-moors and blanket bog. Offshore lie several inhabited islands: Tory Island, where the locals fish for lobster and paint naive art; and Aranmore, more prosperous and biddable, welcoming tourists with holiday cottages.

Third largest county after Cork and Galway, Donegal has the biggest Gaeltacht (Irish-speaking community) in Ireland and nationalist sentiments run high. This is the ancient Gaelic territory of Tir Chonaill – land of Conal. Even after the Flight of the Earls (see pages 34–5), the English never quite got their hands on Donegal's wilder regions, and after partition, though technically part of Ulster, they let it stay with the Republic. Road-signs in rural areas may appear only in Irish. A significant proportion of the population on the eastern side of the county are Protestants, however, who look across the border from their prosaic farmland for their spiritual home.

Leitrim and Sligo Further south, Leitrim has a much lower tourist profile than Donegal, and few foreign visitors could pin-point it on a map. It has pretty enough, but unspectacular, countryside, mostly mixed farmland, lakes and moors on undulating drumlins, with just a few dramatic limestone ridges near Manorhamilton. Lough Allen, the first lake on the Shannon, virtually bisects the county, and provides most of its recreational attractions in the form of boating and fishing. Carrick-on-Shannon, the county town, is now a well-established cruise-boat centre. Leitrim has few significant historic sights.

Sligo, on the other hand, is rich in history, prehistory and mythology, with ancient burial places and cairns. The distinctive shapes of Benbulben and Knocknarea loom above the town, redolent of antique Celtic legends. The poet W B Yeats has strong links with the county, the scene of his childhood and his last resting place. The landscapes and myths of Sligo weave throughout his best work.

The very Irish Errigal Mountain looms above the white marble church of Dunlewy, County Donegal

197

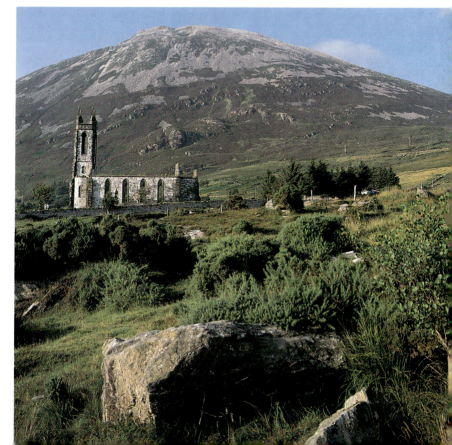

The *Annals of the Four Masters*
During the troubled 17th century a Franciscan monk, Michael O'Cleary, and three lay Gaelic scholars wrote these chronicles of Irish history and mythology. The *Annals* cover the period from before the Flood to the year 1616, and are an important record of Ireland's Celtic heritage. They are now housed in the National Library in Dublin, where facsimiles of the originals are on display.

One of the crafts demonstrated at the Donegal Craft Village is the production of tweed

► ▌ **Ardara**　　　　　*194D2*

Knitwear and tweed are the main concerns of this small town at the head of a deep sea-lough. Outlets vie with each other in the main street, but visitors can, if they prefer, head for any one of half a dozen or so factory shops where you can watch the manufacturing process in action and probably visit a bar or tea-shop at the same time. Prices are generally cheaper here than in high-street retailers. The annual Weavers' Fair in midsummer is a popular local festival with plenty of traditional music and good 'crack'. A heritage centre has recently been set up in the old law courts. The Church of the Holy Family has a fine stained-glass rose window by the well-known artist Evie Hone.

► ► **Carrowkeel, Carrowmore**
　　　　　and Creevykeel　　　　　*194B2*

These confusingly named places are three of the most interesting and important prehistoric sites in the northwestern region. **Carrowkeel**►, in the Bricklieve hills, is an ancient cemetery of circular mounds dating from the late Stone Age (2500–2000BC). There are some splendid views from the exposed hilltop site. **Carrowmore**►► near Sligo is the largest group of megalithic monuments in the whole of the British Isles, containing about 60 tombs, stone circles, dolmens and other antiquities, the earliest of which are alleged to predate the famous passage-grave at Newgrange (see pages 108–9) by about 700 years. Many have been damaged or removed, and incredibly, in 1983, plans were drawn up – and thankfully abandoned – to turn the site into a rubbish tip. **Creevykeel**► near Mullaghmore is a fine example of a neolithic court-tomb dating from about 3000BC, with a double burial chamber surrounded by a wedge-shaped mound of stone. Polished stone axes, worked flints and some bronze Celtic artefacts found here are now in the National Museum in Dublin.

► ▌ **Donegal**　　　　　*194C2*

Surprisingly, Donegal is not the county town of County Donegal (an honour granted to the somewhat unprepossessing town of Letterkenny), but it is nevertheless an attractive and strategic base for exploring the Northwest and, more especially, for shopping. Its main store, Magee's (see panel), is one of the best-known places to buy the regional speciality, Donegal tweed. A short way out of town, on the southern side, a collection of workshops produces a variety of high-quality crafts – jewellery, handweaving, ceramics, batik and crystal (look for signs

199

*The Diamond,
Donegal Town*

indicating the Donegal Craft Village, on the main N15 from Ballyshannon). Several other factory shops can be visited in the area, including those at Ardara (see page 198). **Ballyshannon**, a garrison town to the south, specialises in the region's brand of china, known as Parian ware (because it resembles the clear, white Greek marble from the island of Paros). The **Donegal Parian China Factory▶** and visitor centre stand on the Sligo road. On the Ballyshannon–Belleek road is Celtic Weave China, producing basketware rather similar to the traditional Belleek Parian china produced over the border into Northern Ireland (tours of the factory are free).

Donegal (*Dún na nGall*) means 'fort of the foreigners', a reference to its history as a Viking stronghold. After the Vikings left, the town became the headquarters of Tír Chonaill, the territory of the O'Donnell clan. 'Red Hugh' O'Donnell built a fortress and a Dominican abbey here in the 15th century. Early in the 17th century the Gaelic chieftains left Ireland in the exodus known as the Flight of the Earls (see page 34–5), and their lands and castles were appropriated by English and Scottish settlers. Sir Basil Brooke took over Donegal Castle in 1610 and, in the style of the time, enlarged it to a comfortable, if well-defended, Jacobean home with mullioned windows and imposing fireplaces. Today the castle remains are Donegal's most interesting sight. Sir Basil set about making his mark on the town in other ways too, and Donegal displays typical characteristics of Ulster planning, including a classic Diamond (actually a triangular 'square') in the centre, where a monument stands to the Four Masters (see panel). To the south of town is a lovely stretch of coastline where several rivers flow into Donegal Bay. Here the sun sets amid a maze of tranquil islets and sheltered creeks. St Ernan's Island, reached by a causeway and with an excellent hotel, is one of the best places to enjoy this scenery.

Magee's
This large department store on the north side of the Diamond is an Irish legend, still run by the family who established it in 1866 (the firm has passed to cousins of the original Magee's, called Temple). In the late 19th century, handwoven Donegal tweed was produced on wooden looms, some of which are still in use. Magee's is the only company still weaving and tailoring handwoven tweed in Donegal. High-quality men's clothing and suit fabrics are produced under the Magee's label for world-wide export, in light worsteds as well as the hard-wearing, traditional tweed in the soft colours of the Donegal landscape. Over 600 work in two factories using advanced technology, and visitors are welcome for a short, free tour during opening hours. The upstairs café makes a good place for a coffee or light lunch.

THE ATLANTIC COAST

Drive **The Atlantic Coast**

So complex is north Donegal's coastline that any tour can take many variations depending how much time you have. Best views are from minor roads rather than the N56, but skirting the peninsulas is time-consuming, and roads may be poorly surfaced.

The highlights of the journey are the sculpted rocks at **Crohy Head►►** near Dungloe, the fiery headland known as **Bloody Foreland►►** and the panoramic seascapes around **Horn Head►►** and **Rosguill►►**. If you still have time and a taste for this gorgeous scenery, **Fanad Head►** by the calm fjord of Lough Swilly, or the pastoral **Inishowen Peninsula►** from which Malin Head relays weather reports, are diverse and unspoilt. Inland, the beautiful and lonely routes through the **Glenveagh National Park►►** are well worth exploring (see page 203).

The weather in this part of Ireland is always uncertain, but its very unpredictability is exhilarating, and compensations include amazing sunsets and glorious rainbows. Facilities for tourists along the Donegal coast are limited but steadily increasing.

The section between Dungloe and Crolly is known as **The Rosses▶** (*Na Rosa* means 'the headlands'), a bleak, rocky and fragmented coastline, sometimes worn into stacks and arches. Inland, the terrain is poor, consisting of boulder-strewn bogland waterlogged by myriad tiny lakes and streams. If you have time, you may be able to take a summer boat excursion to **Aran Island▶** (also known as Aranmore, but not to be confused with the Aran Islands off Galway Bay) – a 25-minute trip from Burtonport. There's not much to see except bog and lakes, but there are beaches and quiet walks. **Tory Island▶** to the north is much less accessible, a treeless wilderness with 200 or so inhabitants who eke out their income from fishing with a school of naïve art. Boat trips leave from Bunbeg or Dunfanaghy, but you may be marooned in bad weather, and there is no accommodation on the island. Balor, Celtic god of darkness, is said to have lived here on the eastern cliffs.

Gweedore▶, the next peninsula, is scenically austere but densely populated, with new bungalows springing up along the coast. The most scenic stretch is **Bloody Foreland▶▶**, a mass of red granite that glows a brilliant colour at sunset. The sheer, quartzite cliffs of **Horn Head▶▶** provide terrific views and a windy ledge for thousands of seabirds. Sheep Haven is particularly attractive, and several side-turnings indicate popular holiday resorts. Marble Hill Strand has a fine beach. **Dunfanaghy** is the main resort, a gentle seaside village near an excellent sandy beach offering windsurfing and canoeing, and a blowhole called **McSwyne's Gun** which 'explodes' periodically in rough weather. Beyond Dunfanaghy look out for **Doe Castle▶**, a 15th-century fortress rebuilt in Victorian times. Views from the battlements overlook a wide expanse of Sheephaven Bay. Lackagh Bridge provides another vantage point. Inland, the barren, rocky landscape is scattered with lakes. The next outcrop is **Rosguill**, where an 11km circular tour called the **Atlantic Drive** is signed past dunes and beaches. Highlights of the **Fanad Peninsula** include the neat plantation villages of **Rathmelton** and **Rathmullan**, where Red Hugh O'Donnell, Earl of Tyrconnell, was treacherously lured on to an English merchant ship for a drink, whereupon he was seized and taken to Dublin gaol. On the **Inishowen peninsula▶▶**, don't miss the stone fort called **Grianán of Aileach**, **Fort Dunree** and **Malin Head** (see pages 206–7 for more details of all these).

The splendour of the Donegal coast

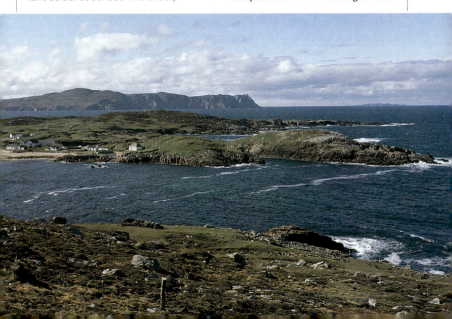

Derek Hill gave Glebe House to the nation in 1980. It makes a short but worthwhile detour from the Glenveagh National Park

Arthur Kingsley Porter
The castle of Glenveagh was once owned by the American art historian Arthur Kingsley Porter, a specialist in medieval sculpture. One day in 1939, he set off on a fishing trip in Donegal; later his boat was found abandoned on an island without a trace of its former occupant. Wagging tongues said he feigned his disappearance to escape an unhappy domestic life; claims that he had been spotted subsequently in the French port of Marseilles and as a Buddhist monk in the Himalayas have never been substantiated, and his real fate remains tantalisingly unknown.

One of more than a dozen early Christian stones in or near Glencolumbcille

▶▶ **Glebe House** *195D3*

This Regency building on Lough Gartan, a rectory dating from 1828, was for 30 years the home of the landscape and portrait artist, Derek Hill, who hailed originally from Southampton. He furnished the house with immense taste and care, using a great mix of styles and art from all over the world, including oriental and Middle Eastern tapestries and ceramics, Victoriana and original William Morris papers and textiles. Donegal folk art is also well represented and in the adjacent gallery are works by Picasso, Bonnard, Kokoschka, Renoir, Augustus John and other leading 19th- and 20th-century artists. A particularly interesting part of the collection contains works by the naïve school of painters on Tory Island, notably James Dixon. Temporary exhibitions are held during the summer opening period (end of May–end of September).

▶ **Glencolumbcille** *194C1*

The scenery is the great draw here; the drive along the north shore of Donegal Bay beyond the fishing port of Killybegs past the grand cliffs of Slieve League is thoroughly spectacular, through sheep-strewn moorland, heather and turf-cut bog to a boiling mass of rocks and sea stacks by the shore. A detour by the coast, for example to the picturesque Gaelic-speaking estuary village of Teelin, is especially recommended. Glencolumbcille, as its name suggests, has many associations with St Columba (Columbcille), the 6th-century saint from Lough Gartan who lived here for a time. On the saint's day (9 June) pilgrims conduct a barefoot procession around the area, pausing to pray at various antiquities such as standing stones and early Christian cross-slabs.

A more recent benefactor, as yet uncanonised, was the energetic priest, Father James MacDyer, who made strenuous efforts to alleviate the area's chronic poverty and unemployment. He was responsible for setting up a number of collective enterprises to provide work. The most high-profile of these is the **Folk Village**▶, on the edge of town, clearly signed. It's a small project using reconstructed cottages to simulate life in bygone Ireland. Three small dwellings are replicas of those typical in the area during the 1720s, 1820s and 1920s, suitably furnished with items of the period. The reception building sells craft souvenirs from all over Ireland, and the Shebeen café offers a variety of curious beverages, including some made from fuchsia or seaweed. A 'famine pot', filled daily with an unenticing brew of maize porridge during the hungry years, stands in the yard.

►► Glenveagh National Park   195D3

Ten thousand hectares of wild scenery make up this park of glaciated valleys and open moorland around Lough Beagh. Parts of the park are wooded with native oak and birch or imported rhododendron and spruce. The approach via Dunlewy at the foot of Mount Errigal gives some of the most spectacular views. Off the main road, an expedition to the Poisoned Glen is worth taking (so called because of a toxic variety of spurge which grows by the waterside). Beside Lough Beagh stands the estate of Glenveagh Castle, created during the mid-19th century by John George Adair who built the romantic castellated mansion in about 1870. He is remembered mostly for the harsh eviction of all his tenants after the murder of one of his estate managers in 1861. He later emigrated to the USA. His wife, however, left much more favourable impressions. She returned to Glenveagh after her husband's death and created the 11ha of glorious gardens around the castle.

During the Civil War the castle was occupied by the IRA and the Free State Army, then restored by a benevolent American owner who later transferred the land to the Irish National Parks Service. The estate contains the largest herd of red deer in Ireland, believed to number about 600 at present. A visitor centre is unobtrusively located on the estate (free minibus service to the castle in summer) with nature trails and an audio-visual show.

Tory Island
A story about the Tory islanders claims that in 1884 a British gunboat, *The Wasp*, was despatched to reprimand the inhabitants and to collect unpaid taxes. The islanders apparently called upon the forces of Balor, the one-eyed Celtic god of darkness, by circling the wishing stones in the centre of the island, and the gunboat promptly sank with all but six hands.

203

Glenveagh castle and gardens

Films set in Ireland

■ Irish cinema, like that in the UK, is in a fairly parlous state, and funding is always difficult. But it has a great stock of talent, Ireland's theatrical traditions raising many fine actors and some noteworthy directors, too. Some delightful low-budget films have been made wholly in Ireland in recent years, such as, *Eat the Peach*, set in Longford .....■

Top: John Wayne and Maureen O'Hara starred in The Quiet Man, *roughly a cross between* The Taming of the Shrew *and* Much Ado about Nothing, *and set in rural Ireland*

Ireland stars In many films, Ireland itself is the star of the big screen. Directors of many nationalities have used Irish locations for movies – even ones not set specifically in Ireland – the soft beauty of its landscapes overcoming the vagaries of its climate. Earliest films included *Life on the Great Southern and Western Railway* (1904) and *In the Days of St Patrick* (1919). Better remembered is Robert Flaherty's *Man of Aran,* made in 1934. This documentary of the harsh lifestyle endured on the Aran Islands has now become a classic, though it was not accurate in all respects – shark-fishing, for example, had not been customary on the Aran Islands for over 60 years. It is regularly shown in Kilronan, the largest community on Inishmore, during the summer tourist season. *The Dawn,* set in Killarney, was made in 1937 by Tom Cooper, a story of the War of Independence using highly effective location sequences. In 1947 a British film was made about the story of Captain Boycott (see panel on page 189), villain of the struggle for tenants' land rights during the 19th century, starring Cecil Parker and Stewart Granger.

Richard Harris in pensive mood in the immensely successful The Field. *Critics, however, could never quite decide whether the plot lived up to the dramatic scenery*

A stunning backdrop Several films of the 1950s used Irish backdrops, too. Most notable of these was probably *The Quiet Man,* a John Ford film of 1952 with John Wayne and Maureen O'Hara. Much of the filming was done around Cong, in County Galway, and some of the stars stayed at the local posh hotel, Ashford Castle. It's a Beatrice and Benedick love-story of an American who returns to Innisfree to find a bride, and good-naturedly perpetuates many Hollywood myths about the Irish. Yet another version of *Moby Dick* appeared in 1956, and the director, John Huston, chose the picturesque Cork town of Youghal for his harbour scenes. Rock Hudson is said to have sampled all the bars of Trim, County Meath, in 1955 during the filming of *Captain Lightfoot,* where the old Norman bridge played a leading role.

The National Film Studios were established at Ardmore in 1975, though lack of capital made this indigenous enterprise still largely dependent on foreign investment.

Films set in Ireland

Only John Boorman's production *Excalibur* (both produced and financed in Ireland) could be descibed as an
'Irish film' of the thirty or so films made there between
1975 and 1980. Stanley Kubrick used Caher Castle,
Tipperary, and Huntington Castle, in County Carlow, for
Barry Lyndon, a gorgeously photographed, if rather static,
version of Thackeray's tale about an Irish adventurer.

1980s and 1990s Many more recent films have featured
Irish locations. *Cal*, by Pat O'Connor, dealt sensitively
with IRA conflicts, *Far and Away* used the Temple Bar district of Dublin to represent 19th-century Boston, and
Educating Rita found Trinity College a more suitable icon
for an English university than either Oxford or Cambridge.
The Commitments and *My Left Foot* (the poignant story
of a severely handicapped writer played in Oscar-winning
style by Daniel Day-Lewis) were also set in Dublin. So
was *The Lonely Passion of Judith Hearne* (though Brian
Moore's novel was set in Belfast), a poignant tale of a
genteel spinster music teacher, played by Maggie Smith,
who falls disastrously in love with a gold-digging ne'er-do-
well – Bob Hoskins. *The Miracle*, directed by Neil Jordan
(recently more famous for *The Crying Game*, which also
has Irish connections) is set in Bray and Dublin, and is one
of his more 'Irish' films.

In sharp contrast, the lush location photography of *The
Field*, filmed in the Connemara village of Leenane, sears
itself on the viewer's retina; that sort of Irish green almost
hurts your eyes. Leenane was a natural choice for this
grim tale written by John B Keane, full of tiny fields and
looming hills. John Hurt and Richard Harris starred, and
once again, the film created a local legend, with many residents earning bit parts as extras. Many of the buildings
and pubs in the village proudly commemorate their
appearance in the film. *December Bride*, a spare tale of
non-conformist passion, is one of the few non-terrorist
films to be set north of the border.

Ryan's Daughter

The blockbuster in 1970 was
unquestionably David
Lean's emotive love story,
Ryan's Daughter. For this an
entire village was built on
the beautiful far western tip
of the Dingle peninsula, at
Dunquin. Few vestiges of
this remain today, but the
film still lives on in the imaginations of local people,
many of whom were used as
extras, and for a while had a
taste of Hollywood glamour.
The story, by Robert Bolt, is
set at the time of the Easter
Rising and tells of an Irish
woman who falls for a
British officer, to the horror
of all. The film had a star
cast (John Mills, Sarah
Miles, Robert Mitchum) and
had great box-office
success, if dismissed as
over-romanticised by the
critics. Certainly Lean
picked his set with care –
Dunquin is a magical place.

205

*Local extras stare
down the street of the
purpose-built village
in* Ryan's Daughter.
*One critic, Pauline
Kael, wrote of the
film, 'Gush made
respectable by mil-
lions of dollars taste-
fully wasted'*

NORTHWESTERN COUNTIES

Some believe that the Grianán of Aileach was designed for sun-worshipping rituals, with hundreds watching the goings-on from the terraces

▶▶ Grianán of Aileach 195D4

This remarkable circular fortress lies about 14km south of Buncrana, perched on a hilltop and reached by a small winding lane. Aerial photographs of it, such as the one below, show the stone ring-fort in an emerald pool of grassland amid scrubby tufts of brownish heather and gorse. The name means 'stone palace of the sun'. Similar *cashel* forts can be seen elsewhere in Ireland, such as Staigue Fort in County Kerry. Its precise age is disputed, some authorities dating it well before the Christian era (about 1700BC), others rather later. Its suspiciously neat appearance is due to enthusiastic restoration during the 1870s by Dr Walter Bernard, a Derry historian. The round enclosure measures about 23m across, with walls over 5m high and 4m thick. A single gate allows access to the interior, which contains four tiers of steps and various passages or storage places. It was recorded by Ptolemy in the 2nd century AD and was used as a stronghold by the O'Neill kings for several centuries before its gradual destruction. If you are lucky enough to visit it on a fine day the views from this hilltop are amazing, stretching for huge distances over Derry, the Fanad and Inishowen peninsulas, and the Swilly estuary.

▶▶ Inishowen peninsula 195E4

Ireland's most northerly point lies in the Republic on this ragged triangular headland, not in Northern Ireland as most people would expect. Lough Foyle and Lough Swilly virtually isolate Inishowen from the rest of the county. The interior is a mix of low white farms and cottages huddling roped against the wind, and grand brown mountains rising toward Slieve Snaght. The scenic 160km route around the edge of Inishowen takes in Malin Head, castles, churches, High Crosses and pre-Christian antiquities. None of these are essential viewing, but the tour, which takes a full day, is a dramatic and varied drive.

Buncrana is the main centre, a popular holiday resort much favoured by inhabitants of Derry. Throughout the centuries it witnessed many clashes between English and Irish. Ireland's remote extremities were always feared (not without reason) as a potential Achilles' heel in English defences against invading Catholic forces from Spain or France, and any hints of disaffection were dealt with ruthlessly. In 1602 the O'Dohertys prepared to welcome a second Spanish armada here and a couple of centuries later Wolfe Tone was held in Buncrana Castle after his abortive rebellion in 1798. Buncrana also has a Vintage Car Museum.

Malin▶ is a 17th-century plantation village built around a green, its most striking feature a long bridge of stone arches. Malin Head relays weather reports from the fishing village of Ballyhillin, sheltered from the worst of the storms by the rocky promontory. Several minor historical sights – crosses, stone circles, etc. – are clustered around Carndonagh.

A premature conclusion
Because of its unexpectedly good acoustics, the stone hill-top fort of the Grianán of Aileach was chosen as the venue for an open-air concert by the New Irish Chamber Orchestra in the 1970s. A special wooden stage was erected for the orchestra, and all was going well until a persistent shower of rain forced the abandonment of the remaining programme. Appropriately enough, the piece being performed was Handel's Water Music.

▶   **Letterkenny**   *195D3*

Donegal's county town is now the main commercial centre of the Republic's northwest region and, as such, has several bustling shopping centres. It guards the lowest bridging point on the River Swilly, just before it widens into the scenic fjord known as Lough Swilly. There are few especially attractive views of this from the town itself, however, which is on the whole not all that interesting. Its main claims to fame are the longest main street in Ireland (one end of which boasts a Sinn Fein office) and the lofty spire of the Victorian neo-Gothic St Eunan's Cathedral which has a handsome altar of Carrara marble and rich stained glass. Look for the Four Masters (see page 198) carved on the pulpit. The Irish patriot Wolfe Tone was captured in Letterkenny in 1798 after his foiled invasion with French allies, and taken to Dublin under heavy guard. The county museum is housed in the old workhouse. Letterkenny makes a useful base for exploring inland Donegal, including the Blue Stack Mountains and the Glenveagh National Park.

St Eunan's Cathedral, Letterkenny, was built by Donegal masons using Donegal sandstone

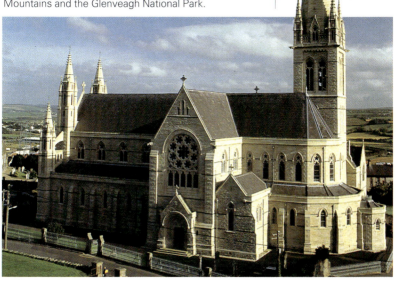

The Lake Isle of Innisfree
I will arise and go now,
    and go to Innisfree,
And a small cabin build
    there of clays and wattles
    made:
Nine bean-rows will I have
    there, a hive for the
    honey-bee,
And live alone in the bee-
    loud glade.

W B Yeats (1865–1939)

Parke's Castle stands on the shores of Lough Gill, considered one of Ireland's most picturesque loughs. About 8km long, Lough Gill resembles a smaller version of the Lakes of Killarney

▶ **Lough Gartan**   195D3

Donegal's local saint, Columba (or Colmcille/Columbcille in Irish), was born by the beautiful shores of Lough Gartan in AD521. A modern building on the eastern shore houses the **Colmcille Heritage Centre**▶, which outlines the saint's life (see page 114) and the rise of Christianity in Ireland. An interesting feature is an exhibition on the preparation of illuminated manuscripts, using parchment and natural pigments. At the saint's alleged birthplace are two sacred stones around which various superstitions have spread. Pregnant women pray at the Natal Stone to ensure a safe delivery, while the Stone of Loneliness warded off the anguish of homesickness and was a popular place of pilgrimage for those about to emigrate.

▶▶ **Parke's Castle**   194B2

A fortified manor house with an interestingly chequered history stands by the calm waters of Lough Gill. Built in 1609 by an Ulster settler, Captain Robert Parke, it occupies the site of a much earlier tower-house belonging to the O'Rourke clan, rulers of the kingdom of Breffni. The last unfortunate O'Rourke laird sheltered a shipwrecked armada officer and was executed at Tyburn, London, for treason. Features of the medieval structure can be seen in the later house. Recently it has been sensitively restored using original materials and local craftsmanship, and now represents a fascinating piece of research and reconstruction. Its witch-hat turrets face the mirror-like lake, and there are splendid views from its ramparts. Beyond the outer defences near the water's edge lies a little beehive hut of stone. This is a sweat-house, or early Irish sauna, used to alleviate various ailments. Exhibitions and an audio-visual show about the castle and many local places of interest, including Sligo's impressive range of antiquities, can be seen inside; free guided tours are available. From the jetty you can take a boat around Lough Gill, calling at the Yeatsian island of Innisfree (see panel).

*The eerie light of
dawn on Lough Gill*

▶ **Rathmelton** 195D3

This dignified plantation town is all stately warehouses and seemly Georgian buildings on a salmon river. It was built by Sir William Stewart for settlers during the early 17th century. The River Leannan was once an important waterway and in earlier times Rathmelton was a significant port exporting grain, salmon, butter and linen (a more unusual product was iodine, made from local seaweed). A new heritage centre in the former Presbyterian meeting house displays information both on the town's history and on the founding of American Presbyterianism.

*An exhibit from the
Flight of the Earls
Heritage Centre,
Rathmullan*

▶ **Rathmullan** 195D3

The eastern side of the Fanad peninsula, overlooking the fjord-like scenery of Lough Swilly, is the most appealing drive, and this fortified harbour village is one of the most interesting places to visit. Before the battery was constructed by the English to ward off Napoleonic attacks, Rathmullan figured twice in Irish history. First, it was the place where 'Red Hugh' O'Donnell, the Ulster chieftain, was treacherously lured on board a disguised merchant ship for a convivial drink, only to find himself in chains on his way to Dublin Castle, where he languished for six years. Twenty years later, the Earls of Tyrone and of Tyrconnell finally left Ireland from Rathmullan in the incident known as the Flight of the Earls (see pages 34–5). Initially they had hopes of raising support against the English from Spanish allies, but their plans came to nothing and they died in exile, leaving their great estates and castles to be occupied by Ulster settlers. A heritage centre in the old fort recounts the history of this period. Another of Rathmullan's attractions is a country house hotel, Rathmullan House (see Hotels and Restaurants, page 276), one of Donegal's most comfortable bases, with a good restaurant.

*The Dominican
Friary, more usually
known as Sligo
Abbey*

The Battle of the Books
A tragic storm in a teacup – but an important principle of copyright – lies at the heart of this curious incident, which took place at Cooldrumman, north of Sligo. In AD561 St Columba borrowed a psalter from St Finian and surreptitiously copied it. When St Finian found out he angrily demanded the copy. St Columba refused and the pair went to arbitration at the court of the High King, Diarmuid. He decided in favour of St Finian, with the famous judgement, 'To every cow its calf; to every book its copy.' St Columba refused to accept the ruling and raised an army against St Finian in which over 3,000 men were killed. St Columba was the victor, but, stricken with remorse, he went to live in exile in Iona off the Scottish coast, where he died in 597.

*The eye-catching
monument to W B
Yeats, winner of the
Nobel Prize for
Literature in 1923, in
Sligo Town*

► ▬▬ **Sligo**   *194B2*

Sligo is one of the largest towns in the Northwest, a lively market town and centre for music pubs and eating places, designed more for its own 18,000 inhabitants than for tourists. Colourful houses stand alongside the River Garavogue which runs through the centre, and the town still has many old quarters and shops of great character. Its literary associations give it a cultural cachet and it now receives a great annual influx of scholars and students on the Yeats trail, especially during August when a Yeats summer school is held.

Sligo was sacked by the Vikings in 807 and, situated as it is on the fringes of Connaught and Ulster, later became a key location for warring clans. The Anglo-Norman Fitzgeralds held sway in the 13th century when the castle (now vanished) and abbey were built. Later the O'Conors and O'Donnells fought for supremacy, and in Cromwellian times the town was one of the last Jacobite strongholds. During the Famine the population fell drastically and massive emigration occurred.

Sligo's main sights are its 13th-century Dominican abbey, sacked in 1641, and its **museum and art gallery**► which houses many documents relating to W B Yeats, together with paintings by his brother, Jack. The town has two cathedrals, the Church of Ireland St John's, designed by Richard Castle in 1730, and the 19th-century Catholic cathedral. Hargadon's pub is a local institution. It recently deigned to allow women inside, but otherwise firmly retains its old-world character and décor, with tiny dark booths and swivelling windows round which noggins could be passed with ease.

Outside the town loom the great hulks of Benbulben (525m) and Knocknarea (330m), like upturned ships. Both hills can be climbed, but can be treacherous in mist because of the deep fissures in the rain-eroded limestone. Benbulben is the legendary death-site of Diarmuid who eloped with Gráinne. Knocknarea to the southwest is supposed to be the burial place of the warrior Queen Maeve (though she died elsewhere), and is surmounted by a massive cairn of 40,000 tonnes of rock.

YEATS COUNTRY

Drive Yeats Country and Benbulben

You're never far from **Benbulben** on this tour, the mountain that so inspired Yeats. The coast is quiet and much broken; inland are lakes and pastures.

This area is called 'Yeats Country' as the poet passed much of his childhood and was eventually buried here, though his adult life was largely spent in Dublin, and in Galway at Thoor Ballylee or at Coole Park. Above Sligo Town the curious hulk of Benbulben looms like a capsized ship, its flat limestone top scored by erosion. Off the N15 north of Sligo is **Drumcliff** churchyard, where Yeats's tomb lies. Minor roads from the N15 lead past the headland of **Rosses Point▶**. Further up, follow the coastal turning to **Lissadell House▶** (open June–mid-September), 19th-century home of the Gore-Booth family. Sisters Eva Gore-Booth and Constance Markie-wicz (see page 66), friends of Yeats,

took part in the Easter Rising. The house, in need of restoration, is surrounded by rampant vegetation. On the promontory of **Mullaghmore** is Classie Bawn (private), former home of Lord Mountbatten who was killed on his boat by the IRA in 1979.

From the resort of **Bundoran▶** a signed leisure drive to Manorhamilton takes you past typical limestone ridge scenery. From here, go west around the north shore of **Glencar Lough,** where a waterfall drops 10m through ferny rocks to a pool (in Yeats's poem *The Stolen Child*). Return to Sligo, then strike east for a circuit of **Lough Gill▶▶**, famous for the lake-isle, Innisfree. Summer cruises are available from Sligo, Dromahair or Parke's Castle (see page 208). Other sites on the lough are the ruined Creevelea Friary, and the Deerpark Monument, a series of stone burial chambers dating from about 3500BC.

Victorian homage to the art of drinking: the Crown Liquor Saloon in Belfast

Map

Rathlin Island
North Channel
Carrick-a-Rede
Rope Bridge Fair Head
Ballycastle
Armoy
Cushendall *Red Bay*
Garron Point
Glens of Antrim
unloy Carnlough
Glenarm
M2 Broughshane
Ballymena *Ballygalley Head*
oghill Moorfields **Larne**
Island Magee
A N T R I M
andalstown **Ballyclare** Ballynure Ballycarry
M22 M2 **Whitehead**
Antrim Templepatrick **Carrickfergus**
Belfast
International **Newtownabbey** Ulster Folk &
Airport Transport Museum **Bangor**
Crumlin M5 Holywood
BELFAST City **Donaghadee**
Glenavy Airport **Newtownards**
Dunmurry Mount Stewart
House NT
Comber Ballywalter
Lisburn Carryduff Greyabbey
Maze Ballygowan
Lurgan Hillsborough Saintfield *Strangford Lough*
Rowallane Portavogie
Dromore Ballynahinch Killyleagh
tford **Castle** Portaferry
Banbridge **Ward NT** Strangford
Loughbrickland D O W N **Downpatrick**
Clough
Castlewellan Ardglass
Rathfriland Dundrum Killough
Hilltown *St John's Point*
Newry **Newcastle**
852m ▲
Slieve Donard
Warrenpoint *M t s* *Mourne*
Rostrevor Annalong
neath
arlingford **Kilkeel**
Greencastle
ooley
Pen
4 5

North Channel

0 10 20 30 km
0 10 20 miles

Northern Ireland The Troubles are inevitably a factor in any decision to visit Northern Ireland. If this is your first trip to the province, you may question the wisdom of going. The ghastly incidents that periodically hit the headlines suggest that sectarian violence and random slaughter are rife. This isn't so. Northern Ireland is, most of the time, in most places, as tranquil as anywhere in the South – and that makes it pretty quiet. Statistically, tourists are much less likely to suffer misadventure than in many other holiday locations; street crime rates are low, personal violence rare. This doesn't mean you shouldn't keep your wits about you, particularly in sensitive zones such as Derry, Armagh, Newry and at any checkpoint. Cars

*The relief of Derry,
see panel on page 224*

Crossing the border
Don't pick up hitchhikers
near the border. Before
driving in Northern Ireland,
check your insurance. If
you have hired a car in the
Republic you must inform
the company when you
collect the car that you in-
tend travelling in the North
(and vice versa). Major
rental companies are fully
covered for all Ireland and
make no extra charge.
   In places the transition
from the Republic to the
North is barely noticeable.
An unmanned or sleepy
check-point, a wave of a
hand and you're through.
At others, the border is a
mass of barbed wire, con-
crete bunkers, automatic
barriers and traffic-lights.
Be ready to stop, state
your destination and pro-
duce a passport or driving-
licence. Security forces on
both sides are unfailingly
courteous to bona fide
travellers and traffic is
rarely delayed for long.

should be parked carefully in official car-parks or in pay-
and-display areas. Some towns and cities have signed
control zones where vehicles must not be left unattended, and illegal parking may cause a security alert. Outside
the trouble spots, Northern Ireland feels, and is, entirely
peaceful. Wherever they come from, visitors receive a
warm welcome. Local people are anxious to show outsiders the good side of the province and, whether
Catholic or Protestant, are extraordinarily hospitable.
Most of them are on perfectly good terms with their
neighbours of whatever creed and it is often baffling to
imagine where the tension lies. The vast majority of people are simply interested in getting on with their lives in
peace.

Scottish connections The closeness of Scotland to
Ulster (a mere 21km at its narrowest point) has always
influenced the province strongly, even before the plantation years (see pages 34–5). Waves of invaders made the
short sea crossing, most notably Edward Bruce, brother
of the famous Scottish leader, Robert, who first arrived at
Carrickfergus with his 'gallowglasses' (mercenaries) in
1315. Settlement hasn't always been one-way: during the
4th and 5th centuries AD, Irish Celts made their way to various westerly parts of Britain. But the people who
returned during the reign of James I were mostly Scottish
Presbyterians – tough, industrious and determined to the
point of intransigence. Northern Ireland has been supported since the plantation years by massive injections of
funds from Britain, but its economic success could not
have been achieved without the settlers' Protestant work
ethic and resourcefulness. These characteristics show in
the many pioneers who left Ulster to seek their fortune in

the New World. The 'Scotch-Irish' who emigrated to the USA have had an influence out of all proportion to their numbers. Two recent and memorable US presidents (John Kennedy and Ronald Reagan) were of Republican Irish stock, but about a dozen former presidents were of Ulster Scottish descent. Theodore Roosevelt was one of these and his mother described her Antrim forebears in these telling terms: 'grim, stern people… relentless, revengeful, suspicious… also upright, resolute and fearless, loyal to their friends and devoted to their country'.

Town and country The scenery of Northern Ireland is its primary attraction and most tourism is concentrated in a few clearly defined rural areas: the Mountains of Mourne; the Glens of Antrim; the Causeway Coast; and the Lakes of Fermanagh. Other less well-known areas such as Lough Neagh and the wild Sperrin Mountains are becoming more popular destinations for walking, fishing, etc., and several forest parks have been created. The Ulster Way is one of Ireland's best long-distance footpaths, leading through the province's most scenic landscapes in all six counties. But it is the cities of the North, especially Belfast and Derry, that give a complete picture of the province and these cannot be ignored if you want to see more than the surface prettiness.

The North is particularly strong on museums and has a fine collection of stately homes and gardens (its Georgian houses are generally better preserved than in the Republic). In many ways Northern Ireland's landscapes are similar to the Republic's, but the North is more intensively industrialised (in parts) and the towns and villages seem generally more prosperous and tidy.

Checkpoints aside, it's easy to get around. Roads are generally good and petrol is quite a bit cheaper than in the South; it is always worth nipping over the border to fill up your tank if you are passing nearby. Except very close to the border, Irish *punts* are not accepted and you must use British currency. Telephones and the postal system are the same as in the rest of the UK.

Approved crossings
Officially, border crossings must be on approved roads where there are checkpoints. There are about 20, all well marked, so no long detours are needed. Many minor roads between the North and the Republic are blocked for security reasons; others are passable, but motorists using them can be subject to penalties. The situation changes according to circumstances and, during an alert, a checkpoint may be closed without notice.

The Red Hand of Ulster
A grisly myth explains the presence of a hand on Ulster's coat of arms. Two great warriors raced each other to the shores of Ulster; whoever touched land first would be king. Neck and neck they sped, until at the last moment one pulled ahead. The other, desperate to win, struck off his hand with his sword and hurled it ashore, so claiming victory. The red hand still stands on the province's coat of arms, a fittingly gory symbol.

215

The Giant's Causeway

BELFAST

▶ **Belfast**   *213B4*

Since Partition, Belfast has been the official capital of Northern Ireland. It is not the seat of government, however; Northern Ireland has been ruled directly from Westminster since 1972 and the grandiose wedding-cake of Stormont, the former Northern Ireland Parliament building, is now administrative offices. With a population of around 360,000, Belfast is much smaller than Dublin and a large exodus of the younger middle-classes during the past two decades to dormitory towns and suburbs has unbalanced the city centre's demography, though it is still a transient home for over 8,000 university students. Apart from its two best museums, none of its sights is hugely compelling, but there is certainly plenty to do for a day or two, and the city has a highly distinctive atmosphere.

Few people unfamiliar with the city will immediately warm to the prospect of a stay here. Religious bigotry, sectarian violence and deliberately high-profile security measures give the impression to outsiders that Northern Ireland's capital is a war-zone. Like many things in Ireland, however, the reality is a surprise. If anything, Belfast is less of a risk for the average visitor than Dublin. The inhabitants have adjusted to their abnormal situation and doggedly refuse to let it affect their lives significantly. Security checks and searches are endured with the stoicism that prevailed during World War II, when Belfast's dockyard targets caused many civilian casualties. Bombs and bomb-threats may periodically damage or close buildings, but the show goes on. Indeed, Belfast hosts one of Britain's liveliest and most acclaimed arts festivals at Queen's University each November, as well as an impressive year-round series of concerts, exhibitions, opera and drama. Restaurants along its Golden Mile bustle; sports events flourish.

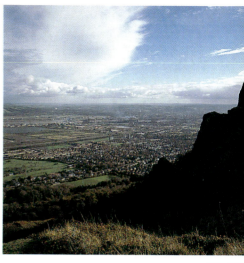

The great engineering works that once made Belfast so prosperous are in sad decline and unemployment figures in the province are among the highest in the UK. Its earliest industries included rope-making and linen, cotton spinning and printing. In 1859 the UK's largest shipyards were established here by the Yorkshire engineer Edward Harland and a marine draughtsman from Hamburg,

Like Dublin, Belfast lies close to hills, in this instance Cave Hill, north of the city

217

The welcome at Larry's Bar is warmer than the ghostly images might imply

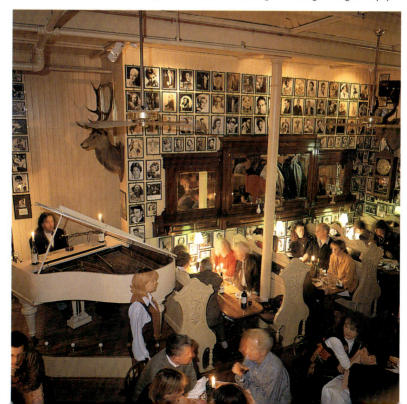

Gustav Wilhelm Wolff. Two vast yellow cranes with the initials 'H & W' painted on them still dominate the dockland skyline as powerfully as any cathedral and are affectionately known as Samson and Goliath. The recent cutbacks in these mighty shipyards was a great psychological blow to the city, as well as an economic one. Other firms closely associated with Belfast are Shorts, the aircraft manufacturers, and Gallahers, the tobacco giant.

Belfast's setting is often praised more than the city itself. The name derives from the Gaelic *beal feirste*, meaning 'mouth of the sandy ford', and Belfast stands proudly at the head of a deep sea-lough surrounded by unspoilt hills, the River Lagan cutting through its heart. Belfast has abundant parks and open spaces, all documented by the tourist authorities (pick up leaflets in their office on North Street). Within minutes fast roads can take you beyond the city to scenic areas like the Ards Peninsula or Strangford Lough; it is a slightly longer journey to the Mountains of Mourne or the Glens of Antrim.

The city's commercial centre and university area lie close to the river on its western side; prosperous residential districts are to the east and south. On the far west of town, beyond the dividing pale of the Westlink motorway, are the notorious sectarian ghettos that have given the

Belfast's City Hall was designed by a certain Crumwell Thomas in 1906; the staircase in the Entrance Hall is lit by seven stained-glass windows depicting scenes from the city's history

city its worst reputation. The overcrowded, run-down areas of Ballymurphy, Falls and Shankill are depressing and can easily be avoided. To some, however, they are oddly fascinating, and intrepid visitors venture there to see their vivid and sometimes highly artistic displays of street mural propaganda (both Catholic and Protestant varieties, incidentally, may be carried out by the same artist!)'. There are slight risks; in 1992 a tourist visiting her family was killed by a stray sniper's bullet. If you want to visit these areas, you can take one of the black cabs which assemble in ranks at the edge of the city centre, plying strictly within either Catholic or Protestant territory.

The City Hall, in the background, is built around a central quadrangle

The *Girona*

Legend has it that one of the strange formations along the Causeway Coast confused the sailors of the Spanish Armada, fleeing after their defeat, who believed it to be Dunluce Castle (3km west). The galleass *Girona* was wrecked in 1588 at Port-na-Spaniagh with all but five hands – a loss of about 1,300 lives. Artefacts salvaged from the ship in 1967 are now on show at Belfast's excellent Ulster Museum, including cannon, rings, coins and a quaint, gold salamander ornament set with rubies.

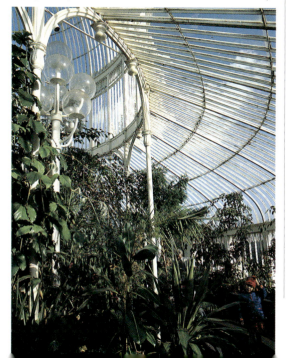

The Palm House at Belfast's Botanic Gardens is one of the oldest examples of a structure made of cast iron and curved glass, dating from 1839–52

NORTHERN IRELAND

To see the Catholic Falls area (Andersonstown), pick up a cab at Castle Street; to visit Shankill, go to North Street. Bear in mind that your fare could possibly be a donation towards some terrorist organisation, to which the driver may (or may not) belong. On the Falls route you will pass the notorious Divis Flats, some of the saddest housing in Europe, and St Peter's Catholic Cathedral in 19th-century Gothic. The Peace Line is a barricade of iron dividing Protestant and Catholic areas. On the Protestant side, murals can be seen all along the Shankill and Donegall roads, the most famous image being King William on a white steed, rearing from the waters of the Boyne.

Main sights

Belfast is essentially a Victorian city, modelled on those robust mercantile centres like Liverpool and Manchester across the water. The late John Betjeman found much to admire in the city's civic architecture, notably its **Custom House▶** near the docks (not open to the public), several palatial bank buildings near the High Street, and the **City Hall▶▶** on Donegall Square, a flamboyant block of white Portland limestone. Inside, the City Hall contains many interesting features and rich decorations of marble and glass – guided tours are available on Wednesday mornings. Donegall Square contains gardens, statues and several other noteworthy buildings, such as the **Linen Hall Library▶**, with a fine collection of volumes in its old-fashioned interior. The Albert Memorial Clock, on Victoria Street, was built in 1865 by William Barre, and depicts Prince Albert in the robes of the Order of the Garter. The tower now leans slightly from the vertical.

Also in the city centre (large parts of which are pedestrianised) is **St Anne's Cathedral▶**, on Donegall Street.

220

The Grand Opera House had fallen into such disrepair that it closed in 1971, eventually reopening in 1980 after five years of restoration. Since then it has sadly fallen victim to terrorist bombs, being badly damaged in both 1991 and 1993

Belfast's Anglican cathedral is austere neo-Romanesque, enlivened inside by mosaics and a floor made of stone from all parts of Ireland. Sir Edward Carson, architect of Partition, is buried here. **St Malachy's►►**, in Alfred Street, was built in 1844, the plainish red-brick exterior of this Roman Catholic church disguising a glorious inner riot of plasterwork in Strawberry Hill Gothic style. **Sinclair Seamen's Church►** in dockland is another of Belfast's most striking churches, with a jaunty nautical theme. The oval **1st Presbyterian Church►**, opened in 1783, has an unusual interior designed by Roger Mulholland. For a truly unforgettable flavour of Belfast, head for the Martyrs' Memorial Free Presbyterian Church, also east of the river, where the Reverend Ian Paisley presides each Sunday, denouncing the Church of Rome and all its works.

Belfast has some extremely florid architecture, particularly at the start of its Golden Mile, stretching along Great Victoria Street towards the university. The **Crown Liquor Saloon►** is a splendidly ornate, gaslit Victorian pub now in the care of the National Trust, all coloured marbles, tiles, mirrors and panelled booths. Good Irish food is served, but lunchtimes can be busy. The **Grand Opera House►►** is a beautiful Victorian theatre, badly damaged in bomb attacks in 1991 and 1993. It contains a typically lavish auditorium and presents performances of many kinds. Of the same era, but in a different style, is **Queen's University►** in University Road. The main building boasts an impressive façade of Tudor Gothic red brick and stone mullions. Close by are the **Botanic Gardens►** in Stranmillis Road, an oasis of lawns and gardens sloping to the river. Its two main structures are the **Palm House►** and the **Tropical Ravine House►**.

In the grounds of the Botanic Gardens is a modern building housing what is certainly one of Ireland's best museums. The **Ulster Museum►►►** has a varied and extensive collection, though anything but wearisome.

Queen's University, with its Tudor-style building, was founded in 1849

Belfast's tropical jungle is to be found at the Botanic Gardens, south of the city

NORTHERN IRELAND

222

Belfast Castle (completed in 1870) was built in the style of Balmoral, the Queen's Scottish residence, and designed by W H Lynn

Flamingos cope with unfamiliar weather at Belfast Zoo

Schoolchildren delight in its dinosaurs; others may prefer its sparkling minerals or exquisite ceramics. The sections devoted to Belfast's industrial heritage are excellent, as is its clear and unpartisan summary of Ulster's history. One of its most popular sections contains treasures and artefacts from the Spanish Armada ship, *Girona*, wrecked on the Causeway Coast. It has a fine collection of paintings, too, including some interesting 18th-century representations of the Giant's Causeway by Susanna Drury.

Outside the city centre lie several other sights. **Belfast Castle►**, on the lower slopes of Cave Hill, is some way north, a Victorian Scottish baronial house, with attractive gardens and fine views of the harbour area. Belfast's **zoo►** is pleasantly set in former gardens near the castle and is just one of many parks and open spaces in and near the city boundaries. **Lagan Valley Park►** is one of the largest of these, with 16km of towpaths and locks; near by is a prehistoric earthwork called **The Giant's Ring►**. On the A20, 7km east, is **Stormont►**, a grand, classical building, once housing the Northern Ireland Parliament and now serving as administrative offices. It stands proudly at the top of a sweeping drive through neat parkland. The Scottish baronial Stormont Castle near by contains the office of the Northern Ireland Secretary of State. Both can be viewed only from outside for obvious reasons. See page 235 for details of Ulster's Folk and Transport Museum in Cultra, on the Bangor road.

If you want to stay in Belfast, the best area to head for is the university area to the south of the centre. In the seemly residential streets of Stranmillis, Malone and Botanic are a number of moderately priced guesthouses – safe, clean and respectable (see Hotels and Restaurants, pages 269–83, for some of the best). Several well-known hotels in the central areas have been terrorist targets in recent years.

►► Armagh   212B3

Armagh has often been the scene of battle, and today, this close to the border, the British Army's presence is noticeable. County Armagh is predominantly Catholic, especially in the South, but the city itself is a Protestant stronghold. The two rival cathedrals, both dedicated to St Patrick, scowl at each other from two of Armagh's seven small hills. The Protestant one sadly has to be kept locked for security reasons, but instructions for obtaining the key are posted on the door. Solid, squat and square, it is mostly 19th century in perpendicular Gothic style, with a fringe of grotesque heads around its otherwise plain exterior. It is the burial place of Brian Ború, the warlike king who finally drove the Vikings out of Ireland. The Roman Catholic cathedral, completed in 1873, stands proudly twin-spired at the top of a long flight of steps. The interior is astonishingly ornate – walls and roof covered with rich mosaics of saints and angels. The Mall, a broad, tree-lined square, is surrounded by some of Armagh's finest Georgian buildings, including the courthouse and the Royal Irish Fusiliers and County Museums. Armagh's most unusual sights are the 18th-century **Observatory**► and neighbouring **Planetarium**►►, where computer displays and models track down heavenly bodies. **Navan Fort**, now just a huge mound to the west, was the ancient palace of Queen Macha, a site which rivalled Tara, and the court of Ulster's chivalrous Red Branch Knights.

223

There are few remaining signs of Eamhain (or palace of) Macha, at Navan Fort, County Armagh. The site is thought to be 4,000–5,000 years old, and is associated with Cuchulainn, the Ulster hero (see page 28 for more details of his exploits)

► Carrickfergus   213C4

The main landmark of this small seaside town is its vast Norman **castle**►►, still mostly intact, on a basalt ledge by the shore. Displays of its history are housed inside and today the castle plays amiably to the gallery by hosting medieval banquets and a Lughnasa festival in August. William of Orange entered Ireland via these shores in 1690 and a Williamite trail can be followed round the town. Just to the east is the Andrew Jackson Centre – an 18th-century cottage with re-created period interiors and displays relating to the 7th US president whose parents lived near by.

Bullets, or road bowls
This ancient game is played along the local roads near Armagh (a version of it can also be seen in Schull, County Cork). A heavy iron ball, about the size of cricket ball, is hurled along the lanes and the aim is to reach the end of the winding 4km course in the fewest number of throws. Betting is fierce. Ask for details in local pubs if you want to see a game – most take place on Sunday afternoons. The first Sunday in August is championship day.

The fine, underrated city of Derry

The siege of Derry
Catholic James II expected a welcome from Derry's governor when his troops arrived in 1688, but 13 Protestant apprentices, fearing reprisals, stole the city's keys and locked the gates against the Jacobite forces. Supporters of William III, who had deposed James II as King of England, joined the apprentices' cause and flocked into the city. They remained under siege for 105 days, the longest siege in British history, during which time the population was reduced to eating a grisly diet of rotting horse-meat, dogs and rats. Over 7,000 of the 30,000 crammed within Derry's walls died from starvation and disease. Yet when offered the chance to capitulate, the defenders merely raised a crimson standard signifying 'No Surrender' – which has since become the rallying cry of the Protestant Unionist cause. The courage of the apprentice boys is still celebrated in Loyalist marches. Eventually William's soldiers raised the siege and James's troops retreated.

▶▶ **Derry**   *212D2*

Formerly 'Londonderry', alluding to James I's gift of the city to the livery companies of London, Derry is now renamed in terms less offensive to its mostly Catholic population. (The county, however, is still referred to as Londonderry.) Derry's notorious Bogside district has seen much unrest, for it is here that Catholic/Protestant tribalism is most sharply polarised. Catholics, unwillingly stranded right on the Republic's border, have suffered much discrimination under gerrymandered Protestant control, while Loyalists find it impossible to cast off their atavistic siege mentality. On a free-standing gable-end near the Bogside (once an IRA no-go area and the scene of 'Bloody Sunday', when 13 Catholic civilians were killed in 1972 during a civil rights march) are the giant words 'You are now entering Free Derry'. Protestants reply a few streets away with the defiant slogan 'No Surrender'.

For all its political ill-feelings, Derry is a fascinating city, retaining intact the **17th-century walls**▶▶ that have played such a significant role in its history. These sturdy ramparts, 8m high and up to 9m thick, have never been breached. Five of the cannons that defended the city during its long siege stand above Shipgate Quay. Derry still has a beleaguered air and some of its eight gates are impassable for security reasons. The Bishop Gate area overlooking the Protestant Fountain quarter is under particularly heavy surveillance, and you can no longer walk all round the walls. None the less the views of the lower city and its great modern bridge spanning the River Foyle are dramatic. Within the walls are an extraordinary little enclave of old-fashioned shops and bars, the Protestant cathedral of St Columb in 'Planters' Gothic' style and a typical Ulster central square known as the **Diamond**▶. A hopeful sign of constructive community spirit is the Derry Craft Village where modern artisanry burgeons in a village-like complex, and a pleasant coffee shop called The Boston Tea Party provides an excuse for a sit-down.

▶ **Downpatrick**   *213B5*

In contrast to Derry, the market town of Down has lengthened its name, in honour of its most distinguished visitor, St Patrick (see page 226). Down Cathedral stands in the highest part of the town amid seemly Georgian buildings.

It is small, mostly 18th century and, perhaps surprisingly, is Anglican, not Catholic. Inside, the original Regency box pews have been preserved.

Not far down the hill is Downpatrick's other major sight, the **Down County Museum**►►, set in the local gaol. The **St Patrick Heritage Centre**►► is well worth seeing for a coherent version of what is known of the saint's life and times (film and exhibition) and there are good local history and wildlife sections. The old prison cells can also be visited. These grim, dark, cramped rooms once housed the leader of the United Irishmen, Thomas Russell, who was convicted and executed here in 1803 for his part in Robert Emmet's rebellion (see pages 38–9).

From Downpatrick the land-locked sea-inlet called **Strangford Lough**►► and the **Ards peninsula**►► can be explored. Both shore roads are attractive, especially the easterly one, but to reach it you must take the car ferry across the straits between Strangford and Portaferry, where the tides rush with great force. The lake is an important wildlife habitat with many unusual species. For more details about this remarkable ecosystem, call in at Portaferry's small **aquarium**► near the quayside, which is devoted to local marine life. At Strangford, on the western side of the straits, is the bizarre house called **Castle Ward**►►, a National Trust property (see page 230).

The gruesome figure of Death makes an appearance at the Derry Festival, held in February/March

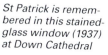

St Patrick is remembered in this stained-glass window (1937) at Down Cathedral

FOCUS ON

The National Trust

■ **The properties and landscape owned by the Northern Ireland branch of the National Trust (NT) are an impressive collection. Ireland's grand houses temper classical orthodoxy with a lively dash of idiosyncrasy, even eccentricity. Besides the well-known set pieces such as Castle Coole or the Giant's Causeway, the National Trust also protects many minor and surprising sights – a glorious Victorian pub in Belfast, a printing press and a beetling mill (used in the old linen industry) in County Tyrone, the curious rope bridge at Carrick-a-rede in County Antrim, and several follies and castles .....**■

Joining and membership
For a small annual fee members of the National Trust (or National Trust for Scotland) gain free admission to almost all the properties managed by the Trust throughout the UK. Membership is open to all, but don't forget to take your card with you. Contact the National Trust, PO Box 39, Bromley, Kent BR1 1NH, UK.

Wellbrook Beetling Mill
The last stage of manufacturing linen is known as beetling, a process in which the flax fibres are hammered to produce a smooth surface. The cultivation of flax was formerly Northern Ireland's largest industry and many deserted mills can be seen. West of Cookstown, in County Tyrone, is Wellbrook Beetling Mill (above) where the machinery is still in working order. It last operated commercially in 1961.

Country Houses The grand Palladian mansion of **Castle Coole►►►**, home of the Earls of Belmore, is the most impressive house of its age in Ireland. Its original cost was enormous (furnishing it was even more expensive than its construction) and it has recently been faithfully restored, at vast expense, by the NT. A masterpiece by James Wyatt, completed in 1798, the house contains magnificent plasterwork and curved doors of ancient mahogany. Entrance to the landscaped parkland is free.

Ardress House►, in parkland near Portadown, dates from the 17th century. The interior contains paintings and good plasterwork. Livestock and farm implements are on show outside; visitors may explore the gardens and woodlands.

Not far away from Ardress House is **The Argory►►**, very little changed since its construction in the 1820s. It has many original contents and a pretty, early-Victorian sundial garden. The interior is still lit by a rare acetylene gas plant surviving in the laundry yard. The surrounding wooded countryside offers many fine walks.

On the shores of Strangford Lough is **Castle Ward►►**, a mansion which clearly displays the diverse tastes of its 18th-century owners, Lord and Lady Bangor. He liked Classical style; she favoured Gothic. Architecture was not all they disagreed on and eventually they separated. Despite its bizarre disparity of styles, the house and contents are of great interest, giving a vivid impression of Victorian life (see the laundry and the playroom). Within the 280ha estate are a 17th-century tower-house, a wildfowl collection and an exhibition about Strangford Lough.

Florence Court►►► is a particularly fine mid-18th-century Palladian house. The seat of the Earls of Enniskillen, it was superbly restored after a disastrous fire in 1956. Splendid plasterwork is the main feature, best preserved on the staircase and dining-room ceiling, which quick-thinking workmen saved from collapse by drilling holes to drain flooded water. The grounds contain a water-powered sawmill and a 220-year-old Irish yew tree, said to be the parent of all Irish-type yews. The 3rd Earl's fossil collection is exhibited in one of the side pavilions.

A thatched 'long-house' dating from about 1691, **Hezlett House**▶ in County Londonderry was probably first used as a parsonage. Its most unusual feature is the cruck-truss roof construction. Inside, it is simply furnished in 18th-century style and contains a display of early building and joinery methods. Further south is **Springhill**▶, former home of the Conynghams, a military family of Ayrshire origins. The edifice dates from the 17th century (with later additions). Outbuildings house a costume museum of 18th-, 19th- and 20th-century clothes. The gunroom contains weapons from Vinegar Hill and the siege of Derry.

Gardens There are two marvellous gardens in County Down. **Mount Stewart Gardens**▶▶ were created by the wife of the 7th Marquis of Londonderry during the 1920s. The mild microclimate engendered by neighbouring Strangford Lough enables many rare and tender plants to flourish. The house is richly furnished and contains political memorabilia. One forebear was Viscount Castlereagh, the 19th-century politician who signed the Act of Union. James Stuart's Temple of the Winds in the grounds echoes a similar building in Athens. The county's other horticultural attraction is at **Rowallane**▶▶. This plantsman's garden was created over the first half of the 20th century on a drumlin site of 21ha and contains specimens from all over the world. Its pride and joy are the azaleas and rhododendrons which flower in May and early June, but the gardens are fine throughout the opening season from April to October.

Gray's printing press
Strabane, in County Tyrone, was an important centre of the Irish printing industry in the 18th and 19th centuries. The National Trust now preserves the only surviving printers, Gray's, in Strabane's Main Street. John Dunlap, printer of the American Declaration of Independence and publisher of America's first daily newspaper, *The Pennsylvania Packet*, is said to have learned his trade here, as is James Wilson, grandfather of President Woodrow Wilson. Visitors may inspect an impressive array of decorative printing presses, all kept in working order, and other antique printing equipment. Gray's Printer's is open in season, afternoons only (not Thursdays and Sundays).

231

Mount Stewart House and Gardens, County Down

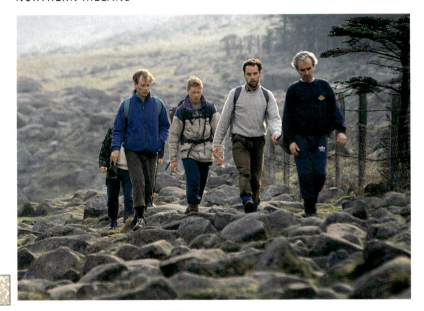

With only one road leading through the Mountains of Mourne, they can only be properly appreciated on foot

Bessbrook
This neat little town north-west of Newry was built during the 19th century by a Quaker linen manu-facturer, John Grubb Richardson. It was designed to house his flax-mill workers, whose living conditions must have been much better than many of their colleagues at other mills. They may have regretted the absence of a pub, however. The tidy, slate-roofed houses are grouped around two village greens.

▶▶▶ **The Mountains of Mourne** *213A4*

These wild, steep-sided granite hills present an unforget-table aspect when seen across Carlingford Lough from the Republic. They reach to an average height of about 600m and are largely inaccessible except on foot, though the range is ringed by roads. Greencastle is a notable landmark near the entrance to Carlingford Lough. It changed hands many times and now stands gaunt and ruined near the rocky shore. Other places of interest along the coastal route are the marine park and restored 19th-century corn mill at Annalong, and the Murlough National Nature Reserve, a stretch of sand-dunes by Dundrum Bay providing an important habitat for many birds.

The border crossing point at Newry is highly politicised and the town is not particularly recommended as a base to stay. If you want to explore the Mourne area, choose one of the eastern coastal resorts or stay in the delightful village of Carlingford over the border in the Republic. **Newcastle** is the main tourist centre for the Mourne Mountains. The resort, though pleasantly set, is of no great interest, but it has a good sandy beach and a wide range of accommodation. There are many walks in the nearby forest parks of Tollymore and Castlewellan.

Slieve Donard is the highest Mourne peak at 852m and it is said that on rare, clear days you can see all the coun-tries of the British Isles from its summit (a relatively safe and easy climb), where there is also a hermit cell. At one time the mountains were a remote and ungovernable area inhabited by smugglers. A maze of ancient tracks lead through open moorland and upland pasture which make excellent walking country. For good maps and infor-mation, make for Newcastle's tourist office or the Mourne Countryside Centre at 91 Central Promenade. Rock-climbing is popular on the steeper cliff faces. The most accessible section is a well-marked tourist route called the Silent Valley which leads up to two reservoirs serving the Greater Belfast region. A visitor centre stands here and shuttle buses take tourists from the car-park to Ben Crom Reservoir (other traffic is banned). The upper sections of the Mourne hills are characterised by tiny fields and dry-stone walls. The Mourne Wall is the largest of these, 35km long and 2m high, enclosing the water catchment area around the Silent Valley. Many semi-precious stones have been mined in the mountains around Hare's Gap.

The Ulster Way Northern Ireland is excellent for walking and its interconnected paths form a magnificent 700km long-distance footpath through all six counties. For most of the way it hugs the perimeter of the province fairly closely, ducking inland across the Sperrin Mountains and briefly touching the shores of Lough Neagh. Obviously some sections are more scenic and easier to follow than others. The paths running through the Mountains of Mourne, the Glens of Antrim, the Causeway coast and the Lakes of Fermanagh are the most popular and most clearly marked, and it is in these well-known tourist areas that you can most easily find accommodation. At various points the Ulster Way links with other routes leading through the Republic. Near the border areas it is advisable not to stray from the waymarked paths. For the most part walking in Northern Ireland is safe and straightforward; no special equipment is needed apart from a good map and sensible footwear and clothing. Route guides and detailed maps are both available from various sources, notably the Sports Council for Northern Ireland, House of Sport, Upper Malone Road, Belfast BT9 5LA (tel: 0232 381222). The Youth Hostel Association of Northern Ireland (56 Bradbury Place, Belfast BT7 1RU, tel: 0232 324733) also organises rambling and hiking holidays throughout the year.

233

Newcastle nestles under the shadow of the Mountains of Mourne

NORTHERN IRELAND

▶▶▶   **Ulster-American Folk Park**   *212C2*

This theme park near Omagh, County Tyrone, has been set up with a generous endowment by the Mellon banking magnates who founded Pittsburgh, Pennsylvania. Thomas Mellon left Ulster in 1818 with his family and became vastly prosperous. The park has been recreated in the peaty bogs around his birthplace at Camphill, a modest whitewashed cottage, and traces the progress of those early Ulster émigrés from the Old World to the New. A guided walk takes visitors from a large reception and exhibition centre through birch groves. In the first section, reconstructed buildings create the atmosphere of a typical 18th-century Ulster village – a blacksmith's forge, a weaver's cottage, a dour Presbyterian meeting house where interminable sermons were preached. Costumed staff cook up griddle cakes over open peat fires, spin wool and organise 'lessons' in the village school (quill pens are used). School parties visit regularly. One of the more imposing buildings is Hugh Campbell's house, where extracts from the journal of 1818, written during his emigration voyage, can be read: 'During the night every moveable in the ship was put in motion by the great heaving,… buckets full of all kinds of filth were hurled in the greatest confusion through the steerage to the great offence of our smelling organs!' On 12 July he wrote, 'This day the anniversary of the Battle of the Boyne was commemorated by a certain part of our passengers to the no small annoyance of another part,' which suggests that not much has changed in the intervening years. Visitors then pass through the Emigration Gallery, a replica emigration ship (complete with sound effects of creaking timbers and roaring seas) and on to the New World, where typical log barns, wagons and farmsteads of the early settlers can be seen. Of its type (and there are many similar projects throughout Ireland) this theme park is highly successful and has a coherent and authentic ring, though some of its amenities (such as the café) could be improved.

Past centuries are imaginatively re-created at the Ulster-American Folk Park

▶▶▶ Ulster Folk and Transport Museum   *213B4*

This museum is located about 8km east of Belfast in the extensive grounds of Cultra Manor on the Bangor road. Typical Ulster buildings have been re-erected or reconstructed here and furnished in turn-of-the-century style. The exhibits include urban terraces, shops and cottages, farmhouses, a flax mill, forge and school. Inside, demonstrations of local crafts such as spinning and weaving take place. An entertaining exhibition of domestic, social and agricultural life in Ulster can be seen in the gallery which functions as an introduction to the park. The section on Ulster marriages is particularly entertaining – exhibits change from time to time. The transport galleries on the opposite side of the main road now house the entire Belfast Transport Museum, which has been relocated from the city centre, and include many exhibits from horse-drawn carts to the ill-fated De Lorean sports car (see panel). Local engineering heroes, such as Harry Ferguson, receive due attention, as do the great Belfast transport firms such as Shorts, the aircraft manufacturers, and Harland & Wolff, the shipbuilders (one of their commissions was the *Titanic*). Ensure that you allow plenty of time to see everything; you could spend the best part of a day here.

▶ Ulster History Park   *212C2*

This new attraction near the Gortin Glen Forest Park traces the history of settlement in Ireland, starting with prehistoric societies dating back to about 6500BC (life-size replicas of *crannógs* and neolithic huts) through early Christian architecture (Round Towers and churches), Norman castles, ring-forts and planters' houses. Further developments are in progress.

A number of drives, parks and beauty spots can be visited in the nearby Sperrin Mountains, a range of ancient and desolate hills in which minute traces of gold have been found. The rare hen harrier flies high above the remoter uplands.

235

The Ulster Folk and Transport Museum

The pioneering spirit lives on at the Folk Park

De Lorean
The famous gull-winged sportscar venture funded by public money to create employment in Belfast caused a major crisis in the Thatcher years when the enterprise crashed spectacularly, amid accusations of business malpractice and fraud. Investors and employees suffered greatly, and confidence in Northern Irish manufacturing projects took a sharp nose-dive.

LAKELAND COUNTIES

Castle Island on Lough Key (County Roscommon) is named after a 19th-century folly

Sionna and the Salmon of Knowledge
This legend echoes the story of Adam and Eve. Sionna, grand-daughter of the great King Lir (see page 236), desired the gift of knowledge, which was granted to men alone. She went to Connla's Well to search for the Salmon of Knowledge. Whoever ate the salmon would acquire its wisdom. As Sionna tried to trap the fish, it lashed its tail and the well over-flowed. Sionna was swept away and drowned in the Shannon Pot (the source of the Shannon in Cavan).

Grand Canal
Until the early 19th century the Grand Canal, running from Dublin through these lakeland counties to the River Shannon at Ballinasloe, was a most important transport route, and it carried freight until 1959. The heyday of the Royal and Grand Canals, however, occurred before the Act of Union in 1801, which effectively destroyed Ireland's ability to compete with the Industrial Revolution in Britain. Horses would gallop along the towpaths, hauling barges at speeds of up to 16kph. In recent years many canals have enjoyed something of a renaissance, thanks to their recreational use.

Lakeland counties These smallish, watery counties – Cavan and Monaghan near the Northern Ireland border, and Westmeath, Laois, Offaly, Roscommon and Longford – form the geographical heart of Ireland, yet are usually portrayed as places to get *through* on the way to somewhere more interesting. Initially they are not prepossessing. Dreary main roads blast through on radial routes from the capital, often slow with heavy traffic. Closer exploration of these unsung plains is surprisingly rewarding, however. There are historic towns, abbey ruins and grand houses to visit, and masses of outdoor activities. Highlights include Strokestown House, Birr Castle Gardens and the monastic ruins of Clonmacnois.

Facilities for visitors are limited compared with parts of the more popular western or southeastern counties. Budget accommodation, especially campsites or hostels, is scarce, but the area has some highly distinctive and good-value country house hotels. These central counties also offer a less stereotyped picture of the Emerald Isle. Visitors are welcomed with true Irish hospitality, with no pressure to buy sweaters or shamrock table linen.

Waterlands The landscape seems at first monotonous – a shallow saucer of endless unremarkable arable and pasture land, broken up by a maze of lakes and river systems. Few grand vistas can be seen; the eyeline generally stops at the first gappy hedge. The small-scale, piecemeal landscape appears intimate and domesticated, though its most significant geographical feature, the River Shannon, is the longest in the British Isles, carving its ponderous course through the brimming flood plains and water meadows of several counties. It provides many things – scenic interest, wildlife habitats, an important navigable waterway and a profitable playground for fishermen and boat-lovers. As if more water were needed, long canals slice through the bogs – the Grand Canal in the heart of Offaly and the Royal Canal linking Dublin with the Shannon. These waterways and the massive lakes of the Shannon and its major tributaries are extensively exploited for recreational use. Myriad smaller pools dot the wavering horizons of Monaghan and Cavan. A practised topographical eye will quickly identify this borderland area as drumlin country, where glacial deposits have been left in distinctive ridges, or eskers (the only geological term to be derived from the Irish language) and pear-shaped hills (drumlins) forming a classic 'basket of eggs' landscape.

Laois has the highest hills, the Slieve Blooms, which rise to a modest maximum of 527m. Amid these low-lying plains, however, they seem grand indeed and the long-distance footpath called the Slieve Bloom Way attracts many walkers.

Settlers, invaders and bandits Patterns of settlement are complex. Invaders and adventurers throughout the centuries tramped across these mournful boglands to find out what lay beyond, and the fierce clans who established themselves here posed a constant threat to the Anglo-Normans walled up in the Pale around Dublin. The area is full of castles, dour planters' churches and the demesnes of great families. In Elizabeth I's time many estates were confiscated from their original Gaelic owners and parcelled out to Scottish and English landlords.

The wild border counties of Monaghan and Cavan harbour further resentment. Once part of the old kingdom of Ulster, they were torn from their ancient allegiances by Partition. Complex geography makes a national frontier virtually impossible to police, and parts well deserve the sobriquet 'bandit country'. Political activists and smugglers criss-cross the uncertain border on unofficial, pot-holed tracks. The bizarre course of the boundary between North and South seems to epitomise, by its perverse loops and twists, the irrationality of the present dividing line. There is not much reason to linger on this section of the border and, while there, it is prudent to adopt the local habit of remaining tight-lipped on political opinions.

Bog Butter
Butter has always been eaten in Ireland in great quantities. In medieval times it was sometimes flavoured with garlic or onions. Before the days of refrigeration, it was discovered that Irish peat-bogs conserved food remarkably well, and caches were often buried in wooden barrels where they were safe from plunderers. It developed a distinctive cheesy flavour but would last for hundreds of years. Bog butter from long ago is still occasionally unearthed during turf cutting.

239

14th-century Clough-outer Castle stands in Lough Outer (Cavan)

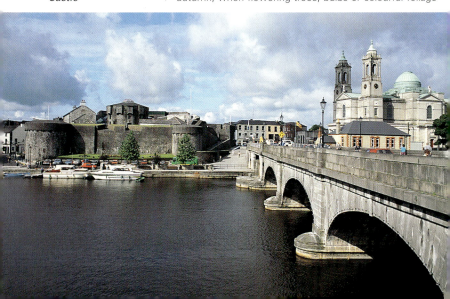

BIRTHPLACE OF COUNT JOHN McCORMACK, WORLDS FAMOUS TENOR.

John McCormack
A legend in his own life-time, John McCormack (1884–1945) is still regarded as one of the greatest lyrical tenors in recorded history and, fortunately, he lived in an era when his voice could be captured on early gramophone discs. He quickly achieved fame and was internationally recognised in Italy, London and America. He made a fortune from his repertoire of popular music and spent it on his other two oddly varied passions: horse-racing and the Catholic Church. For his charitable services he was awarded the unusual honour of being made a Papal Count.

240

The Anglo-Norman fortress of Athlone Castle

▶ **Athlone** *236C2*

The 'capital of the Midlands' stands at one of Ireland's most central points, midway along the Shannon and an important rail, road and river junction on the border between Leinster and Connaught. The town was besieged and badly damaged by Williamite forces after the Battle of the Boyne when the defeated Jacobites retreated here and were finally routed at nearby Aughrim. Unsurprisingly, its strategic location necessitated a stronghold, and one of its most significant historic buildings is a 13th-century castle▶ in the market square, whose curtain walls, towers and keep are still intact. The castle has been put to good modern use as the setting for a museum of local history; its most interesting section is an exhibition on the famous tenor, John McCormack, who was born in the town. Recordings of McCormack's voice can be heard on his own 78rpm gramophone. Elsewhere in the town is his birthplace, in a narrow street called The Bawn. Apart from the castle, a handful of abbey ruins and a fine Jacobean house (Court Devenish) dating from 1620, there is no very pressing reason to visit Athlone, but it makes a good base for boat excursions on Lough Ree and its various islands. Of these, Inchclearaun and Inchbofin both have churches and Early Christian graveslabs; Inchclearaun is also associated with the legendary warrior Queen Maeve, who met her death here bizarrely, struck by a missile of cheese!

▶ **Birr** *236B2*

This pleasant, quiet Georgian town was formerly known as Parsonstown, after the family name of the Earls of Rosse, whose seat is Birr Castle▶▶. The building is 17th-century Gothic and not generally open to the public, but the 40ha of gardens are open all year and heartily reward a visit. They contain many rare specimen trees and shrubs, and the tallest box hedges in the world (10m high). The gardens are particularly fine in spring and autumn, when flowering trees, bulbs or colourful foliage are at their best. Walks lead beside the lake and rivers, around which the grounds are landscaped. The most fascinating feature of Birr Castle, however, is the remains of a remarkable early telescope. Built by the 3rd Earl of Rosse in the 1840s, it was then the largest and most powerful in the world, its 183cm lens enabling the aristocratic astronomer and his son, the 4th Earl, to study the spiral nebulae and measure the heat of the moon. The supporting walls that held this massive instrument can still be seen; taped information provides background history. Birr Castle's Dower House, Tullanisk, is an exceptionally attractive place to stay (see Hotels and Restaurants, page 278). Several fine Georgian houses and streets survive in the town.

The grounds of Birr Castle straddle the boundary between Counties Offaly and Tipperary

► **Boyle**   236D2

The main reason to visit Boyle is to see the ruined **Cistercian abbey►** dating from 1161, founded by the same group of monks who built Mellifont. Though central and near one of the town's main streets, the abbey seems tranquil beside its rushing stream, and a good proportion of it is still intact, despite innumerable attacks by warring Irish clans. The Abbey Guesthouse, just beside the ruins, keeps the keys if the gatehouse is locked. The 12th-century church within the compound shows Gothic and Romanesque arches and interesting carvings. For a couple of centuries from Elizabethan times the abbey housed a military garrison. A short distance east of Boyle is the **Lough Key Forest Park►►**, part of the Rockingham estate, an enormous demesne which once belonged to the King family (Edward King, drowned in the Irish Sea in 1636, was the subject of Milton's elegiac poem *Lycidas*). Rockingham originally belonged to the MacDermots, the local chieftains and Lords of Moylurg, but was handed to the King family in 1617. The big house in what is now the forest park was burned down in 1957, but the King family's town mansion in the main street is being restored. There is little else to see in this quiet town, but with the Curlew Mountains close by and its excellent opportunities for walking and fishing, Boyle is an increasingly popular holiday base.

An Irish Romeo and Juliet
Castle Island in Lough Key, near Boyle, is traditionally taken to be the burial place of two young lovers, Una MacDermott and Thomas Costello, the subject of a famous traditional Irish poem (*Úna Bhán – White Una*). Her parents would not allow the match and Thomas departed grief-stricken from her home, promising to return only if he were recalled before he crossed a nearby river. He tarried at the ford, but finally crossed – too late to learn that Una had died of a broken heart. She was buried on Castle Island, where Thomas used to swim his horse each night to lament his lost love until he collapsed lifeless over her grave. Two ash trees grew above the tomb and entwined over this Irish Romeo and Juliet, united at last in death.

Interesting places to stay

■ **Ireland is one of the most hospitable countries in the world. Tourist accommodation is big business and there is a vast range of places to stay at all price levels, from modest cottages to great castles. A genuinely warm welcome, a home-like atmosphere, and an excellent breakfast is a feature of many of them .....■**

Characterful houses
Cheaper options include Blanchville in County Kilkenny, Bruckless House in County Donegal, Ballycormac House in Tipperary and several Glebe Houses (once providing accommodation for Church of Ireland clergy) – those in Ballinakill, County Laois, Dowth, County Louth, and Ballinadee, County Cork are highly recommended.More modest but excellent value are Fergus View, convenient for the Burren, Church Villa or Dunmore Lodge (both in Dunmore East, County Waterford), Kille House in County Galway, Hanora's Cottage in County Waterford, Larchwood House in Cork, or Rosturk Woods in County Mayo.

The dining-room at Tullanisk, near Birr, in County Offaly

Useful publications Anonymous business hotels or luxury castles will give you reliable hot water and TV, but little of the real Ireland of conversation and idiosyncrasy that you will find in more personally run places. To meet the increasing demand for places with something special, several useful listings have been made. Pick up the booklets in any tourist office. *The Blue Book* lists a fine range of country-house hotels and restaurants, often with some historic interest or culinary distinction. Staying in most of these places is a memorable, but generally expensive, experience. Some of the outstanding ones are mentioned on pages 160–1.

The Hidden Ireland provides an even more interesting selection of *homes* offering hospitality (as opposed to commercially operated hotels). In many of these you may dine *en famille*, join a country-house-party atmosphere, get to know the owners or join in locally available sports such as hunting or fishing. All the places are rural and of some architectural distinction, many are fascinating and distinguished old houses filled with family mementoes and antiques. *Friendly Homes of Ireland* is a personal choice (by John Colclough, a well known journalist) of generally less expensive places offering family hospitality in interesting settings. (There is some overlap between these listings.) Many visitors base their whole holiday around these selected houses, and although not every establishment may be to your taste, they all have merit,

242

The elegance of
Clohamon House,
Bunclody, County
Wexford

and if you have little idea of where to start looking, are of great help. Here are just a few places offering exceptional and typically Irish hospitality – informal, effortless, unsnobby and warm. (For details see pages 269–83.)

Luxurious mansions At the more expensive end of the price-range, **Hilton Park** in Clones, County Monaghan, overlooking extensive parkland which includes a golf course and three lakes, offers a splendid Anglo-Irish country-house stay. Four-poster beds, elegant furnishings and many memorabilia add to the interest of the house, home of the Madden family for some 250 years. Organic produce from the gardens appears on its excellent dinner menus. **Bantry House** in Cork is a magnificent stately home still owned by descendants of the White family who lived there in 1739 and helped to foil Wolfe Tone's invasion. Accommodation is provided in a separate wing of newly refurbished rooms, all very comfortable, overlooking the lovely Italianate gardens. Concerts are a speciality. The state rooms are open to the public, so don't expect complete seclusion. Slightly less expensive are **Ballyvolane House** (also in County Cork), dating from 1728, elegantly remodelled in early Victorian times. It has lovely peaceful grounds, private fishing and excellent Irish country cooking. **Clohamon House** in Wexford is an 18th-century house in the Slaney valley surrounded by beechwoods and gardens of rare trees. The estate land is farmed, and contains a Connemara pony stud. Antiques and family portraits lend a gracious air, though the atmosphere is entirely unstuffy. **Newbay House**, closer to the Wexford coast, is another cheerful, relaxing Georgian home in sweeping parkland. **Ballinkeele House** was designed by Daniel Robertson (of Powerscourt fame) in 1840, and is the ancestral home of the Maher family, who dispense effortless hospitality and excellent cooking amid 140ha of farmland. **Roundwood House** in Laois is one of the best of all Irish country houses for character and idiosyncratic charm. It is also one of Ireland's finest Georgian homes, in the Palladian style. **Tullanisk**, also in Lakeland (County Offaly) is the former Dower House of the Earls of Rosse, who own Birr Castle. **Gurthalougha House** on the shores of Lough Derg, Tipperary, dates from the early 19th century and stands in a private forest.

Ballymaloe House
This rambling, Georgian mansion with a Norman keep is in farming country east of Cork. Owned by the Allen family, produce from the 160ha farm is used to good effect, for Myrtle Allen is one of Ireland's most celebrated chefs, happy to pass on her skills in books, television broadcasts, and through the Ballymaloe cookery school, run by her son and daughter-in-law, Timothy and Darina Allen. The hotel has many facilities and is lavishly furnished, but retains the feel of a family home and is utterly relaxing.

243

Tullanisk, in the Birr
Castle Estate; guests
are given free
admission to the
Castle gardens

Clonalis House (1878), seat of the O'Conors

Castlerea   236D1

The town itself is not in the least riveting, but **Clonalis House►**, on the southwestern outskirts, is worth a look. Guided tours are conducted by the family owners, and you can even enjoy an unusual, if expensive, brand of aristocratic B&B in its palatial bedrooms, or self-catering in nearby cottages. Clonalis House is a late-Victorian mansion in fine parkland whose main interest consists in its contents and its inhabitants. It is a rare example of a clan house, the seat of an ancient Gaelic family which can, it claims, trace its line back through 60 generations to the Kings of Connaught and the last High Kings of Ireland. The O'Conors have owned the local land for the best part of two millennia and many castles and abbeys in the region are associated with the clan. The house is sumptuously furnished with antiques, and full of archive material and family memorabilia, including silver, porcelain, costumes and manuscripts. One of its most prized items is a harp belonging to the great 18th-century bard Turlough O'Carolan.

►►► Clonmacnois   236B2

These extensive and impressive monastic remains stand in velvety, emerald water-meadows by a rushy bend in the River Shannon, a place of almost tangible stillness, especially at dawn or dusk when the few visitors who venture here are absent. In earlier centuries it was even more isolated by the river and surrounding bogland, and was accessible only by boat, or along the esker (see caption) ridge known as the Pilgrims' Causeway. Founded by St Ciarán (or Kieran) in about AD548, this Celtic site became the most important religious establishment of its time in Ireland and was renowned as a place of art and learning throughout Europe. St Ciarán himself died of plague at the age of only 33, just seven months after the monastery site had been established, but news of his good works eventually spread beyond Irish shores. Several ecclesiastical treasures produced here are now on display at the National Museum in Dublin. The gold and silver Crozier of Clonmacnois, decorated with strapwork and animal patterns, is one of these. The *Book of the Dun Cow*, one of the earliest and most famous manuscripts in the Irish language, was also produced here.

Clonmacnois was once a royal city and the burial place of the High Kings of Tara and Connaught, including the last High King, Rory O'Conor (see Castlerea). Like most settlements of its type, it suffered constant depredations

Goldsmith country
The poet and playwright, Oliver Goldsmith (1728–1774) was born at Pallas, County Longford, and spent much of his childhood in Lissoy parsonage, near Auburn crossroads. Villages most associated with Goldsmith's writings (particularly his long poem, *The Deserted Village*) include Tang, where he went to school, and Ballymahon, his widowed mother's home. Most of his adult life was spent in London, but he recalled his Irish childhood and the gentle, humdrum lifestyle of this rural area in idyllic terms. The Three Jolly Pigeons pub, immortalized in *She Stoops to Conquer*, can be seen on the Ballymahon road near Athlone.

at the hands of Vikings and Normans and was devastated by English forces in 1552. Still visible within its enclosing walls are the remains of a cathedral, eight churches, two Round Towers, many carved gravestones (the oldest now displayed in the visitor centre) and several High Crosses. The splendid Cross of the Scriptures, erected in the 9th or 10th century, depicts, amongst the usual biblical scenes, King Dermot helping St Ciarán erect the first corner-post of the monastery at Clonmacnois.

The Nuns' Church stands beside a quiet lane outside the main enclosure and is reached via a path through the modern cemetery and out into the road beyond. It is worth making the short excursion to this pleasant spot; the tiny church with its finely carved arches is sheltered by tall trees in a peaceful little meadow. It was built by Dervorgilla, Ireland's equivalent of Helen of Troy, whose abduction by Dermot MacMurrough provided the excuse for Strongbow's Anglo-Norman invasion (see page 32–3). On the other side of the monastic buildings, not far from the car-park, vestiges of a Norman castle also survive on the slopes beside the river. Little of the castle survives except for its courtyard and a crazily leaning tower.

A new interpretative centre at Clonmacnois has recently been opened, offering a range of facilities.

The Dead at Clonmacnois
In a quiet water'd land, a land of roses,
Stands Saint Ciarán's city fair;
And the warriors of Erin in their famous generations
Slumber there.

T.W. Rolleston (1857–1920); from the medieval Irish poem by Enóg Ó Gilláin.

Clonmacnois, strategically sited on an esker beside the Shannon. (An esker is a winding ridge of gravel deposited by a meltwater stream running beneath a glacier)

245

Lakeland activities

■ **Many of the sporting activities of this central region are based upon its rivers, lakes and forests. Several forest parks have been created, partly for environmental conservation, but also for recreation and to increase the region's tourism potential. Some of these designated parks are rather over-organised, with plentiful picnic tables and similar amenities. If you prefer a slightly wilder scene, head for the Slieve Bloom Mountains .....■**

246

Lacemaking

County Monaghan is famous for its lace industry. Carrickmacross and Clones are the two main centres and, in both cases, the craft was introduced during the 19th century by local rectors' wives, partly as a means of relieving the area's chronic poverty. The fortunes of the industry waxed and waned as a result of changing fashions and periodic over-production. Lace is still made by hand in these centres, though the genuine article is extremely labour-intensive and correspondingly expensive. Carrickmacross lace incorporates hundreds of intricate fine loops. Clones lace is crocheted and often features small raised knots known as Clones dots.

Lace-making, County Monaghan

Forest parks Lying just outside Boyle, in the grounds of the former Rockingham estate, the **Lough Key Forest Park**►► ranges over about 340ha along a lake shore and includes a cypress grove, deerpark, ice-house, temple, bog garden full of peat-loving plants such as azaleas, and many waymarked paths. Boats tour the lake from Rockingham Harbour, and rowing boats can be hired. There are ring-forts and islands to explore, and a vantage point called the Moylurg Tower can be climbed for views of the surrounding scenery. The gateway and lodge of the old estate still exist, though the main house, designed by Nash, was burned down in 1957.

Northwest of Cavan on the N3, the 240ha **Killykeen Forest Park**► is set amid the complex Chinese puzzle of water and islets that forms Lough Oughter. Waymarked walks, nature trails, etc., enable visitors to enjoy fishing, birdwatching and exploring early fortifications.

Rossmore Forest Park lies near Monaghan Town on the Newbliss road and consists of 280ha of gentle hills and lakes interconnected by forest walks through rhododendron plantations. Just beyond Newbliss is the Victorian Annaghmakerrig House, former home of theatre director, Sir Tyrone Guthrie, and now left to the nation as a centre for writers and artists. Visitors can picnic and walk in its beautiful surroundings.

Haunted by red squirrels, **Dún A Rí Forest Park**► provides 230ha of wooded walks southwest of Carrickmacross. From the hilltop car-park are views of the Mourne Mountains and a ruined Elizabethan fortress. A wishing-well called Tobar na Splinnc is set into a rocky ledge above the River Cabra, and Sarah's Bridge supposedly commemorates a lady who was so startled by a belated proposal of marriage from a man she had been meeting for 30 years that she fell off and drowned!

Lough Muckno Forest Park is a former Georgian estate near Castleblayney. Situated beside Monaghan's largest lake, it offers signposted walks through beautiful grounds of mixed woodland and gently undulating drumlins. Caravans and campers can be accommodated near by.

The Slieve Bloom Mountains Though not particularly high, the Slieve Blooms►► rise quite dramatically from the low-lying boggy plains which surround them, their looming purple shoulders a backdrop to many a view in this area. It is said that they are named after Bladhma, an

Killykeen Forest Park lies on the shores of Lough Outer in County Cavan

ancient hero, who once took refuge from his enemies in these hills. Later, in Cromwellian times, the Slieve Blooms again became a place of hiding for men whose lands had been confiscated by the Parliamentary forces.

The slopes are rounded rather than steep, many covered in conifer plantations, and the high density of well-marked paths and tracks (so unusual in Ireland) make them ideal for walking. A long-distance footpath called the Slieve Bloom Way runs for 30km or so around these hills, on a route past waterfalls and glens, through bog and moorland, conifer woods and an ancient (pre-Ice Age) river valley. Though the hills are mostly too gentle for really dramatic views, the slopes do in some places drop away sufficiently to reveal the great plains below stretching mistily into the distance. Look out for the rare pine marten which haunts the mountains, together with Irish hares, fallow deer and mountain goats. Good starting points for the walk are Glen Barrow or the standing stone at Forelacka. Despite their unthreatening altitude (maximum 527m), these hills can be treacherously misty and waterlogged, so adequate footwear, clothing and equipment are essential.

247

Boating
An excellent way to enjoy the peaceful Midland scenery is from the deck of a boat, and you can charter boats in many centres on the 500km of navigable lakes, rivers, or canals in the region. Tullamore, on the Grand Canal linking Dublin and the Shannon, is one of the most popular starting points for narrow boats, and the scenery spans flower-filled banks, gentle pasture and open bogland (Celtic Canal Cruisers, tel: 0506 21861). Other good centres include Athlone (Athlone Cruisers Ltd, tel: 0902 72892, for boat trips round Lough Ree), Banagher, or Glasson.

Lough Key, a perfect place to enjoy some of Ireland's finest fishing

LAKELAND COUNTIES

The seven wonders
Fore is famous for its seven wonders:
1. The monastery on a quaking scraw.
2. A mill without a mill-race.
3. Water that flows uphill.
4. An ash tree that won't burn.
5. Water that never boils.
6. The great stone above the old church door.
7. The Holy man in a stone (an anchorite's cell).
Many stories are told to explain the origin of these, but the grains of truth in some should be mixed with pinches of salt in others.

St Brigid's Chapel in Mullingar Cathedral

► ▅▅▅▅ **Monaghan** 237E4

This garrison town shows a strong Scots Presbyterian influence, with solid mercantile buildings and a central square known as the Diamond, similar to those in Derry and Donegal. Its location close to the Northern Irish border is not fortunate and, although it prospered from the linen industry introduced mainly by Ulster settlers in the 18th century, it has been a hotbed of unrest from time to time. Charles Gavan Duffy, one of its most famous inhabitants who eventually became Prime Minister of Victoria, Australia, characterised the town's political awareness by founding the Irish Tenant League and a nationalist newspaper called *The Nation*. The flamboyant 19th-century Gothic spire of **St Macartan's Catholic Cathedral** lords it over the more sedate classical and Regency buildings of the town centre. In the Diamond, the elegant 1792 Market House, with its fine, carved decorations, is now the tourist office. The Rossmore Memorial, a huge Victorian drinking fountain, with eight grey marble columns and a sandstone canopy, also in the Diamond, necessitated the removal from here of the old 17th-century market cross, once a sundial, to another square in the town (Old Cross Square). The town's most interesting sight is its **County Museum►** on Hill Street near the tourist office, an award-winning collection of local history and art. One of its prize exhibits is the processional Cross of Clogher, beautifully embossed with figures and ornaments, and dating from about 1400.

▅▅▅▅ **Mullingar** 237C3

This busy county town is the centre of a prosperous commercial and cattle-raising area. The main reason to visit the town, otherwise, is to see its museums and its modern Catholic cathedral. Best of the museums is the **Military Museum►**, with a section devoted to the old IRA, a more idealistic and honourable organisation than it is today. The **Cathedral of Christ the King►**, not in itself a remarkable building, contains two famous mosaics by a Russian artist, Boris Anrep, and an ecclesiastical museum

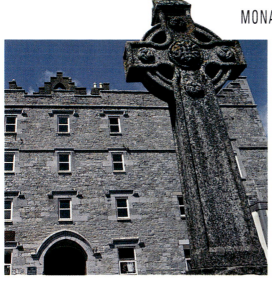

The Old Gaol, Roscommon

Adolphus Cooke
Not far from Mullingar on the road to Delvin is the small village of Reynella, where the graveyard contains a strange tomb in the shape of a beehive. This is the grave of a celebrated local eccentric, Adolphus Cooke, who believd that one of his flock of turkeys was his re-incarnated father. He also tried his favourite dog, Gusty, for the crime of repeatedly straying and cavorting with the common dogs of Mullingar. The setter was eventually reprieved when the hangman claimed that the dog addressed him in a foreign tongue, thereby proving Cooke's theory of reincarnation. Market Hall Museum in Mullingar contains a few relics relating to this extraordinary person.

housing the vestments of St Oliver Plunkett (see page 114). North of Mullingar and near the underrated Lough Derravaragh is **Tullynally Castle▶**, seat of the Earls of Longford, a castellated stone building much remodelled in the 19th century, with fine gardens. Inside is an interesting collection of domestic utensils and a celebrated private library, indicating the literary bent of the Pakenham family, whose scions include the present Lord Longford's gifted daughters, Antonia Fraser and Rachel Billington. The castle is open only from mid-July to mid-August, the grounds from June to September. Near by is **Fore Abbey▶**, founded in the 7th century by St Fechin. This large religious community was destroyed many times during the Dark Ages, but a church dating from the 10th century survives, along with a 13th-century Benedictine priory built by the de Lacy family.

▶   Roscommon   *236C2*

The huge **Norman castle▶**, standing in fields on the edge of Roscommon, seems out of proportion to anything else in this little county town. It dates from the 13th century, though was altered much in later years, with refined Tudor mullions added in the 16th century. The quarrelsome O'Kelly and O'Conor clans seized it periodically, but its last definitive remodelling took place at the hands of Cromwellian troops and its drum towers now stand lopped and hollow around a rectangle of neatly mown turf. In the town are the **Dominican priory ruins**, last resting place of the priory's 13th-century founder Félim O'Conor, a king of Connaught, whose tomb is decorated with effigies of gallowglasses (Irish or Scots mercenaries). The main street, with attractively restored Georgian and Victorian shops, bifurcates around a copper-domed Georgian courthouse (now a Bank of Ireland branch). Near by is the castellated county gaol, where Roscommon's redoubtable lady hangman carried out her civic duty (see panel). Another curiosity is James J Harlow's Funeral Requisites and Furniture Stores, a beautifully restored ironmonger's shop and bar crammed with household gadgets and nostalgic examples of advertising.

Lady Betty
Roscommon's condemned prisoners faced a female executioner during the 18th century. Condemned to death herself, allegedly for the unwitting murder of her only son, she volunteered to step into the breach when the hangman was ill, on condition that her life be spared. She was subsequently appointed as the town's 'hangwoman' with a salary and accommodation at the prison, and there she remained for about 30 years, performing her grisly duty with apparent efficiency and detachment. She drew charcoal portraits on her walls of some of her clients, whom she dispatched from a hinged board outside her third-floor window.

Richard Cassels or Castle
This architect (1690–1751) was one of the formative influences on Anglo-Irish architecture during Georgian times. Among his great works are Powerscourt and Russborough in County Wicklow, Westport in Mayo, Newbridge in Dublin and Strokestown House in Roscommon. He came from a Huguenot family settled in Hesse-Kassel in Germany. He first arrived in Ireland in 1728 to work on a project in County Fermanagh and soon became known to Lord Burlington and his circle. Before long he was the most sought-after architect in Ireland. His style was Palladian, with heavy mouldings and muscular sculpted stonework. His name appears most often in its anglicised form – Castle.

▶▶   **Strokestown**   *236D2*

Many Irish towns and villages reveal their Georgian origins in wide streets, but Strokestown's is certainly exceptional – originally modelled on Vienna's Ringstrasse which had greatly impressed one of the local landowners, it is said to be the widest provincial main street in Ireland. The village is little more than an adjunct to the enormous **Strokestown House**▶▶ which lies beyond the Gothic triple arch on this main street. Home of the Pakenham Mahon family, their 17th-century farmhouse was reconstructed by Richard Castle (see panel) in the 1730s in Palladian style for the Anglo-Irish MP, Thomas Mahon. Its most famous (and infamous) proprietor was Major Denis Mahon, who presided over the Strokestown estate during the unproductive Famine years, and found himself so short of cash that he pressed his tenants to emigrate to the New World. Rumours spread that he was chartering the dreaded 'coffin ships' in which so many Irish emigrants perished, and Mahon was shot dead near Strokestown in 1847. In 1979 the dilapidated house was sold to an enterprising local garage firm, who gallantly resisted the mood of the times to let all traces of 'British imperialism' (i.e. its superb Georgian heritage) lapse into ruin. The company energetically restored the premises, replanted the parkland and established the Famine Museum in the house, which is now open to the public. Strokestown House is one of Ireland's finest and most authentic Palladian buildings and gives a real flavour of the life and times of the Anglo-Irish families and their tenants. One of its most fascinating features is the galleried kitchen in the south wing from which the lady of the house could drop menus and instructions to the kitchen staff without troubling herself by any closer proximity. Tunnels allowing tradesmen and staff to perform their duties unseen link the main house to the kitchen and stables located in the wings.

At the far end of Strokestown, the County Heritage and Genealogical Centre (open only from May to September) offers regional displays and an audio-visual show about County Roscommon.

The library at Strokestown House

TRAVEL FACTS

Arriving

Entry formalities British visitors entering the Republic or the North do not need a passport. The best advice, however, is to take it anyway. It provides useful and convincing identity for changing money, hiring a car, obtaining medical treatment and at security checkpoints. British nationals not born in the UK, or non-Caucasians, will find a passport cuts the red tape considerably.

EC and North American or Australasian visitors simply need a valid passport and can stay for up to three months. Other nationals should check to see if they require a visa. In the North, British regulations apply and EC residents or travellers from English-speaking or Commonwealth countries can usually stay for up to six months with a passport or suitable identity documents.

By Air Ireland's international airports are Dublin, Shannon, Cork, Belfast International (well linked by public transport to the city-centres) and Knock. All transatlantic flights to the Republic land at Shannon, near Limerick, since airlines are required under controversial Irish regulations to stop over in Shannon as part of a scheme to bring tourism and employment to the western regions. If you are visiting the West anyway, Shannon makes a convenient landing point. Most European flights land in Dublin or Belfast, but other airports are served from the UK. Flying time from London is an hour to Dublin or Belfast (90 mins to Shannon, Cork or Knock). You can fly to Ireland from many regional UK airports. Both Shannon and Dublin have well-stocked duty-free outlets with many Irish products on sale.

Since deregulation of air transport, air fares from Britain to all parts of Ireland have become extremely competitive, to the point of damaging the profitability of the Republic's national carrier (Aer Lingus). Many promotional fares are available, making air travel an attractive option unless you need to take a car. Fare structures are complex and constantly changing according to the market. In general, though, competition keeps the main

operators more or less in line from any particular airport. If flying from London, check with British Airways, Aer Lingus, Ryanair or British Midland. Apex fares are generally the cheapest; you need to book these in advance and stay a Saturday night. Other airlines serving Ireland from the UK include Loganair, Brymon and Manx Airlines. These, plus Air UK, Gill Air, Titan, Britannia Airways and British Airways, serve the North.

From North America, it may be cheaper to fly to London and reroute to Ireland from there, though this will add time to your long journey. In the US and Canada many discount fares are available. Aer Lingus and Delta operate scheduled services to Dublin, America Trans Air to Belfast; there are many charter flights. Boston–Shannon flying time is around five and a half hours. Direct flights are available from many European cities.

Aer Lingus offices can be found at the following addresses:
- Australia: Level 5, 36 Carrington Street, NSW 2000 (tel: 02 299 6211)
- Republic of Ireland: 42 Grafton Street, Dublin 2 (tel: 01 377777)
- UK: Aer Lingus House, 83 Staines Road, Hounslow, Middlesex (tel: 081 569 5555), and 223 Regent Street, London W1
- US: 122 East 42nd Street, New York 10168 (tel: 212/557 1090)
- Northern Ireland: 46 Castle Street, Belfast (tel: 0232 245151)

By sea Poor sailors beware, the Irish Sea is a notoriously uncomfortable crossing in bad weather. The main reason to opt for a sea crossing is to take a car, so cutting out the high costs of car hire in the Republic. Budget travellers may also use cheap rail/ferry or coach/ferry inclusive packages (student or youth reductions are considerable), though cheap air travel has severely dented even this market, and the Irish ferry scene has been marked by economic uncertainty in recent years. The main routes in the Republic are Holyhead–Dun Laoghaire (Dublin), Pembroke or Fishguard–Rosslare, or Swansea–Cork; in the North you can travel from Liverpool to Belfast, Stranraer or Cairnryan to Larne. A SeaCat fast catamaran service runs between Stranraer and Larne, and Holyhead and Dun Laoghaire. Services also operate between Cork and Rosslare to certain ports in Normandy and Brittany. In summer you need to book in advance for a place on many crossings. Ask your rail or bus travel centre about combined train/ ferry or bus/ferry fares. London–Dublin coach fares can be extremely cheap. Slattery's (tel: 071 482 1604) and Supabus (National Express, tel: 071 730 0202) are the main operators, serving Ireland from many UK cities. Getting to the North is more expensive; check with Ulsterbus (tel: 0232 333000) or Scottish Citylink (tel: 071 636 9373).

Quarantine Ireland is part of the British Isles quarantine area, which means that pets resident in Britain, the Channel Isles or the Isle of Man for at least six months can be taken to Ireland without requiring isolation. Indeed, being able to take the family dog on holiday is an important attraction for many British visitors. Animals from other places, of course, will be placed in quarantine. The following breeds of dog must wear muzzles and be kept under tight control:

Dun Laoghaire harbour, the port of entry for many visitors from Britain

- American pit bull terrier
- English bull terrier
- Staffordshire bull terrier
- ban dog
- bulldog
- bull mastiff
- Doberman pinscher
- German shepherd (Alsatian)
- Rhodesian ridgeback
- Rottweiler
- Japanese akita
- Japanese tosa.

Camping and caravanning

Lists of caravan parks and campsites are available from both national tourist boards; those in Bord Fáilte's brochure are regularly inspected and graded. All these sites have facilities, including mains water and electricity, showers, WCs, and sometimes restaurants and play areas. Unofficial camping is widespread in Ireland, however, and as long as you have the landowner's permission and cause no disturbance you may camp in any field. You may be asked to pay a *punt* or two in tourist areas. Many hostels will allow cheap camping on nearby land with use of showers and kitchens. State-run forest parks in the Republic do not permit camping; many in the North do.

Caravans can be hired, sometimes in conjunction with ferry deals. These vary from luxuriously furnished mobile homes to the picturesque,

253

horse-drawn Romany caravans of the Irish brochures (see below for more information).

Horse-drawn caravans If you want to hire a horse-drawn caravan, it is best to arrange third party liability insurance. Expect to cover no more than 15km per day, and stick to the quiet, flatter lanes of rural Ireland. Most caravans are four-berth. Don't expect luxury facilities aboard (bed linen and simple cooking utensils are provided, but no WCs, for example. Take your own towels and matches for lighting gas burners). Before you set off, hiring companies give you full instructions on routes, and handling and looking after the horse. Prices are seasonal; a deposit is required, and you should allow IR£5–7 for each overnight stop. Riding horses can be hired to accompany the caravan. Two of the best-known companies are Slattery's Horse-Drawn Caravans, 1 Russell Street, Tralee, County Kerry (tel: 066 26277, fax: 066 25981) or Clissman's Horse-Drawn Caravans, Carrigmore Farm, Wicklow (tel: 0404 48188, fax: 0404 48288). CIE Tours International, based outside London, can also arrange hire (tel: 081 667 0011).

The road between Glengarriff in County Cork and Kenmare in Kerry

Car breakdown

If the car is rented, contact the rental company (their nearest contact number should be on your contract or other rental documents). Automobile Association (AA) members, or members of affiliated motoring organisations belonging to the AIT (*Alliance International de Tourisme*), may call on the AA rescue services (provided in the Republic by the Automobile Association of Ireland). Both the AA and the RAC operates a breakdown service for its members in Northern Ireland.

Car rental

Hiring a car in the Republic is expensive – rates are among the highest in Europe, although they are cheaper in the North. Tariffs vary and, as elsewhere, small local firms will often give you a cheaper deal than the major international companies. To offset this, the vehicle may in some cases be less roadworthy, collection points less convenient, and service less efficient. You may also have to return the car to the point of collection rather than dropping it off in another town (check drop-off charges in advance). The large companies are geared to a nationwide operation, so if you hire in Dublin and break down in Donegal you won't have a problem. Just ring the nearest office. Major companies also insure you automatically to drive on either side of the border, though you should always specify this when you accept the car; check the booking conditions and insurance cover carefully. Most multinational companies have offices at the main airports and ferry terminals, as well as in large cities. Rental charges at Northern Ireland airports, however, may be more expensive than hiring with the same firm in the city. The tourist offices or the Automobile Association will be able to offer advice concerning approved rental companies.

Avis/Johnson & Perrott (based in Cork but with offices in most airports and cities) are the largest operators in the Republic, supplying cars for several major travel firms, airlines, etc. They provide clean, reliable cars and a good back-up service. Other large firms include Hertz, Murray's, Europcar and Budget. Rates are very seasonal. The cheapest way to book a rental car is to arrange an inclusive package-deal in advance with a tour operator, airline and ferry company (fly-drive or rail/ferry-drive) rather than waiting until you arrrive in Ireland.

To hire a car you must have a valid driving licence (an international licence with an English translation if you are a non-EC resident). Some companies specify age limits for drivers (usually a minimum of 23 or 25 and a maximum of 70 or 75). Make sure you take out collision damage waiver (CDW) as well as tne standard third-party insurance. Manual transmission vehicles are usually supplied unless automatics are specifically requested. Almost all rental cars use unleaded fuel. The best-value deals include unlimited mileage.

Climate

No one goes to Ireland for a tan. It has a fine climate (mild, free from extremes, good for plants), but per-haps too much weather. As the pres-sure-systems sweep in from the Atlantic, Ireland gets the lot – and rain follows shine with immense rapidity. Ireland's 'soft days' of fine drizzle and low cloud are unavoid-able, but it is unfortunate if you should happen to be touring the Ring of Kerry on one. Be prepared for the four seasons in a single day. The Southeast is appreciably sunnier and drier than the west coast. July and August are the warmest months (average temperatures 10°C at night, 18°C during the day), but May, June or September may well be drier. Ireland has the added advantage of being less crowded in late spring and early autumn. It is impossible to pre-dict fine days at any time of year. If the sun comes out, enjoy it while you can. If it rains, tog up or head for the pub. It probably won't last long.

Crime

In general, rural areas of both the Republic and Northern Ireland are extremely safe. Unpleasant sectarian incidents or terrorist attacks hit the

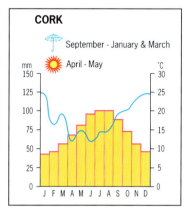

255

headlines at regular intervals, and occasionally visiting tourists have been caught up, but this is very rare. The main problems occur in cities, particularly in the deprived areas of

Dublin, where car theft is rife. Limerick also has a significant problem of violent crime and theft. Large gatherings (festivals, markets, horse-sales, etc.) attract a criminal element, as anywhere, and it is sensible to take precautions with your belongings. In particular, don't leave tempting valuables visible in a car. Personal violence or sexual assaults on strangers are fortunately rare, though women travelling alone should not take unnecessary risks (for example, by hitch-hiking).

Customs regulations

The Republic now operates the same rules on duty-free goods as the rest of the EC. From 1 January 1993, EC travellers have been able to import increased quantities of *duty-paid* goods for personal use only: up to 50 litres of beer; 25 litres of wine; and 800 cigarettes. *Duty-free* allowances (not available when travelling between Britain and Northern Ireland) are lower: 200 cigarettes; 1 litre of spirits; 2 litres of wine, 50g of perfume and 250ml of toilet water, plus other dutiable goods to the value of IR£34 (IR£17 if under 15 years of age). There are restrictions on importing certain food items into both the Republic and Northern Ireland (the latter if travelling from

The Irish are enthusiastic cyclists

outside the UK). For more information, contact the Custom House either in Dublin (tel: 01 873 4555) or in Belfast (0232 234466).

Cycling

Cycling is one of the best ways to get about in Ireland, especially granted decent weather. The secondary roads are mostly empty, built-up areas limited, and open countryside all around. Most airlines will carry bikes free if you don't exceed your weight allowance. If you bring your own bike it's advisable to bring a spare tube and tyre with you, as Irish sizes are unusual. It is very easy to hire a bike when you arrive in Ireland. Raleigh are the biggest operators, with a nationwide organisation of pick-up and drop-off points, but local dealers, hotels and hostels can provide them too. Cycle helmets can be hired in some places, but not everywhere. Check brakes and tyres and get a pump and repair kit. Bikes can be carried on buses and trains, if room, but there is a charge. Collect leaflets on cycling from Bord Fáilte or the Northern Ireland Tourist Board (NITB). Several companies in Britain and Ireland arrange cycling holidays, with accommodation, transport of luggage, lunches and guides, including: Celtic Cycling, Bagenalstown, County Carlow (tel: 0503 75282), Bike Events (in Avon, England, tel:

0225 480130) and the Irish Travel Bureau, Manchester (tel: 061 976 3887).

Disabled people

Associations for the disabled can give advice on travel and mobility problems. Contact the Disabled Drivers Association (in Ireland, tel: 050 841449) for details of travel discounts on ferries, etc. Registered disabled drivers may park free of charge with an orange badge. The national tourist boards both produce useful literature (Bord Fáilte's *Accommodation Guide for Disabled Persons* is available free). Increasing numbers of hotels and guest-houses cater for people in wheelchairs, and access to many sights, museums, etc., is being adapted. Useful addresses include:

● National Rehabilitation Board, 25 Clyde Road, Dublin 4 (tel: 01 668 4181)
● Irish Wheelchair Association, Blackheath Drive, Clontarf, Dublin 3 (tel: 01 338241, fax: 01 333273)
● Disability Action, 2 Annadale Avenue, Belfast BT7 3JR (tel: 0232 491011).

Driving

Motorists drive on the left in Ireland, though driving habits are erratic, particularly in rural areas. Hazards include slow-moving farm vehicles, often without lights, that lurch suddenly into the roadway from field gates – or equally suddenly, turn into farm entrances without indicating. Herds of cows, flocks of sheep, seemingly endless loose chippings and unexpected roadworks are all part of Irish motoring. Farm dogs enjoy chasing cars. There is no need to swerve or brake for them; they know exactly how far to go. Poor public transport networks and the importance of the pub in Ireland result in a high incidence of drivers on the roads with alcohol on board, though penalties for drinking and driving are severe. In short, care is required at all times on Irish roads.

Documents required A valid driving licence is required (with an English-language translation if you wish to

hire a car). Non-EC residents should obtain an international driving licence from their country of origin. If you bring your own vehicle, take the registration document with you, and a letter of authorisation from the owner if he or she is not with the vehicle. Both the car and any trailer or caravan should carry an appropriately sized nationality sticker. Insurance is compulsory; a Green Card is a well recognised international proof of cover.

Regulations Irish residents are not insured to drive non-Irish visitors' cars, other than a garage hand with written permission. A red warning triangle or hazard lights should be used if you break down. Use full or dipped headlights in poor visibility. Front seat-belts should be worn in the Republic; rear seat-belts (if fitted) in the North. Children under 12 must travel in the back. Offences such as speeding may attract an on-the-spot fine. Motorcyclists and passengers must wear helmets.

Speed limits: Despite most signposts in the Republic being in kilometres, speed limits are defined on both sides of the border in miles per hour. In the Republic:
● 30mph (48kph) in built-up areas
● 60mph (96kph) in country areas unless otherwise indicated
● 70mph (113kph) on motorways.

In Northern Ireland:
● 30mph (48kph) in built-up areas
● 40–60mph (64–96kph) in country areas
● 70mph (113kph) on dual carriageways and motorways
In both the limit for vehicles with trailers is 64kph (40mph).

Roads In the Republic there are very few stretches of motorway, though roads are being rapidly improved with the aid of EC grants. There are three road classifications: National Primary (labelled N, plus a number of between 1 and 50); National Secondary (N plus a number over 50) and Regional (R). These categories give little indication of how good the road actually is. Roads near large cities

257

TRAVEL FACTS

(Dublin, Cork, Waterford and Limerick) may suffer from congestion in rush hours. Elsewhere roadworks or border checkpoints may cause delays, but generally speaking roads are empty and driving in Ireland is a relaxing affair. Roads in Northern Ireland are much better, whether motorways, A-roads or B-roads.

Road signs In the Republic a single signpost may be cluttered with up to a dozen signs, some broken or turned the wrong way, in a mix of English and Gaelic. Distances are in kilometres on green Euro signs, but in miles on older black-and-white signs – even in Irish miles (equal to 2.05km or 1.3 miles) on some milestones – so the distance from your destination alters as you travel! Part of the entertainment of driving in Ireland is finding your way in these circumstances, helped by local directions, often of the 'I wouldn't be starting from here' variety.

Fuel Petrol is cheaper in the North; if you are anywhere near, it is worth hopping over the border to fill up. The differences are even more marked for unleaded fuel, which is now widely used on both sides of the border. Petrol stations usually stay open till around 8pm (later in built-up areas) in the Republic and some are open on Sundays. In the North petrol stations stay open longer, some 24 hours.

An unavoidable hazard on Irish lanes

Parking Several larger cities in the Republic have a disc parking system. Buy a disc from local shops or garages which allows you to park for a specified time. Elsewhere, multistorey or pay-and-display car-parks are the norm. In Belfast or Northern Irish towns, park only in authorised places. Many towns have control zones where you may not leave a vehicle unattended. If you do, you may cause a security alert.

Crossing the border (See panels on pages 214–15 for more details.) You should use only approved roads for border crossings, and be prepared to stop at checkpoints, state your destination and show identification. A passport, is useful, especially if you have hired a car with Irish Republic plates. Check your insurance covers you across the border.

Automobile Association Offices
The main AA offices in Ireland are at:
- 23 Rockhill, Blackrock, Dublin South (tel: 01 283 3555)
- 23 Suffolk Street, Dublin 2 (tel: 01 677 9481)
- 12 Emmet Place, Cork (tel: 021 276922)
- Fanum House, 108–10 Great Victoria Street, Belfast (tel: 0232 328924).

Electricity
The standard supply is 230 (240 in Northern Ireland) volts AC (50Hz), with mostly flat 3-pin sockets as in Britain (occasionally older round 2- or 3-pin ones may be found). North American appliances require both a transformer and an adapter – bring them with you.

Embassies and Consulates
Embassies in the Republic:
- Australia: Fitzwilton House, Wilton Terrace, Dublin 2 (tel: 01 676 1517)
- Canada: 65 St Stephen's Green, Dublin 2 (tel: 01 478 1988)
- UK: 33 Merrion Road, Dublin 4 (tel: 01 269 5211)
- US: 42 Elgin Road, Dublin 4 (tel: 01 668 8777).

Consular offices for Northern Ireland:

● Australia High Commission: Australia House, The Strand, London WC2B 4LA (tel: 071 379 4334)
● Canada High Commission: McDonald House, 1 Grosvenor Square, London W1X 0AB (tel: 071 258 6600)
● New Zealand High Commission: New Zealand House, Haymarket, London SW1Y 4TQ (tel: 071 930 8422)
● US: Queens House, 14 Queen Street, Belfast 1 (tel: 0232 328239).

Irish consulates abroad
● Britain: 17 Grosvenor Place, London SW1X 7HR (tel: 071 235 2171)
● Australia: 20 Arkana Street, Yarrulumla, Canberra 2600, ACT (tel: 062 733 022).
● Canada: 170 Metcalfe Street, Ottawa K2P 1P3, Ontario (tel: 613 233 6281)
● US: 2234 Massachusetts Avenue NW, Washington DC 20008 (tel: 202 462 3939/40/41/42). Also in Chicago, Boston, New York and San Francisco.

Emergency telephone numbers
Dial 999 throughout Ireland for police, fire or ambulance, or rescue services (coastal, mountain, cave).

Health
There are no special health requirements or recommended inoculations for visitors to the Republic or to Northern Ireland, and no particular hazards or diseases. EC residents are entitled to reciprocal health care (bring Form E111 or equivalent with you, obtainable from post offices). Make it clear you want to be treated under EC reciprocal arrangements if you need medical attention.

If you are a British citizen you are technically entitled to reciprocal free health care in the Republic, just as Irish citizens are entitled to use the NHS in Britain; in practice this may be difficult to obtain unless you have an E111 with you, and you may not find a doctor registered with the Health Board Panel who is prepared to treat you without charging. British citizens are of course entitled to free National Health Service treatment in Northern Ireland – if you're British, your best bet is to get yourself over the border if at all possible.

It is advisable for any visitor to take out adequate medical insurance. A good travel policy will cover loss and theft of property, cover you for any legal emergency, and get you home if you're stuck. If you have to have medical treatment, keep all bills and medical receipts for any subsequent claim. Take some convincing identification with you when you ask for treatment, and proof of insurance.

Language
Everyone in Ireland speaks English, but officially the Republic is bilingual, and Gaelic is the first language in areas of Cork, Waterford and parts of the West (especially Dingle and

A detail from a mural at the Irish Life Centre in Dublin

TRAVEL FACTS

Connemara). Every Irish citizen can be heard in Irish if summoned to court, and it is an entry requirement for university (except TCD). Radio, television and newspapers all have features in Gaelic.

In practice you don't need to speak a word as a visitor, but you may find a warmer welcome if you show an interest. Pronunciation is difficult, bearing scant relation to spelling, and it is frustratingly hard for a non-native even to attempt a rendering of some place-names without hearing an Irish speaker first. There are several dialects of Gaelic and pronunciation varies from place to place.

Lost property
Serious losses should always be reported to the police, who should give you a copy of your statement if you wish to make an insurance claim. Inform your embassy if you have lost a passport; a bank displaying the Eurocard symbol if you have lost credit cards or traveller's cheques (be sure to keep a note of the numbers and your purchase receipt *separate* from the cheques in order to obtain replacements rapidly).

❏ Here are a few of the words and phrases you are most likely to come across:

Bord Fáilte (Irish Tourist Board, literally 'board of welcomes') – pronounced 'bord fawlcha'
Céad míle fáilte (literally, 'a hundred thousand welcomes') – 'kay-d mille fawlcha'
céilídh (Irish dance night) – 'kaylee'
Gaeltacht (Irish-speaking region) – 'gale-tackt'
Garda Síochána (police) – 'gawr-da sheekawnah'
poteen (alcohol distilled from potatoes, illegal and often dangerous) – 'potcheen'
sláinte (cheers, good health) – 'slawn-cha'
slán (goodbye) –'slawn'
Taoiseach (Prime Minister) – 'teeshock'
uisce beatha (whiskey, literally 'water of life') – 'ishka baha'
Most importantly, *Mná* means women and *Fir* means men on WCs.

And a few words that appear in place-names:
ard height (Ardmore, Ardglass)
ath ford (Athlone, Athlumney)
bal, baile, bally town (Ballymena, Ballinrobe)
carrick rock (Carrickfergus, Carrickmacross)
drom, *drum* ridge (Dromahair, Drumcondra)
dún fort (Donegal, Dungannon)
ennis, inis island (Enniskillen, Innisfree)
glen vale, glen (Glendalough, Glengarriff)
kil, cille church (Killarney, Kilkenny)
lios, liss mound, ring-fort (Lismore, Lisdoonvarna)
rath fortified homestead, ring-fort (Rathmullen, Rathkeale). ❏

260

The Irish seem particularly keen to get as much use as possible from each of their signposts – this one stands at Dromahair in County Leitrim

Media

Republic of Ireland television broadcasting is operated by a state-sponsored body called RTE (Radio Telefís Éireann). It has three radio and two television channels (RTE1 and RTE2). You can receive them all over Ireland, including the North. In much of the Republic, you can pick up BBC (radio and television) and Ulster Television. Local radio, including many independent stations, offers blasts of Irish music, chat, and lilting Gaelic (also useful for traffic and weather reports, and events). British visitors will hear a new slant to Irish or world affairs – or the problems of the North – on Irish news broadcasts.

The main newspapers available in the Republic are the *Irish Times*, the *Irish Press* and the *Irish Independent* – all slim publications which are expensive by UK standards, but a great insight into Irish life and politics. Another respected newspaper is the *Cork Examiner*, which comments on world affairs with *gravitas*. Sunday papers include the *Sunday Tribune* (good arts reviews and listings), the *Sunday Press*, *Sunday Independent* and *Sunday Business Post*. British newspapers are available the same day in Dublin and major cities, and of course on sale all over the North. The most widespread local paper there is the evening *Belfast Telegraph*. In the mornings you have a choice of the nationalist *Irish News*, or the loyalist *News Letter*.

Money matters

Currency: In the North the currency used is the pound sterling (as in the rest of the UK). In the Republic it is the *punt* or Irish pound (written IR£), divided into 100 pence. When the UK was forced out of the European Monetary System and devalued sterling sharply in late 1992, the *punt* was left badly exposed to every economic chill wind, though many southern Irish found it hard to restrain their glee at the sight of an Irish pound worth considerably more than a British one for almost the first time in history. Eventually the *punt* has settled down to its customary level (very roughly five per cent below sterling). In a few border outlets such as petrol

261

CONVERSION CHARTS

FROM	TO	MULTIPLY BY
Inches	Centimetres	2.54
Centimetres	Inches	0.3937
Feet	Metres	0.3048
Metres	Feet	3.2810
Yards	Metres	0.9144
Metres	Yards	1.0940
Miles	Kilometres	1.6090
Kilometres	Miles	0.6214
Acres	Hectares	0.4047
Hectares	Acres	2.4710
Gallons	Litres	4.5460
Litres	Gallons	0.2200
Ounces	Grams	28.35
Grams	Ounces	0.0353
Pounds	Grams	453.6
Grams	Pounds	0.0022
Pounds	Kilograms	0.4536
Kilograms	Pounds	2.205
Tons	Tonnes	1.0160
Tonnes	Tons	0.9842

MEN'S SUITS

UK	36	38	40	42	44	46	48
Rest of Europe	46	48	50	52	54	56	58
US	36	38	40	42	44	46	48

DRESS SIZES

UK	8	10	12	14	16	18
France	36	38	40	42	44	46
Italy	38	40	42	44	46	48
Rest of Europe	34	36	38	40	42	44
US	6	8	10	12	14	16

MEN'S SHIRTS

UK	14	14.5	15	15.5	16	16.5	17
Rest of Europe	36	37	38	39/40	41	42	43
US	14	14.5	15	15.5	16	16.5	17

MEN'S SHOES

UK	7	7.5	8.5	9.5	10.5	11
Rest of Europe	41	42	43	44	45	46
US	8	8.5	9.5	10.5	11.5	12

WOMEN'S SHOES

UK	4.5	5	5.5	6	6.5	7
Rest of Europe	38	38	39	39	40	41
US	6	6.5	7	7.5	8	8.5

A Kilkenny pub sign

stations you can use either currency at parity, whatever the exchange rate; elsewhere you must use the appropriate currency or lose heavily in the conversion process. Have a supply of both currencies if you are crossing the border. Traveller's cheques or a Eurocheque book and card are the safest way to carry your cash. There is no limit to the amount of currency you may take in with you.

Changing money This is best carried out at a bank; see below for opening hours. Exchange facilities are also available at international airports, travel agencies, hotels and some tourist offices, though the rates may not be as favourable.

Credit cards: Major credit cards (those bearing the Eurocard/Master-card and Visa symbols), are widely accepted all over Ireland, particularly in shops catering for tourists. Charge cards, such as American Express and Diners Club, are also acceptable in some outlets (less so in the North). You can use Visa to withdraw cash from banks displaying the card's symbol. Smaller retailers or restaurateurs and bed-and-breakfast owners prefer cash. Personal cheques drawn on British banks and backed by a cheque guarantee card may be cashed to the value of IR£50.00 in the Republic.

National holidays
New Year's Day, St Patrick's Day (17 March), Easter Monday, Christmas Day and Boxing Day (known as St Stephen's Day in the Republic) are public holidays in both the North and the Republic. In addition the Republic has the following public holidays:
● first Monday in June
● first Monday in August
● last Monday in October.

Northern Ireland also takes these days as holidays:
● first Monday in May
● last Monday in May
● Orange Day (12 July)
● last Monday in August
Good Friday is not a statutory holiday, but is observed as a holiday in most parts of Ireland.

Opening hours
Times given below are general and subject to local variations. In the Republic – particularly in rural areas – shop hours may be erratic, but shop-keepers are also flexible and may be willing to open up specially. In Dublin and Belfast, hours may be longer, with late-night shopping on Thursday or Friday. Museums and other tourist sights vary greatly: the largest stay open all year; others close from mid-September or October until Easter. Summer opening hours are usually longer than in winter. Some muse-ums close on Monday; *always* check with the tourist office before making a long journey. Published times may be unreliable, or sights closed for renovation, etc. The following open-ing hours apply in the Republic:
● shops: 9–5.30, Monday–Saturday, with partial closing on Monday, Wednesday or Thursday
● banks: 10–12.30; 1.30–3, Monday–Friday (closed national holi-days). Many banks stay open until 5 on Thursday in Dublin, some now open at lunchtime
● post offices: 8–5.30 or 6, Monday–Saturday (usually closed at lunchtime). Sub-post offices close early one day a week
● pubs: 10.30a.m.–11.30p.m., Monday–Saturday; 12.30–2, 4–11.30, Sunday (during the summer months). Pubs tend to close at 11 in winter.

Opening hours in the North are slightly different:
● shops: 9–5.30, Monday–Saturday, with one mid-week early closing day (Wednesday or Thursday). Some close for lunch, while many Belfast stores open late (until 9) on Thursday
● banks: 10–3.30, Monday–Friday. Some banks close 12.30–1.30
● post offices: 9–5.30, Monday–Friday; 9–1, Saturday. Some close for lunch, or, alternatively, all day Wednesday
● pubs: 11.30a.m.–11p.m., Monday–Saturday (some pubs in Belfast have a late licence until 1a.m. on Friday and Saturday nights); 12.30–2.30, 7–10, Sunday (at the landlord's discretion).

Pharmacies

Besides medicines, these also stock cosmetics and photographic products. When closed, they should display a notice outside giving the rota of chemists open late. In an emergency, contact the local hospital. Contraceptives (condoms) are much more widely available in the Republic than they were a few years ago (when they were illegal!) but you may still find them hard to obtain in some rural areas, and they are still products to be kept under the counter, not on general display.

The view from the Rock of Dunamase, County Laois

Places of worship

Ireland naturally has many churches, though it may surprise visitors to see how many are Church of Ireland (Protestant), not Roman Catholic. Some churches open only for services and are otherwise locked. You can usually obtain the key by asking someone near by where it is kept. If you cause no disturbance it is acceptable to slip in and out of a church during mass for a quick look round (don't barge about during the service, of course). There are few non-Christian places of worship, but Belfast and Dublin have synagogues, Dublin a mosque (check with tourist boards for details). Marian shrines, such as the one at Knock, or grottoes like Ballinspittle, attract many pious Catholics, the majority of whom are women.

Police

In the Republic, the police are called the Gardaí ('gardee'), wear blue-and-black uniforms, and are unarmed. In the North the police force is the Royal Ulster Constabulary, in green uniforms. They carry arms, and police stations in the North have very tight security.

Post Offices

Easily identifiable, even in the Republic, by the word 'Post' in green. The postal services are notoriously unreliable in the Republic, and postage is expensive (postcards are cheaper than letters). In the North postal rates are the same as in the rest of the UK (a two-tier system is used: first and second class, the former purportedly buying speed). Pillar boxes are red in the north, green in the south. The correct stamps must be used either side of the border. The GPO in O'Connell Street, Dublin, is open longer hours than elsewhere, including Sundays and bank holidays. See also the opening hours section, above.

Public Transport

In general, local public transport in the Republic is very limited, which is why you see so many young people hitch-hiking. Things are better in the North, though it is still immeasurably more convenient to have your own transport.

Air Regular air services connect Dublin with the West (Shannon and Cork) and if money is no object, it is a very quick journey (30–40 mins). Regular flights also connect Galway and the Aran Islands (15–25 mins), operated by Aer Arann, weather permitting. Business travel and tourism have opened up a number of provincial airports with regular internal services and flights to the UK run by Aer Lingus and Ryanair.

Train The rail network in the Republic is controlled by the state-owned Irish Rail (Iarnrod Éireann), the rail division of CIE (Coras Iompair Éireann). Trains are fairly slow and

infrequent, but generally reliable and comfortable. Most routes radiate from Dublin. The only service connecting the Republic and the North is the Dublin–Belfast Express (about six trains each way a day). Large parts of the country are not covered by the rail network at all, such as Donegal and the border counties, Clare, Connemara, and southwest Cork. Fares are complex and not especially cheap – consider a discount pass if you plan to do much rail travel (see Passes, below). The Dublin area has its own transport system, DART (Dublin Area Rapid Transit), a suburban electric rail service operating between Howth and Bray. In Northern Ireland there are three routes run by Northern Ireland Rail. You can take a bike on trains if there is room, but there is a charge.

Bus Bus Éireann and Ulsterbus respectively provide the Republic's and Northern Ireland's national express coach systems, supplemented by Dublin Bus in the Dublin area, and by many private bus lines (sometimes cheaper and faster than the national buses, though insurance cover may be dubious). Various coach operators offer sightseeing tours (such as Grey Line). Bus travel in the Republic is often very slow, but fares are much cheaper than train fares. Off-season services may be very infrequent, but conversely weekend services may be oversubscribed. Small villages are sometimes served by only a couple of buses a week. Many bus indicators are in Irish, so check your destination carefully. Midweek 'single' tickets can be used for a free return journey and remain valid for a month. Bikes can be carried (for a charge) at the driver's discretion – if there is room. Bus travel in the North is generally reliable and serves most areas not reached by train.

Ferry or boat Three useful car ferries across estuaries cut down long detours inland. One is at Waterford (between Ballyhack and Passage East), linking Counties Waterford and

Post boxes are green south of the border, and red to the north

The DART at Dun Laoghaire station

Wexford. The second is across the Shannon estuary between Killimer and Tarbert, linking Kerry and Clare and cutting out the bottleneck journey through Limerick. The third is between Strangford and Portaferry in County Down.

Most of Ireland's islands can be reached by ferry, too. There are regular services to the Aran Islands from Galway City, Spiddal, Rossaveal (further west along the south Galway coast) and Doolin in County Clare. The islands off Donegal (Inishbofin, Aran Island) and those of Cork (Bear, Sherkin and Clear Island) are also linked with regular ferries. Others can be reached by private charter services (such as the Blaskets, Skelligs, and Tory Island), usually in the summer only. Get the tourist office leaflet *Island Boat/Air Services* (No IS50C) for further details. Rathlin is reached from Ballycastle.

Passes Many different discount schemes operate, but you need to assess your probable usage carefully before investing in a pass. Ask the tourist office which would be most appropriate for you. Emerald Cards cover unlimited bus and rail travel throughout Ireland for eight or fifteen days. Rambler Tickets buy you unlimited travel on Irish Rail for so many days within a given period.

Runaround tickets are valid on Northern Irish trains. These various offers are constantly changing and you should check at tourist offices for up-to-date information.

More information Irish Rail (Iarnrod Éireann) (tel: 01 366222); Bus Éireann (tel: 01 366111);Ulsterbus (tel: 0232 333000); Northern Ireland Railways (tel: 0232 230310). For guided tour information, contact CIE Tours International, 35 Lower Abbey Street Dublin (tel: 01 873 1100) or, in Northern Ireland, the Ulsterbus Travel Centre, Glengall Street, Belfast (tel: 0232 333000).

Security
Most of Ireland is extremely relaxed, but inevitably in the tension zones of the North security measures are tight. Leave no baggage unattended, be vigilant, and always park in authorised places (some central areas are controlled zones where unattended vehicles will be removed or possibly detonated by security forces). If there is an alert, you may have to move very fast. Be prepared to show identification (a passport or driving licence). Always stop at road checks, and use only approved roads for border crossings. There are no public places to leave luggage in the North, but lockers are usually available at bus and rail stations in the Republic. It is generally illegal to take photo-

graphs of police or military barracks in the North and if you are noticed you may be suspected of terrorism. Security forces on both sides of the border are usually extremely polite to bona fide travellers, and if you have nothing to hide, you have nothing to fear.

Student and youth travel

Discounts are available for young people and students. Check fares through specialist agencies such as British-based STA Travel or Campus Travel, or ask ferry and airline companies direct. Tickets may be subject to availability (only bookable the day before you travel for example) so you need to be more flexible than you might like during busy periods. Check youth fares against other types of saver tickets – there are many cheap fares available. You may need an international student identity card (ISIC), Youthcard or Travelsave Stamp to obtain these low fares; in some cases a passport or driving licence will do. Eurail and Transalpino passes (for under 26 year olds) are valid in Ireland.

Cheap travel concessions (such as combined accommodation and rail or bus tickets) are also available from The Irish Youth Hostel Association, **An Óige**, based at 61 Mountjoy Square, Dublin 1 (tel: 01 304555). It has about 50 hostels all over the Republic, some in attractive old buildings and beautiful settings. The Youth Hostel Association of Northern Ireland runs six hostels (YHANI, 56 Bradbury Place, Belfast BT7 1RU, tel: 0232 324733, fax: 0232 439699). The 76 hostels of the Independent Hostel Owners group (IHO Information Office, tel: 027 51050) are run along rather more relaxed lines, with private double, single and family rooms as well as traditional dormitory accommodation. Bord Fáilte runs an inspection scheme for independent hostels; the Irish Approved Independent Hostels (IAIH, tel: 01 269 7696, fax: 01 269 7704). Budget accommodation can become overcrowded during peak season.

Telephones

You can find public STD payphones in street booths and bars or shops (some with a sign saying 'you can phone from here'). Older-style call boxes in the Republic are blue and cream and marked in Gaelic 'Telefón'. Some are antique; follow the instructions carefully. Northern Irish call boxes are red. Newer automatic glass and metal boxes are replacing both types. International calls must be made from newer machines, or from some post offices. Calls connected by the operator – dial 10 (100 in the North) – are much more expensive than directdial calls (no cheap rate in the Republic, after 6p.m. and at weekends in Northern Ireland); so are those made from hotels. Calls to Britain and parts of Europe (including EC countries) *are* cheaper after 6p.m.; to US or Canada after 10p.m.; both are cheaper at weekends. Lower rates operate between the Republic and Britain than elsewhere (cheapest of all between midnight and 8a.m. – direct-dial from an ordinary phone only). Other countries have no reduced-rate call times. Cardphones are a new and convenient way of making long-dis-

The older style of Irish phone box

tance calls (buy cards at newsagents or post offices). Dublin numbers are changing from six to seven digits; if you dial a six-figure number, the operator *may* tell you to add a prefix. A useful booklet summarising telephone information and listing international codes can be picked up at airports, post or tourist offices.

Time

Ireland is on UK time: Greenwich Mean Time (GMT) in winter; GMT plus one hour in summer (British

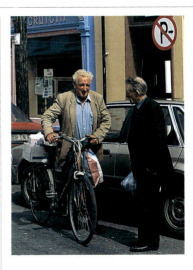

The greener form of transport

❑ International Dialling
Omit the initial zero of the local code when dialling internationally.
Access codes to Ireland from:
● Britain 010
● Australia 0011
● New Zealand 00
● Canada 011
● US 011
followed by 353 for the Republic or 44 for Northern Ireland.

Access codes from the Republic:
● Britain 0044
● Australia 0061
● New Zealand 0064
● Canada 001
● US 001.

● To dial the North from the Republic, dial 08, followed by the local code (in full, including the initial STD zero). Check in the phonebook or dial 1190 for local codes.
● To dial the Republic from the North, local codes are used, but not the same ones as used when dialling internationally! Ask the local operator for assistance.
❑

Summer Time or Central European Time). Summer, in this sense, runs from March to October. Irish time, however, may bear little relation to the clock – allow plenty of leeway!

Tipping

If service is not included (it often is, at 12 or 15 per cent), leave a 10–15 per cent tip on restaurant bills. Taxi drivers, hotel porters, lounge bar waiters and so forth like receiving tips as much as anyone, but in general help and advice to strangers is proffered as a natural courtesy in Ireland, without expectation of reward. Tipping is not customary in pubs.

Toilets

Public conveniences (rest-rooms) are generally available in towns and tourist sites throughout Ireland. You may see the Gaelic signs *Mná* (women) or *Fir* (men) on some, but ideograms usually leave you in no doubt which is which. Loos in traditional spit-and-sawdust bars may not be particularly well kept.

Tourist information

A list of all Ireland's tourist information offices can be picked up in any tourist office, North or South. All these centres can supply maps, town plans, timetables, brochures and information on all local sights, events, sports facilities etc., though for many items a charge is made. Bord Fáilte's green information sheets give useful summaries on many topics (such as fishing, car hire, horse-drawn caravans, Irish folklore). Maps of Ireland are often out of date and inaccurate, fine for general motoring, but not ideal for exploring in detail. Local maps, such as those produced by Tim Robinson to Connemara, the Aran Islands and the Burren, are the best bet for walking.

Northern Ireland has plenty of well-produced and very useful information, mostly distributed free of charge. Most tourist offices will book accommodation for you, though you have to pay a fee for the telephone calls – it is often better to get the lists and do your own phoning. A ten per cent deposit is taken at the time of booking, later deducted from your final bill. Accommodation unlisted by Bord Fáilte is not necessarily substandard.

Bord Fáilte (Irish Tourist Board)
● Britain: 150 Bond Street London W1Y 0AQ (tel: 071 493 3201); also at All-Ireland Tourism, 12 Regent Street, London SW1Y 4PQ (tel: 071 839 8416/7)
● Australia: 5th Level, 36 Cannington Street, Sydney, NSW 2000 (tel: 02 299 6177)
● Canada: 160 Bloor Street East, Suite 1150, Toronto, Ontario, M4W 1B9 (tel: 416 929 2777)
● US: 757 Third Avenue, New York NY 10017 (tel: 212 418 0800)

Northern Ireland Tourist Board
● Britain: Northern Ireland Business Centre, 11 Berkeley Street, London W1X 5AD (tel: 071 493 0601 or 0800 282662); also at All-Ireland Tourism, 12 Regent Street, London SW1Y 4PQ (tel: 071 839 8416/7)
● Canada: 111 Avenue Road, Suite 450, Toronto, Ontario (tel: 416 925 6368)
● Republic of Ireland: 16 Nassau Street, Dublin 2 (tel: 01 679 1977)
● US: Suite701, 515 5th Avenue, New York NY 10001 (tel: 212 922 0101 or 800 326 0063)

Within the Republic there are about 100 tourist offices marked with the information symbol 'i' on a green background. Those in major towns usually stay open all year, Monday to Saturday. Dublin's main tourist office is at 14 O'Connell Street (tel: 01 874 7733). Northern Ireland has about 30 tourist information centres; NITB

A Kinsale character

head office is at St Anne's Court, North Street, Belfast (tel: 0232 246609).

Useful things to bring
Warm clothes, comfortable footwear, and rain gear are essential. Bring wellingtons if you are planning to explore the boglands, sensible walking shoes or boots and a compass if you are planning to do any serious walking. A torch can be handy for dark churches, caves or castle ruins, or simply for finding your way home from the pub late at night. Take a sheet sleeping bag for staying in hostels. A good flower or bird identification guide and binoculars are musts for keen naturalists. If you are planning to visit the North, don't forget your National Trust membership card if you have one. Camera film is quite expensive in the Republic. Bring any prescribed medicines or contraceptives you need; they may not be available locally. Non-British visitors with electrical appliances will need an adaptor and possibly a transformer. Take your driving licence if you want to hire a car. A passport provides useful identification, even if you don't need to bring it (see entry formalities above). Leave room in your suitcase, though, for an Irish sweater or some tweed. You will almost certainly want to take home something from the Emerald Isle.

268

ACCOMMODATION

Accommodation registered with the Irish Tourist Board (in the Republic) has a green shamrock sign outside. All accommodation in the North is inspected and graded by the NITB. This isn't always a guarantee of excellence, but it does indicate that some basic standards have been met. Standards of accommodation have risen dramatically recently. Many establishments have been totally renovated in the last few years, with modern bathrooms and all mod cons. Some may feel the old-style charm and period interest has consequently been lost.

There are many splendid country-house hotels in Ireland, and lots of good-value, friendly B&Bs. Middle-range accommodation offering character and value is harder to find – there are many dull and shabby commercial hotels and seedy guest-houses with few attractions for the tourist. In high season all available accommodation can be very busy and it is advisable to book ahead, especially if some popular event or festival is taking place (the Kinsale Food Festival or the Cork Jazz Festival, for example). All the Bord Fáilte and Northern Ireland Tourist Board offices will ring round to book a room for you for a small fee.

Three leaflets are well worth looking out for: *The Blue Book*, *The Hidden Ireland*, and *Friendly Homes of Ireland* (see pages 236–7). The Tourist Office publications *Town and Country Homes*, *Farm Holidays in Ireland* and *Be Our Guest* also have useful if less discriminating selections. In addition it may be worth getting hold of a copy of *Where to Stay in Northern Ireland*, published by the NITB, and listing all the recommended accommodation in the province. If you want to stay really cheaply, look for the leaflet *Irish Hostel*

270

Guide, a list of approved independent hostels, or contact An Óige, the Irish Youth Hostel Association (61 Mountjoy Square, Dublin 1, tel: 01 304555) in the Republic, and the Youth Hostel Association of Northern Ireland (56 Bradbury Place, Belfast, tel: 0232 324733) in the North. You need an international youth hostel membership card to stay in these hostels. *Self-catering*, a guide to just that, is also available. Irish Rent a Cottage plc (85 O'Connell Street, Limerick, tel: 061 411109) is one of the largest specialist companies.

The list of accommodation that follows has been divided into three price categories, based on rates in high season:
● budget (£): you are likely to find a double bedroom for less than IR£45, including breakfast for two;
● moderate (££): you are likely to find a double bedroom for between IR£45 and IR£80, including breakfast for two;
● expensive (£££): you are likely to pay more than IR£75 for a double bedroom, including breakfast for two.

DUBLIN
(the code for Dublin is 01)
Ariel House (££) 52 Lansdowne Road, Ballsbridge, 4 (tel: 6685512). Well-run Victorian guest-house, with garden.
Avalon House (£) 55 Aungier Street, 2 (tel: 4750001). Cheering modern budget accommodation, bright, neat, practical. Self-service café. Rooms sleep 2–6.
Avondale House (££) Scribblestown, Castleknock (tel: 386545). Elegant 18th-century house near Phoenix Park. Country-house atmosphere (former estate hunting lodge). Rail transport to centre. Good home-cooking.
Buswells (£££) Molesworth Street, 2 (tel: 6764013). Gracious town-houses in heart of Georgian Dublin. Family-run, formal but relax-

ing, popular with journalists and politicians.
The Georgian House (££) 20–21 Lower Baggot Street, 2 (tel: 6618834). Stylishly converted town-house near St Stephen's Green. Elegant lounge, cosy brasserie and seafood (see also restaurant section).
Grey Door (£££) 22–23 Upper Pembroke Street, 2 (tel: 6763286). Restaurant-with-(newly opened)-rooms in Georgian setting. Accommodation is smart, if somewhat impersonal (see also restaurant section).
ISAAC'S (£) 2–5 Frenchman's Lane, 1 (tel: 363877/8749321). Pleasant hostel in converted 18th-century warehouse. Accommodation simple but adequate. Good self-service restaurant. Friendly and well-run.
Kinlay House (£) 2–12 Lord Edward Street, 2 (tel: 6796644). Simple, friendly USIT (Union of Students in Ireland Travel) hostel for young travellers near Dublin Castle.
Leeson Court (££) 26–27 Lower Leeson Street, 2 (tel: 6763380). Intimate, cheerfully furnished Georgian house. Patio/beer-garden at rear; night-club in basement; evening bar music (well insulated).
Longfield's (££) 9–10 Fitzwilliam Street Lower, 2 (tel: 6761367). Attractively furnished Georgian town-house with intimate basement restaurant (see also restaurant section).
Merrion Hall (£) 54–56 Merrion Road, Ballsbridge, 4 (tel: 6681426). Clean, tastefully furnished Victorian guest-house. Breakfast served in conservatory.
No 31 (££) 31 Leeson Close, 2 (tel: 6765011). Unusual and stylish house, secluded off smart Georgian street. Architect-designed interior. Lavish bathrooms. Friendly, unassuming owners. Excellent breakfasts. Roof garden.
Raglan Lodge (£) 10 Raglan Road, Ballsbridge, 4 (tel: 6606697). Attractive Victorian guest-house in

quiet residential area. Antiques. All bedrooms have private bathrooms.
Shelbourne (£££) 27 St Stephen's Green, 2 (tel: 6766471). Dublin's grandest hotel in a prime location, immortalised in *Ulysses*. The interior is smartly comfortable, but not daunting (see restaurants). Good for morning coffee and pre-dinner drinks.
Simmonstown House (£) 2 Sydenham Road, Ballsbridge, 4 (tel: 6607260). One of Dublin's least-known but most elegant guesthouses, preserving its civilised Edwardian atmosphere. Bedrooms individually designed.
Stephen's Hall (££) 14–17 Lower Leeson Street, 2 (tel: 6610585). Georgian exterior; bland modern furnishings within. All suite accommodation with good facilities for business visitors.

EASTERN COUNTIES
County Kildare
Barberstown Castle (£££) Straffan (tel: 01 6288157). Newly poshed-up restaurant-with-rooms in a mix of medieval, Elizabethan and Victorian surroundings. Expensive repro and heavy fabrics; large, sumptuous bedrooms (see also restaurant section).
Moyglare Manor (£££) Moyglare, Maynooth (tel: 01 6286351). Sybaritically furnished Georgian house in extensive parkland, an easy run from Dublin (see also restaurant section).
Silken Thomas (£) The Square, Kildare (tel: 045 22232). Well-kept central inn with ornate conservatory reception rooms and lavish Victoriana. A rear annexe, the Lord Edward Guest House, contains practical modern accommodation. Some may find the décor overdone, but it is certainly effortful. Decent bar food.

County Louth
Boyne Valley Hotel (££) Drogheda (tel: 041 37737). Rambling terracotta

Victorian mansion in waterside grounds. Traditionally comfortable interior. Conservatory bar and Swiss restaurant.
Carlingford House (£) Carlingford (tel: 042 73118). Welcoming family home quietly set in village centre. Attractively decorated bedrooms with easy chairs, some with original fireplaces.
The Gables (£) Ardee (tel: 041 53789). The main focus of attention is on the food here. Accommodation in this suburban roadside house is plain and unfrilly, but the welcome is warm (see also restaurant section).
McKevitt's Village Hotel (££) Market Square, Carlingford (tel: 042 73116). Cosy inn, the social heart of this charming village. Firelit bars where snacks are served. Well-equipped, sensibly planned bedrooms in cottagey style with modern pine.
Red House (£££) Ardee (tel: 041 53523). Georgian house in parkland, once the home of Lord Carlingford.
Viewpoint (£) Omeath Road, Carlingford (tel: 042 73149). High-quality, split-level, motel-style accommodation with restaurant; superlative views of Carlingford Lough and the Mountains of Mourne. Friendly welcome.

County Meath
Annesbrook (££) Duleek (tel: 041 23293). Imposing Georgian house offering relaxed family hospitality.
Conyngham Arms (££) Slane (tel: 041 24155). Unpretentious but comfortable stone-built village hotel, newly renovated in Edwardian style with modern facilities. Good bar-snacks and cakes.
The Glebe House (£) Dowth, Drogheda (tel: 041 36101). A splendidly hospitable, beautifully furnished country house right next to the great passage grave at Dowth (Newgrange is just down the road). Peaceful, tasteful, and comfortable,

with excellent views and good home-cooking.
Station House (££) Kilmessan (tel: 046 25239). This rambling, white Victorian house was indeed once a station linking lines from Dublin with County Meath. Now it is attractive and comfortable in restful florals, overlooking peaceful grounds. The Hill of Tara is just up the road (see also restaurant section).

County Wicklow
Ballyknocken House (£) Glenealy (tel: 0404 44627). Simple 80ha working farm with peaceful gardens, transformed by its welcoming hostess into a charming guest-house.
Corner House (£) Enniskerry (tel: 01 2860149). Small guest-house over the village shop offering good-value B&B with showers in each room. A cheap base for Powerscourt or the Wicklow Mountains.
Derrybawn House (£) Glendalough, Laragh (tel: 0404 45134). Attractive and peaceful guest-house a little way from the tourist traps of Glendalough. Modest facilities, but good value. Log fires and a full-size snooker table. Dinner by arrangement.
Enniscree Lodge Hotel (££) Glencree Road, Enniskerry (tel: 01 2863542). Homely if unremarkable interior redeemed by a spectacular location and views. Popular for Sunday lunch.
Hunter's Hotel (££) Newrath Bridge, Rathnew (tel: 0404 40106). Splendid, old-fashioned coaching inn of unspoilt character and with a long history. Still family-run and idiosyncratic, with luscious gardens, cosy fires and relaxing charm (see also restaurant section). Close to Mount Usher Gardens.
Lissadell House (£) Ashtown, Wicklow (tel: 0404 67458). White detached house on working farm. Modest interior but a warm family welcome.
Old Rectory (£££) Wicklow (tel: 0404 67048). Smartly

271

furnished Regency-style house with good facilities and a secluded atmosphere, on the edge of town (see restaurants).

Rathsallagh House (£££) Dunlavin (tel: 045 53112). Rambling country-house hotel in parkland. Converted from a Queen Anne stable-block when the original house was burned down, this is now a supremely comfortable and appealing place. Tastefully and imaginatively furnished throughout, with gorgeous gardens. Self-catering annexe, tennis and indoor pool (see also restaurant section).

Tinakilly (£££) Rathnew (tel: 0404 69274). Once the house of Captain Halpin, that Victorian sea-farer who commanded the *Great Eastern*. Though now somewhat businesslike in style, the house retains the imposing dimensions specified by its creator, and overlooks lovely gardens to the sea (see also restaurant section).

SOUTHEASTERN COUNTIES

County Carlow

Lorum Old Rectory (£) Kilgreaney, Bagenalstown (tel: 0503 75282). Comfortably furnished house in scenic Barrow Valley.

County Kilkenny

Abbey House (£) Jerpoint Abbey, Thomastown (tel: 056 24166). Strikingly modernised guest-house very close to the abbey.

Blanchville House (£) Dunbell, Maddoxtown (tel: 056 27197). Elegant Georgian country house with spacious and tasteful rooms. House-party atmosphere.

Butler House (££) 16 Patrick Street, Kilkenny (tel: 056 22828). Interesting Civic Trust restoration of the former Dower House of Kilkenny Castle, this now combines stylish mod cons with gracious 1770 proportions. Walled garden. Small conferences sometimes held.

Cullintra House (£) Inistioge (tel: 051 23614). Idiosyncratic but thoroughly interesting creeper-covered farmhouse in wooded valley. Candlelit dinners and open fires. Lovely walks and views.

Garranavabby House (£) The Rower (tel: 051 23613). Simple but appealingly quaint farmhouse dating from 17th century, in glorious scenery. Fresh home cooking.

Lacken House (££) Dublin Road, Kilkenny (tel: 056 61085). Comfortable modern bedrooms with good facilities in this Victorian roadside restaurant-with-rooms (see also restaurant section).

County Tipperary

Aherlow House (££) Glen of Aherlow, Bansha (tel: 062 56153). Chintzy interpretation of old hunting lodge in lovely forest scenery. Antiques and modern furnishings.

Ballycormac House (££) Aglish, near Borrisokane (tel: 067 21129). Charming country house run on informal but decidedly upmarket house-party lines. Equestrian holidays a speciality. Excellent food.

Bansha Castle (£) Bansha (tel: 062 54187). Imposing early 19th-century house, a former residence of the Butler family. Now run as a friendly and informal guest-house.

Bansha House (£) Bansha (tel: 062 54194). Pleasant Georgian guest-house in 40ha of farmland where brood mares and foals roam. Modest modern furnishings.

Cappamura House (£) Dundrum (tel: 062 71127). Agreeable pink-washed farmhouse in quiet Golden Vale surroundings, comfortably furnished in a mix of traditional styles.

Cashel Palace (£££) Cashel (tel: 062 61411). Architecturally imposing bishop's residence in quiet setting below the Rock, somewhat staid inside (see also restaurant section).

Clonmel Arms (££) Clonmel

(tel: 052 21233). Reliable if unremarkable town-centre hotel.

Gurthalougha House (££) Ballinderry, Terryglass (tel: 067 22080). Delightful Regency farmhouse in forest by Lough Derg. Very peaceful and relaxing. Tastefully furnished and home-like. Good cooking. Outdoor pursuits.

Inch House (£) Bouladuff, Thurles (tel: 0504 51348). Distinguished 300-year-old manor in demesne of 140ha. Furnished carefully in period style with antiques and log fires.

Riverrun House (£) Terryglass, (tel: 067 22125). Quality new B&B venture in peaceful village setting. Light, spacious bedrooms furnished in tasteful modern styles. Log fires. Good breakfast.

County Waterford

Church Villa (£) Dunmore East (tel: 051 83390). Friendly and comfortable B&B opposite church. Very good value.

Clonea Strand (££) Clonea Strand, Dungarvan (tel: 058 42416). Recently modernised resort hotel on lovely beach. Leisure and fitness centre; no antique charm but lots for families.

Diamond Hill (£) Slieverue, Waterford (tel: 051 32855). Very competently run modern guest-house just outside town centre – somewhat impersonal accommodation but an Irish welcome with award-winning gardens.

Dunmore Lodge (£) Dunmore East (tel: 051 83454). Well-furnished and civilised accommodation in welcoming guest-house overlooking the bay. Good breakfasts.

Foxmount Farm (£) Halfway House, Waterford (tel: 051 74308). Pleasant 17th-century house in mature gardens. Homely furnishings. Good value and convenient for exploring Waterford City or the attractive harbour scenery.

Hanora's Cottage Guesthouse (£) Ballymacarbry, Nire Valley,

via Clonmel (tel: 052 36134). Unusual formula offering glorious peaceful valley scenery, modest but pleasant accommodation, afternoon teas and a short, careful dinner menu. Lots of activities nearby (fishing, riding, golf etc.). Friendly family atmosphere. Riverside gardens.
Hillfield House (£) Ballymabin, Dunmore East (tel: 051 83565). Enterprising modern B&B venture in quiet open farmland. Attractive, well-equipped bedrooms. Spacious and light.
Richmond House (££) Cappoquin (tel: 058 54278). Civilised and interesting Georgian house, once part of the Earl of Cork's estate. Antiques and individual furnishings.
Waterford Castle (£££) The Island, Ballinakill, Waterford (tel: 051 78203). Deluxe hotel on private island (reached by ferry). Lavish Tudor repro supplements genuine antiques and tapestries. Many sports facilities (see also restaurant section).

County Wexford
Ballinkeele House (££) Ballymurn, Enniscorthy (tel: 053 38105). Delightful, welcoming house built (imposingly) in 1840. Early Victorian-period feel and many interesting features. Excellent country-house cooking. The owners farm local land and take a great interest in the Wexford Opera Festival.
Clohamon House (££) Bunclody (tel: 054 77253). Charming 18th-century house in 70ha of land; aristocratic ownership. Dairy farm and pony stud. Private fishing rights and local country activities. Furnished with antiques, family portraits and romantic four-posters. Irish home cooking.
Clonard House (£) Clonard Great, Wexford (tel: 053 43141). Peaceful location just outside Wexford. Above-average country-house B&B in elegant

Georgian building (dairy farm). Unassuming hospitality. Informal dinners. Good value.
Kelly's Strand (££) Rosslare (tel: 053 32114). This rambling hotel looks brashly modern, but has a surprisingly long family pedigree. Today it houses predictable modern furnishings and good leisure facilities. Many awards for service and food.
Marlfield House (£££) Gorey (tel: 055 21124). Opulently furnished with flair. Both bedrooms and public areas of this aristocratic country house are a memorable experience (see also restaurant section).
Newbay Country House (££) Newbay, Wexford (tel: 053 42779). Civilised but relaxing country-house hospitality in tastefully furnished Georgian house. Parkland and woods around. Excellent food.
Whites Hotel (££) George Street, Wexford (tel: 053 22311). Solid, comfortable hotel with good facilities, slap in the middle of town. Modern box-like additions spoil the original 19th-century core.

SOUTHWESTERN COUNTIES
County Cork
Arbutus Lodge (££) Montenotte, Cork (tel: 021 501237). Victorian villa in hilly suburbs. Fine city views. Some antiques and interesting plasterwork; other sections are practical and modern. Solid comfort in the bedrooms and renowned food (see also restaurant section).
Assolas Country House (£££) Kanturk (tel: 029 50015). One of Ireland's most charming country houses – and one of the oldest (17th-century in parts). Serene surroundings, period features and antiques throughout. Welcoming atmosphere and lovely gardens. Excellent food (see also restaurant section).
Bailick Cottage (£) Midleton (tel: 021 631244). Charming

B&B in a creeper-clad house overlooking the estuary. Tasteful and attractive throughout. Excellent breakfasts and a welcoming hostess. Simple meals by arrangement.
Ballylickey Manor House (£££) Ballylickey, Bantry Bay (tel: 027 50071). Peaceful 17th-century manor, now luxuriously furnished in country-house style. Lovely gardens and bay views.
Ballymakeigh House (£) Killeagh, Youghal (tel: 024 95184). Excellent value guest-house with superb views down to the sea. Very comfortable and well-furnished throughout. Welcoming atmosphere and good cooking.
Ballymaloe House (£££) Shanagarry, Midleton (tel: 021 652531). A well-loved hotel, offering peace and some of the best food in Ireland (see also restaurant section). The keep of an old castle stands by the mellow creeper-covered farmhouse. Several outbuildings now house extra accommodation. Modern paintings add to the hotel's imaginative and tasteful décor, including many works by Jack Yeats. Superbly relaxing bedrooms. Family-run with enthusiasm and enterprise.
Ballyvolane House (££) Castlelyons, Fermoy (tel: 025 36349). Georgian mansion offering classy but completely unpretentious hospitality in a fine Italianate setting. Beautiful park and gardens and country house cooking. House-party style dining at one table.
Bantry House (£££) Bantry (tel: 027 50047). Classy B&B offered in a stately home. Recently refurbished bedrooms are spacious and well equipped in light modern colours. Incomparable views of the bay.
Blue Haven (££) Kinsale (tel: 021 772209). Very central small hotel, ever-popular for its excellent, good-value food (see also restaurant section) and attractive

273

accommodation. Bedrooms may be small but are well equipped. Lively and welcoming.

Conna House (£) Ballynoe, Conna, Tallow (tel: 058 59419). Exceptional B&B in Victorian house set in 4ha of woods and lawns. Beautiful furnishings, including Asian and Middle-Eastern rugs and curios.

Dunauley (£) Seskin, Bantry (tel: 027 50290). Delightful B&B in a pleasantly designed modern house overlooking Bantry Bay.

Glebe House (£) Ballinadee, Kinsale (tel: 021 778294). Attractive Georgian rectory, beautifully furnished, very welcoming hosts. Accommodation is simple, but civilised and very good value.

Innishannon House (£££) Innishannon (tel: 021 775121). White-painted house in peaceful riverside setting. Bright, attractive, tasteful furnishings and some interestingly shaped bedrooms. Undaunting, straightforward hospitality.

ISAAC'S (£) 48 MacCurtain Street, Cork (tel: 021 500011). One of the best budget options in the city centre. A pleasant, sensibly run hostel in a converted warehouse, with basic, but attractive facilities in dormitory, family, double and single rooms. Good self-service restaurant (open to non-residents, see also restaurant section).

Larchwood House (£) Pearsons Bridge, Ballylickey, Bantry (tel: 027 66181). Attractive modern house with light, well co-ordinated colour schemes. The main attractions of this apparently modest guesthouse, however, are its welcoming owners, beautifully landscaped gardens and exceptional food (see also restaurant section). Very peaceful.

Longueville House (£££) Mallow (tel: 022 47156). One of Ireland's most renowned country manors, a grand building overlooking many hectares of parkland. Inside it is predictably elegant, but

has a warm, welcoming feel. Conservatory extension, formal dining room where oil-painted worthies watch you eat superb food, and many period features (see also restaurant section).

Marine (££) Glandore (tel: 028 33366). Simple village hotel in idyllic location overlooking cove.

The Moorings (££) Scilly, Kinsale (tel: 021 772376). Large modern bungalow, somewhat suburban in style but with magnificent glazed extensions giving unparalleled views over Kinsale Harbour. Comfortable and welcoming.

Morrisons Island (£££) Morrisons Quay, Cork (tel: 021 275858). Suite accommodation in a warehouse-styled building overlooking the harbour. If you prefer the unrestricted aspects of a self-contained apartment, this could be the answer. Restaurant and all mod cons. Business facilities.

O'Donovan's (£) Clonakilty (tel: 023 33250). Time-warp hotel of the old commercial type, emphatically family-run. Furnishings are old-fashioned and basic, but the hotel has many interesting features, including a museum of historical associations. The Republican hero Michael Collins was born just up the road.

Old Bank House (££) Pearse Street, Kinsale (tel: 021 774075). Well-run and tastefully furnished Georgian building near the quayside, offering discreetly upmarket B&B. The owners run one of Kinsale's best restaurants (the Vintage, see also restaurant section).

Old Presbytery (£) Cork Street, Kinsale (tel: 021 772027). Personally and interestingly furnished, welcoming and home-like B&B in quiet (but central) location. Warmly recommended, and with excellent breakfasts. Good evening meals occasionally available.

Scilly House (£) Scilly, Kinsale (tel: 021 772413). Charming and beautifully located guest-house with romantically opulent bed-

rooms.

Sea View House (££) Ballylickey, Bantry (tel: 027 50462). Large white house in lovely gardens, well furnished in traditional style with some more modern additions. Bedrooms are large and light, some overlooking the sea. Genteel and welcoming air.

Seven North Mall (££) 7 North Mall, Cork (tel: 021 397191). Classy B&B in a listed Georgian building. Accommodation is attractive and practical enough for business people, with all mod cons. Breakfasts are excellent. A good location for exploring Cork City, overlooking the river.

County Kerry

Benner's Hotel (££) Main Street, Dingle (tel: 066 51638). Solid, well-furnished town hotel in distinguished Georgian building.

Captain's House (£) The Mall, Dingle (tel: 066 51531). Charming B&B in town centre, tastefully furnished.

Cleevaun Country Guest House (£) Lady's Cross, Dingle (tel: 066 51108). Simple but welcoming B&B in modern bungalow. Rural setting.

Doyle's Seafood Bar and Townhouse (££) John Street, Dingle (tel: 066 51174). This sophisticated establishment is well known in the West for its excellent, tastefully furnished accommodation and brilliant food (see also restaurant section). Unstuffy and informal.

Kathleen's Country House (££) Madam's Height, Tralee Road, Killarney (tel: 064 32810). Modern building, comfortably furnished. What makes it special is Kathleen's brand of effortless hospitality which engulfs you as soon as you set foot inside.

Muxnaw Lodge (£) Castletownbere Road, Kenmare (tel: 064 41252). Characterful and welcoming B&B just outside town.

Park Hotel (£££) Kenmare (tel: 064 41200). All the trimmings of this fine hotel in lovely grounds make it

274

expensive, but its particular brand of luxury is more than merely professional. It is also remarkably friendly. Excellent food (see also restaurant section).

Royal Hotel (££) College Street, Killarney (tel: 064 31853). If you have to stay in the centre of Killarney this is a safe bet, a well run, traditional town hotel, recently refurbished.

Sheen Falls Lodge (£££) Kenmare (tel: 064 41600). Newly opened and very large luxury hotel hogging the views of these spectacular waterfalls.

Smugglers Inn (£) Cliff Road, Waterville (tel: 066 74330). Simple, inexpensive option on the Ring of Kerry. Enjoy the sea, or a game of golf. Seafood available.

Tahilla Cove (££) Tahilla (tel: 064 45204). Charming guest-house overlooking bay. Pretty gardens.

Towers Hotel (£) Glenbeigh (tel: 066 68212). Modest, homely hotel in popular resort village. Many local activities.

County Limerick

Adare Manor (£££) Adare (tel: 061 396566). Elaborate Victorian Gothic pile, former seat of the Earls of Dunraven, now a luxury hotel under American ownership. All mod cons and baronial flourishes. Palatial bedrooms.

Dunraven Arms (££) Adare (tel: 061 396209). A well-known village inn, unspoilt by its hordes of coach-trippers. Tasteful décor, some antiques and cosy public rooms. Refurbished bedrooms. Good food, formal and informal (see also restaurant section).

WESTERN COUNTIES
County Clare

Carnelly House (££) Clarecastle (tel: 065 28442). Beautifully proportioned Queen Anne style building in 40ha of farmland, designed by Francis Bindon. As elegant inside as out, it now provides smart guest-house accommodation and classy din-

ners. Bedrooms are spacious and very tasteful.

Dromoland Castle (£££) Newmarket-on-Fergus (tel: 061 368144). Luxuriously appointed castle hotel in large estate, mostly favoured by the wealthy. Private golf course.

Fergus View (£) Kilnaboy, Corofin (tel: 065 27606). Good-value guest-house quietly set above lakes. Exceptionally wholesome cooking. Pleasant, simple décor.

Gregan's Castle (££) Ballyvaughan (tel: 065 77005). The smartest country house hotel on the Burren, overlooking a classic scene of grey limestone. Comfortable, cottage-look décor with all mod cons. Attractive, well-kept gardens.

Hyland's Hotel (££) Ballyvaughan (tel: 065 77037). Simple (but homely) village inn with comfortable bedrooms and good public areas. Music sessions in bar.

Lahardan House (£) Crusheen (tel: 065 27128). Modern farmhouse in peaceful countryside, offering slightly bleak accommodation but a family atmosphere.

Rusheen Lodge (£) Knocknagrough, Ballyvaughan (tel: 065 77092). Highly thought of guest-house in white bungalow on edge of village. Inexpensive base for exploring the north of the Burren. Modern furnishings.

Sheedy's Spa View (££) Lisdoonvarna (tel: 065 74026). Large complex offering unexceptional accommodation but renowned for its food (see also restaurant section).

Smyth's Village (£) Feakle (tel: 061 924002). Modern complex of cottage-like buildings in lovely countryside. This unusual enterprise offers simple accommodation and restaurant facilities for a moderate price. Private functions may take over at times. Activities can be arranged. Evening

music in summer.

Thomond House (££) Dromoland (tel: 061 368304). The former laird of Dromoland, Lord Inchiquin, now lives in this modest Georgian pastiche on the estate grounds and will share it with you for a nominal fee. It is very comfortable, though lacks the authenticity of Ireland's many genuine Georgian country houses.

County Galway

Ardagh (££) Clifden, Connemara (tel: 095 21384). Modern, stylish Dutch-owned hotel overlooking a splendid chunk of Connemara's coastal scenery from the upper restaurant windows. Pleasing décor (lots of plants) and extensive public rooms. Bedrooms are comfortable, spacious and well-equipped.

Ardilaun House (££) Taylors Hill, Galway (tel: 091 21433). Smartly furnished mid-market hotel near the resort of Salthill. Considerable business trade.

Ballynahinch Castle (££) Recess, Connemara (tel: 095 31006). Somewhat on the coach party circuit at lunch or tea-time, but this large estate house (once bought by a Maharajah) in beautiful scenery is very comfortable indeed for residents (see also restaurant section).

Cashel House (£££) Cashel Bay, Connemara (tel: 095 31001). Luxuriously furnished small hotel in white-painted Victorian house by coast. Lush, sheltered sub-tropical gardens. Many antiques and excellent food and wines. Peaceful, upmarket atmosphere.

Crocnaraw (££) Moyard, Connemara (tel: 095 41068). Attractively furnished and very quiet country house in splendid Connemara countryside. Stylish throughout, with lovely gardens.

Currarevagh House (££) Oughterard, Connemara (tel: 091 82312). This secluded country house offers

275

utter lakeshore peace – it may even be too quiet for some. A slightly staid air prevails, and some furnishings are a little dowdy. However, it is comfortable and the views from spacious bedrooms are splendid.

Delphi Lodge (££) Leenane (tel: 095 42211). House-party atmosphere in relaxingly informal family home. Seven guest-rooms all have bathrooms and lovely views. Extremely peaceful, with good country cooking. Good for fishing and walking. Some self-catering.

Erriseask House (££) Ballyconneely, Connemara (tel: 095 23553). Attractively decorated modern farmhouse in lovely coastal scenery. Light, airy bedrooms. Stylish but informal public areas.

Kille House (£) Kingstown, Clifden, Connemara (tel: 095 21849). Pleasantly furnished guest-house in distinguished early Victorian house in isolated location off the beautiful Sky Road northwest of Clifden. Very peaceful. Good cooking by arrangement.

Moycullen House (££) Moycullen, Connemara (tel: 091 85566). Secluded white-painted house in lush grounds. Interestingly furnished inside, each bedroom is different. Welcoming atmosphere. Good home-cooking by arrangement.

Rock Glen Manor House (££) Clifden, Connemara (tel: 095 21035). This traditional hotel occupies a lovely setting above the bay. Inside it is solidly comfortable, springing no decorative surprises, but has a relaxing and friendly air.

Rosleague Manor (££) Letterfrack, Connemara (tel: 095 41101. Imposing Georgian house overlooking Ballinakill Bay, now converted into a peaceful and comfortable country-house hotel with a fine reputation for good food (see also restaurant section).

St Ciarán's (£) Oughill,

Kilronan, Inishmore, Aran Islands (tel: 099 61238). Delightful B&B with cats, a designer's eye for décor, and generous breakfasts (or tea to revive you after the boat journey).

County Mayo
Ashford Castle (£££) Cong (tel: 092 46003). Sister hotel of Dromoland, it offers substantially the same package of Gothic-revival grandeur and a splendid parkland and lakeshore setting.

Enniscoe House (££) Castlehill, near Crossmolina, Ballina (tel: 096 31112). One of Ireland's finest Georgian mansions 'the last great house of North Mayo'. Many period features remain intact, and the house is furnished and decorated throughout with great taste, though it feels informal too. Good cooking. Heritage centre and small museum on estate.

Healy's (£) Pontoon (tel: 094 56443). Low-slung old stone building in scenic lakeshore setting. Simple bar food and hearty Irish cooking in the restaurant. Clean, comfortable bedrooms. Good site for bird-watching.

Newport House (££) Newport (tel: 098 41222). Elegantly furnished country-house hotel, formerly the seat of a branch of the O'Donnell family, Earls of Tyrconnell who were dispatched west of the Shannon by Cromwell. The house is full of history and interesting objects. A good fishing base.

Olde Railway Hotel (££) The Mall, Westport (tel: 098 25166). Old-fashioned town hotel, now comfortably refurbished in traditional style.

Rosturk Woods (£) Mulrany (tel: 098 36264). Exceptionally pleasant guest-house in quiet location, furnished with taste and flair throughout.

NORTHWESTERN COUNTIES
County Donegal
Bruckless House (£) Bruckless (tel: 073 37071).

Attractive 18th-century farmhouse in large grounds of well-kept gardens and woodland. Sea views from some windows. Good home cooking.

Castle Murray House (££) St John's Point, Dunkineely (tel: 073 37022). Acclaimed restaurant-with-rooms in splendid location (see also restaurant section).

Gortfad (£) Castlefinn (tel: 074 46135). Family home in Victorian/Edwardian house. Peaceful touring base.

Harvey's Point Country Hotel (££) Lough Eske, Donegal Town (tel: 073 22088). Modern luxurious Swiss restaurant-with-rooms on shores of lough. Many sports facilities (see also restaurant section).

Kee's Hotel (££) Main Street, Stranorlar, Ballybofey (tel: 074 31018). Family-run hotel in village near the Bluestack Mountains. 19th-century coaching inn, recently refurbished. Leisure centre.

Rathmullan House (£££) Rathmullan (tel: 074 58188). One of Donegal's few country-house hotels, dating from the 18th century. Lovely gardens stretch towards the beach. Rooms overlook Lough Swilly, a fjord. Saltwater pool. Good food (see also restaurant section).

St Ernan's (££) St Ernan's Island, Donegal Town (tel: 073 21065). Beautifully situated on a wooded island linked to the mainland by a causeway, this 19th-century pinkish-cream house is a haven of peace. Furnishings echo the Regency theme of the house. Good food (see also restaurant section).

Sand House (££) Rossnowlagh (tel: 072 51777). Long-established and family-run resort hotel on one of Donegal's best beaches. Castle-like architecture. Inside it is lively but relaxing, with roaring fires and bright furnishings.

Smuggler's Creek (£) Rossnowlagh (tel: 072 52366). Cheerful and popular bistro-style bar overlooking the bay. Bedrooms are fresh and clean with spriggy wallpapers and modern pine. Breakfast served in conservatory extension with lovely views (see also restaurant section).

County Leitrim
Glebe House (£) Mohill (tel: 078 31086). Attractive rectory guest-house in 16ha of farmland and woods. Many local activities.
Stanford's Village Inn (£) Dromahair (tel: 071 64140). Simple village pub with accommodation in the heart of Yeats country. Bedrooms are small and modest but have showers. Period interest in the museum-like time-warp bar next door.

County Sligo
Coopershill (£££) Riverstown (tel: 071 65108). One of Ireland's best-loved and most hospitable country-house hotels, peacefully set in extensive wooded grounds. The handsome Georgian house retains many period features, including splendidly antique bathroom fittings. House-party atmosphere and notable food. Family-run for several generations.
Cromleach Lodge Country House (££) Castlebaldwin, near Boyle (tel: 071 65155). Purpose-built restaurant-with-rooms taking advantage of beautiful hilltop views. Bedrooms are very spacious and comfortable with smart modern furnishings (see also restaurant section).
Markree Castle (££) Collooney (tel: 071 67800). Impressively castellated in the 19th century, this house, seat of the Cooper family, is none the less genuinely old. Inside it is in parts draughty and cavernous, but mostly comfortable and relaxing, with lovely views of gardens and parklands (see also restaurant section).
Ross House (££) Riverstown (tel: 071 65140). Friendly farm B&B offering simple, good-value accommodation with some character.
Temple House (££)

Ballymote (tel: 071 83329). Unusual Georgian mansion revamped to contain 100 rooms in Victorian times, overlooking a lakeside Templar castle. Good local produce served.
Urlar House (£) Drumcliffe (tel 071 63110). Simple but civilised farmhouse accommodation in the shadow of Benbulben. Peaceful.

NORTHERN IRELAND
County Antrim
Ash-Rowan Guest House (££) 12 Windsor Avenue, Belfast (tel: 0232 661758). Above-average B&B in quiet, roomy Victorian house. Each bedroom individually decorated with private facilities. Good breakfasts. No-smoking house.
Auberge de Seneirl (££) 28 Ballyclough Road, Bushmills (tel: 02657 41536). Stylishly furnished restaurant-with-rooms converted from an old country school-house. Indoor pool, sauna, solarium (see also restaurant section).
Ballygally Castle (££) 274 Coast Road, Ballygally (tel: 0574 583212). A Scottish planter castle, complete with ghost, converted to a comfortable modern hotel. Sea views from some windows.
Camera House (££) 44 Wellington Park, Belfast (tel: 0232 660026). Charming B&B, a bright spark amid streets of unremarkable guest-houses in the university area. Clean, personal and friendly.
Dobbins Inn (££) 6 High Street, Carrickfergus (tel: 09603 51905). Ancient family-run inn in town centre, offering plain accommodation with private baths. Popular, lively bar – good snacks and morning coffee.
Dukes (£££) 65 University Street, Belfast (tel: 0232 236666). Stylish new hotel in university area with good facilities and plenty of vegetation in public areas.
Dunadry Inn (£££) 2 Islandreagh Drive, Dunadry (tel: 08494 32474). Whitewashed building

incorporating country-club facilities. Large gardens. Handy for airport.
Londonderry Arms (££) Harbour Road, Carnlough (tel: 0574 885255). Creeper-covered coaching inn with seaside garden, and antique furnishings in Georgian style. Some rooms are modern and functional. Hearty Irish food served, with traditional music in summer.
Malone Guest House (£) 79 Malone Road, Belfast (tel: 0232 669565). Simple but clean and practical accommodation offered in a residential district near the university.
Stranmillis Lodge (££) 14 Chlorine Gardens, Belfast (tel: 0232 682009). Quiet suburban location near university and botanic gardens. Inside, furnished to a high and practical standard with modern, inoffensive furnishings. Evening menu available.
Whitepark House (£) Whitepark Bay, Ballintoy (tel: 02657 31482). Certainly one of the more imaginatively furnished country guest-houses within striking distance of the Giant's Causeway. Secluded setting and attractive gardens.

County Down
Culloden (£££) 142 Bangor Road, Holywood (tel: 02317 425223). Grand baronial mansion in palatial woods and parkland. Luxurious facilities and décor. High-profile security. Close to Ulster Folk Museum.
Glassdrumman Lodge (££) 85 Mill Road, Annalong (tel: 03967 68451). Stylishly furnished modern house at the foot of the Mountains of Mourne. Very comfortable light bedrooms with all mod cons. Relaxing and secluded atmosphere. Acclaimed food (see also restaurant section).
Portaferry Inn (££) The Strand, Portaferry (tel: 02477 28231). Whitewashed inn overlooking Strangford Lough, a stone's throw from the ferry. Well kept modern rooms with

277

predictable but enjoyable seafood.

County Fermanagh
Jamestown House (££) Magheracross, Ballinamallard (tel: 036581 209). Fine Georgian house near Lough Erne. Spacious well-furnished bedrooms. Private fishing. Good food. **Killyreagh** (££) Tamlaght, Enniskillen (tel: 0365 87221). Lord Hamilton's elegant 19th-century house in parkland.

County Londonderry
Beech Hill Country House (£££) 32 Ardmore Road, Derry (tel: 0504 49279). Grand Victorian pile comfortably furnished and in lovely gardens. Serious food (see also restaurant section).
Blackheath House (££) 112 Killeague Road, Blackhill, Coleraine (tel: 0265 868433). Listed 18th-century rectory amid extensive landscaped gardens. Furnished in traditional styles with some antiques. Good food (see also restaurant section).
Greenhill House (£) 24 Greenhill Road, Aghadowey, Coleraine (tel: 0265 868241). Georgian country house in secluded countryside. Homely and welcoming atmosphere with substantial country cooking.
Camus House (£) 27 Curragh Road, Coleraine (tel: 0265 42982). Charming stone farmhouse overlooking River Bann near salmon leap, dating back to 1685. Bedrooms are decorated in light colours.
Coolbeg (££) 2e Grange Road, Coleraine (tel: 0265 44961). Modern bungalow in suburban setting, quiet and well-equipped. Suitable for disabled visitors.

LAKELAND COUNTIES
County Laois
The Glebe (£) Ballinakill (tel: 0502 33368). Superbly hospitable Georgian country house, in size a modest version of the breed, but with exceptionally interesting food and masses of charac-

ter. Parkland setting with horses. (See also restaurant section.)
Roundwood House (££) Mountrath (tel: 0502 32120). Delightful Georgian house, intriguing both for its Palladian villa architecture (splendidly intact thanks to its owners' keen support for the Georgian Society), and its food (see also restaurant section). The atmosphere is always cheerful, hospitable, informal and very, very Irish. The preservation of its period character takes precedence over 20th-century superfluities such as television. Try good conversation or a book instead.

County Longford
Carrigglas Manor (££) Longford (tel: 043 45165). Gothic-revival house near the Shannon, grandly furnished within. Excellent trout fishing and many other outdoor pursuits. Good traditional cooking. Some self-catering. Non-residents visit the house to look around. Tea-rooms, costume museum, guided tours.

County Monaghan
Hilton Park (£££) Clones (tel: 047 56007). Palatial mansion set in fine parkland, home of the present occupants for many generations. Run very much as a family home; furnishings are full of character and the food is excellent. House-party atmosphere.

County Offaly
Tullanisk (££) Birr (tel: 0509 20572). The former dower house of Birr Castle estate has a reputation far and wide as one of the most charming and hospitable country houses in the Midlands. Many sporting opportunities. Beautifully furnished, excellent cooking.

County Roscommon
Clonalis House (££) Castlerea (tel: 0907 20014). Ancestral home of the O'Conors of Connaught (last High Kings of Ireland). The house, though not especially old, is full of interest.

Bedrooms are palatially sized and have good park views. Some self-catering.

County Westmeath
Mornington House (££) Multyfarnham (tel: 044 72191). Delightful late Victorian house (with Georgian core) offering most comfortable accommodation and excellent cooking, using fresh local produce. Dinner is by candlelight. Fine views across Lough Derravaragh to Knock Ion. Sporting opportunities, including croquet, hunting and fishing.

RESTAURANTS

The following restaurants have also been divided into three price categories: budget (£); moderate (££) and expensive (£££).

DUBLIN
(the code for Dublin is 01)
Aisling (£££) (the restaurant of the Shelbourne Hotel, see accommodation). Distinguished, expensive menu worth smartening up for.

Ante Room Seafood Restaurant (££) (the restaurant of the Georgian House, see accommodation). Intimate setting, sophisticated atmosphere. Music some nights.
Bad Ass Cafe (£) Crown Alley, Temple Bar, 2 (tel: 6712596). Lively pizza place in converted warehouse where Sinead O'Connor was once a waitress. Popular with all age groups.
Beshoff's Ocean Foods (£) 14 Westmoreland Street, 2 (tel: 6778026). One claimant to Dublin's fish-and-chip crown. Edwardian bistro décor.
Bewley's Oriental Café (£) Four central locations: South Great George Street, Mary Street, Westmoreland Street, and the main one in Grafton Street (tel: 6776761). Coffee shop *par excellence*, embellished with mahogany and stained glass. Sticky

buns or full meals. Upstairs (in Grafton Street) it's less crowded, with a museum. All walks of life end up here.

The Commons (£££) Newman House, 85–86 St Stephen's Green, 2 (tel: 4752597). Urbane, classic French cooking served amid a fine collection of commissioned modern art and startling furnishings.

Le Coq Hardi (£££) 35 Pembroke Road, 4 (tel: 6684130). Gentleman's club surroundings and ultra-serious gourmet food and wine. Popular with business fraternity.

Eastern Tandoori (££) 34 South William Street, 2 (tel: 6710428). Popular authentic Indian cuisine, décor and music. Extensive vegetarian choice.

Elephant and Castle (£) 18 Temple Bar, 2 (tel: 6791399). Bustling, chic venue for drinks or dinner. Eclectic, Californian-style cuisine – burgers, guacamole and tortilla chips, pasta, omelettes. Good for people-watching.

Fat Freddy's Pizza Warehouse (£) Crow Street, Temple Lane, 2 (tel: 6796769). Good, cheap pizzas fly round this white-washed warehouse. Mostly students and folk with no ear-drums. Quiches, pasta and chilli supplement the pizzas.

Fitzers, National Gallery Restaurant (£) Merrion Square, 2 (tel: 6686481). Good self-service restaurant to stave off hunger brought on by cultural overdose. Reasonably priced wine. Daytime only.

Gallagher's Boxty House (£) 20 Temple Bar, 2 (tel: 6772762). A new formula based on griddled Irish potato cakes (boxties) wrapping up all kinds of savoury fillings. Bacon and cabbage, champ, smoked fish and other Irish fare. Always popular. Homely (modern) country décor of pine and pottery.

Imperial (££) 12a Wicklow Street, 2 (tel: 6772580). Superior Chinese, specialis-

ing in dim sum. Popular at Sunday lunchtime. Good value if you stick to tea rather than wine.

Kapriol's (£) 45 Camden Street Lower, 2 (tel: 4751235). Vibrant North Italian cooking amid Dolomite décor.

Kilkenny Kitchen (£) Nassau Street, 2. (tel: 6777066). On first floor of Kilkenny Design Centre. Excellent self-service coffee shop and restaurant, capitalising on the success of the stylish original in Kilkenny. Always busy at lunchtime.

Leo Burdock's (£) 2 Werburgh Street, 2 (tel: 540366). A legend in fish and chips. Closed Tuesday and Sunday.

Les Frères Jacques (£££) 74 Dame Street, 2 (tel: 6794555). Ambitious and expensive food – mostly French with Irish farmhouse cheeses.

Mitchell's Cellars (££) 21 Kildare Street, 2 (tel: 6680367). Bistro style wine-bar and restaurant. Pâtés, quiches, casseroles. Lunchtime only.

No 10 (£££) (the restaurant of Longfield's, see accommodation). Intimate basement dining room with smart white linen and crystal. Elegant atmosphere. Successful blend of French and Irish cooking.

Pasta Fresca (££) 3–4 Chatham Street, 2 (tel: 6792402). Stylish Italian cuisine, including good versions of well known favourites and more unusual things. The pasta, of course, is *fresca*.

Patrick Guilbaud (£££) 46 James Place, Lower Baggot Street, 2 (tel: 6764192). Hushed, reverential atmosphere indicates that this is *cuisine serieuse*, and the only place in Dublin with a Michelin rosette. Business clients dine in discretion here. Mostly classic French, with the odd pig's trotter thrown in for regional interest.

Periwinkle Seafood Bar (£) Powerscourt Centre, South William Street, 2 (tel: 6794203). Bar-counter

restaurant popular with grazing shoppers. Good chowder.

Pigalle (££) 14 Temple Bar, 2 (tel: 6719262). Good French *paysanne* food like gratins, tarts, mousses and soups in cramped bistro setting.

Rajdoot (££) 26–28 Clarendon Street, Westbury Centre, 2 (tel: 6794274). High quality Moghul specialities here, in elegant, discreetly formal setting.

Royal Kilmainham Hospital (£) Kilmainham Gaol (tel: 6718666). The coffee shop restaurant is good here, especially at Sunday lunchtimes, when whole families appear. Simple home-cooking.

Shalimar (££) 17 South Great George's Street, 2 (tel: 6710738). Yet another of Dublin's surprising ethnic winners. North Indian and Pakistani cooking.

Sichuan (££) 4 Lower Kilmacud Road, Stillorgan (tel: 2884817). State-owned Chinese restaurant (owned by the People's Republic of China, that is). Authentic ingredients and real Chinese chefs.

Thornton's Wine Epergne (£££) 147 Upper Rathmines Road, 6 (tel: 962348). Post-nouvelle cuisine using the best quality products, often highly elaborate. Old-fashioned, Victorian décor.

EASTERN COUNTIES
County Dublin

Abbey Tavern (££) Abbey Street, Howth (tel: 01 390282). Olde-worlde tavern specialising in fish. Traditional Irish music most nights (separate annexe).

Ayumi-Ya (££) Newpark Centre, Newtownpark Avenue, Blackrock (tel: 01 283 1767). Acclaimed Japanese food.

Il Ristorante (££) 18 Coliemore Road, Dalkey (tel: 01 2840800). Small, discreet, with highly competent Italian cooking. Lots of plants and fresh flowers.

Na Mara (££) Railway Station, Harbour Road, Dun Laoghaire (tel: 01 2806767). Meat and fresh seafood in

one of Ireland's earliest railway stations.
King Sitric (£££) East Pier, Howth (tel: 01 325235). Celebrated seafood in delightful harbourside setting. Dinner only.
Red Bank (££) 7 Church Street, Skerries (tel: 01 8491005). Relaxing family-run seafood restaurant in converted bank. Dinner only.

County Kildare
Barberstown Castle (££) Straffan (tel: 01 6288157). Imaginative dishes served in the 16th-century stone banqueting hall (see also accommodation section).
Doyle's Schoolhouse (££) Castledermot (tel: 0503 44282). Modern country cooking in 1930s school.
Lawlor's Restaurant (££) Poplar Square, Naas (tel: 045 97085). Hearty steaks and fish for the racing crowd. Lighter meals in the bar.
Moyglare Manor (£££) Moyglare, Maynooth (tel: 01 6286351, see also accommodation section). Elaborate French menu complements the sumptuous décor.

County Louth
Buttergate (££) Millmount, Drogheda (tel: 041 34759). Spirited French cuisine on the upper floors of the converted barracks buildings by the museum.
Forge Gallery (££) Collon (tel: 041 26272). Well-established restaurant, decorated with the work of local artists. Generous portions of French provincial and traditional Irish cooking.
The Gables (££) Ardee (tel: 041 53789, see accommodation section). French country cooking served with a generous spirit in traditional surroundings of velvet, linen, lace and silver.
Jordans (£) Carlingford (tel: 042 73223). Village centre pub bistro. Good fish and some exotic surprises.

County Meath
Station House (££) Kilmessan (tel: 046 25239,

see also accommodation section). Local fresh produce served in calm, unflashy setting.

County Wicklow
Hunter's (££) Newrath Bridge, Rathnew (tel: 0404 40106, see also accommodation section). Traditional country-house cuisine using local produce, such as Wicklow lamb. Afternoon teas in the garden.
Old Rectory (££) Wicklow (tel: 0404 67048, see also accommodation section). Talented and imaginative fare served in intimate surroundings. Interesting Spanish wines. Local organic produce.
Rathsallagh House (££) Dunlavin (tel: 045 53112, see also accommodation section). Small but classy dining-room serving hearty but utterly interesting country cooking.
Tinakilly (£££) Rathnew (tel: 0404 69274, see also accommodation section). Smart Irish/French cooking in rather formal surroundings.
Tree of Idleness (£££) Seafront, Bray (tel: 01 2863498). Unusually excellent Greek-Cypriot cooking in Victorian house. Dinner only.

SOUTHEASTERN COUNTIES
County Carlow
Lord Bagenal Inn (£) Leighlinbridge (tel: 0503 21668). Famous old inn now serving a good range of undemanding food in the bar with more sophisticated French cuisine in the restaurant. Open fires and rustic décor.

County Kilkenny
Kilkenny Design Centre (£) Castle Yard, Kilkenny (tel: 056 22118). Sparkling self-service restaurant in attractive upper floors of the castle stable block, housing a fine selection of Irish craft products.
Lacken House (££) Dublin Road, Kilkenny (tel: 056 61085, see also accommodation section). Traditionally furnished cellar dining-

rooms, serving imaginative international cuisine.

County Tipperary
Bee's Knees Bistro (£) Clonmel (tel: 052 21457). Good wholefood café for daytime snacks.
Cashel Palace (££) Cashel (tel: 062 61411, see also accommodation section). The Buttery restaurant downstairs is one of the cosiest places in Cashel for a snack, full meal or drink. Open fires in winter.
Chez Hans (££) Cashel (tel: 062 61177). Parisian bistro-style in the setting of an old Baptist church. Generous portions. Cashel blue cheese figures on the menu.

County Waterford
Dwyers (££) Mary Street, Waterford (tel: 051 77478). Pleasantly intimate restaurant a block or two back from the waterside. Small, interesting menu. Evenings only.
Ship Inn (£) Dunmore East (tel: 051 83141). Nautically decorated pub with interesting fishy dishes.
Waterford Castle (£££) The Island, Ballinakill, Waterford (tel: 051 78203, see also accommodation section). Classily presented gourmet food (lobster, asparagus, poached salmon) and homely classics like bread-and-butter pudding.

County Wexford
Cellar Restaurant (££) Horetown House, Foulksmills (tel: 051 63771). Fine country cooking in the splendid setting of a 300-year-old Georgian manor.
The Galley (££) New Ross (tel: 051 21723). Mobile, cruising restaurants operate between Waterford and New Ross during the summer, offering fresh local produce.
Marlfield House (£££) Gorey (tel: 055 21124, see also accommodation section). The style of the food matches the rest of the house – rich, opulent, complicated.
Neptune (££) Ballyhack (tel: 051 89284). Near the castle and the car ferry that plies to Passage East, this agreeable

little seafood restaurant is worth crossing the water for. Harp recitals.

Oyster Restaurant (££) Rosslare Strand (tel: 053 32439). Wine bar and seafood restaurant in the heart of the resort.

SOUTHWESTERN COUNTIES
County Cork

Aherne's (££) Youghal (tel: 024 92424). Excellent range of seafood produced in various levels of elaboration in this thriving enterprise. Modern, well-equipped accommodation available.

Arbutus Lodge (££) Montenotte, Cork (tel: 021 501237, see also accommodation section). Classic Cork favourites are done best here, though ambitious chefs strive for perfection in many directions.

Assolas House (££) Kanturk (tel: 029 50015, see also accommodation section). Skilful use of the best available local produce ensures the success of this country-house restaurant.

Ballymaloe House (£££) Shanagarry (tel: 021 652531, see also accommodation section). An Irish legend which now dispenses the talent and experience of the Allen dynasty through its cookery school. Superbly accomplished and good-value food, using local produce to full advantage.

Blairs Cove House (££) Durrus (tel: 027 61127). Buffet-style seafood starters, local fish and meat and splendid puddings served on the grand piano. A lovely Georgian house overlooking the sea.

Blue Haven (££) Kinsale (tel: 021 772209, see also accommodation section). Excellent range of undemanding, filling seafood, snacks and meat.

Chez Youen (££) Baltimore (tel: 028 20136). Popular seafood restaurant near harbour.

Cliffords (£££) 18 Dyke Parade, Cork (tel: 021 275333). Smart, formal, French-style restaurant in

town centre.

Crawford Gallery Café (££) Emmet Place, Cork (tel: 021 274415). A scion of the Allen family of Ballymaloe House (see above) masterminds this attractive gallery restaurant Whether you call in for a cake or a full meal, excellence is assured. Now open several evenings a week too (Wednesday–Friday).

Dunworley Cottage Restaurant (££) Dunworley, Butlerstown, Clonakilty (tel: 023 40314). News of this isolated restaurant has steadily filtered through to the foodies of West Cork. Dynamic food served in modest surroundings.

Finins (££) 75 Main Street, Midleton (tel: 021 631878). Simple meat and seafood dishes, filling soups etc. unpretentiously served.

ISAAC'S (£) 48 MacCurtain Street, Cork (tel: 021 500011, see also accommodation section). Good-value hostel self-service restaurant. Mostly wholefoods.

Larchwood House (££) Pearsons Bridge, Bantry (tel: 027 66181, see also accommodation section). Imaginative and satisfying Irish country cooking in a modest guest-house .

Longueville House (£££) Mallow (tel: 022 47156, see also accommodation section). August and formal food for serious eaters.

Quay Coop (£) 24 Sullivans Quay, Cork (tel: 021 317660). Thoroughly imaginative wholefood and vegetarian specialities.

Shiro (£££) Ahakista, near Bantry (tel: 027 67030). Remarkably situated restaurant serving exquisitely presented authentic Japanese food. Attentive service. Advance booking always essential.

The Vintage (££) 50 Main Street, Kinsale (tel: 021 772502). Cosy and romantic setting for a Hamburg chef to conjure up some of Kinsale's best cuisine.

County Kerry
Doyle's Seafood Bar (££) John Street, Dingle (tel: 066

51174, see also accommodation section). Excellent and highly praised seafood dishes (and other things) served with minimal ceremony.

Lime Tree (££) Kenmare (tel 064 41225). Intimate setting for uncomplicated fish and meat dishes.

Nick's (££) Killorglin (tel: 066 61219). Relaxed beamed dining room where excellent fish dishes are prepared.

Park (£££) Kenmare (tel: 064 41200, see also accommodation section). Gourmet food in serene surroundings.

Strawberry Tree (££) 24 Plunkett Street, Killarney (tel: 064 32688). Lively and generous meals are served (with plenty of calories) by friendly staff.

281

County Limerick
Dunraven Arms (££) Adare (tel: 061 396209, see also accommodation section). Reliable Irish cooking, whether a sandwich in the bar or a full meal in the restaurant.

Mustard Seed (££) Adare (tel: 061 396451). Inventive food in charming cottage setting.

WESTERN COUNTIES
County Clare
Bunratty Castle (££) Bunratty (tel: 061 360788) Classic medieval banquets in castle setting with full programme of entertainment. There are two sittings; book at any tourist office.

Claire's Restaurant (££) Ballyvaughan (tel: 065 77029). This simple dining-room at the back of a crafts shop dispenses attractive combinations of Burren goat's cheese, Ballyvaughan crab or plain (but delicious) Galway Bay oysters.

The Cloister (££) Abbey Street, Ennis (tel: 065 29521). Simple seafood and snacks are available in the bar from lunchtime onwards; more complex fish dishes in the dining-room. Treacle bread and

Inagh goat's cheese salad are specialities.

Knappogue Castle (££) near Quin (tel: 061 360788) Medieval feasting in well-restored castle accompanied by entertainers recounting stories of Celtic Ireland; book at any tourist office.

MacCloskey's (£££) Bunratty House Mews, Bunratty (tel: 061 364082). In the middle of Bunratty's shamrock-and-leprechaun version of Ireland, this hard-headed and competent restaurant is a breath of fresh air. Classical and *nouvelle cuisine* combine local ingredients with skill and flair in intimate, romantic surroundings.

Manuel's Seafood (££) Corbally, Kilkee (tel: 065 56211). If you find yourself exploring the south Clare coast you might try this place at dinnertime for local seafood or vegetarian specials in a small modern hill-top restaurant.

Sheedy's Spa View (££) Lisdoonvarna (tel: 065 74026, see also accommodation section). The Orchid Room restaurant is often praised for its outstanding five-course set dinner – French/Irish cuisine prepared by the family owners. Friendly atmosphere and hearty servings.

County Galway
Ballynahinch Castle (££) Recess, Connemara (tel: 095 31006, see also accommodation section). The dining-room produces formal and correct food here, a serene and relaxing setting. If you want something simpler, there is an excellent range of bar food available in the Fisherman's pub.

Drimcong House (££) Moycullen (tel: 091 85115). A fine 17th-century house provides the setting for this attractive restaurant which produces carefully thought out concoctions of local products in imaginative combinations of sweet and savoury flavours. One of the West's foremost restaurants, and acclaimed

throughout Ireland.

Dunquaire Castle (££) Kinvara (tel: 091 37108) Banquet fare accompanied by literary gleanings from Synge, Shaw and O'Casey; book at any tourist office.

Fat Freddy's (£) Quay Street, Galway (tel: 091 67279). One of the best places for pizza, cheerful, youthful, informal.

McDonagh's Seafood Bar (£) 22 Quay Street, Galway (tel: 091 65001). A great place for seafood, relaxed and informal, with long opening hours.

Moran's Oyster Cottage (££) The Weir, Kilcolgan, Clarinbridge (tel: 091 961113). Oysters are what they do best here, as the name suggests, from their own beds just outside. But you can get a great chowder, and lots of other seafood besides, accompanied by delicious soda bread and chilled white wine – or decent Guinness.

O'Grady's Seafood (££) Clifden (tel: 095 21450). Good-value seafood in reassuringly unpretentious surroundings.

Paddy Burke's (££) Clarinbridge (tel: 091 96226). Another great location for oyster-sampling, but you can find plenty of other seafood and hearty Irish cooking here. Always popular and bustling.

Rosleague Manor (£££) Letterfrack, Connemara (tel: 095 41101, see also accommodation section). Award-winning restaurant featuring seafood and home-grown vegetables.

Aran Islands Hostel Restaurant (£) Kilronan Harbour, Inishmore, Aran Islands (tel: 099 61255). A good place for inexpensive daytime snacks and vegetarian evening meals.

County Mayo
Chalet Seafood (£) Keel, Achill Island (tel: 098 43157). Simple versions of fresh local seafood (such as home-smoked salmon).

Continental Café (£) Westport (tel: 098 26679). Simple home-made fare, including soups and cakes.

Glosh House (£) Murrisk, Westport (tel: 098 64839). A surprising place to find after you have climbed Croagh Patrick – or perhaps just looked at it! An amazing range of food appears in this tiny doll's-house of a dining-room, including seafood and healthy vegetarian options. It also produces good Irish breakfasts and afternoon teas. Open June–September.

Quay Cottage (££) The Quay, Westport (near entrance to Westport House) (tel: 098 26412). Atmospheric high-ceilinged wine-bar and shellfish restaurant converted from a waterside cottage. Open fires and nautical nick-nacks on the rafters.

NORTHWESTERN COUNTIES
County Donegal
Castle Murray House (££) St John's Point, Dunkineely (tel: 073 37022, see also accommodation section). Thierry Delcros's smart French cooking is served amid distracting views.

Danby Restaurant (££) Rossnowlagh Road, Ballyshannon (tel: 072 51138). The oddly staid décor of this Georgian guest-house belies its imaginative and challenging cuisine. Family-run and memorably competent.

Harvey's Point (££) Lough Eske, Donegal (tel: 073 22208, see also accommodation section). French cuisine in *nouvelle* style. Fairly formal atmosphere.

Landhaus (££) West End, Bundoran (tel: 072 41915). Interesting Germanic flavours here, and a lively patronne to keep things buzzing smoothly.

Rathmullan House (£££) Rathmullan (tel: 074 58188, see also accommodation section). *Table d'hôte* menus available in the evenings. Hearty Irish home cooking. Seafood and farm-house cheeses.

Restaurant St John's (££) Fahan (tel: 077 60289). Simple, traditional food with well-priced wine in a strangely suburban outpost of wildest Donegal.

St Ernan's House (££) St Ernan's Island, Donegal (tel: 073 21065, see also accommodation section). Attractively presented five-course dinners served in Irish country-house style. Smart, traditional décor of crisp linen and Regency stripes.

Smuggler's Creek (£) Rossnowlagh (tel: 072 52366, see also accommodation section). Imaginative range of bistro fare in simple stone-built inn. Fresh seafood and organically-grown vegetables.

Water's Edge (££) Rathmullan (tel: 074 58182). Glorious views over Lough Swilly enhance the local ingredients here – mostly fresh fish.

Country Sligo

Cromleach Lodge (£££) Castlebaldwin, near Boyle (tel: 071 65155, see also accommodation section). Accomplished if expensive food served with lovely views.

Markree Castle (££) Collooney (tel: 071 67800, see also accommodation section). Knockmuldowney Restaurant has moved (with its owner) from its former address to the medieval-looking setting of this castle. The food is just as assured.

Truffles (££) 11 The Mall, Sligo (tel: 071 44226). New Age pizzas of distinction.

NORTHERN IRELAND
County Antrim

Auberge de Seneirl (££) 28 Ballyclough Road, Bushmills (see also accommodation section). Accomplished French cuisine in decidedly generous portions.

Crown Liquor Saloon (£) 46 Great Victoria Street, Belfast (tel: 0232 249476). The National Trust's superbly restored Victorian pub is a must for any visitor; good lunchtime food, including oysters throughout the year. Irish dishes also available.

Front Page (£) 106 Donegall Street, Belfast (tel: 0232 324269). Good seafood, to the accompaniment by live music.

Nick's Warehouse (£) 35–39 Hill Street, Belfast (tel: 0232 439690). Morning coffee, lunchtime or evening snacks or full meals are all available here either in wine bar or formal restaurant settings. Terrines a popular speciality.

Ramore (£££) The Harbour, Portrush (tel: 0265 823444). Streamlined décor accompanies some sophisticated food. There is a good-value wine list.

Restaurant 44 (£££) 44 Bedford Street, Belfast (tel: 0232 244844). Smart colonial décor and accomplished French food. Good selection of vegetarian dishes.

Roscoff (£££) Shaftesbury Square, Belfast (tel: 0232 331532). Chic and renowned, one of the best in the province. Vaguely marine décor, befitting the fishy specialities. Wide range of ingredients. Good value.

County Down

Bistro Iona (££) 27 Church Road, Holywood (tel: 0232 425655). Informal, comfortable place to bring your own wine and enjoy a range of healthy dishes from the menus chalked up on a blackboard.

Glassdrumman House (£–£££) 242 Glassdrumman Road, Annalong (tel: 0396 768451, see also Glassdrumman Lodge in accommodation section). There are no less than three restaurants in this establishment: the Gallery serves light snacks, coffee and teas; the Kitchen Garden is fully licensed and à la carte; Memories serves gourmet French blowouts on Saturdays.

The Gaslamp (££) 47 Court Street, Newtownards (tel: 0247 811225). Popular, especially with business people. Generous portions of French cuisine, mostly with claret.

County Fermanagh

Blake's of the Hollow (£) Enniskillen (tel: 0365 322143). Good sandwiches in Victorian pub.

The Cedars (££) Castle Archdale, Drumall, Lisnarick (tel: 036 56 21493). Home-cooking and classic favourites, including really blue steak (if you want it that way).

Florence Court House (£) Florence Court (tel: 036 582 249). National Trust tea-rooms; wholesome lunches and snacks.

The Sheelin (££) Bellanaleck (tel: 036 582 232). Thatched-cottage bakery serving teas and snacks, and set Saturday dinner.

County Londonderry

Beech Hill Country House (£££) Ardmore Road, Derry (tel: 0504 49279, see also accommodation section). Carefully prepared food using mostly organic produce.

Blackheath House (££) 112 Killeague Road, Blackhill (tel:0265 868433,see also accommodation section). MacDuff's Cellar Restaurant is open to non-residents, offering pricey but well-prepared concoctions of local meat, game and seafood.

Linenhall Bar (£) Derry City (tel: 0504 371665). Good for lunchtime pub food.

LAKELAND COUNTIES
County Laois

Glebe House (££) Ballinakill (tel: 0502 33368, see also accommodation section). Welcoming family atmosphere and assured country cooking.

Roundwood House (££) Mountrath (tel: 0502 32120, see also accommodation section). Accomplished cooking by a natural hostess in magnificent Palladian surroundings.

County Westmeath

Crookedwood House (££) Crookedwood, Mullingar (tel: 044 72165). Copious and good, interesting food served in relaxing fireside setting.

Index

INDEX

287

INDEX

Picture credits

The Automobile Association would like to thank the following photographers, libraries and associations for their assistance in the preparation of this book.
BORD FÁILTE 22a horse-racing, 22b hurling, 23 football, 30a Muiredach's Cross, 102–3 Punchestown races, 105 Malahide Castle, 112b Slane Abbey, 122 Ardmore Round Tower, 127b Rock of Cashel Museum, 141 cannon, Rosslare, 142 Georges St, Waterford, 164b Ashford Castle Hotel, 165 Adare Manor Hotel, 175 banquet, Knappogue Castle, 179a flora, 190a Thoor Ballylee, 202a Glebe House, 202b Glencolumbcille standing stone, 207 St Eunan's, 249 Old Gaol. H CHEVALLIER 177b Aran Island gate. G GOSSIP 164a Bantry House, 242a Hilton Park Hotel, 243a Clohamon House, 242b, 243b Tullanisk. CHRISTOPHER HILL PHOTOGRAPHIC 3 Glencolumbcille, 5c Roundstone, 7a lobster fishing, 10b Dunluce Castle, 15 Irish dancing, 16a W B Yeats, 18a Irish fry, 18–19 seafood, 20b farming, 24b Roundstone Bog, 32a Boa Island Figure, 79a seafood, 155b Rowallane Gardens, 182–3 Clifden, 186 Oyster Festival, 190b Westport, 199 Donegal, 200–1 Atlantic Drive, 206 Grianán of Aileach, 208 Parke's Castle, 209a Lough Gill, 210a Sligo Abbey, 210b W B Yeats, 212 Crown Liquor Saloon, 214 Relief of Derry, 217a Belfast, 217b Larry's Bar, 218, 219a City Hall, 219b Palm House, 220 Opera House, 221a Queen's University, 222a Belfast Castle, 222b Belfast Zoo, 223 Navan Fort, 224 Derry, 225b St Patrick's window, 226a Stone, 230b Wellbrook Mill, 232 Mourne Mountains, 235b Transport Museum, 238 Lough Key, 247b Lough Key, 251 Giant's Causeway, 256 cycles. KOBAL COLLECTION 204a *The Quiet Man*, 204b *The Field*, 205 *Ryan's Daughter*. MARY EVANS PICTURE LIBRARY 17a Samuel Beckett, 17b G B Shaw, 26a creatures, 27 Cuchulainn, 36b William III, 37 James II, 39 Lord Kilwarden, 40b de Valera and Lloyd George, 42b Sir Edward Carson, 63a G B Shaw, 63b W B Yeats, 114 St Columba, 138 James Joyce. NATIONAL MUSEUM OF IRELAND 66 Tara Brooch. NATURE PHOTOGRAPHERS LTD 180a mountain avens (R Bush), 180b fly orchid (P Sterry), 181a pine marten (W S Paton), 181b corncrake (P Sterry). NORTHERN IRELAND TOURIST BOARD 227b Marble Arch Caves. OFFICE OF PUBLIC WORKS, DUBLIN 34a Silken Thomas. REX FEATURES 12b Mary Robinson. ROYAL GEOGRAPHICAL SOCIETY 28a map. STROKESTOWN PARK 250 Strokestown Park. THE SLIDE FILE 4 cottages near Moate, 10a children, 24–5 turf cutting, 126 Cashel Rock, 179b Burren, 194 *currach*, 198 weaving, 239 Lough Oughter Castle, 245 Clonmacnois, 247a Killykeen Forest Park. THE MANSELL COLLECTION 34b Richard II campaign, 35 Oliver Cromwell, 36–7 Siege of Londonderry, 38b Emmett, 40a Sackville St, 41 signing treaty, 43a Parnell, 43b Liberation of O'Connell, 54a Easter Rising, 54b GPO 1916, 55a Easter Rising, 62 Oscar Wilde. WATERFORD CRYSTAL 143a Copper Wheel Engraver, 143b Master Cutter. ZEFA PICTURE LIBRARY (UK) LTD (Cover) shopfront, 12a UK flag, 13a Irish flag.

All remaining pictures are held in the Association's own library (AA PHOTO LIBRARY) with contributions from: L BLAKE 11, 110, 115a, 145, 184, 185, 187, 188, 191, 226b, 240a, 241, 244, 246a, 260. J BLANDFORD 9b, 21, 25, 121, 136, 146, 148, 149d, 152, 154, 155a, 159, 161, 163a, 163b. D FORSS 33, 51, 149a, 152–3, 162. S HILL 5a, 5b, 14b, 30b, 150a, 150b, 151, 156, 157, 158, 167a, 167b, 168, 169, 170, 171, 172, 174, 176, 177a, 189, 192a, 193a, 266, 268. J JENNINGS 19b, 38a, 192b, 193b, 196, 225a, 235a, 246b. T KING 46, 55b, 83a, 98. G MUNDAY 6, 26b, 29, 49a, 52, 53, 57a, 57b, 61a, 68a, 68b, 69a, 69b, 70a, 70b, 72b, 76, 96, 104, 112a, 116, 213, 219b, 215, 221b, 227a, 228, 230a, 231, 233, 234, 269. M SHORT 7b, 9a, 13b, 16b, 20a, 28b, 32b, 44–5, 48a, 48b, 49b, 50, 56, 58b, 59, 60, 64, 65b, 67, 71, 72a, 74a, 74b, 75, 78, 79b, 80, 81a, 81b, 82, 83b, 84a, 84b, 85, 87, 88, 89a, 89b, 91b, 92, 94, 95, 97a, 97b, 99a, 99b, 100b, 101, 102a, 103, 106a, 109, 111, 113, 115b, 117, 123a, 124a, 124b, 130a, 130b, 131, 132, 133, 135, 137, 139a, 140, 236, 248, 253, 258, 259, 262, 263, 264, 265. W VOYSEY 42a, 58a, 61b, 65a, 77a, 77b. P ZOELLER 91a, 107, 108a, 108b, 118, 120, 123b, 125, 127a, 129, 144, 166, 267.

Acknowledgements

The author would like to thank the following for their help in the production of this book: Bord Fáilte; Aer Lingus; Avis/Johnson & Perrott; and British Midland Airways Ltd.

Contributors

Series advisor: Ingrid Morgan   **Designer:** Tony Truscott
Joint series editor: Susi Bailey   **Indexer:** Marie Lorimer
Copy editor: Tessa Lecomber   **Verifiers:** Ian Hill, Letitia Pollard